TEMPLE ARCHITECTURE AND SCULPTURE OF THE NOḶAMBAS

(Ninth-Tenth Centuries)

Temple Architecture and Sculpture of the Noḷambas

(Ninth-Tenth Centuries)

ANDREW L. COHEN

MANOHAR
2026

First published 1998
Reprinted 2026
First eBook edition 2025

ISBN 978-81-7304-222-5 (hardbound)
ISBN 978-93-6080-963-8 (eBook)

Published by
Ajay Kumar Jain for
Manohar Publishers & Distributors
4753/23 Ansari Road, Daryaganj
New Delhi 110 002

Printed and bound in India

To

THUY

Contents

Illustrations

PLATES

MAP AND FIGURES

Acknowledgements

I was inspired to study Noḷamba monuments during a visit to the Madras Government Museum. There a curious set of sculptures from Hemavati demand attention, for they are aesthetically engrossing and historically distinctive. These images, along with all other Noḷamba monuments, are marginalized in scholarly studies. This neglect, however, became my inducement to research the topic. Noḷamba monuments were the focus of my 1989 University of Chicago doctoral dissertation and this book is a revision of that thesis.

Over the years this study has been improved through conversations and comments by Cathy Asher, Rick Asher, Carol Bolon, Richard Davis, Vidya Dehejia, Mark DeLancey, Dan Ehnbom, Susan Huntington, George Michell, Stanley Murashige, Michael Rabe, Ajay Sinha, Gary Tartakov, Phil Wagoner, and Michael Willis among others. Portions of my Noḷamba research have been presented to the American Council for Southern Asian Art Symposia (1991, 1994), the College Art Association Conference (1997), and the Center for South Asian Studies, University of Virginia (1995); these fora provided enrichment and encouragement.

In India my debts are many. Often during field work I visited small villages in search of the elusive Noḷamba and along the way usually someone, bemused by my quest, would offer kindness. Hemavati, though rich in Noḷamba history and essential site for this study, today is a modest village. I spent considerable time roaming Hemavati and environs—because no lodging is available, I usually slept in the Siddēśvara compound—and I thank the many people who helped. My travels throughout Noḷambavāḍi were made easier thanks to S. Prasad who often accompanied me.

I am grateful to the following who made my India research possible: at the Directorate of Archaeology and Museums in Karnataka, M.S. Nagaraja Rao, A. Sundara (both former Directors), and C.S. Patil; at the Epigraphy Office, Archaeological Survey of India, K.V. Ramesh and M. Kitti (both former Directors); and at Mysore University, A.V. Narasimha Murthy and M.S. Krishna Murthy.

I appreciate the financial support provided by the Samuel H. Kress Foundation, awarded through the University of Chicago Art Department, which allowed for research in India during 1985-6, and for dissertation writing in 1988-9. And I am grateful to the American Institute of Indian Studies for funding my 1986-7 year in India, and for their Senior Fellow award which allowed me to revisit sites in the summer of 1994. I am thankful to Pradeep Mehendiratta, Director, AIIS, who was instrumental in the transformation of this study and introduced me to Ramesh Jain, owner of Manohar Publishers. Also at the American Institute of Indian Studies I thank M.A. Dhaky, especially for his scholarship.

For their funding of research time and text preparation I thank the University of Central Arkansas Research Council. My colleagues at the UCA Department of Art have been helpful; especially Anna Lee, who as departmental secretary has patiently aided my work; Tonya Ward-Davis who helped with the index; and Pooi Yin Chong, a former student, who redrew the groundplans for the manuscript with the assistance of Lyn Brand-Wallace. Originally the groundplans were prepared by G. Jayaprasad Rao in India.

To Thuy, thanks for her precious support.

ANDREW L. COHEN

Abbreviations

ARE	*Annual Report on Indian Epigraphy*
ASI	Archaeological Survey of India
EA	*Epigraphica Andhrica*
EC	*Epigraphica Carnatica*
EI	*Epigraphica Indica*
EITA	*Encyclopaedia of Indian Temple Architecture*
LP	*Liṅga Purāṇa*
MAR	*Annual Reports of the Mysore Archaeological Survey*
SII	*South-Indian Inscriptions*
SP	*Śiva Purāṇa*

CHAPTER ONE

Introduction

ISSUES AND METHOD

When discussed, Noḷamba[1] monuments are presented as provincial copies of the more central works of the Deccan tradition, that is, those of Cālukyas, Rāṣṭrakūṭas, or the southern Pallava and Cōḷa traditions; or, as a combination of influences from these larger nearby traditions. I, too, during much of my fieldwork expected the time honoured method of seeking artistic origins and influences from territories controlled by large dynasties outside of Noḷambavāḍi would somehow explain the appearance or 'style' of Noḷamba period monuments. However, after completely surveying Noḷambavāḍi—encompassing present-day south-east Karnataka and contiguous portions of Andhra Pradesh and Tamil Nadu (see map)—I realized that I needed not only primary documentation, but also a better way to talk about the formation of art in areas controlled by minor—which usually means less studied—dynasties.

I suggest historians of Indian art need to question the 'essentialism' in dynastic and regional studies that assumes there exists some 'spirit' or 'nature' of a dynasty—either an artistic spirit, or a nature of each dynasty expressing itself in certain shapes, images and motifs identifiable with (and the property of) that dynasty. This essentialism allows one to arbitrarily define an artistic spirit and then assume this spirit spreads outwards, transcending all other criteria. The problem with this sort of thinking is that it allows generalizations of the characteristics of a Cōḷa temple, for instance, to truly define 'Cōḷa', so that when the same (more likely, similar) characteristics are seen elsewhere, it is assumed that we are still witnessing 'Cōḷa' (or, at least, Cōḷa-influenced art). The stronger the spirit (i.e. larger dynasties have more powerful artistic essences) the more 'influence' it has over others. It is as if there were only room for major dynastic personalities or major styles and all others had to be seen as dependent styles. Art then is recreated in scholarship to reflect a modern aesthetic recapitulation of the supposed regional political hierarchy under consideration. This approach disregards the diverse and complex factors that contribute to why a temple looks the way it does.

How should we address art developed in the peripheral regions of India's great dynastic capitals? Must the stylistic character of every local art be attributed to the 'essential character' of neighbouring macro-centres, or can we understand the art better as locally-based and relatively autonomous? Are Noḷamba monuments only the provincial imitations of their more powerful military and political neighbours, or are they somehow appropriate expressions of their own local circumstances? I suggest that monuments in smaller regions need to be recognized not as the commingling of 'influences' from the larger and more familiar dynasties, but, rather as autonomous local expressions revealing a dialectical response to neighbouring monuments and not a simple subordination to them. Or, to be more precise, it is not the monuments that are responding to others, but the human agencies responsible for the monuments. To understand temple art it must be seen as the product of human agents, expressing the interests of those agents, not as concealed essences. Local, 'minor', polities have autonomous wills and interests quite distinct from their larger more powerful neighbours and so their expressions, whether political or aesthetic, will be their own and not merely miniature reproductions of the interests or wills of their nearby powerful neighbours. Even if we cannot identify all the agencies involved and their motivations for involvement we might benefit from remembering that the temple is a complex monument, both in its form and in its purpose.

Centrality and periphery here is defined as a fluctuating opposition rather than, as has more commonly been the practice, as a continuum or a diminishing extension.[2] Political and artistic centres do not always coincide, but I am arguing that issues of polity and centrality need inclusion in the discourse. Of course an obvious point, but one that I think should not be dismissed as trite, is that what is considered peripheral relative to a 'major' centre, becomes central within another context. Within Noḷambavāḍi (considered peripheral by (art) historians) I call the Noḷamba capital, Hemavati, central. As this study demonstrates, artistic periphery need not be considered inferior, or unoriginal. Even if monuments are based on models from other localities (or 'influenced'[3] as it is often used), the resulting product, due to training of artisans, available materials, patron demands and other requirements, are reshaped according to immediate needs.

After studying artistic developments in peripheral regions of a cultural context other than India, that of medieval and Renaissance eastern Europe, Jan Bialostocki observes:

> Periphery is an area situated far away from the powerful center and not dependent on the influences coming from one place, but which receive inspirations from many regions and centers. Periphery is an area where various influences mix and merge and where no one of them obtains decisive superiority; that allows the artist of the peripheral regions to make the choice to develop the independently chosen elements and to create out of various influences an art autonomous and original.[4]

Although I found his observations helpful, it essentializes central and periphery as fixed places. Another approach to the same situation, or at least how I see it for medieval south India, would be to recognize the great centres as autonomous yet connected and in a world of slow limited communication—contrasted to today's immediate maximum communication—all centres, major and minor, are peripheral to each other: responding to one and another if or when found to be required or helpful. Artists distant from major dynastic centres are aware of divergent forms that might come from any number of localities. They reshape designs, within the limitations of their training and skill, to satisfy the specific needs and demands of any given situation unbeholden to any particular tradition but susceptible to all those nearby. When building a temple there are many complex agents involved in varying stages of the construction contributing to the final appearance. Local tradition and autonomy predominate, but do not block other elements from potential use.

There is a teleological formalism predominating in most art historical accounts that explains artists, works or periods influencing subsequent artists, works and periods as if some style or period essence proceeds uninterrupted. Art historians' search for origins and evolutions might at times misrepresent the art and ideas rather than explain.[5] Although some art historians feel uneasy with the evolutionist approach, many implicit assumptions concerning essences in Indian art historical scholarship remain intact.

One problem (as many art historians today acknowledge) is that the conventional models for non-Western studies are based on Eurocentric paradigms, and, specifically in art history, the predominant normative model for (world) art history has been based on assumptions regarding the Italian Renaissance.[6] As Svetlana Alpers shows, even areas of Western art have been significantly distorted by scholars operating on the assumption that the mode of making art during the Italian Renaissance is correct for other (pre-modern) cultures.[7] On the Western standard India, of course, did not 'correctly' evolve artistically (or in any manner, according to some). As was the case in the Renaissance, proper art should be rational, scientific, proportional, balanced: it is based on the human figure, which, of course, means man. Unbalanced, or irrational, art is hence feminine[8]—which, as it is used, becomes a derogatory term. In orientalist scholarship the term 'feminine' has also been used in describing the essence of the mind of India.[9] The subtle survival of Western evolutionist, Renaissance model implicit in most Indian art historical scholarship is a serious problem that we have only begun to debate.

The intellectual manipulations which try to reconstitute knowledge of other peoples (i.e. orientalism) is not a new topic.[10] In *Imagining India,* Inden thoroughly critiques Indological discourse as it has constructed India. I have little to add but to point out that historiography engenders modes of discourse: revisions to commonly accepted models of south Indian polity could help in new approaches to dynastic or regional art studies.

The available histories of medieval south Indian are presented as hegemonic texts in both form and content. The authors' intentions are to present studies that are empirically comprehensive and authoritative; their primary concern is for the dynastic histories of major kings, their political networks, and the competition among dynastic powers. Often these studies have an inherently biased political agenda. The British presented countless studies which subtly justified their historic role in India. And following their lead many English educated (directly or indirectly) Indian scholars carried on in this vein though with different objectives.[11] Using European empiricism to demonstrate historical parallels between Indian and European political institutions, many historians wanted to present medieval Indian government more like that of constitutional monarchs than as oriental despots.[12] Most notable for contributions to south Indian and Deccan history are K.A. Nilakanta Sastri and A.S. Altekar.[13] Although there is much to be admired in these studies, their adoption of European models has given an unwarranted emphasis on efficient, centralized dynastic power. According to Nilakanta Sastri and Altekar, lesser dynasties remain subjugated powers, inconsequentional except according to the situation as allies or foes to the dominating dynasties. Scholars following the conventional history see the centralized large dynasty (in the case of my study, that would be the Rāṣṭrakūṭas or Cōḷas) as dominating, hence, politically and artistically independent: creative, innovative and superior. Obviously what follows is that smaller peripheral dynasties, and art from those areas, are depicted as unimaginative, derivative, inferior.

This historical model, even when written by 'nationalist historians', is an extrusion of discourse that originates out of orientalist thinking. Many Indian scholars trying to regain a sense of agentic past, denied by earlier British historians, have adopted methods embedded in European political thought that unwittingly perpetuate models that emphasize centralized political domination. Most historians of Indian art have accepted this conventional thinking as accurate. I believe this is why many temples have been labelled 'Cōḷa' (or 'Rāṣṭrakūṭa', etc.) when the validity of such attributions are questionable. My earlier point regarding the Italian Renaissance as the normative model for art studies ties in here. Much art is judged by a Western and especially a Renaissance ideal. This way of looking at art, through a lens that defines normacy, was extended to India. Art associated with dynasties that in conventional historical models were predominate (e.g. Cōḷas, Rāṣṭrakūṭas) also became the standard upon which to judge other modes of artistic work.

The validity of the large centralized, bureaucratic dynastic model is challenged by the work of some recent scholars. Burton Stein shows how decentralized the actual political authority was within the Cōḷa realm and presents the king's overlordship as mostly symbolic.[14] Ronald Inden sees the Rāṣṭrakūṭa king's authority intact but explains the 'imperial formation' as dialectically and eristically constituted, with the emphasis on complex, shifting human agencies which compose the formation.[15] Nicholas Dirks discusses 'little kingdoms', those of the periphery, in relation to large kingdoms.[16]

In contrast to Nilakanta Sastri's view that the Cōḷa realm was controlled by Cōḷa kings, who organized an efficient, centralized, bureaucratized administrative structure, Stein concludes that the Cōḷa realm was a 'segmentary state' of locally controlled nāḍus ('self-sufficient ethno-agrarian micro regions'), and that their leaders' relation with the Cōḷa kings were ritualistic.[17] A complex balance existed between local groups including the dominant agriculturalists, local chieftains, Brahmins, and merchants, in order to perpetuate relatively autonomous nāḍus. Here authority was decentralized. There was no powerful central bureaucracy overseeing everything, including temple construction.

As our understanding of Cōḷa polity becomes clearer, maybe the more problematic study of local artistic forms will reveal that the convenient attribution of 'Cōḷa' (or Cōḷa-influenced) to temples, especially those at the perimeter of Cōḷamaṇḍalam, needs rethinking.

Inden presents a much different model of polity. He argues that an essentialism—which he explains as inherent in academic discourse on Indian state, religion, caste, etc.,—should be replaced by a theory of human agency. Agents are complex and shifting, they reconstitute one another through a dialectical and eristical process in changing and overlapping situations. At length, Inden's critique of Indological discourse exposes major assumptions and, in his opinion, fallacies intrinsic in most of these works, including his own earlier work on caste.

Using the same historical sources such as epigraphs and other available materials that historians employ, Inden demonstrates how one period of medieval history, that of the Rāṣṭrakūṭas, can be presented. He discusses how the king, councils, assemblies and other complex agencies dialectically and eristically composed the Rāṣṭrakūṭa formation which was continually being completed, contested and remade during specific cyclic processions. The same process and similar agencies that constituted the Rāṣṭrakūṭa imperial formation also, but on a lesser scale, composed smaller kingdoms like the Noḷambas. To a greater or lesser degree, depending on the strength of the involved agents, simple kingdoms functioned within the dialectics of the imperial formation.

Inden discusses temple building as a political as well as religious act, and shows how certain temples are integral to rituals which constitute the imperial formation. For example, he argues that Kailāsanātha at Ellora was the finale of Rāṣṭrakūṭa King Kṛṣṇa I's conquests, and the enshrined deity was intended as the imperial overlord. His discussion helps put the monument in historical context, possibly in a clearer manner than most. Still, his concern with only imperial temples raises a plethora of unanswered questions (which were not of his concern) regarding temples without known imperial affliation. For instance, who built temples within the Rāṣṭrakūṭa realm such as the Jaina temples at Hallur and Paṭṭaḍakal, or the other temples in Karnataka usually labelled 'Rāṣṭrakūṭa' at Kukkanur, Sirval, Aihole? And, a question of peculiar interest for art historians: how should we discuss the modal diversity of forms encountered in this imperial formation which expands over areas controlled by simple kingdoms? Inden's discussion seems to reintroduce the imperial king as the arbiter of temple shape. None the less, his provocative model offers a way for art historians to re-evaluate their assumptions regarding polity, dynasties, and how we discuss monuments.

Dirks' study explains the interdependency of 'little kingdoms' and 'large kingdoms' and discusses how 'symbolic' acts (ritual gifts) are the substance which binds the two. Although Dirks' main focus is on the Pudukkottai state during the British Raj, his discussion explains kingship in south India from the Pallavas onwards. His study demonstrates how authority fluctuates and how little kings became large, contradicting centralized dynastic models.

> The sovereignty of a subordinate lord, thus, is always dependent on, indeed part of, the sovereignty of the greater lord. However, the king's gift is at once binding and potentially divisive. The more gifts of honors and right the overlord makes to his subordinate, and—in what is a logical and political consequence of this—the more the subordinate participates in the sovereignty of his overlord, the more the subordinate is represented as sovereign in his own right. While gift giving articulates relations both of solidarity and hierarchy, simultaneously creating by its own internal dynamic the transactional poles of center and periphery, the possibility implicit in every gift is the cessation of the gift relationship. This possibility is made real by the very substance of the gift: authority itself.[18]

Once a subordinate, now a sovereign, the shift of authority is relative to context. The Noḷamba king of my study was sovereign within his realm and made gifts to subordinates and temples and, I argue, his relation to an overlord was only as binding as required during specific situations. Indian cosmology and polity is much more fluid than the western 'medieval' construct yet there is a tendency to apply the same rigid hierarchic model to both. Dirks, like Stein and Inden, discusses the integral role of temple to kingship and society.

Conventional dynastic art studies, I believe, unjustifiably assume that the art affiliated with smaller dynasties are derivative of the regionally dominating centralized dynasties. This approach incorrectly assumes that an artistic essence can be attributed to dynasties, just as it assumes that an unchanging centralized bureaucracy controls regional polity. The common understanding of Noḷambavāḍi is restricted by conventional studies that do not question south Indian polity and art; hence this epistemological closure has perpetuated a reductionist history that misrepresents the regional complexities and often ignores the human agencies responsible for temples.

I suggest that within a given region, including a peripheral region such as Noḷambavāḍi, defined by socio-political circumstances extended over a related period, a relatively autonomous art could be perpetuated while still sharing artistic elements from neighbouring regions. Sharing implies that a vast body of knowledge, in this case modes of artistic representation and of iconography, was known among artisans and that this knowledge was not restricted by political borders. Shared or new artistic forms and ideas from all directions could interact with concerned complex agents—be they the king as patron or other types of patronage, temple officials and priests, possibly merchants or other suppliers of materials, and, especially, the artisans and their own interaction among themselves and with other artisan families. Together, in accordance with the demands and conditions within a given time and location, the art was formed and reconstituted. Sometimes, however, even though images were known, because they were signs of political power, they were contested rather than shared. Artisans, and other concerned agencies, chose which artistic elements were required according to the needs and demands of a particular monument. Similarities in temple forms (i.e. sharing) then were not the result of divergent influences.

Dissimilarities in temple forms, I suggest, are the result of agents deciding which elements to utilize or to omit, and which elements to recompose in response to other monuments—hence, we might say, temples are dialectically constituted. Instead of seeing how one temple 'influenced' another temple (can a temple influence?), we might ask why one temple is built in a manner that purposely restructures elements seen at another temple while still maintaining the same basic temple form. For instance, instead of the evolutionist approach which says that the (Pallava) Kailāsanātha at Kāñcī influenced the (Cālukya) Virūpākṣa temple at Paṭṭadakal, which influenced the (Rāṣṭrakūṭa) Kailāsa temple at Ellora, we could discuss reasons why the creators of one temple, in response to another temple, chose to reject some attributes, reshape other attributes, while retaining the basic form. Continuity and change need not be explained as essences, but rather in accordance with the circumstances and agencies that compose monuments.

Other dissimilarities in surface appearance, and probably the major contributor to diversity, can be attributable to the collective training and the working method of locally based artisan workshops. Modes of artistic representation are determined by contributing artisans within a given locality. Hence I agree with those that advocate the study of style or idiom regionally,[19] but I do not believe a regional artistic essence exist which can be explained separate from the complex agencies which dialectically compose regional polity. When discussing 'idiom' all the contributing external factors probably are not identifiable; yet, this does not excuse us from at least remembering that temples are more than artistic essences. More documentation of local traditions in south India and Deccan is required to clearly discuss regional diversity and modal interchange. Temples in south Karnataka, northwest Tamil Nadu, southwest Andhra Pradesh (i.e. Gaṅgavāḍi, Koṅgu, Renāṇḍu, etc.) which often are labelled 'Cōḷa', and temples in Karnataka labelled 'Rāṣṭrakūṭa' especially need study. My study will document monuments in Noḷambavāḍi and discuss the forms and variations within this region. It is my hope that this information will help future studies expand the art historical discourse to include other lesser-known monuments and we will begin to have a clearer understanding of how monuments are shaped, and why.

REVIEW OF NOLAMBA-RELATED STUDIES

While critical and comprehensible accounts of Noḷambavāḍi monuments are unavailable, some general observations regarding isolated temples or sculptures are published. Various issues of the *Mysore Archaeological Reports* (*MAR*) note a few Noḷamba period monuments, particularly the temples at Nandi, Avani, and Aralaguppe.[20] The ceiling panels of Naṭēśa surrounded by Aṣṭadikpālas at the Kallēśvara temple, Aralaguppe, have received praise for their sculptural refinement by Seshadri[21] (twice in articles which are almost identical) Sivaramamurti[22] and De Lippe.[23] Scattered among a few general publications, reference to Noḷamba art is available, though none can be considered significant contributions. Soundara Rajan, *Indian Temple Styles,* summarizes features of the temples at Hemavati, Avani and Nandi.[24] Rajendra Prasad mentions Hemavati in two very similar books concerned with the art of Andhra Pradesh.[25] In his recent Indian art survey, Harle includes the Bhōgaṇandīśvara and Aruṇācalēśvara temples at Nandi in his discussion on Deccan temple development.[26] And mention is made of Hemavati sculptures in Huntington's recent survey.[27]

The section on Noḷambavāḍi temples in the American Institute of Indian Studies *Encyclopaedia of Indian Temple Architecture* (*EITA*) is relatively limited. A pithy summary of the architectural features is followed by a description of a few important temples. The Hemavati Virūpākṣa temple is incorrectly called Mallēśvara temple.[28] Orientation of the Doḍḍēśvara temple at Hemavati is stated incorrectly; consequently the description is confused and the sculptures mislabelled.[29] The superstructure of the Aruṇācalēśvara temple in Nandi is mistakenly described as having brick and mortar images,[30] when, in fact, it is granite, rebuilt in an archaizing manner during the Vijayanagara period. Generally, the abridged temple descriptions do not accurately portray the monuments. Though it provides an account of available resources pertaining to the Noḷambas, the encyclopaedia is a testimony to the acute need for a thorough investigation.

K. Krishna Murthy's *Noḷamba Sculptures: A Cultural Study* sounds promising from the title, but it is disappointingly concerned with 'costumes', 'personal ornaments', 'hair styles and hair dress', and other material paraphernalia (e.g. 'furniture', 'weapons', etc.).[31] While this book might be useful to those who are interested in identifying Indian garments and jewels, it offers no new information or insights regarding Noḷamba period art.[32]

M.S. Krishna Murthy's study is the most comprehensive Noḷamba dynastic history.[33] Its chapter on art is mostly limited to information available in *Mysore Archaeological Reports* or Sivaramamurti, though it does provide the first published account of the important Mahēndrēśvara temple at Baraguru. His more successful accomplishment is the analysis of Noḷamba political history. Though limited in number, Noḷamba dynastic history is the topic of a few articles beginning with Rice.[34] Other contributors include Lakshminarayan Rao,[35] Mahalingam,[36] Sompath[37] and Balambal.[38]

Douglas Barrett (in 1958) was the first to note Hemavati, the Noḷamba dynastic capital, as a topic of interest.[39] Limited to a few introductory pages, the publication's importance is its photographs. Sivaramamurti's catalogue of sculptures from Hemavati at the Madras Government Museum is the best known study on Noḷamba art.[40] Because his perception of Noḷambavāḍi monuments is so often repeated, I will now turn to his presentation.

When I speak of the conventional (mis) represention of Noḷambavāḍi monuments, it is Sivaramamurti's work (and like-minded adherents) to which I refer. Sivaramamurti did not recognize that the monuments from Noḷambavāḍi have relatively autonomous traits, consciously chosen by concerned human agents to fulfil their immediate needs (which change over time and locality within the region), while at the same time display characteristics and elements shared (and contested), or in dialectics with, neighbouring monuments. He saw instead a derivative style, dependent on more powerful neighbours for impetus. He and like-minded scholars assume that select major dynasties somehow arbitrate modes of artistic form which subsidiary dynasties in the cultural penumbra of those major dynasties then copy (in a provincial manner); this, as I discuss above, is a result of following conventional hegemonic historical paradigms. It also assumes there is a correct modality: this is similar to having world art judged according to an arbitrary model like the Italian Renaissance. Art of smaller dynasties, according to the convention model, mimics features of the larger ones; it is a politically submissive and artistically passive process.

According to Sivaramamurti, Noḷamba art is essentially a copying of the Cālukya style with some Pallava elements added.[41] A 'distinctiveness' or 'charm' is conceded, but not defined. In order to particularize Noḷamba period art he identifies the elements that are derived from greater (better known) dynasties. 'The peculiar features noticed in Noḷamba sculptures call for a careful comparative study of features in late Pallava, early Choḷa and Rāshṭrakūṭa carvings.'[42] With that objective in mind, Sivaramamurti seeks origins in Cālukya, Rāṣṭrakūṭa, Pallava and Cōḷa elements to explain features seen in Hemavati (Madras Museum) sculptures. A hairstyle might be Pallava or Cōḷa, and a necklace Cālukya.

For example, he compares a Hemavati Dakṣiṇāmūrti to figures from Kaveripakkam, a site which he calls '. . . late Pallava influenced to a great extent by Chalukya Rāshṭrakūṭa traditions.'[43] He sees the jaṭās of the hair as 'Pallava and Choḷa type', and the yajñopavīta is worn in a manner that 'is at once suggestive of the Pallava tradition both from the Pallava and Chalukya territory [*sic*]'.[44] One is bewildered by these ambiguous attributions: The hair is like the Pallava and Cōḷa type, but the Pallava image from Kaveripakkam is 'influenced' by Cālukyas and Rāṣṭrakūṭas. Is the hair then a Pallava-Cōḷa-Cālukya-Rāṣṭrakūṭa type? The yajñopavīta is from the Pallava tradition but also seen in Cālukya territory. Sivaramamurti uses dynastic appellations to explain styles to the point of meaninglessness. His knowledge of Pallava, Cōḷa, Cālukya and other motifs seems more the topic of his Noḷamba catalogue than an understanding of Noḷamba period art.

The propensity for seeking origins—as if finding the source of an element then explains the new context—or attempting to explain elements as analogous to other similar appearing elements in order to explicate form is a tendency in some scholarship. Take for example Sivaramamurti's quote from his *Nataraja* (p. 362). In reference to a Naṭarāja from Cham Museum, Danang (ancient Champa, Vietnam):

> Here also Śiva carries the vina. One cannot but recall the famous Naṭarāja known as Nartēśvara in Bengal from Sankarbandha dancing on the back of Nandi. But with twist of the body, which is usually found in the Chalukyan and Noḷamba figures, there is here a happy combination of elements from areas like Karṇāta, Kaliṅga, Trilinga and Vaṅga.

This pronouncement disregards historical possibility: he dates the Danang piece eighth century, the Bengal Naṭarāja eleventh century, and inexplicably assumes the commingling of diverse forms in a foreign sculpture, without consideration to the local idiom and traditions. Sivaramamurti's method is not an isolated example, rather it is the normative model, one which makes little attempt to understand the complex dialectics which formulates regional polity and monuments.

Since most Noḷamba monuments are unpublished elsewhere, my main goal is to present a comprehensive listing and description, including iconographic, of the temples and sculptures. After a summary of Noḷamba dynastic history, in chapter two, I will delineate the ninth-tenth centuries Noḷambavāḍi monuments, dividing the territory into subregional groupings (and chapters) in order to explicate style variations. Temple descriptions are lengthy; some readers might find the minutia tedious, but at least now Noḷamba monuments are available for study as expressions from within the regional dialectics rather than as a provincial conglomeration of external influences.

NOTES

1. For convenience I retain dynastic names for periods and, although I discuss the modes of artistic representations regionally, I believe dynastic polity contributes to artistic formations.
2. Although my discussion focuses specifically on the question of centrality and periphery in medieval south Indian polity, I am also questioning the way conventional art histories have assigned certain art or the field of study of certain arts to the (hopefully silent) periphery of art history.
3. For one of the only articles to consider critically the notion of 'influence' as it is used in Indian art history, see Gary Tartakov and Vidya Dehejia, 'Sharing, Intrusion, and Influence: The Mahisasuramardini Imagery of the Calukyas and the Pallavas', *Artibus Asiae* 45 (1984): 287-345.
4. Jan Bialostocki, 'Some Values of Artistic Periphery', in *World Art: Themes of Unity in Diversity* (Pennsylvania State University Press, 1989), p. 50.
5. This problem, especially regarding the history of ideas, is explained by Michel Foucault, *The Archaeology of Knowledge* (New York: Pantheon Books, 1972).
6. To note the obvious: predominately the discipline and language of art writing is inherently loaded and the product of Western philosophical debate.
7. Svetlana Alpers, 'Style Is What You Make It', in *The Concept of Style*, ed. by Berel Lang (Ithaca: Cornell University Press, 1979), pp. 137-62. Cf., Alpers, *The Art of Describing* (Chicago: University of Chicago Press, 1983).
8. Alpers, 'Style', pp. 150-4.
9. Ronald Inden, *Imagining India* (Oxford: Basil Blackwell, 1990), pp. 85-9 for discussion and its implications to India.
10. See Edward Said, *Orientalism* (New York: Pantheon Books, 1978). For a history of the reception of

Indian art in the West see Partha Mittar, *Much Maligned Monsters* (Oxford: Clarendon Press, 1977).

11. For a detailed discussion see Gyan Prakash, 'Writing Post-Orientalist Histories of the Third World: Perspectives from Indian Historiography', *Comparative Studies in Society and History* 32: 1990: 383-408.
12. Cf. Inden, *Imagining*, pp. 192-8.
13. K. A. Nilkanta Sastri, *The Colas* (Madras: Madras University, 1955). Also *A History of South India* (London: Oxford Press, 1966). A.S. Altekar, *The Rashtrakutas and their Time* (Poona: Poona Oriental Series, 1934).
14. Burton Stein, *Peasant State and Society in Medieval South India* (Oxford: Oxford University Press, 1980).
15. Inden, *Imagining*.
16. Nicholas Dirks, *The Hollow Crown* (Cambridge: Cambridge University Press, 1987).
17. Stein's 'segmentary state' theory is partially challenged by Noboru Karashima, *South Indian History and Society* (Oxford: Oxford University Press, 1984). Also see James Heitzman, 'State formation in South India, 850-1280', *The Indian Economic and Social History Review* 24 (1987): 35-61. For comments by Inden, *Imagining*, pp. 205-10.
18. Dirks, *Hollow Crown*, pp. 47-8.
19. For some of the issues and an advocacy for regional (opposed to dynastic) labels see: Pramod Chandra, *On the Study of Indian Art* (Cambridge: Harvard University, 1983), pp. 70-2.
20. Nandi: *MAR* 1914, 1932, 1940; Avani: *MAR* 1911, 1923, 1927, 1930, 1935, 1940, 1945; Aralaguppe: *MAR* 1912, 1935.
21. M. Seshadri, 'Sandhya Tandava', *Artibus Asiae* 18 (1955): 117-20. 'Astadikpala Figures from Aralaguppe, Mysore State', *Journal of the Mysore University* 23 (1967): 70-1.
22. C. Sivaramamurti, *Nataraja in Art, Thought and Literature* (New Delhi: National Museum, 1974), fig. 128. *Panorama of Jain Art* (New Delhi: Times of India, 1983), fig. 211. He labels the temple Late Cālukya.
23. A. De Lippe, *Indian Mediaeval Sculpture* (Amsterdam: North Holland Pub., 1978) pls. 291-3.
24. K.V. Soundara Rajan, *Indian Temple Styles* (New Delhi: Munshiram Manoharlal, 1972), pp. 130, 143-5.
25. B.R. Prasad, *Temple Sculpture of Andhra Pradesh* (Hyderabad: Government of Andhra Pradesh, 1978), pp. 36-9. *Art of South India: Andhra Pradesh* (Delhi: Sundeep Prakashan, 1980), pp. 161-3.
26. J.C. Harle, *The Art and Architecture of the Indian Subcontinent* (Middlesex: Penguin Books, 1986), pp. 183-4.
27. Susan Huntington, *The Art of Ancient India* (New York: Weatherhill, 1985) pp. 338-40.
28. *EITA*, 2: 213, pl. 635. K. V. Soundara Rajan is the section contributor. Adding to the confusion, there is a Mallēśvara temple at Hemavati but it is not the one described.
29. *EITA*, 2: 212-3, pls. 628, 630.
30. *EITA*, 2: 210. Only the apex *śikhara* has brick and mortar images (see Nandi section).
31. K. Krishna Murthy, *Nolamba Sculptures: A Cultural Study* (Delhi: Sundeep Prakashan, 1987). The content of this study differs little from the author's other works, to name a few: *Material Culture of Sanchi* (Delhi: Sundeep Prakashan, 1983), *Ancient Indian Furniture* (Delhi: Sundeep Prakashan, 1982), *Mirrors of Indian Culture* (Delhi: Sundeep Prakashan, 1982).
32. The author's incessant quest to identify material objects led him to believe that a musician playing a three-headed drum was actually a merchant with 'three gunny bags filled with edibles. . . .' (p. 121, fig. XLI, pl. XLIII). The figure is carved on a Hemavati pillar at the Madras Museum. The drummer, with other musicians beside him, accompany Naṭēśa who dances to the proper right of the musicians.
33. M.S. Krishna Murthy, *The Nolambas: A Political and Cultural Study* (Mysore: University of Mysore, 1980). The monograph is a revision of his doctoral thesis submitted to the University of Mysore in 1975.
34. B.L. Rice, *Mysore and Coorg From the Inscriptions* (London: Archibald Constable and Co., 1909). Also see Rice's introductions to *EC*, vols., 10, 11, 12.
35. N. Lakshminarayan Rao, 'Genealogy and Chronology of the Nolamba-Pallavas', *The Quarterly Journal of the Mythic Society* 47 (1956-7): 28-42.
36. T.V. Mahalingam, 'The Nolamba Pallavas: Their Origin', *Journal of Indian History* 36 (1958): 131-41.
37. M.D. Sompath, 'New Light on Nolambas', *Professor K.A. Nilakanta Sastri Felicitations Volume* (Madras: Prof. K.A. Nilkanta Sastri Felicitation Committee, 1971), pp. 165-79.
38. V. Balambal, *Feudatories of South India* (Allahabad: Chugh Pub., 1978).
39. Douglas Barrett, *Nolamba Temples at Hemavati* (Bombay: Bhulabhai Memorial Institute, 1958).
40. C. Sivaramamurti, *Nolamba Sculptures in the Madras Government Museum* (Madras: Government of Madras, 1964).
41. Sivaramamurti, *Nolamba*, p. 2; *Nataraja*, p. 212; *The Art of India* (New York: Harry Abrams, 1977), p. 223.
42. Sivaramamurti, *Nolamba*, p. 8. In discussing style he considers Cālukya and Rāṣṭrakūṭa synonymous.
43. Ibid., pp. 8-9.
44. Ibid.

CHAPTER TWO

Summary of Noḷamba Political History

Though a lesser-known dynasty in comparison to their better-known contemporary dynasties such as the Rāṣṭrakūṭas, Pallavas, and Cōḷas, the Noḷambas were, nevertheless, a critical power in the fluctuating politics of south India during the eighth through eleventh centuries. The family commonly referred to themselves in epigraphs as Noḷamba-Pallava, but scholars have not found evidence which establishes a consanguineous relation between the Noḷambas and the Pallavas. Sometime in the eighth century, the Noḷambas settled in Noḷambaḷige (portions of Chitradurg and Tumkur districts in present day Karnataka and Anantapur district in Andhra Pradesh). While serving as a feudatory to the Gaṅgas, or, as the flux of power demanded, to the Rāṣṭrakūṭas, the Noḷambas were able to consolidate local control. By 878 (CE) the powerful Noḷamba ruler Mahēndrādhirāja conquered neighbouring families, especially the Telugu Cōḍas, the Bāṇas, and the Vaidumbas, severed his ties with the Gaṅgas, and declared himself independent. From that date to the beginning of the eleventh century, the Noḷambas remained either fully independent or minimally subservient to other dynasties. They ruled from their capital, Hemavati, over the territory known as Noḷambavāḍi which at its height encompassed Tumkur, Chitradurg, and sections of Kolar, Bangalore, and Mysore districts in Karnataka; a substantial portion of Anantapur district in Andhra Pradesh; and the northern part of Dharmapuri district in Tamil Nadu (see map). The following dynastic history is based on my reading of over 250 stone inscriptions issued by the Noḷambas and relevant epigraphs from coeval dynasties.[1]

A dated pillar (942) from Hemavati which gives the genealogy of the early Noḷamba kings begins, 'born in the Īśvara-vaṁśa was Trinayana, from whom was born the king of Kānchī, Pallava'.[2] The Noḷambas emphatically claim their descent from the Pallavas. Birudas (epithets) such as 'glory of the Pallavakula', 'the Pallava roarer', and 'the Pallava master champion' frequently occur in Noḷamba epigraphs. Occasionally the Noḷamba ruler will claim the boastful, but dubious, title 'the lord of Kāñcī'.

Trinayana Pallava does not appear in any known Pallava of Kāñcī genealogies, nor is he mentioned in other Noḷamba epigraphs. Trilocana Pallava occurs in some early inscriptions from Andhra Pradesh. H. Krishna Sastri observes: 'Trilochana, Trinetra, Trinayana and Mukkaṇṭi are synonymous terms and occur frequently in Telugu epigraphs with the suffix Pallava, as the name of a mythical ruler of Pallava origin who held sway over the Telugu country at some period of its early history'.[3] Although Krishna Sastri calls Trilocana a mythical ruler, he dates him to the end of the fifth century.[4] In the Hemavati inscription Trinayana is considered the progenitor of the Pallavas, but no further exploits are attributed to him and he should probably be viewed as a legendary figure.

Trinayana means 'he with three eyes', an epithet of Śiva.[5] The Īśvara vaṁśa, from which Trinayana was born, probably refers to Śiva.[6] The Noḷambas were avid followers of Śiva; most of their temple records are Śaiva. The Hemavati genealogy inscription praises the priest Cilluka bhaṭāra, who is considered to be an incarnation of Lakulīśa.[7] The founder or systematizer of the Pāśupata sect of Śaivism, Lakulīśa was an incarnation of Śiva. Apparently the Noḷambas legitimized their dynasty by claiming descent from Śiva, acknowledging a Pallava intermediary. The Pallavas of Kāñcī, however, claim descent from Brahmā not Śiva.[8]

It is not known when or how the Noḷambas became a political force in Noḷambaḷige (portions of Chitradurg, Tumkur and Anantapur districts). One suggestion is that after Pallava Narasiṁhavarman I invaded the Cālukya capital Vātāpi (Badami) in 642, the Noḷambas settled in a border area which was ceded by the Cālukyas to the Pallavas.[9] Another suggestion is that after the death of Pallava Paramēśvara II (731), when the Pallava control over Toṇḍaimaṇḍalam (northern Tamil Nadu) was in disarray, Mangaḷa, the first Noḷamba king, led a junior branch of the Pallavas west and occupied an area in Anantapur district.[10] Since the Noḷambas proudly insist on a Pallava family connection, it is highly probable that they migrated from the Pallava territories. There is, however, no solid information on the circumstances of the migration.

The first historical Noḷamba king is Mangaḷa. No epigraphs are available from his reign, but the Hemavati genealogy inscription gives useful information. 'Born in his [Trinayana's] family, conqueror of the Kirāta king, worshipper of Caṇḍikā, world-renowned for the victory over enemies, was Noḷambādhirāja, praised by the Karṇṇāṭas, the king named Mangaḷa, reverenced by the learned'.[11]

Mangaḷa, according to the Hemavati record, defeated the Kirātas. Kirāta is a generic name for hunting tribes which populated areas of south India. It appears that Mangaḷa settled in a new territory and displaced local families while establishing control. It is generally assumed that the Karṇṇāṭas who praised Mangaḷa were the Cālukyas of Vātāpi (Badami). The nature of the relationship between the Cālukyas and the Noḷambas is not known. With the aid of Gaṅga Śrīpuruṣa, Cālukya Vikramāditya II conquered Kāñcī (*c.* 735) and on their return left an inscription (badly abraded) in the Tumkur district which mentions the seizure of some territory(?) in Noḷambavāḍi.[12] Significantly, the term Noḷambavāḍi was used, revealing that this area already was associated with the Noḷambas. The coeval Noḷamba ruler might have been Mangaḷa.

Mangaḷa's son and successor was Siṁhapōta, alternatively known as Kali Noḷambādhirāja Kolliarasa and Kolli Pallava Noḷamba. Siṁhapōta served as a feudatory first to Gaṅga Śivamāra II and later to Rāṣṭrakūṭa Gōvinda III.

Under the Gaṅgas, Siṁhapōta became a powerful figure. Three undated vīrakaḷs (memorial stones) from Doddaulvarte, Chitradurg district refer to the reign of Siṁhapōta.[13] Two mention no suzerain but the third reveals that Siṁhapōta Kali Noḷambādhiarasa, 'entitled to the five great sounds, favourite of the earth', was ordered by Permmanaḍi to battle Duggamāra.[14] Possession of the five great sounds (pañcamahāśabda) is a privilege reserved for special feudatories:[15] it demonstrates that Siṁhapōta enjoyed high status and, at least locally, wielded authority. His obligation, nevertheless, was to act according to his overlord's command. Permmanaḍi is an honorific kingship title and in this particular inscription it is thought to designate Gaṅga Śivamāra II.[16] Duggamāra Ereyappa, the younger brother of Śivamāra, made an unsuccessful attempt to seize the Gaṅga throne.

Rāṣṭrakūṭa Gōvinda III conquered Gaṅgavāḍi (*c.* 798) and imprisoned Śivamāra. Stambha Raṇāvalōka (Kambarasa), elder brother to Gōvinda, was appointed to rule Gaṅgavāḍi (southern Karnataka which was controlled by the Gaṅgas of Talakad) and held the area until his death in 802.[17] Rāṣṭrakūṭa sovereignty extended over Siṁhapōta who responded to Gōvinda's call to battle Citravāhana II of the Āḷupa family.[18]

The next Noḷamba ruler was Cāruponneṛa. He remained a vassal to Rāṣṭrakūṭa Gōvinda III during the early years of his reign. Two informative inscriptions from the Mallēśvara temple at Chikkamadhure (Chitradurg district) which commence with an acknowledgment to Gōvinda (here identified as Jagattuṅga Prabhūtavarṣa Pratāpāvalōka Śrī Vallaha), state that Cāruponneṛa (here identified as Siṁhapōta Rāja's son Paramēśvara Pallavādhirāja) ruled Noḷambaḷige 1000, Nirggundanāḍ 300, Iṛigalvāḍi 300, Gaṅgavūr 30, and Nelliguṇḍi 12.[19] They also state that Cāruponneṛa's son Pallavamalla (Poḷalcōra) ruled Madarikal, Toṇḍūr, Malchar 12, Ammavaḷḷi 12, Kōḷūr 12, and Gaṅgavūr 30. Extensive portions of Chitradurg and Tumkur districts were directly under Noḷamba control. Iṛigalvāḍi 300 (present day Pavugada taluk, Tumkur district) has been identified as Eṛigalvāḍi, part of the traditional territory of the Telugu Cōḍas.[20] Evidently the Noḷambas had expropriated land from the Cōḍas.[21] The Chikkamadhure epigraphs also mention that Cāruponneṛa's wife Gavagaṇabbe had a Śiva temple named Gavagaṇēśvara built in Madarakal.[22]

Rāṣṭrakūṭa Gōvinda died in 814 and was succeeded by Amōghavarṣa Nṛpatuṅga, a six-year-old boy. The unstable leadership of the youth substantially weakened the Rāṣṭrakūṭas and created a power void which allowed many Rāṣṭrakūṭa feudatories to attain independence. In Gaṅgavāḍi, and surrounding areas, an intense struggle for control ensued with the Gaṅgas and Noḷambas allied against the Bāṇas. The Manne plates of Gaṅga Rācamalla, dated 828, claim a major victory over the Bāṇas.[23] However, the battle for supremacy in Gaṅgavāḍi continued throughout the rest of Cāruponneṛa's years and into his successor's reign.

Poḷalcōra, Cāruponneṛa's son, enhanced the Gaṅga-Noḷamba alliance by marrying Jāyabbe, the daughter of Gaṅga Rācamalla.[24] Poḷalcōra probably assisted Rācamalla in his campaign into Bāṇa territory. Rācamalla's expedition through Pulināḍu (North Arcot district in Tamil Nadu and Chittoor district in Andhra Pradesh) reached at least as far as Vaillimalai, North Arcot district, where he had carved and inscribed two large groups of Jain images on the walls of a natural cave.[25]

During the reign of Rācamalla's son Gaṅga Nītimārga Permmanaḍi, Noḷambādhirāja Poḷalcōra governed Gaṅgarusāsira (Gaṅga 6000).[26] Nītimārga and Poḷalcōra made a land grant to the family of Pompalla, a hero in Poḷalcōra's army who died fighting the Bāṇas at Murggepadi.[27] Gaṅgarusāsira, consisting of Kolar district and possibly adjacent parts of Chittoor and Dharmapuri districts, considerably expanded the Noḷamba realm. Poḷalcōra also controlled a portion of Anantapur district. An inscribed pillar found at Kambaduru states that Poḷalcōra bestowed on Ajjaparvara Bhidiyeṛya (probably an architect) the name Noḷambadoḍḍa (servant to Noḷamba) in honour of his construction of a temple dedicated to Mahādēva (Śiva).[28] An epigraph during Nītimārga's reign, dated 853, mentions that his subordinate, Noḷamba, ruled as far as Kāñcī.[29] Although the statement is probably an exaggeration, it does suggest that the Noḷambas had become a significant political power in south India. Therefore it is not surprising to learn that Gunaga Vijayāditya III, the Cālukya of Vēṅgī king and ally to the Rāṣṭrakūṭas, penetrated into Noḷambavāḍi in order to weaken the Gaṅgas and the Noḷambas.[30] Many Cālukya of Vēṅgī epigraphs pridefully exclaim that Vijayāditya killed 'Maṅgi', who in one of the inscriptions is called the ruler of Noḷambarastra.[31] Some scholars believe Maṅgi to be Poḷalcōra because the term Noḷambarāṣṭrapati appears in the inscription and because the event corresponds to Poḷalcōra's known reign period (*c.* 870).[32] Alternatively it has been suggested that Maṅgi was a relative to the ruler of Noḷambavāḍi and general of the army.[33] Whoever Maṅgi might have been, his defeat did not alter the strength of the Noḷambas.

Poḷalcōra's successor Mahēndra inherited his father's territories, his subsidiary position to the Gaṅgas, and his animosity towards the Bāṇas. Eventually Mahēndrādhirāja became fully independent, defeated the Bāṇas and other families, and greatly expanded his territorial rule.

Two vīrakaḷs (undated, *c.* 870) state that Mahēndra ruled Gaṅgarusāsira (Gaṅga 6000).[34] The Gaṅga-Noḷamba alliance remained secure during Mahēndra's early reign. Consequently Mahēndra defended Gaṅga Rācamalla II against Pṛthvīpati (member of the collateral Gaṅga family), a contestant for the Gaṅga throne. Pṛthvīpati formed a strategic alliance with Bāṇa Vikramāditya and Vaidumba Gaṇḍatriṇētra.[35] Together they fought at Mudimaḍuvu, Tiruvuḷa and Māndāvuda, with the pivotal battle at Sōremaḍi against Rācamalla, Mahēndra, Mayindamacōḷa (a Telugu Cōḍa king) and Danḍiga(?).[36] Epigraphs referring to hostilities previous to the battle at Sōremaḍi were issued by the Bāṇas or Vaidumbas, but both families were conspicuously silent in regard to the outcome. The allied Gaṅga-Noḷamba forces appear to have scored a major victory.[37] Mahēndra continued to attack the Bāṇas, seized portions of Pulināḍu, and by 893 claimed to have 'destroyed the Mahābali race' (Mahābalikulavisvaṁśa).[38] Mahēndra's records after 878 indicate that he had achieved independence: a pillar inscription from the Mahēndrēśvara temple in Baraguru, Tumkur district states that, 'the crowns of all the bowing feudatories rolling before his jewel throne . . . glory of the Pallavakula, Śrī Mahēndrādhirāja, having uprooted and destroyed Chōra and other rivals, was ruling the kingdom of the world . . . rejoiced to have increased the kingdom. . . '.[39] Mahēndra had the Mahēndrēśvara temple built in 878 (Śaka 800) and granted land for temple maintenance and for worship of the god Mahēndrēśvara. The grant to the priest Dinakarasōma bhaṭāra stipulates that the teacher and his disciples must be Brahmacārīs (celibates), for a 'maṭhapati who is not a Brahmachāri, has ruined the king who rules him, the *nāḍ*, and the assembly of the village, and is guilty of the five great sins'.[40]

The Telugu Cōḍas (Cōras) were defeated by Mahēndra and became his feudatory.[41] At the battle of Sōremaḍi the Cōḍas fought alongside Mahēndra. The Kālahastīśvara temple at Nidugal, Tumkur district, has an inscription which explains that Cōrarasa had the temple built while Mahēndra ruled the kingdom of the world.[42]

In 883 Mahēndra was in Kambaduru, Anantapur district where he granted land to an Āditya (Sūrya) temple.[43] To his south-east, in Toṇḍaimaṇḍalam, conditions were unstable due to the ongoing struggle between the Pallava brothers, Nṛpatuṅga and Aparājita.[43] As the Pallava territorial hegemony deteriorated, peripheral families seized available territories. The Cōḷas, for one, began their rise during this period. It is at such times as these that excursions into weaken territories might be economically beneficial (i.e. booty). Quick to exploit the disharmonious conditions, Mahēndra campaigned into Toṇḍaimaṇḍalam: according to the testimony of two vīrakaḷs dated the twenty-sixth regnal year of Pallava Nṛpatuṅga (885), Mahēndra raided Ambur, North Arcot district.[45] He continued on the offensive through Pulināḍu and after destroying the Bāṇas, Mahēndra established himself at Tagaduru (present-day Dharmapuri, Dharmapuri district).

In Dharmapuri Mahēndra made grants to both Śaiva and Jain temples. Mahēndra granted a tank(?) to the Śaiva teacher Ponnera goravar in 878.[46] While residing at his royal mansion at Tagaduru in 893, Mahēndra granted the village Mulapalle to a basadi (Jain temple) in order to provide for worship and maintenance.[47] A third fragmentary pillar inscription from Noḷambādhirāja's (Mahēndra) reign, records a donation by Bhairavaśakti bhaṭāra of Nandi.[48] Nandi, where the priest comes from, can be identified as Nandi in Kolar district, location of the Bhōgaṇandiśvara and Aruṇācalēśvara Noḷamba temples.[49]

The earliest temple inscription at Hemavati is from Mahēndra's reign. Near the Doḍḍēśvara temple a broken pillar records a grant of land given to feed the Jain priests (tapasvins), and to upkeep a tank, issued by Mayindamma (Mahēndra) and which also mentions his son Ayyabba (Ayyapa).[50]

Finally, Mahēndrādhirāja's expansionist policy focused on Gaṅgavāḍi. His unsuccessful campaign against his one-time suzerain, Gaṅga Rācamalla II, ended with his death.[51] Vīrakaḷs from Kolar, Bangalore and Mandya districts record the heroic death of soldiers in Noḷamba-Gaṅga battles.[52] An inscription from Chittoor district reveals that Noḷambadiyarasa (Mahēndra) marched on Taḻekāḍu (Talakad, the Gaṅga capital).[53] Mahēndra in 895 granted land to a temple in central Gaṅgavāḍi (Tayalur, Mandya district).[54] Rācamalla was aided by his brother Būtaga and his nephew Nītimārga Eṟeyappa. The Gattavadipur plates state that Eṟeyappa, through the aid of spies, was able to capture Tippēru, Sūṟūr, and the Noḷamba capital Penjaru (present-day Hemavati), and put Mahēndra to death.[55] The plates are dated 904 but the event probably took place between 895, the last dated epigraph from Mahēndra, and 897, the first dated inscription of Mahēndra's son Ayyapa.

Ayyapa succeeded Mahēndra; however, the epigraphs from his early reign years are difficult to piece together coherently. An inscription dated 897 found in the Tumkur district refers to Ayyapa (Noḷambādhirāja Nolippa) as being independent (ruling the kingdom of the world).[56] A grant from Chikmagalur district was made by a 'Noḷambamahādēva of Asandināḍ' in 899-900 during the reign of Gaṅga Rācamalla II.[57] If Noḷambamahādēva and Ayyapa are the same person, then Ayyapa was ruling a minor area in Gaṅgavāḍi as Rācamalla's feudatory. No other epigraphs during Ayyapa's reign acknowledge Gaṅga suzerainty. Some Ganga heroes died fighting Ayyapa at Kakikatte during Rācamalla's reign.[58] This event transpired before 907 (the last known dated inscription for Rācamalla); possibly the hostilities were before 900, at which time Ayyapa accepted Rācamalla as an overlord.[59] But a confusing vīrakaḷ dated 907 from Chitradurg district (Noḷamba territory), issued during the reign of Rāṣṭrakūṭa Kṛṣṇa II, mentions that 'by the order of Gaṅga' two heroes died fighting Noḷamba.[60] Hostilities between the Gaṅgas and Noḷambas appear to have occurred intermittently during the early years of Ayyapa's reign. The tension between the families might have eased after Ayyapa married the Gaṅga princess Pollabbarasi, mother of Aṇṇiga who succeeded Ayyapa.[61]

The Gaṅgas suffered defeats by Rāṣṭrakūṭa Kṛṣṇa II during the early tenth century. In 903 Damapàiya, a Rāṣṭrakūṭa general, occupied Gaṅgavāḍi.[62] Ayyapa's status at this time is unknown. The Rāṣṭrakūṭa epigraph found in Chitradurg district, dated 907, has been mentioned above.[63] Ayyapa is not encountered again in a dated record until 918 at which time he ruled Noḷambavāḍi independently.

From Bagenahalu, Chitradurg district, a partially effaced inscription (on an Īśvara temple) dated 918-19, states that 'Nannigaśraya (the asylum of truth) Śrīmat Ayyapadēva ruled the kingdom of the world'.[64] In the same year Ayyapa's son Mayda Noḷipa ruled from Jakkasandra, Bangalore district.[65] Also that year, on the occasion of the solar eclipse, in honor of his wives Nāgiyabbe and Heleyabbe ('the beloved of his heart and eyes'), Ayyapa granted land to the two temples at Baraguru (Tumkur district) and gave a gift to the god Mahēndrēśvara.[66] The event was witnessed by the leaders of the five maṭhas of Penjeru (Hemavati); evidently the Noḷamba capital was a thriving religious centre. Another Chitradurg record, from Mushtur, Kallēśvara temple dated 920 states that Ayyapa ruled Noḷambavāḍi 32,000 and his son Aṇṇayya (Aṇṇiga) ruled Paduma and Muttuvur.[67] The record further states that a temple with a ruined foundation was rebuilt in stone by the god's servant, Nāthavarmmā.

Dharmapuri remained within Ayyapa's realm of control. To the same basadi that Mahēndra had granted land, Ayyapa awarded the village Buduguru.[68] Undated epigraphs from Ayyapa's reign also are found in Kolar district.[69]

In 922 the Noḷambas made an expedition into Rāṣṭrakūṭa territory. Two vīrakaḷs found at Kadabagare (Harapanahalli taluk), Bellary district and issued in the reign of Indra III state that Māḷayya and Nākalokka of the Kadamba family died when Aṇṇiga, son of Ayyapa from Noḷambavāḍi, attacked at Padugallu.[70] The following year Aṇṇiga succeeded to the Noḷamba throne.[71]

It has been asserted that Ayyapa remained alive during Aṇṇiga's reign, moved north, and ruled the Harapanahalli taluk area (Bellary district) under the Rāṣṭrakūṭas while Aṇṇiga controlled Noḷambavāḍi.[72] This claim is probably based on a confusion. A vīrakaḷ from Harapanahalli taluk dated 931-2, during the reign of Gōvinda IV, tells that a Paḍiganomba died defending the village. 'Ayyapayya', who ruled Māsevāḍi 140 and Kōlalināḍ, made a grant to the hero's family.[73] Ayyapa is also said to have fought the Cālukya of Vēṅgī King Bhīma II (*c.* 934). An inscription from Bangalore district issued by Gaṅga Eṟeyappa refers to an 'Ayappadēva' who combined forces with him and fought against Bira Mahēndra (Bhima II) at Tumbepāḍi.[74] Bhīma is said to have killed the 'excessively powerful Ayyapa'.[75] This Ayyapa has been identified as the Noḷamba Ayyapa.[76] Although the Ayyapa in the above two records might be the same person, it is questionable to identify him with Ayyapa Noḷambādhirāja. Conclusive evidence exists which shows that Aṇṇiga's reign began in 923 (Śaka 845).[77] It is implausible that Noḷamba Ayyapa ceded all control of Noḷambavāḍi to his son Aṇṇiga in 923, re-emerged a decade later as a ruler of a minor area under the Rāṣṭrakūṭas, and then, as an aged man, fought a battle in Bangalore district.

A vīrakaḷ from Dharmapuri district, dated 925 (Śaka 847) is also labelled the second regnal year of Aṇṇiyan Vīra-Nuḷamba (Aṇṇiga).[78] Aṇṇiga inherited and maintained control throughout Noḷambavāḍi until his later years when some territory was ceded to the Rāṣṭrakūṭas. He married the Cālukya princess Attiyabbarasi; she bore their son Iruḷacōra, who is mentioned only once (in 929 from Dharmapuri) and must have predeceased his father.[79]

During Aṇṇiga's reign two Śaiva priests, Varuṇaśiva-bhaṭāra and Tribhuvanakartara-bhaṭāra, occupied prestigious and influential positions. In Anantapur district, during 936, Bīranoḷamba Aṇṇayyadēva (Aṇṇiga) granted land for the upkeep of a tank.[80] Varuṇaśiva, the administrator of the Noḷambēśvara temple (sthāna), witnessed the gift. The privilege of being entitled to the five great sounds and other lofty titles (e.g. paramēśvara, mahāsāmantādhipati, etc.) were conferred upon Varuṇaśiva. In Hemavati his name appears on the south wall of the Doḍḍēśvara temple, as does his teacher's name, Rudraśivācārya.[81] On the east basement of the Lakṣmaṇēśvara temple in Avani, Kolar district, is inscribed 'svasti Śrī Vīra Noḷamba' (Aṇṇiga) and 'svasti Śrī Tribhuvanadēvam'.[82] Tribhuvanakartaradēva was the guru to the Avani sthāna. In 961 Tribhuvanakartara died after ruling the Avani area for forty years and having built fifty temples.[83] His name frequently appeared in records during Iṛiva's reign. A sculpted image of Tribhuvanakarata is delineated next to his name on the north exterior wall of the Lakṣmaṇēśvara temple.[84]

The Śāntara family attacked Noḷambavāḍi. Aṇṇiga, with the aid of his ally Nanniya Gaṅga (from the collateral Gaṅga line), defeated and killed the Śāntara king.[85]

In the latter part of his reign Aṇṇiga Bīranoḷamba made an ill advised assault on Gaṅgavāḍi.[86] Aṇṇiga penetrated as far as Kottamaṅgaḷa, Mysore district, where he was overwhelmed by Gaṅga Rācamalla III, causing Aṇṇiga to become subordinate to Rācamalla.[87] Shortly thereafter (*c.* 937), the Rāṣṭrakūṭa Yuvarāja Kṛṣṇa III raided Gaṅgavāḍi, killed Rācamalla and installed Būtaga II upon the Gaṅga throne (Būtaga was Rācamalla's younger brother and son-in-law to Kṛṣṇa).[88] Also 'the Pallava [king] Aṇṇiga was beaten and reduced to a sad condition' by Kṛṣṇa.[89] The last known dated records of Aṇṇiga are three vīrakaḷs from Dharmapuri district dated the fifteenth regnal year of Bīranoḷamba (938).[90]

Iṛiva Noḷamba Diliparasa succeeded his elder brother Aṇṇiga. The Hemavati genealogy epigraph issued in 942 (Iṛiva's first dated inscription) records a gift of land to sustain the god Naninnēśvara.[91] Cilluka-bhaṭāra, an incarnation of Lakulīśa, was entrusted with the grant.

The Noḷamba hegemony contracted during Iṛiva's reign. Portions of Chitradurg district, the ancestral home of the Noḷambas, were ceded to the Rāṣṭrakūṭas after Aṇṇiga's defeat. Records are conspicuously absent from Dharmapuri, which had been a Noḷamba stronghold since Mahēndra's time. However, Kolar, Anantapur, Tumkur, and a portion of Bangalore districts remained in Iṛiva's domain. His epigraphs speak of him 'ruling the kingdom of the world' (an independent ruler), but he did serve as a feudatory to Rāṣṭrakūṭa Kṛṣṇa III during the latter's campaigns against the Cōḷas.

Iṛiva joined Ponnayya, a servant of Ballaha (Kṛṣṇa) in the battle of Ipīḷi (948) against Gajāṅkuśacōḷa.[92] K.V. Ramesh suggests that Gajāṅkuśacōḷa was a member of the Telugu Cōḍa family, but that the battle was part of the Rāṣṭrakūṭa offensive against the imperial Cōḷas which climaxed at Takkōlam (in 949) with the death of Cōḷa Rājāditya at the hand of Gaṅga Būtaga II.[93] Kṛṣṇa remained in Toṇḍaimaṇḍalam, as is evident from his inscriptions.[94] During Iṛiva's reign his son Nanni and his grandson Poḷalcōra II aided the Rāṣṭrakūṭas. A grant from Anantapur district, dated 965, states that Poḷalcōradēva (grandson of Iṛiva Noḷambādhirāja, 'the lord of Kāñcī') served as an officer to Rāṣṭrakūṭa Kṛṣṇa during the latter's conquest of Cōḷanāḍu.[95] During Kṛṣṇa's twenty-sixth regnal year (*c.* 966), Nuḷamba Tribhuvanādhīra, also called the glorious Pallavamurāri (Viṣṇu among the Pallavas) and his son Nuḷamba made a donation in Velur, North Arcot district, to a temple.[96] Nuḷamba Tribhuvanādhīra must be the contemporary Noḷamba king, Iṛiva.

The Vaidumbas and the Bāṇas, evicted by the Cōḷas from their homelands, became feudatories to Kṛṣṇa who made them subordinate to Iṛiva. An inscription on the Vijayaraṅgasvāmī temple at Betamaṅgala in Kolar district records that Iṛiva ordered Vaidumba Vikramādityan Tiruvayya to repair a tank and grant land to the five hundred Brahmans of Kayvāra.[97] In 961, while Iṛiva was ruling the kingdom of the world, Sambayya, born into the Mahābali kula (Bāṇas), granted land for a tank.[98]

Iṛiva was the first Noḷamba king to be supportive of Vaiṣṇavism. He continued the traditional patronage of Śaiva temples at Hemavati and Avani, and in addition he granted land to a Viṣṇu temple at Madhudi, Anantapur district in 959-60.[99] Iṛiva permitted Kōtayya, a Rāṣṭrakūṭa official, to construct a Visnu temple at Agali, Anantapur district.[100] Iṛiva occasionally employed Vaisnava birudas—Pallavarāma and Pallavamurāri.

The Noḷamba throne was passed to Iṛiva's son Nanni in an orderly fashion. During Iṛiva's reign Basavayya, a minister of Nanni called Chaladaṅkakāṛadēva, erected a mānastambha (pillar of fame) in Avani which celebrates Nanni's martial abilities.[101] The last dated inscription of Iṛiva was issued in 966-7; two vīrakaḷs are also dated the twenty-seventh year of his reign, which correspond to *c.* 967.[102] Nanni's first dated independent record is from 969.[103]

Nanni's reign coincided with a dramatic upheaval in the power structure of south India. After Kṛṣṇa's death in 968, the Rāṣṭrakūṭa empire began to collapse. From the north, the Paramāras delivered a devastating defeat onto the Rāṣṭrakūṭas and by 973-4 Taila II, the Cālukya of Kalyana king, weakened the Rāṣṭrakūṭas to the extent that, soon after, the former Rāṣṭrakūṭa realm was ruled by Taila. In the deep south, the Cōḷas had become a formidable power constantly trying to expand their rule.

Nanni, after Kṛṣṇa's death, regained former Noḷamba territories. From Chitradurg district an inscription reads 'while Kaṭṭānamalla, the illustrious Chaladaṅkakāra was ruling Gaṅgarusāsira', a temple pillar was set up for Noḷambagāvuṇḍa.[103] Presumably this record refers to Nanni who used the name Chaladaṅkakāra in his Avani record. Gaṅga Mārasiṁha who remained loyal to the enfeebled Rāṣṭrakūṭas, decided to humble Nanni. Kaṭṭānemalla and other Noḷambas were wounded in battle against Mārasiṁha in 971 and in the same year Mārasiṁha arrogantly began to use the epithet *Noḷambakulāntaka* (annihilator of the Noḷambas).[105] Apparently the Noḷambas were substantially weakened; the following years were a chaotic period and they never fully regained control of Noḷambavāḍi. After Mārasiṁha's death in 974, an inscription from Kolar district states: 'Pallavāditya, Noḷambādhirāja and Chōraya Noḷamba's father, these 3 halted in Sūryya Miniyūr—hearing that Mārasiṁha—Permmadi was dead'.[106] The identity of Noḷambādhirāja is uncertain, possibly it is Nanni, but neither he nor his son Poḷalcōra II are ever mentioned again as rulers.

Noḷambavāḍi remained in the possession of the Gaṅgas during the reign of Pāñcāḷadēva (Mārasiṁha's successor) and after his death by Cālukya (of Kalyana) Taila II in 977, Gaṅga Rācamalla IV temporarily held control.[107] The Noḷamba successor Vīramahēndra made advances back into Noḷambavāḍi. An inscription dated 977 in the reign of Maydammarasa (Vīramahēndra) states that he was ruling from Baraguru (Tumkur district), and again that year a Noḷambādhirāja made a grant in the Kolar district.[107] Vīramahēndra Noḷambādhirājadēva left a record in Chittoor district which states that he returned from Cōḷanāḍu, entered Noḷambavāḍi, and camped at Kōḷāla in the Gaṅgarusāsira area, at which time he appointed Kīrigāvuṇḍa to the position of Noḷambagāvuṇḍa of Pulināḍu.[109] Evidently during this period Vīramahēndra exercised considerable control in the region. His expedition into Cōḷanāḍu transpired due to an alliance with Cālukya Taila who often warred with the Cōḷas.

As feudatory to the Later Western Cālukyas, the Noḷambas gradually migrated north, especially after the Cōḷa intrusion into Noḷambavāḍi (*c.* 990). In the Bellary district an epigraph dated 981, during the reign of Cālukya Āhavamalladēva (Taila II), states that Rēvaladēvī, a queen of Vīranoḷamba Pallava Permānaḍidēva who bore the title 'lord of Kāñcī', granted land to two Viṣṇu temples and to the god Kāḷapriyadēva.[110] During this time, Vīramahēndra was involved in a campaign to the south. A vīrakaḷ from Bangalore district might speak of his death: 'Noḷambādhirāja was ruling the kingdom of the world—Cōḷa fighting with Noḷamba force (stationed at) Bijayitamangala—in Peṛdeḷe, Noḷambarasa fighting died. . . '.[111]

Controversy surrounds the identity of Vīramahēndra's successor. Two genealogy inscriptions claim that Vīramahēndra's son was Ekavākyadēva and his younger son was Iṛiva Noḷamba (II) Ghaṭeyaṅkakāṛa.[112] Both records were issued during Iṛiva's reign. But records are not known from the reign of Ekavākya and Iṛiva's first dated inscription is in 1010. Thirty years are void of datable epigraphic evidence. The matter is complicated by an undated inscription from Avani which states that Poḷalcōra's queen, Dīvabbarasi (of the Kadamba family), built a temple to Īśa (Śiva) and one to Mukunda (Viṣṇu), plus a tank, after the death of her son Vīramahēndra.[113] At that time she was waiting for her younger son Pallavēndra Iṛiva Noḷamba to come to rule. According to the Avani record Vīramahēndra and Iṛiva are brothers (not father and son).[114]

The genealogy records correctly state the Noḷamba ancestry for four generations (Iṛiva-Nanni-Poḷalcōra II-Vīramahēndra). It is reasonable to assume that they would be correct with the most recent generation (Vīramahēndra's son was Ekavākya whose younger brother was Iṛiva). This would also explain why Iṛiva is not heard of until 1010; his older brother Ekavākya probably ruled during the interim between Vīramahēndra's death and Iṛiva's ascension. But the fact remains that no Noḷamba epigraphs are available to explain their activities for thirty years, regardless of who ruled.

The Cōḷas aggressively expanded their territorial control and seized portions of Noḷambavāḍi in the late tenth century. Iṛiva II expediently allied his family as a subordinate to the Cālukyas. The sister of Cālukya Vikramāditya V was married to Iṛiva. An inscription of Iṛiva's issued in 1010, from Dharwar district, praised his suzerain Vikramāditya. Iṛiva pridefully exclaimed his marriage alliance and called himself a Trinetra (Śiva) of feudatory princes. He retained the title 'lord of Kāñcī' and claimed rule of Noḷambavāḍi 32,000, Keṁgaḷ 500, Bellakunda 300, Kukkanūr 30 and five towns in Māsiyavāḍināḍu.[115] Only northern Noḷambavāḍi and parts of the Bellary district, however, remained in Iṛiva's care.

The next two generations of Noḷamba kings remained under Cālukya suzerainty, often partaking in campaigns against the Cōḷas. They continued as influential feudatories, frequently granting generous endowments to temples in the Bellary district.[116] Jagadēkamalla Noḷamba Pallava Permanḍi Udayādityadēva succeeded Iṛiva, ruled from Kampali (Bellary district) and claimed control of Gaṅgavāḍi 96,000 among other areas.[117] But this dubious boast was probably only a remembrance of past Noḷamba grandeur. He was followed by his son Jagadēkamalla Irmadi Noḷamba Permanddi, who was succeeded by his younger brother Trailokyamalla Nanni Noḷamba. During his reign Cōḷa Rājādhirāja penetrated Rattamanḍalam (Cālukya territory) and destroyed Kampali.[118] Nanni Noḷamba died in battle at Koppam against Rājendra (younger brother of Rājādhirāja) in 1052.[119] Noḷamba names are found in later epigraphs but their direct relationship to the royal Noḷamba line cannot be determined.

NOTES

1. *MAR*, 1947-56, p. 16, reported the discovery of the first known Noḷamba copper-plates. They did not publish the plates nor give a summary of its contents. The one known set of Noḷamba plates, presumably the same one referred in *MAR*, is considered 'spurious' by M.S. Krishna Murthy, *Noḷambas: A Political and Cultural Study* (Mysore: Mysore University, 1980), p. 8.
2. *EC*, 12: Si 28. Dates are all in the 'common era' (*CE*), unless otherwise specified.
3. *EI*, 11: 340.
4. Ibid.
5. The Kadambas of Goa derive their origin from a three-eyed, four-armed Jayanta, also known as Trilocana Kadamba, who sprang from a drop of sweat from the forehead of Śiva after the conquest of Tripura. J.F. Fleet, 'Dynasties of Kanarase District', *Bombay Gazetteer* 1, pt. 2 (1896): 286. A similar origin from Śiva might have been associated with Trinayana Pallava.
6. Īśvara is an epithet of Śiva. The Īśvara vaṁśa is not known from other family lineages.
7. *EC*, 12: Si 28.
8. Fleet, 'Dynasties', p. 317. The Pallavas of Kāñcī give their descent as: Brahmā-Aṅgiras-Bṛhaspati-Śaṁyu-Bharadvāja-Drōṇa-Aśvathāman-Pallava.
9. Fleet, 'Dynasties', p. 318. Fleet did not recognize the Noḷambas as a family separate from the Pallavas. However, he did suggest: 'The Pallavas had also a province in Western India, known as Noḷambavāḍi . . . this was doubtlessly acquired by them about the middle of the 7th century AD, when they invaded Badami'. Krishna Murthy, *Noḷambas*, pp. 1-2, repeats this suggestion.
10. V. Balambal, *Feudatories of South India, 800-1070 A.D.* (Allahabad: Chugh Pub., 1978), p. 68.
11. *EC*, 12: Si 28.
12. *MAR*, 1941, pp. 220-1.
13. *EC*, 11: Cl 5, 7, 8.
14. *EC*, 11: Cl 8.
15. *EI*, 5: 216 (according to Fleet). The Noḷambas even as independent rulers retained the title '*samadhigatapañcamahāśabda*'.
16. T.V. Mahālingam, 'The Noḷamba Pallavas: Their Origin', *Journal of Indian History* 36 (1958): 131-41, disagrees. He thinks Permmanḍi refers to Pallava Nandivarman II who, according to Mahālingam, was the overlord of Siṁhapōta.
17. *EC*, 9: Nl 61. A. S. Altekar, *Rashtrakutas and their Times* (Poona: Poona Oriental Series, 1967), p. 62.
18. *EC*, 8: Sb 10.
19. *EC*, 11 Cl: 33-34.
20. *EI*, 27: 221-22.
21. Ibid. An epigraph from Tumkur district (*MAR*, 1918, p. 43) states that Ponneṛa (Cāruponneṛa) and Cōḷa Mahārāja made a grant(?) together. Probably this Cōḷa Mahārāja is a Telugu Cōḍa king; if so, this would suggest that the Noḷambas and Cōḍas were on amicable terms.
22. This is the earliest surviving Noḷamba epigraph which claims royal temple patronage. Madarakal was the traditional name for Chikkamadhure. At this village a dilapidated Īśvara temple survives which probably is the Gavagaṇēśvara temple.
23. *MAR*, 1910, p. 25.
24. *EC*, 12: Si 38; *EI*, 10: 68.
25. *EI*, 4: 160.
26. *EC*, 10: Kl 79.
27. Ibid. Although the inscription clearly identifies Pompalla as a Noḷamba subordinate Krishna Murthy, *Noḷambas*, p. 59 misidentifies Pompalla as a Bāṇa subordinate.
28. *SII*, 9 (pt. 1): 17. Today there is not a Noḷamba period temple at Kambaduru.
29. *ARE*, 1913, no. 588; and pt. 2, pp. 90-2.
30. Altekar, *Rashtrakutas*, pp. 91-4.

31. *EI*, 5: 162; *EI*, 4: 239; *EI*, 9: 55; *SII*, 1: 38-9, 42.
32. Krishna Murthy, *Noḷambas*, pp. 60, 192-3; Balambal, *Feudatories*, p. 75.
33. Altekar, *Rashtrakutas*, p. 94.
34. *EC*, 10: Bp 64; *EC*, 9: Ht 9.
35. Pṛthvīpati strengthened his alliance with the Bāṇas by marrying his daughter Kundavve to Bāṇa Vidyādhara, a Bāṇa prince, *EI*, 24: 187.
36. Battle at Mudimaḍuvu: *EI*, 24: 192; *ARE*, 1922, no. 314. Tiruvuḷa: *ARE*, 1923, no. 309. Māndāvuda: *EI*, 7: 23; *EC*, 10: Mb 228. Sōremaḍi: *EI*, 24: 192; *ARE*, 1922, no. 308. The date of the Sōremaḍi battle and its participants has been much debated. Jayaranga Rao (*EA* 4: 21-24) dates the battle to *c.* 825 and believes Rācamalla I (not II) was the Gaṅga king. R.S. Panchamukha (*EI*, 24: 183-93), *c.* 885 and has Pṛthvīpati's son Nanniya Gaṅga involved (Krishna Murthy, *Noḷambas*, p. 80, denies Nanniya Ganga ever existed). Balambal, *Feudatories*, p. 76, *c.* 875. Krishna Murthy, *Noḷambas*, pp. 70-84, dates the battle between 878-83 and discusses the issues at length.
37. *EI*, 24: 189; Krishna Murthy, *Noḷambas*, pp. 83-4.
38. *SII*, 9 (pt. 1): 4; *EI*, 10: 68.
39. *EC*, 12: Si 38. See Baraguru section regarding the Mahēndrēśvara temple.
40. Ibid.
41. *EC*, 12: Si 38; *EC*, 12: Si 24.
42. *EC*, 12: p. 45. This epigraph is built into the Kalahastīśvara temple which was reconstructed in 1670 by Harati Timmaṇṇa Nāyaka (*EC*, 12: p. 46).
43. *SII*, 9 (pt. 1): 18.
44. Nṛpatuṅga and Aparājita were in contention for the Pallava throne. Nṛpatuṅga ruled Toṇḍaimaṇḍalam and had as his ally Pāṇḍa Varaguṇa. Aparājita had Pṛthvīpati I of the collateral Gaṅga family and probably Cōḷa Āditya I as allies. The forces battled at Sripurambiyam in *c.* 885 and Aparājita's side won. K.A. Nilakanta Sastry, *A History of South India* (Bombay: Oxford Press, 1964), pp. 174-5.
45. *EI*, 4: 180-3.
46. *SII*, 7: 580. The suffix goravar is mostly associated with Saiva ascetics, although Jain priest occasionally claimed the title.
47. *EI*, 10: 69. The grant was actually received by the merchants Candiyaṇṇa and Nidhyaṇṇa, the patrons of the temple, who transferred it to the priest Kanakasēna Siddhāntadabhaṭāra. No Noḷamba period Jain temples survive in Dharmapuri but a few loose Jain sculptures remain in the vicinity.
48. *SII*, 7: 532.
49. See Nandi section in chapter four.
50. *SII*, 9 (pt. 1): 19. Loose Jain sculptures remain in Hemavati but not basadis.
51. Mahēndra had a consanguineous relation with the Gaṅgas; his mother Jāyabbe was from the Ganga family (as was his wife, Gāmabbe), *SII*, 9 (pt. 1): 23.
52. *EC*, 10: Sp 19; *EC*, 10: CT 116; *EC*, 9: DB 3; *MAR*, 1926, p. 71; *EC*, 3: Nl 139 (dated 891-2 *CE*).
53. *SII*, 9 (pt. 1): 20.
54. *EC*, 14: Md 13 (rev.).
55. *EC*, 12: Nj 269.
56. *EC*, 12: Mi 52. It is not inconceivable that Nolippa is other than Ayyapa, but the name Nolippa does not appear in any known Noḷamba genealogies. Nolippa is also used in *EC*, 12: Mi 27.
57. *EC*, 6: Kd 141.
58. *EC*, 6: CM 129; *EC*, 15: Ak 215.
59. Krishna Murthy, *Noḷambas*, p. 97 holds this opinion but he does not discuss a vīrakaḷ dated 907 (EC, 11: Jl 19) which mentions Gaṅga-Noḷamba hostilities.
60. *EC*, 11: Jl 19.
61. *SII*, 9 (pt. 1): 23.
62. *EC*, 16: Tm 81.
63. *EC*, 11: Jl 19.
64. *EC*, 11: Cd 62. This epigraph was found at an Īśvara temple in Bagenahalu. During my visit, only a loose mātṛkā panel, a vīrakaḷ, and the epigraph in question remained where the temple once stood.
65. *EC*, 9: DB 9.
66. *EC*, 12: Si 39.
67. *EC*, 11: Jl 29.
68. *EI*, 10: 70.
69. *EC*, 10: Sp 29; Bp 42.
70. *SII*, 9 (pt. 1): 57-8.
71. *EI*, 39: 14. Aṇṇiga's reign begun in 923 (Śaka 845).
72. Krishna Murthy, *Noḷambas*, pp. 100, 102.
73. *SII*, 9 (pt. 1): 61.
74. *EC*, 9: Bn 83; *EI*, 6: 47-8.
75. *EI*, 7: 190.
76. *EI*, 6: 47-8 (by Fleet). Krishna Murthy *Noḷambas*, pp. 100, 103-4. Balambal, *Feudatories*, p. 80, believes that the Ayyapa mentioned in the above two records is the same person, but not Ayyapa Noḷambādhirāja. It should be noted that a grant issued by Ereyappa in Mysore district (*EC*, 4: HS 92) was witnessed by Ayyapa of Kedalegar. Possibly this is the Ayyapa that participated in the Tumbepadi battle.
77. *EI*, 39: 13-16.
78. *EI*, 39: 14. The spelling 'Nuḷamba' is common in Tamil epigraphs.
79. *SII*, 9 (pt. 1): 23.
80. *EI*, 39: 27-33 (=*SII*, 9 [pt. 1]: 24).
81. *ARE*, 1917, no. 13 (app. c). See Doḍḍēśvara temple discussion.
82. *EC*, 17: Mb 293-4. See section on Avani.
83. *EC*, 10: Mb 45.
84. *EC*, 10: Mb 43.
85. *EC*, 10: Gd 4; Sp 64.
86. *EC*, 12: Tp 10; Mg 71.
87. Ramesh, *Inscriptions of Western Gaṅgas*, p. 427, Kadulur plates. 'Rācamalla defeated and put to flight the Noḷamba chief Aṇṇiga in the famous battle of Kottamaṅgaḷa, and taking pity on the trembling enemy, took him under his protection.'
88. *EC*, 11: Cd 76; *EI*, 5: 188-97; *EI*, 4: 278-90.
89. *EI*, 5: 188-97; *EI*, 4: 278-90.
90. *EI*, 39: 13-16; *ARE*, 1972-3, nos. 277-8.
91. *EC*, 12: Si 28.
92. *EI*, 33: 77-8 (=*SII*, 9 [pt. 1]: 25 = *EC*, 12: Si 35).
93. *EI*, 33: 77-8.
94. Altekar, *Rashtrakutas*, p. 116.
95. *SII*, 9 (pt. 1): 30.

96. *EI*, 4: 81-3.
97. *EC*, 10: Bp 4. Iṛiva and Tiruvayya together made a grant in 951, *EC*, 10: Ct 49. Noḷamba period sculptures remain in Betamaṅgala.
98. *EC*, 10: Mb 126.
99. *SII*, 9 (pt. 1): 28. I did not find any Noḷamba remains at Madhudi.
100. *SII*, 9 (pt. 1): 33. No Noḷamba period temples remain at Agali, but I found loose sculptures: a Gaṇeśa, a broken mātṛkā panel, and an effaced Kālī.
101. *EC*, 10: Mb 59.
102. *EC*, 10: Kl 245; *MAR*, 1923, p. 49; *MAR*, 1941, p. 156.
103. *EC*, 10: Mb 122.
104. *MAR*, 1947-55, p. 72.
105. *EC*, 15: 237 (MV) Hassan District. Noḷambakulāntaka used in *EC*, 5: Ch 267; *EC*, 4: Ng 51; *EC*, 12 Tp: 103, all dated Śaka 894, and in later records.
106. *EC*, 10: Mb 84.
107. *EC*, 10: Sp 59.
108. *SII*, 9 (pt. 1): 40; *EC*, 10: CB 45.
109. *SII*, 9 (pt. 1): 39.
110. *SII*, 9 (pt. 1): 74.
111. *EC*, 9: Ht 47.
112. *SII*, 9 (pt, 1): 41; *ARE*, 1932, no. 208.
113. *EC*, 10: Mb 38.
114. Krishna Murthy, *Noḷambas*, p. 45, believes that the correct relationship is the one stated in the Avani record, Iṛiva was Vīramahēndra's younger brother, but that the scribe in the genealogies incorrectly stated this fact. Balambal, *Feudatories*, p. 87, believes the genealogies are correctly stated and that Ekavākya ruled during the dark period between *c.* 980-1000 (?).
115. *EI*, 16: 27-31.
116. *SII*, 9 (pt. 1): 80, 81, 82, 85, 87, 88, 90, passim.
117. *SII*, 9 (pt. 1): 80.
118. *SII*, 3: 28.
119. *SII* 3: 29.

CHAPTER THREE

Central Noḷambavāḍi Monuments

INTRODUCTION

This chapter is concerned with the monuments in central Noḷambavāḍi, primarily in Hemavati (Anantapur district, Andhra Pradesh). Hemavati, or Heñjeru as it is referred to in epigraphs, was a capital to the Noḷamba dynasty. I will describe and analyze the temples of Siddēśvara, Doḍḍēśvara, Virūpākṣa, Mallēśvara, Akka and Taṇgi, as well as other miscellaneous shrines and loose sculptures in Hemavati.[1] The Siddēśvara temple's importance is the enshrined Bhairava: Bhairava is not only an artistic masterpiece—testimony to the central Noḷambavāḍi idiom at its finest—he also is an iconographic rarity, known locally as Heñjerappa. The largest temple in central Noḷambavāḍi, in fact all of Noḷambavāḍi, is the Doḍḍēśvara temple. The other temples are in various degrees of disrepair. The mukhamaṇḍapas to the twin Akka and Taṇgi temples are demolished. These temples, the Doḍḍēśvara, and portion of the Siddēśvara are the only surviving granite monuments in central Noḷambavāḍi. Other shrines have plain granite adhiṣṭhānas (base mouldings) and brick walls. Evidently the more common construction material was the less expensive brick.

Central Noḷambavāḍi temples are generally simple shrines architecturally, yet embellished with sculptural elements which provide grace to the monuments. Consisting of a garbhagṛha ('womb-house', i.e. sanctum), an antarāla (vestibule), and a mukhamaṇḍapa (front hall), some temples have a later period Nandi maṇḍapa (pavilion to house Nandi) and/or an agramaṇḍapa (porch) addition. The Doḍḍēśvara, an unusually large temple, has a mukhamaṇḍapa with sixteen free-standing pillars and, instead of an antarāla, an ardhamaṇḍapa (half hall) with four more pillars, whereas the other temples have four pillar mukhamaṇḍapas and two additional pillars to demarcate the antarāla entrance. No Noḷamba period temples have antarāla doorways. Although the garbhagṛha doorways tend to be relatively simple—usually with three decorative bands (śākhās) and small door guardians (dvārapālas) at the base—the mukhamaṇḍapa entrances are sculpturally intricate. Commonly, five band (pañcaśākhā) doorways are adorned with miniature relief musicians, dancers, loving couples, gaṇas and other mythical creatures, etc., entwined within meandering lotus vines (kalpavallis), or other decorative motifs, and are protected by dvārapālas at the base, and auspicious signs (often Naṭēśa—dancing Śiva—and host) above.

In some temples, ceiling panels with figural sculptures pleasantly distract from the temples' austerity. Although only two temples in central Noḷambavāḍi (at Pathasivarama and Aralaguppe) have such panels surviving in their mukhamaṇḍapas, loose panels also are preserved in Hemavati. In fact, mukhamaṇḍapa coffered ceilings divided into nine bays with Śiva encircled by Aṣṭadikpālas (except in some loose Hemavati panels) are commonly found throughout Noḷambavāḍi. Mukhamaṇḍapa ceilings without figural panels often are divided into nine bays, but are plain except for a large central lotus medallion relief.

Because of their sculptural refinement and because of their iconographic presentation pillars are critical to central Noḷambavāḍi monuments.[2] The most characteristic Noḷambavāḍi pillar is of the citrakhaṇḍa order with caturasra relief carvings (figs. 7 and 8). These pillars have square shafts with a small upper cylindrical section leading to a cushion capital. The centre of the shaft, the caturasra portion, has square panels with reliefs. The caturasra sections have kīrttimukhas which spew jewelled strands in the centre and sides of the panels. The strands form the outline of two panels where figural sculptures invariably appear. Sometimes the left and right panels directly relate thematically, other times they function independently. Above the kīrttimukha there is a kalpavalli which usually has figural sculptures at the top and sides. Sometimes this upper section has autonomic scenes occupying the space. Above the caturasra area on the four corners, ubiquitous small lions are represented. Below the lower panels a vertical band of a kalpavalli usually emerges, and occasionally the band has figural carvings which might relate to the panels.

Found throughout Noḷambavāḍi, the central

Noḷambavāḍi citrakhaṇḍa pillars have especially elaborate reliefs. Because the pillar carvings are the most important iconographic remains *in situ*, and because Hemavati is irrefutably a Noḷamba centre, I describe the reliefs in great detail, usually specifying attributes held by each deity. Prior to this study the identity of the pillar reliefs at Hemavati, and in fact all of Noḷambavāḍi, have been neglected except for isolated examples. I intend to indicate the iconographic diversity available and to demonstrate that in Noḷambavāḍi a repertoire of themes were delineated independently of the 'standard' themes represented elsewhere. Obviously the iconography, which shows Śiva or Devī or Viṣṇu in their various manifestations and other epic or Purāṇic scenes, is shared throughout India. My point, however, is that the manner of representation often differs from neighbouring regions both in form (pose and attributes held) and stylistic idiosyncracies. Contrary to Sivaramamurti's repeated assertion that Hemavati (Noḷamba) sculptures are a copy of Cālukya and/or Pallava (and Rāṣṭrakūṭa and Cōḷa) 'styles', the central Noḷambavāḍi sculptures are, indeed, products of the central Noḷambavāḍi idiom. Sivaramamurti would have us believe that Noḷamba period (Hemavati) sculptures are no more than the result of 'influences' from diverging 'styles'. The 'atomistic' approach of Sivaramamurti, and others, which identifies a motif or an ornament, such as a necklace, or an anatomical part, as indicative of other styles (sometimes many) somehow operative in another style (e.g. Noḷamba) is of questionable value and in my study not considered a useful analytical tool. I believe central Noḷambavāḍi sculptures are identifiable as works of a relatively independent idiom.[3] In iconography, this is apparent by the diverse and sometimes incongruous scenes. In style, it is even more apparent if one studies the idiomatic mannerisms. As should be expected, the idiom is not homogeneous in appearance; rather a few manneristic propensities are distinguishable. Hence, idiom characterizations might often seem contradictory or vague: this I discuss further in the 'loose sculptures' section.

In addition to Hemavati monuments, I consider the Noḷamba period temples in neighbouring villages. Many of the villages I surveyed no longer have Noḷamba period remains, in spite of inscriptional allusions which suggest temples once existed. Occasionally I found loose sculptures, but many more throughout central Noḷambavāḍi, I am convinced, are lost or available only through excavations (especially in Hemavati). Included in this chapter is the Mailarēśvarasvami temple at Pathasivarama. Though a modest shrine, it has (unpublished) ceiling panels of Naṭēśa and Aṣṭadikpālas which are splendid examples of mature Noḷamba period sculpture. The Raṅganāthasvāmi temple on Pailabanda hill has citrakhaṇḍa pillars with caturasra reliefs, unmistakably from the Noḷamba period, built in the mukhamaṇḍapa. Probably these were pillars incorporated into a later period temple; however, because of the pillars, I note the temple. Also included is the Mahēndrēśvara temple at Baraguru. It is a surprisingly humble monument, built of brick, yet it is one of the only temples to have irrecusable Noḷamba royal sponsorship of construction.[4] The earliest temple to have an inscriptional record of construction by Noḷamba royalty, by the Queen Gavagaṇabbe, is a temple in Chikkamadhure, Chitradurg district.[5] Finally, included in this chapter is the Kallēśvara temple at Aralaguppe. Not in immediate proximity of Hemavati (almost 100 km between the two villages), Aralaguppe is included as a central Noḷambavāḍi monument because of stylistic considerations. I argue that the exquisite Naṭēśa and Aṣṭadikpāla ceiling panels in the Kallēśvara temple exemplify traits of the central Noḷambavāḍi idiom. The Naṭēśa-Aṣṭadikpāla panels at Aralaguppe, Pathasivarama and Hemavati (loose panels) are superb works that, though sculpted by different hands and during separate times, are idiomatically related and representative of the sculptural excellence often achieved in central Noḷambavāḍi.

SIDDĒŚVARA TEMPLE

The Siddēśvara is the only Noḷamba temple at Hemavati which currently is in worship.[6] Enshrined in the sanctum is an imposing Bhairava, locally known as Heñjerappa, which has been in perpetual, or intermittent, worship for over a millennium. The west-facing temple consists of a garbhagṛha ('womb-house', i.e. sanctum), an antarāla (vestibule), a gudhamaṇḍapa (closed hall), a mukhamaṇḍapa (front hall) constructed at a slightly later date, and a modern agramaṇḍapa (porch) with four typical Noḷamba period citrakhaṇḍa pillars reconstructed into it (fig. 2). A prākāra (enclosure walls), maybe constructed in the sixteenth century or later, circumscribes the temple.

Bhairava (Heñjerappa)

Certainly the most remarkable feature of the Siddēśvara temple is the enshrined Bhairava (pl. 1). More than just a 'powerful' or 'beautiful' image, this Bhairava demands consideration to function. But before discussing signification, I will first describe the image's appearance. The Bhairava enshrined in the Siddēśvara garbhagṛha sits in lalitāsana, the right leg pendant, holding[7] triśūla (UR), ḍamaru (drum, UL), abhaya-mudrā (LR), and kapāla (skull bowl,

LL). The attributes are held in a naturalistic manner: the fingers around the triśūla are relaxed, the ḍamaru rests in the palm and fingers of the hand, not held by two fingers which often is the manner of placement. Stylized hair ringlets encircle the head in two rows, appearing like a halo. The apex of the head is adorned with a muṇḍa (skull), a nāga entwines the forehead. Nāgas also form the keyūra (upper armlets). He wears a muṇḍa-yajñopavīta (sacred-thread composed of skulls). Other ornaments include a siṁhamukha mekhala (lion-headed belt) with jewels, a ratnadāma (jewelled necklace), a kaṭibandha (waist band), kuṇḍalas (earrings), and circular bracelets and anklets. The youthful, round, fleshy face has two small fangs protruding from the mouth.[8] This is not a Bhairava emphasizing his ugra (ferocious) nature; rather it is a welcoming figure. However, at 152 cm heigh and 92 cm at the widest point, this large, black schist figure has a dominating presence which rivals other Bhairava images in Indian art.

No surviving information (i.e. epigraphs) states the image's origins and purpose nor information regarding the complex agents' intentions when they had this image composed. Nor is there even positive evidence available to prove that this Bhairava, locally called Heñjerappa, is in his original home. Heñjerappa's size indicates he was created for temple worship. It is doubtful that he was made for a subshrine: no surviving Noḷamba period temples have subshrines, nor do their temple layouts suggest one could have existed. Enshrined and fixed within the Siddēśvara garbhagṛha, Heñjerappa is the central and only temple icon. Yet, in this geographic region, it is rare to find an anthropomorphic form of Śiva in a garbhagṛha. During the Vīraśaiva movement of the twelfth century onwards almost all enshrined Śiva images (mūrti) were replaced by liṅgas. Vīraśaivas (Liṅgāyats), however, currently control this temple and, evidently, a traditional respect towards Heñjerappa has kept him from being removed.

The function of an image may vary over time as people reinterpret the image and their own needs, but, even today, the high regard with which local people show towards Heñjerappa supports my suspicion that he had special status from inception. Present-day Hemavati, the Noḷamba capital, is called Heñjeru in Noḷamba epigraphs. Appa, in Kannaḍa, means father (also it is a respectful suffix): Heñjerappa is the father, or protector, of Heñjeru. People regularly seek Heñjerappa's blessing and in times of trouble petition him for resolution. As mentioned, Vīraśaivas—people who wear a small liṅga and consider the liṅga as the proper form of Śiva to worship—ritually maintain Heñjerappa. Although Vīraśaivas are strict vegetarians, the priests to Heñjerappa allow on special occasions goat sacrifice (Bhairava is, after all, a wrathful deity) and the meat is cooked and eaten within the Siddēśvara compound.[9] It appears that their own Vīraśaiva teachings are subordinate to Heñjerappa's traditional needs.

From inscriptional remains it is known that the Pāśupata Śaivas were in Heñjeru (Hemavati) and patronized by Noḷamba kings. There is good reason to believe the more enigmatic Kālāmukhas also were present. As religious agencies within Noḷamba polity they were charged with ritual maintenance of royal monuments. The rituals, incidentally, are serious actions which, if not performed properly, can have serious consequences for the doer, the king, the realm.[10] According to a Noḷamba inscription Lakulīśa, the premier teacher of the Pāśupatas, was himself incarnated and lived in Hemavati as Cilluka-bhaṭāra: 'Lakulīśa, fearing that his own name and works of dharmma would be forgotten, became incarnate and was born again on the earth as the muninātha Chilluka.'[11] The Noḷamba King Iṛiva entrusted to Cilluka-bhaṭāra a land grant in order to maintain the god Naninnēśvara. Iṛiva's father Ayyapa had the biruda Nanni, 'the asylum of truth', and Naninnēśvara probably was the royal deity (and protector) of Ayyapa.[12]

A supreme deity—a divine overlord—whose grace and sustenance legitimized a king and his realm was a critical aspect of regional polity.[13] A ferocious form of Śiva, feared even by time himself (Kāla),[14] Bhairava is an able protector and overlord for a king seeking to consolidate his realm (as is Vīrabhadra, see below). Heñjerappa, I suspect, was chosen by one or more of the Noḷamba kings as their paramount deity. Responsibility for proper ritualistic maintenance to the deity, which is extended to the king and his realm, was charged to the Pāśupatas and/or Kālāmukhas.

In reference to Karnataka, the Pāśupatas and Kālāmukhas are considered synonymous by some scholars. In Kālāmukha epigraphs they sometimes refer to themselves as adherents to the Lakulāgamas,[15] and Handiqui concludes: 'The Lakula or Pāśupata system is generally mentioned in the Mysore inscriptions in connection with the Kālāmukha sect; and there is no doubt that the Pāśupatas were known as Kālāmukhas in the Kannaḍa country.'[16] Another scholar suggests that Cilluka, the incarnation of Lakulīśa was, indeed, a Kālāmukha preceptor.[17] The earliest Kālāmukha inscriptions in Karnataka (806 and 810 CE) are from Nandi, a Noḷamba centre; however, besides the Tandikonda grant of *c.* 958, few epigraphs specify Kālāmukha affiliation again until the eleventh century, at which time some Noḷamba grants do specify Kālāmukhas.[18] There remains much confusion regarding the Kālāmukhas, little is known about their practices and no surviving texts have rectified this problem.[19] The ugra forms of Śiva were definitely important to the Kāpālikas, another Śaiva sect coeval with the Kālāmukhas, and sometimes the two are confused. Bhairava is the paramount deity to the Kāpālikas; it remains uncertain if Bhairava occupied a similar position in Kālāmukha doctrines.[20]

At Mulgund (Dharwad district), a site alleged to have been a Kālāmukha centre in the mid-tenth century and later, there is a Kālabhairava temple. An enormous (H: 3.50 m.) standing six-armed Bhairava, flanked by two four-armed female attendants, is enshrined in the temple. Sundara has identified this image as Vīrabhadra because a small goat-headed figure projects from the base in between the Bhairava's feet.[21] Sundara states that Vīrabhadra, in the form of Bhairava, was worshipped by the Kālāmukhas and that the Vīrabhadra/Bhairava at Mulgund was created in conformity to Kālāmukha practices (he dates the sculpture and temple to the second half of the tenth century).[22]

Vīrabhadra, the destroyer of Dakṣa's sacrifice, also was important to the Pāśupatas[23] and in Purāṇic texts sometimes Vīrabhadra and Bhairava are interchangeable or analogous.[24] It has been suggested that Heñjerappa is Yajñarīśvara, that is, Vīrabhadra.[25] Though none as imposing as Heñjerappa, many Bhairava images survive from the Noḷamba period, possibly due to Kālāmukha ritual needs. Maybe Kālāmukha rites at Hemavati required pūjā to Bhairava, hence his presence in the garbhagṛha of the Siddēśvara temple; or, Pāśupata rites required pūjā to Vīrabhadra. Maybe Heñjerappa is both Vīrabhadra and Bhairava and worshipped by the Kālāmukhas and/or the Pāśupatas. However, without definite information regarding Kālāmukha rituals—or, proof that it was indeed the Kālāmukhas, in addition to the related Pāśupatas at Hemavati—this question remains open.

The protective and potentially destructive aspect of Heñjerappa, as recognized today, might help support my suggestion that Heñjerappa's original function was as overlord to Heñjeru in Noḷamba times. Probably a royal deity to one or more Noḷamba kings and made in conformity with Pāśupata/Kālāmukha rites, Heñjerappa is an example of an image formulated and his appearance composed in response to the needs and demands of the complex agencies within the dialectics of Noḷamba polity. Additionally, he should now be recognized as a product of local artisans, working during the Noḷamba period, who shaped the image according to their own skills and knowledge. There is nothing about the image's surface design, or the various parts and motifs which together formulate the image, that suggests a copying or reliance on models from 'major' dynastic centres.

Exterior

The vimāna and antarāla walls are constructed of plain granite slabs. The remaining temple walls are now assembled of rubble with a covering of plaster and without base mouldings (adhiṣṭhāna). The vimāna adhiṣṭhāna has jagatī, tripaṭṭa (three-sided) kumuda and paṭṭika mouldings which project at the bhadra and karṇa (i.e. central and corner) sections of the walls. Above the walls is a kapōta (cornice) that has a few simple nāsikā reliefs. A brick Phaṁsanā (tiered) superstructure with square grīvā-śikhara tops the vimāna. Extending over the antarāla is a śukanāsa (antefix at the front of the superstructure) The Kallēśvara temple at Aralaguppe also has a brick Phaṁsanā tower with a śukanāsa, suggesting that this arrangement might have been common for central Noḷambavāḍi temples.

The main mukhamaṇḍapa entryway is in the south, but there are front (west) and north entrances as well. The elaborate pañca-śākhā (five-band) doorway in the south has at its inner base, to the left, Yamunā on her kūrma vāhana (tortoise vehicle), and, right, Gaṅgā on her makara (sea animal, mostly crocodilian). The two śākhās above the river goddesses have kalpavallis (wish-fulfilling vine); one of the bands has gaṇa musicians within the meandering swirls. At the base of the third śākhā, Nidhis, both holding padmas (lotus), sit on elephants which have the front half of their bodies projecting beyond the door surface. A stambha (pillar) śākhā decorated with a kalpavalli is above each Nidhi. Next, there is a yāḷimālā (row of leonine creatures) followed by a ratna-padma (jewelled bead and rope motif) śākhā. Beyond the śākhās two Śaiva dvārapālas (door guardians) stand: they are over one meter in height, the largest surviving Noḷamba period dvārapālas. They stand in tribhaṅga (triple bend) pose with their legs in svastikāpasṛta (legs cross without touching) on top of large nāgas, holding triśūla, nāga and gadā. A vidyādhara (flying celestial) is over each dvārapāla. Gajalakṣmī is above the doorway, topped by a haṁsamālā and, next, a kapōta that has two kirttimukhas-nāsikās and lotus-design reliefs. Above the kapōta is a panel portraying Naṭēśa and attendants, including Brahmā and Viṣṇu. Eight-armed Naṭēśa is in lalita pose, holding in his right hands abhaya-mudrā (main), padma (?, UR), nāga (LR), and the middle right hand is unclear. In the left hands are gajahasta (main), ḍamaru (UL), agni (?, mid L), and triśūla (LL). To Śiva's right there are musicians, gandharvas and Brahmā; to his left, dancing Bhṛṅgi, Pārvatī (Śivakāmasundarī), musicians, Viṣṇu, and a female dancer. The north entrance is a simple triśākhā (three band) doorway. A few meters in front of this entrance there is a crude shrine with a (post-Noḷamba period) standing Bhairava enshrined. The front (west) entrance is hidden by modern metal covering.

In front the temple has a porch (agramaṇḍapa), built within the last century or two. Erected within this space are four Noḷamba period citrakhaṇḍa pillars with caturasra carvings (described below). Written on three of the pillars, in the same area for each of the pillars, are faintly incised Kannaḍa letters. I suggest these markings, which paleographically are only 100-200 years old,[26] helped workmen place the pillars in the desired directions. On the north-west pillar, 'va' is incised to connote Vāyu, the directional name of the north-west; on the north-east pillar, 'yi' for Īśāna, the name of the north-east direction; on the south-west pillar its directional name is conveyed by a 'na' for Nirṛti; and the fourth pillar did not require a marking. The pillars are marked either because the porch was disassembled, repaired, and reassembled, or, more likely, the pillars were taken from another (ruined) temple and employed in the construction of a new porch. The porch extends further west, ending with a small open elevated platform topped with a śikhara.

Interior

The four free-standing pillars in the mukhamaṇḍapa are of the proto-śrīkāra (cylindrical, 'lathe-turned') order. Śrīkāra pillars are employed at many Noḷamba period sites (e.g. Hemavati, Baraguru, Avani, Aralaguppe, etc.) in a number of variations: the Siddēśvara pillars are akin to the ones at Baraguru, Mahēndrēśvara temple in the mukhamaṇḍapa, dated 878 CE. The central portion of the maṇḍapa ceiling is divided into nine sections by crossbeams. The outer bays are plain but the central bay has a lotus medallion. Four lotus pendants project from where the cross beams intersect around the central bay. This ceiling arrangement also is found at the Mahēndrēśvara temple, Baraguru, and other Noḷamba period temples.

The entrance to the gudhamaṇḍapa is hidden behind modern metal-work. The four free-standing pillars are simple miśra (mixed order) pillars of alternating square and octagonal sections with an apex two-sided abacus. The ceiling is plain.

The antarāla and garbhagṛha doorways are without decorations. The same type of 'lantern roof' (or 'square and diamond system') ceiling with a central lotus medallion is constructed in the antarāla and garbhagṛha. It is likely that the ceilings are the result of repairs. The lantern roof became popular after the Noḷamba period, especially during the Vijayanagara era. This type of ceiling is constructed in the temple at Pailabanda (see Raṅganāthasvāmī temple discussion) during Vijayanagara times by a local leader. Also the eastern Noḷambavāḍi Aruṇācalēśvara temple has a lantern roof; however, there too the ceiling was repaired during the Vijayanagara period.

Pillar reliefs

The agramaṇḍapa's citrakhaṇḍa pillars are later additions to the Siddēśvara temple. Because the pillars are Noḷamba period carvings, I specify in the following listing the iconography of the reliefs found in the caturasra portions—that is, the square, central panels of the pillars. An arbitrary, but logical, manner to discuss the pillar carvings is to first describe the left panel (i.e. the proper right of the pillar), then the right side; next, if there is activity in the kalpavalli (meandering lotus motif) above, it will be discussed, and if necessary information is supplied in the lower kalpavalli, it, too, will be mentioned.

North 1, west face. Carved in the left and right panels are naked females with long, flowing, unadorned hair, standing in tribhaṅga pose. They could be devotees to Durgā (above) or members of her entourage, such as yoginīs. Above, Mahiṣāsuramardinī. Her left foot steps on the theriomorphic Mahiṣāsura's back; her attributes are cakra (UR), śaṅkha (UL), triśūla (LR) embedded into the asura's neck and her lower left hand twists the asura's head. Gaṇas are delineated in the two side swirls of the kalpavalli.

North 1, north face. Left, a Śaiva ascetic/teacher (or gaṇa?) sits with a yogapaṭṭa around his legs and has a book (pustaka) in his left hand. Right, another sitting Śaiva ascetic (or gaṇa) holding a triśūla. Above centre, two gaṇas at play with two more gaṇas in the side kalpavalli swirls.

North 1, east face. Left, a female with a pot (R) and alms (L) to be offered to Bhikṣāṭana in the right panel. Naked Bhikṣāṭana wears only a yajñopavīta (sacred-thread) and a snake is wrapped around his waist. He has a kapāla in his right hand, a triśūla against his left shoulder and a kaṅkāladaṇḍa (?) in the left hand. Above, a female dancer accompanied by three gaṇa musicians playing cymbals, flute, and drum.

North 1, south face. Left, a chubby female dances with snakes in her hands, as does a chubby male in the right panel. Above, Caṇḍēśvara(?) stands in samabhaṅga with a paraśu (axe) in the right hand, and the left hand in kaṭihastamudrā. The only identifying attribute is the paraśu, also a sign of Paraśurāma, an avatāra of Viṣṇu. The overwhelmingly Śaiva iconography of these pillars would suggest this image is Caṇḍēśvara rather than Paraśurāma.

North 2, west face. Kirātārjunīyam.[27] Left, Śiva, as a plump kirāta (hunter), has a bow and arrow ready for discharge. Right, with his bow in hand, Arjuna turns backwards to look at the kirāta. Above, in ekapādāsana Arjuna performs tapas. In the side swirls, to the left, is a liṅga with a garland, and right, the boar which was the object of contention between Śiva and Arjuna.

North 2, north face (pl. 2). Left, seated Gaṇeśa holding pāśa (noose, UR), danta (tusk, UL), laḍḍu (sweets, LR); lower left hand is unclear. Right, a Nidhi with a padma in his right hand, the left hand on his knee, with a śaṅkha placed to the left of his head. Maybe he is meant to represent both Padmanidhi and Śaṅkhanidhi. Seated on a pillow, he has three legs, two to the proper right. It seems that the Nidhi was first put into pralambapadāsana (both legs hanging down) and then (ardha) utkaṭikāsana (right leg on the pedestal, left leg held down). Possibly it is intended to suggest both Nidhis occupying the same space. Above, there is a recumbent Nandi with the royal emblems, a chattra (umbrella) and two caurīs (fly whisk), suspended overhead. A similar Nandi with royal symbols is depicted on the one known Noḷamba coin and is considered the Noḷamba royal insignia.[28] Below the lower panels, a long lotus stalk blossoms into a seat for Lakṣmī who holds kalaśa (UR, waterpot), padma (UL), abhaya (LR), and has the lower left hand on her thigh. Auspicious signs—the Goddess of fortune (Lakṣmī), the remover of obstacles (Gaṇeśa), a bestower of wealth (Nidhi)—benignly converge on this pillar to bless the Noḷamba family, conveyed by their emblem Nandi. This is one of the few tangible signs of association between the Noḷambas, who in epigraphs repeatedly claim descent from the Pallavas, and the Pallavas (of Kāñcī) whose emblem also was Nandi.

North 2, east face. Left, a male embraces a liṅga. The figure has a small animal on his back.[29] Right, standing Śiva embraces Devī. Śiva, identified by his third eye, is without recognizable attributes; a bowl might be in his upper right hand, the upper left is in vismaya-mudrā (?), he embraces Devī with the lower right, and the lower left hand is on his hip (kaṭihastamudrā). Above, sitting Yogēśvara Śiva (probably Yoga-dakṣiṇāmūrti) has a yogapaṭṭa around his waist and left leg, and the right leg is pendant. He holds a mālā (UR), a small triśūla (UL), varada-mudrā (LR), and padma (?, LL). Below him sits two ascetics (or gaṇas?) with triśūlas and pustakas. To the sides, makaras with gaṇas in their mouths and more gaṇas above.

North 2, south face. Left, a dancing gaṇa with his right hand in cin-mudrā and a pustaka in his left hand. Right, an elderly man with a walking stick and an umbrella. Above, an ugra form of Devī sits on a padmapītha in yogāsana surrounded by a fire prabhāvalī. She has a skull diadem, a snake around her chest; in her hands she holds akṣamālā (UR), kapāla (UL), abhaya (LR), and the lower left hand is on her thigh.

South 1, west face. Left and right panels have yālīs with riders. Above, Padmanidhi rides an elephant, and gaṇas are in the side kalpavalli swirls.

South 1, north face. Left, a female, to the right a male. Both attractive, dignified figures, they are an aristocratic couple. The bejewelled female has especially lovely ornamented long hair. The male has hair over his shoulders, wears a mukuṭa (crown) and holds a śakti (spear). Above, a female dancer in the centre, and to the sides, gaṇa musicians with cymbals and drum.

South 1, east face. Left, Viṣṇu, in samabhaṅga pose, is holding his attributes in the sequence most commonly presented in Noḷamba period Viṣṇus, cakra (UR), śaṅkha (UL), gadā (LR), kaṭihastamudrā (LL). Right, Sūrya in samabhaṅga with padmas in his two hands. Above, gaṇas, one is presenting a garland.

South 1, south face. Left, turned towards the right panel a male is offering a fruit (?). Right, a female has a lotus in her right hand, and her left hand holds the lower section of her garment which seems to be unraveling. Above, Dakṣiṇāmūrti(?) Śiva seated in ardhayogāsana, holds pustaka (?,UR), nāga (UL), akṣamālā (LR), and a bowl (?, LL). Below the panels, a Kinnara mithuna couple with avian lower bodies.

South 2, west face. Left and right panels have females in tribhaṅga pose holding lotuses. Above, a finely carved Manmatha stands in tribhaṅga holding his attributes a lotus arrow (R) and sugar cane bow (L). Gaṇas are in the side kalpavalli swirls. Below the panels is a Kinnara.

South 2, north face. Left, Gaṅgā is standing on her vāhana the makara, with a kalaśa in her left hand. Right, standing on her vāhana the kūrma, Yamunā has a kalaśa in her right hand. Above, Ardhanārīśvara. The right, masculine side has a triśūla in his upper hand and a nāga in his lower hand. The Devī feminine side has one arm held to the side. Gaṇas frolic in the side kalpavalli swirls. Below the panels is a Kinnarī.

South 2, east face. Left, Padmanidhi, to the right

Śaṅkhanidhi. Above, within kalpavalli swirls there are four frolicking gaṇas, one dances with a nāga in hand.

South 2, south face. Left, a female dancer accompanied by a male drummer in the right panel. Above, four playful *gaṇas* are in the kalpavalli swirls.

Conclusion: Dating of Siddēśvara

The vimāna and antarāla are the only portions of the Siddēśvara temple which definitely constitute the original temple (except the ceilings which are later repairs). The gudhamaṇḍapa probably was constructed at the same time, but the severe austerity of the hall and its simple pillars are inexplicable. Soon after, the mukhamaṇḍapa was attached. This hall and the mukhamaṇḍapa in the Mahēndrēśvara temple at Baraguru, constructed by Mahēndra in 878, closely resemble each other. The ceilings in the two temple's mukhamaṇḍapas are the same in design and the proto-śrīkāra pillars are akin. Because of this consideration, the suggested construction date for the mukhamaṇḍapa is *c.* 875-85. The original temple portions might have been built during the beginning of Mahēndra's reign, *c.* 870, or earlier, during the reign of Mahēndra's father Poḷalcōra. This chronology is based on tenuous information; however, it does appear to me that the Siddēśvara antecedes the Doḍḍēśvara which I suggest dates from *c.* 920-30s. The Bhairava enshrined in the garbhagṛha also appears to be from the late ninth or early tenth century. The agramaṇḍapa was appended in the last century or two, but the citrakhaṇḍa pillars in the porch are Noḷamba period, probably from mid-tenth century, slightly earlier or coeval with the pillars in the Virūpākṣa temple (Hemavati).

DOḌḌEŚVARA TEMPLE

The Doḍḍēśvara temple has received notice by some scholars, although none of the accounts have been thorough discussions.[30] The temple is the largest (sixty meters in length), best preserved Noḷamba monument in central Noḷambavāḍi. Central Noḷambavāḍi temples commonly feature an elaborate entrance doorway with jambs, or śākhās, of detailed reliefs (e.g., Siddēśvara, Virūpākṣa, Mallēśvara at Hemavati and Kallēśvara at Aralaguppe); yet, the Doḍḍēśvara doorway is outstanding due to the sophisticated manner in which the miniature figures, such as the yāḷis, gaṇas, gandharvas, apsarās, mithunas and maithunas, combine to make the entrance monumental (pl. 3). Another temple distinction is the windows. Found throughout Noḷambavāḍi, finely sculpted perforated windows are characteristic of many Noḷamba period monuments. Unfortunately, in central Noḷambavāḍi most of the windows have not survived times' pillages, hence the Doḍḍēśvara windows are, presumably, representative of an important, now lost, central Noḷambavāḍi temple trait. The ubiquitous citrakhaṇḍa pillars with caturasra reliefs, another typical feature throughout Noḷambavāḍi, are present in the Doḍḍēśvara temple.

Inscriptions

Three epigraphs are inscribed on the Doḍḍēśvara temple exterior walls. At the base of a perforated window (jāla-vātāyana) on the front (west) wall a badly abraded inscription states that the maṇḍapa was built (caused to be constructed) by Mārayya, son of Lak[ṣma]yya.[31] An embracing couple, sculpted in the window, probably represents the temple patron Mārayya and his spouse (pl. 4). Gaṅgā is carved in the other front perforated window (pl. 5). Although Yamunā would be the obvious iconographic counterpart to Gaṅgā on the front wall, on this temple a couple with the name of the patron incised below is placed here.[32] The names Mārayya and Lak[ṣma]yya are not known from surviving Noḷamba genealogies. Yet the presentation of the couple, especially the crown worn by the male, suggests that the patron—if it is a patron's portrait—had aristocratic affiliation. The original name of the temple might have been Noṇambēśvara. An inscription found beside the Doḍḍēśvara refers to the god Noṇambēśvara and states that the Noṇambēśvara temple is the 'great ghaṭikā-sthāna (great learning centre) of Heñjera'.[33]

On the south maṇḍapa wall a second epigraph records an donation to Māpayya by Varuṇaśivabhaṭāra from Moraga[gē]ri, a disciple of Rudraśivācārya.[34] From a dated inscription (936 CE) found on a broken pillar in a field at Gunimorubagalu, Anantapur district, it is known that Varuṇaśiva was an influential Śaiva teacher during the reign of Bīra-Noḷamba Aṇṇayyadēva (Aṇṇiga).[35] Varuṇaśiva, the administrator of the Noḷambēśvara temple,[36] and ruler of Paḷivāḷa-bāḷu (unidentified area name), was allowed to use in the Gunimorubagalu epigraph such lofty epithets as paramēśvara and paramabhaṭṭāraka (a supreme sage, a title also used by paramount sovereignty), suggesting he was a royal preceptor. Possibly Māpayya, the donation recipient, and Mārayya, the temple patron, are one and the same; however, no explanation for the spelling variation is offered other than it is an orthographic mistake (or that the names in the records, which are hardly legible, are not accurately read). If Māpayya and Mārayya are the same then the dated

Gunimorubagalu inscription helps to date approximately the Doḍḍēśvara temple.

A third inscription, also on the south maṇḍapa wall, records that the Gāvuṇḍa (village leader) from Belturu gave as tribute forty-five gold gadyāṇa (coin unit) to Noḷamba Candrāditya.[37] Although this information is inconsequential, it is noteworthy that the name Candrāditya does not appear in known Noḷamba genealogies.

Exterior[38]

Constructed of granite, the west facing Doḍḍēśvara temple consists of a garbhagṛha, ardhamaṇḍapa, mukhamaṇḍapa, and an open-sided Nandi maṇḍapa (fig. 3). The large black schist Nandi is contemporary with the temple but the Nandi maṇḍapa is a recent addition. As is the case with other central Noḷambavāḍi temples, the adhiṣṭhāna mouldings are modest: a jagatī, a multi-faced (dharavṛta) kumuda, and a paṭṭika compose the temple base. The otherwise simple walls (pāda) are divided by karṇa, pratikarṇa, and wide bhadra projections, with each section having engaged brahmakānta (rectangular) pilasters. Recesses between the pratikarṇa and bhadra on the west, north, and south walls of the mukhamaṇḍapa and ardhamaṇḍapa have jāla-vātāyanas (perforated windows) carved with deities or kalpavallis interspersed with figural sculptures. Framed on both sides by engaged pilasters, topped by a kapōta, the windows with deities essentially serve the same function as dēvakōṣṭhas.

The jāla-vātāyanas in pradakṣiṇāpatha order (clockwise) starting with the front (west) window on the north side are as follows: In the first window the river goddess Gaṅgā stands in tribhaṅga on top of her vāhana, a makara (pl. 5). The two Nidhis, śaṅkha and padma, sit at the window outer base, flanking the makara. Gaṅgā's right hand rests on her full hip and the left hand holds a water pot (kamaṇḍalu). She wears a beaded belt (mekhalā) around a tight-fitting dhotī, upper armlets (keyūra) with a creeper design, plain bangles, a necklace (hāra) of pipal leave pieces, and heavy circular earrings (kuṇḍala). The hair, especially, is often rendered in a charming manner in the more refined central Noḷambavāḍi figures: Gaṅgā's hair is in a large ornamented bun at back, tight curls elsewhere, and is further decorated with jewels in the front and sides. The simple but elegant treatment of her ornaments and the refined balance of her body with its soft contour combine to place this sculpture among the masterpieces of Noḷamba art.

The first, north side maṇḍapa window has a three-headed, youthful and beardless, Brahmā standing in samabhaṅga posture.[39] He holds in his upper right hand a mālā, and in the upper left a kamaṇḍalu (water pot); the lower right hand holds a daṇḍa (staff), and the lower left hand is in kaṭihastamudrā (on his hip). The Nidhis, distinguished by the padma in the hand of Padmanidhi to the proper right, and by the śaṅkha held by Śaṅkhanidhi to the left, flank the base and they have a halo of coins overhead here and in the other windows in which they appear. The second north maṇḍapa window is a later replacement showing a simple double-swirl kalpavalli. It does not fit correctly in the window space and the crudeness of this piece is incongruous with the style of the Doḍḍēśvara temple. The original window might be the one brought to Tanjavur by Cōḷa Rājēndra during his victorious excursion through Noḷambavāḍi.[40] The Noḷamba window at Tanjavur (Rājarajēśvara temple) has a kalpavalli with mithunas within its three swirls, and Nidhis on elephants flanking the base. Stylistically, the window compares nicely to works at the Doḍḍēśvara temple, especially to the following two windows.

The north ardhamaṇḍapa window has a beautiful kalpavalli with Nidhis sitting on elephants to the sides.[41] The kalpavalli stalk forms three circles having within them a male drummer in the lower swirl, a female dancer accompanied by a male playing the cymbals in the middle and above, a male musician with a vīṇā. The south ardhamaṇḍapa window also has a kalpavalli. This one has two circles, a male drummer within the lower swirl and a female dancer in the upper section. Instead of having Nidhis, two female attendants, both with padmas in one of their hands, stand in tribhaṅga flanking the window's base.

In the window on the south side in the rear of the temple Kārttikeya stands in samabhaṅga with his vāhana, a peacock (mayūra), depicted behind him. Nidhis flank the base. In Kārttikeya's upper right hand a snake twines around his fingers, and the attribute once held in the upper left hand is now destroyed. The lower right hand shows varada-mudrā, the lower left hand is in kaṭihastamudrā. Viṣṇu in samabhaṅga posture stands in the front, south maṇḍapa window. Nidhis also flank the base of this window. As is typical with most Noḷamba period Viṣṇus, this one holds in his upper right hand a cakra, in his upper left a śaṅkha, lower right a gadā, and the lower left hand is on his hip.

Finally, sculpted in the front (west) window towards the south side is an embracing couple (pl. 4). With one hand on their hip, and their other arm around their partner's shoulders, they stand in tribhaṅga. As mentioned earlier, this couple probably represents the temple patron, Mārayya, and his wife. It is inscribed on the base of this window that Mārayya caused the construction of the maṇḍapa.[42]

Above the walls, the kapōta is decorated with low

relief nāsikās that have pinnacle kīrttimukhas. Below the kapōta a bhūtamālā is carved; haṁsas, yāḷis, or, even rarer, elephants are occasionally interspersed among the bhūtas. Śiva and Pārvatī sit with Nandi to their side under the kapōta in a section on the west wall, south end.

No superstructure is now in existence. However, the vimāna walls are extremely thick: presumably they at one time supported a tower. Found near the Doḍḍēśvara temple, three sculptures, a Naṭēśa, a Vyākhyāna-Dakṣiṇāmūrti, and a Gaṅgādhara, have thick portions of stone protruding horizontally out of the back of the sculptures which would have inserted into sockets, possibly in the superstructure of this temple. Sculptures intended to be inserted in a pedestal have vertical stone protrusions below the piece, not horizontal extensions from the back of the sculptures.

A reconstructed Nandi pavilion is in front of the temple, built on a platform connecting to the temple entrance. The large Nandi (pl. 6) is carved with a concern for naturalism and surely coeval with the Doḍḍēśvara temple. Nandi's face has incised lines to suggest veins, the mouth is partly open showing his teeth, and the eyes are attentively opened wide. He wears jewels on his head, a simple rope pattern necklace with a bell in front, and a heavy ghaṇṭamālā extends from behind his hump to the front of his body, resting on the ground. Seen from the front, his dewlap forms a few S-curves which add to the naturalism. Some central Noḷambavāḍi Nandis, such as the one at the Virūpākṣa temple, Hemavati, are more stylized and embellished. Like the Gaṅgā window, this Nandi is sculpted without overly emphasizing the decorative. A balanced amount of ornamentation accentuates the form, rather than distracts from the figure. This balance between the elements—form and adornment—is idiomatic of one propensity in central Noḷambavāḍi. Not all sculptures display this trait; the ones that do are a product of a 'mature' strain in the central Noḷambavāḍi idiom, which is not necessarily indicative of time (relative chronology) as much as skill.

The temple entrance is approached by stairs placed at the north and at the south of the front platform. The doorway was widened at some point. The capital elements of the doorway pilasters correspond correctly to the pilaster pedestals at the doorway base, but the actual stambhaśākhās, which should line up vertically with the capitals and pedestals, are extended approximately fourteen cm to the north and south.

Emphatic stress on dance is expressed at this doorway and elsewhere in the Doḍḍēśvara temple. Above the door on a frieze, the paramount dancer, Naṭēśa, manifests the quiddity of dance. Beside Naṭēśa his son Gaṇeśa joins the dance. Elsewhere on the doorway and interior pillars gaṇas display their enthusiastic dances. Human dancers dance on the pillars and windows. Gaṇapati (Gaṇeśa), lord of the gaṇas, also dances on one of the door pilasters.

The doorway has five jambs (pañca-śākhā) of superb relief sculptures (pl. 3). The first śākhā has a kalpavalli with dancing gaṇas, mythical animals, and lotus flowers within the meandering lotus swirls. Next śākhā, on each side of the base, female figures stand in tribhaṅga, holding water pots and padmas. If they are river goddesses, they cannot be differentiated as Gaṅgā and Yamunā because they lack their vāhanas, the makara and kūrma. Above, within the swirls of a kalpavalli, there are gandharva-apsarās couples (celestial musicians), mithunas (loving couples), and maithunas (or ratikrīḍā mithuna, couples in coitus) (pl. 7). It is appropriate that gandharvas and apsarās, the celestial lovers famed for their seductive abilities, and maithunas appear together in the same śākhā. The third śākhā is a slightly projecting engaged pilaster (stambha-śākhā) that has a lotus meander relief. Towards the top of the north pilaster there is a Mahiṣāsuramardinī, and on the other pilaster, a dancing Gaṇeśa. The next śākhā has at the base on each side, four-armed Śaiva dvārapālas in atitribhaṅga holding triśūla, nāga, and gadā; the guardian on the north displays sūci-mudrā, the other, vismaya-mudrā. Above the dvārapālas is a row of yāḷis that have varying physiognomy, in one instance, a human face. The last śākhā is a jewelled strand engraved with a bead and rope motif, bordered by lotus leaves (i.e. a ratna-padma śākhā).

Above the doorway lintel is placed a sculptural frieze delineating Naṭēśa flanked by the Aṣṭadikpālas. In the centre an eight-armed Naṭēśa in lalita pose, holds in his hands abhaya-mudrā (main right), ḍamaru (upper right), khaḍga (middle right), ghaṇṭā (lower right), gajahasta (main left), nāga (upper left), pustaka (?, middle left), and triśūla or khaṭvāṅga (lower left). Śiva dances upon a sprawled Apsamāra who holds a nāga. Gaṇa musicians accompany Naṭēśa, and to Naṭēśa's right, Gaṇeśa dances and Pārvatī watches (Śivakāmasundarī). The guardians of the eight directions, the dikpālas, also witness the event. Riding on their vāhanas, to the north (from inner to outer), Īśāna on a bull (guardian of NE), Kubera on a ram (N), Vāyu on a deer (NW), and Varuṇa on a makara (W) are portrayed; to the south, Indra on Airāvata, his elephant (E), Agni on a goat (SE), Yama on a buffalo (S), and Nirṛti on a man (naravāhana, SW). Devī's normal placement when represented with Śiva is to his left, yet in this frieze and many other Noḷamba period pieces, Devī stands to Śiva's right.

Interior

In the interior, the mukhamaṇḍapa has sixteen free-standing citrakhaṇḍa pillars. In a west-east axis the pillars are divided into four rows: the outer north and south rows are plain or with simple ornamentation; the inner rows, but for two exceptions, have elaborately carved caturasra reliefs, a trait of most Noḷamba period citrakhaṇḍa pillars. Four more citrakhaṇḍa pillars with caturasra carvings stand in the ardhamaṇḍapa. The pillar reliefs are described in detail below.

The ceiling in the centre of the mukhamaṇḍapa has six large lotus medallions in two rows of three to the north and south of the centre. The ardhamaṇḍapa intended to have six lotus medallions but only three are carved in a row to the south of the ceiling centre. The ardhamaṇḍapa does not have an entrance doorway.

Enshrined in the garbhagṛha is a large black schist liṅga with a square pīṭha. A lotus medallion is on the ceiling. The garbhagṛha doorway has at its base two Śaiva dvārapālas holding the same attributes as the mukhamaṇḍapa door dvārapālas. The first śākhā has a row of gaṇa musicians and dancers inside the circles of a kalpavalli, bordered at one side by lotus leaves. Next, is a stambhaśākhā, followed by a meandering lotus. The next and outer rows have ratnapadma śākhās. Between those śākhās there is a projecting tripartite band with four-petal lotus flowers carved at regular intervals up the shaft.

Pillar reliefs

The mukhamaṇḍapa and ardhamaṇḍapa pillars in the inner west-east axis have reliefs on the caturasra portion of the pillars portraying an eclectic array of themes. Critical scenes of the *Rāmāyaṇa* and *Mahābhārata* are alongside erotica, dancers and musicians, deities and Purāṇic episodes (and scenes unknown). I describe the four sides of each pillar, in clockwise order (i.e. west, north, east, south), starting with the first, north row (west face) mukhamaṇḍapa pillar. The discussion first details the north row of pillars, which includes four in the mukhamaṇḍapa and two in the ardhamaṇḍapa, and then the south row.

North 1, west face. Left, a seated male drummer plays for Naṭēśa who is in the right panel. Naṭēśa dances in lalita pose and displays triśūla (UR), ḍamaru (UL), abhaya (LR), and gajahasta pose (LL).

North 1, north face. Left, a female dancer. Right, three-headed Brahmā in samabhaṅga holds mālā (UR), padma (UL), kamaṇḍalu (LR), and LL in kaṭihastamudrā. Above, in the centre, Narasiṁha disembowels Hiraṇyakaśipu with his lower hands, the UR holds a cakra and a śaṅkha is in the upper left.

North 1, east face. Left, Viṣṇu in samabhaṅga displays his standard attributes cakra (UR), śaṅkha (UL), gadā (LR), and on the hip (LL). Right, Sūrya stands with padmas in his two hands. Above centre, Mahiṣāsuramardinī with cakra (UR) and śaṅkha (UL), has a triśūla (LR) through the back of the completely theriomorphic Mahiṣāsura, and her lower left hand stretches upward the asura's head.

North 1, south face. Left, a female dances. Right, musicians: a male drummer accompanied by a female cymbals player, perform for the dancer to the left side. Above, in the three swirls of the kalpavalli, gaṇas frolic.

The second north pillar is devoted to the *Rāmāyaṇa.* It appears that a chronological development of the story was not sought because, according to sequential progression, one would have to view the pillar sides first south, then north, east, west order.

North 2, west face. Left, Lakṣmaṇa stands behind Rāma who aims an arrow towards the right (Rāvaṇa). Right, Rāvaṇa with ten arms, but only one head, charges towards Rāma. Although Rāvaṇa's ratha is not depicted, it is implicitly present because of the swan below Rāvaṇa. Above, monkeys (vānaras) climb through the swirls in the kalpavalli. Below the panels, monkeys battle a rākṣasa. One monkey, limp on rākṣasa's leg, apparently is dead.

North 2, north face. Left, Jaṭāyu attacks three-headed, six-armed Rāvaṇa. Right, Sītā sits in lalitāsana, probably in Aśokavana, Laṅkā. This programme repeats on the first north ardhamaṇḍapa pillar, north face, with an additional attendant beside Sītā indicating that the setting is in Aśokavana. Above, Gaṇas play, obviously unrelated to the scene below.

North 2, east face. Left, Rāma and Lakṣmaṇa standing together are greeted by Hanumān (to the right) who kneels with his hands in añjalī. Above, in the centre, a ṛṣi sits at ease on a small throne, his right hand in vyākhyāna-mudrā (teaching), the left hand rests on his thigh. To the ṛṣi's side, below him, four figures sit listening to his discourse. Superseding the normal upper kalpavalli section, this scene is stressed. Possibly the ṛṣi is Valmiki expounding the *Rāmāyaṇa.*

North 2, south face (pl. 8). Left, Śūrpaṇakhā, rendered in an attractively young and sweet manner, sits beside Rāma as they converse. Right, with his face in a repugnant grimace, Lakṣmaṇa stands over

Śūrpaṇakhā and with his sword maims Śurpaṇakhā's face. Above, Gaṇas frolic. Below the panels, delineated within two kalpavalli swirls, Rāma shoots an arrow at the golden deer who actually is Mārīca, the Rākṣasa ascetic that sacrificed his own life helping Rāvaṇa abduct Sītā. Pivotal episodes of the *Rāmāyaṇa* are represented on this pillar face: the rejection of Śūrpaṇakhā which subsequently inspired Rāvaṇa's desire to abduct Sītā, and the diverting of Rāma's attention by the golden deer which allowed Rāvaṇa to succeed with the abduction.

North 3, west face. Left, Gajāsurasaṁhāramūrti, Śiva's terrifying (raudra) victorious dance after the slaying of Gajāsura. Śiva holds over his head the hide of Gajāsura with the elephant's head below Śiva's left leg. Right, in horror, Pārvatī recoils from Śiva's frenzied dance. In this scene usually baby Kārttikeya is pulled away with Pārvatī, the small faded figure behind Pārvatī probably is Kārttikeya. Above, Gaṇas play.

North 3, north face. Mahābhārata battle between Arjuna and Vṛṣasena: Left, Arjuna, identified by his Kapidhvaja (monkey banner) in the rear of his ratha, aims his arrow towards Vṛṣasena (in the right panel), identified by his Mayūradhvaja (peacock banner).

North 3, east face. Left, Śaṅkhanidhi and right, Padmanidhi are seated. Above, Gaṇas.

North 3, south face. Left, Mahiṣāsuramardinī holds cakra (UR), śaṅkha (UL), triśūla through the theriomorphic Mahiṣāsura, and LL twist the asura's head (similar to the Mahiṣāsuramardinī on north pillar 1, east face). Right, seated, two-armed Gaṇeśa with laḍḍu (sweetmeat) in his left hand, the right is unclear. Above, Gaṇas frolic.

North pillar 4 is not completely carved: the east side is plain, the north side has only the central kīrttimukha partially incised. The west and south sides depict erotic scenes. At this temple interior erotic scenes are also found on the north 6 pillar (second ardhamaṇḍapa pillar which is in front of the garbhagṛha) and south 5 pillar. Usually erotic representations are restricted to the exterior of temples, as is the case for later Cālukya and Hoysaḷa examples.[43] However, earlier, during the period of the Cālukyas of Badami, interior erotic scenes occurred at Paṭṭaḍakal, Yeni temple and Mallikārjuna temple (eighth century), and still earlier at Badami Cave 1 (sixth century).[44]

North 4, west face. Left, a couple standing together, the female lifts her right leg over the hip of her partner and, probably (sculpture is faded), she pulls his hair. According to Desai this is a love-play position fondly described by poets and kāmaśāstra writers.[45] Right, badly abraded, but it appears to be an embracing couple seated together, facing each other, possibly in coitus. Above, Gaṇas.

North 4, south face. Left, a couple in mutual oral congress. In south India the only earlier known display of this posture is the anomalous example from the mid-sixth century, on a door jamb at the Kont-guḍi, Aihole, where it is crudely carved.[46] Right, a couple in coitus, the female sits on the lap of the male. Above, Gaṇas.

The ardhamaṇḍapa pillars (north and south pillars 5 and 6) in comparison to the mukhamaṇḍapa pillars are carved in a distinctly more refined manner. The figures are crisper, more slender and better articulated; obviously a master sculptor worked on the ardhamaṇḍapa pillars, possibly because of the closer proximity to the garbhagṛha.

North 5, west face. A dispute is portrayed on this side but the specific event is abstruse. Left, two men converse, one holds a shield. Right panel, to the left, two men face each other, one person's leg crosses the leg of the other person's, and one has his arm lifted overhead as if ready to strike (a fight sequence?). To the side, a person has fallen and has an arm raised in protection(?) from the other man who stands over the first man. Above, Gaṇas.

North 5, north face. Same iconography as north pillar 2, north face, showing Rāvaṇa battling Jaṭāyu to the left, and Sītā in Aśokavana to the right, except this pillar has an additional female attendant standing beside Sītā.

North 5, east face. Probably represents Arjuna and Vṛṣasena in battle, as was depicted on north pillar 3, north face. The dhvaja in the right ratha appears to be a mayūradhvaja, identifying the figure as Vṛṣasena, however, the right dhvaja is unclear. Above, standing Ardhanārīśvara, the right Śiva side holds a triśūla (UR) and abhaya (?, LR), the left Pārvatī side has one arm at ease to her side.

North 5, south face (pl. 9). Left, three males stand, the taller, central male has a chattra (umbrella) held overhead by an attendant, suggesting he is a king. The king has one arm around the shoulders of his companion. Right, A female sits while two female attendants stand to the sides holding bowls. Tentatively, I propose that the central lady is being bathed prior to her presentation to her groom, who stands in the left panel. This could possibly be the wedding of Rāma and Sītā, or maybe it celebrates an actual historical royal wedding: it might even show Mārayya, inscribed as patron of the maṇḍapa, and his wife who are depicted in the front window. Below the panels, two mithuna couples sit in a kalpavalli. Mithunas might have been included to emphasis the romantic scene above. Above, Gaṇas.

Love and fertility pervades the following pillar. Portrayed are Nāga-Nāginīs (south face), symbols of fecundity, as are erotic couples (east face). Manmatha (Kāma, south face) inspires love and desire in all, and no one is immune, not even Śiva (east face) or Viṣṇu (north face) both shown embracing their lovers.

North 6, west face. On this side only the contour of the kīrttimukhas are incised, and, above, the pillar is plain. Left, outline of a couple in a close embrace, possibly kissing and in coitus. Right, similar to north 4 pillar, west face, here a loving couple stand together with one of the female's legs raised to the male's thigh and one of her hands pulling his hair. Above, Gaṇas.

North 6, north face. Left, Viṣṇu on Garuḍa holding cakra (UR), śaṅkha (UL), gadā (LR), and LL on his thigh. Right, Viṣṇu in tribhaṅga pose with his lower left arm wrapped around Lakṣmī's shoulders, and his other hands have cakra (UR), śaṅkha (UL), and the LR hand is on his hip. Viṣṇu usually stands in samabhaṅga, and I am unaware of another Noḷamba period example of Viṣṇu embracing his wife. Above, Gaṇapati (Gaṇeśa) dances in the centre and is accompanied by two flanking Gaṇas.

North 6, east face. Left, Śiva and Pārvatī stand together, both in tribhaṅga, Śiva holds a triśūla (UR), upper left arm is around Pārvatī's shoulders, his lower right arm leans on Nandi, and his lower left arm is not visible. Right, Viṣṇu in samabhaṅga, displays cakra (UR), śaṅkha (UL), abhaya (LR), and kaṭihastamudrā (LL). Above, one Gaṇa dancer and two Gaṇa musicians.

North 6, south face (pl. 10). Left, Manmaṭha in tribhaṅga pose holding his attributes, a lotus arrow (R), and a sugar cane bow. To his left, his wife Rati affectionately looks to him. A chubby male stands to the other side holding Manmaṭha's peacock dhvaja. Right, in tribhaṅga posture, a Nāgarāja lovingly looks down at his female companion to his left who returns his glance. On the other side another female watches. Above, Mahiṣāsuramardinī. She displays the same attributes shown in north 1 and 3 pillars; however, the greater skill of this sculptor is evident. Gaṇas holding small clubs flank Mahiṣāsuramardinī.

In general, the workmanship skill on the south side pillars is inferior to the north side. Some of the details on the south pillar sides are not completed; often the panels are now faded due to the fact that the scenes were carved in very low relief and not well articulated. However, the ardhamaṇḍapa pillars are equally skillful on both north and south sides and chiselled by the same sculptor.

South 1, west face. Left, Śāṅkhanidhi, right Padmanidhi and above, a plain kalpavalli.

South 1, north face. Left, Kṛṣṇa walks carrying a flute. Right, a female nurses a baby, probably baby Kṛṣṇa with Pūtanā, the demoness that unsuccessfully attempted to poison Kṛṣṇa with her milk and died in the process.

South 1, east face. Left, a bird with a fish in his beak and other fishes, a tortoise (?) and a crocodile are present. Possibly this is the Pañcatantra episode in which a bird tricks fishes into allowing him to transport them, only to eat the fishes when out of sight.[47] Right, a two-armed man without embellishments, stands alone. Above, Gaṇas.

South 1, south face. Left, badly abraded, maybe an embracing couple. Right, a man performing tapas.

South 2, west face (pl. 11). Mahābhārata battle, death of Bhīṣma: Left, Arjuna, with his kapidhvaja visible at the rear of his ratha, shoots an arrow towards the right panel where Bhīṣma lies on a bed of arrows. Above, Gaṇas carrying weapons.

South 2, north face. Mahābhārata battle of Vṛṣasena and Arjuna (?): Vṛṣasena's mayūradhvaja can be identified in the ratha to the right; however, the man and ratha to the left is faded and the dhvaja is not visible. Above, Gaṇas.

South 2, east face. Vindyādharas, one to each side, bearing garlands and, above, Gaṇas.

South 2, south face. Kirātārjunīyam: Left, Śiva as a kirāta (hunter) with Pārvatī to his right. Right, Arjuna performing tapas. Above, Gaṇas. This pillar is faded and badly carved, a superior rendering of the Kirātārjunīyam is portrayed on the south 5 pillar, south face.

South 3, west face. This pillar is faded and thematically unidentified. Left, a male sits with two female attendants to his right(?) Right, a monkey with a squatting male behind him (?) Maybe this is Vāli with a bound Rāvaṇa. Above, Gaṇas.

South 3, north face. Left, Mahiṣāsuramardinī and, right, Naṭēśa; however, the pillar is faded and the deities' attributes are not distinct.

South 3, east face. Trivikrama with his left leg and arm lifted towards the sky, holding cakra (UR), śaṅkha (UL), and gadā (LR). Right, Viṣṇu in samabhaṅga pose having in his hands cakra (UR), śaṅkha (UL), abhaya (LR), and gadā (LL). Figures, unfortunately abraded and indistinct, are to Viṣṇu's sides. Above, Gaṇas.

South 3, south face. Left, Vindyādharī with a padma. Right, a faded two-armed male seated. Above, Gaṇas.

South 4, west face. Left, three-headed Brahmā in samabhaṅga pose; he is four armed, the lower arms are to his sides and its unclear if attributes are in the upper hands. Right, a female dancer in a slight variant posture of the dancers on north 1 pillar. Above, Gaṇas.

South 4, north face. Left, a male drummer who is also dancing. Right, female dancer, similar to the previous dancer. Above, Gaṇas.

South 4, east face. Left and right, Śaṅkha and Padmanidhis. Above, Gaṇas.

South 4, south face. Left, a seated male drummer. Right, a female dancer similar to the other pillar dancers. Above, Gaṇas.

South 5, west face. Left, a male drummer dancing. Right, with an exaggerated twist of the hips, a female dancer performs. Above, Naṭēśa in catura pose, holds in his hands triśūla (UR), gajahasta (UL), abhaya (LR), and nāga (LL). In the kalpavalli swirls below him, to the left, are two dancers and to the right, two musicians.

South 5, north face. On this pillar face, the two episodes portrayed represent Śiva in his anugrahamūrti (boon-bestowing manifestation). Left, Kirātārjunīyam: Śiva as a kirāta (hunter) holding a bow and arrow and, to his right, accompanied by Devī who holds an animal hide. Right, Arjuna performing tapas. Above, Rāvaṇānugrahanmūrti: Rāvaṇa attempts to shake Mt. Kailāsa where Śiva and Pārvatī are seated. In the side two kalpavalli swirls musicians perform.

South 5, east face. Left, A couple in coitus, the female sits on the male's lap. Right, a couple sits together, the female touches the male's thigh, and the man, whose appearance suggests that he is a guru, has his right hand in vyākhyāna-mudrā (teaching) (a lecture in erotics?). Above, in the centre a gaṇa, and to the sides two attractive females.

South 5, south face. Left, a female holding a parrot(?). Right, a male. Both figures are seated at ease. Above, dancing Gaṇas and a female dancer.

South 6, west face. Left, Sūrya in samabhaṅga pose holding padmas in both hands. Right, Vaiṣṇavī in tribhaṅga, her hands display cakra (UR), śaṅkha (UL), abhaya (LR), and kaṭihastamudrā (LL). Above centre, Śiva posed in tribhaṅga, holds paraśu (UR), mṛga (deer, UL), abhaya (LR), and kaṭihastamudrā. Two frolicking Gaṇas flank Śiva.

South 6, north face. Left, a male stands in between two females. The one to the left is a seductress(?): her arms are wrapped around the male's waist and her left foot is placed on the male's right foot. The other female in profile facing the others looks away. Right, the central male has rejected(?) the female to the left who is in a squatting position; his arm is around the shoulders of his companion to the right. Above, this section is mostly uncarved, but in the centre, in very low relief, an emerging form of Gaṇeśa is delineated. The east and south faces of this pillar are uncarved.

Conclusion

The Doḍḍēśvara temple, perhaps originally named the Noṇambēśvara, is the largest, best preserved temple in central Noḷambavāḍi. Whereas most central Noḷambavāḍi temples are constructed of brick, this temple is built of granite, one reason for its durability. Granite also indicates that expense was not a confining consideration. Mārayya, an inscription tells us, financed (caused to be constructed, i.e. patronized) the maṇḍapa. His portrait, along with his wife's, probably is sculpted in one of the front maṇḍapa windows where the epigraph is written. Mārayya's name does not appear in surviving genealogies of direct royal Noḷamba descent; this does not eliminate the possibility that he was a member of the royal family, or an allied affiliate, such as a minister or general. Whoever he was, he must of had the means to accumulate and disperse wealth. Because the record states that the maṇḍapa was built instead of the complete temple (sthāna), it might indicate that the sanctum was already in existence at the time of Mārayya's enterprise. None of this information helps to date the temple.

Another inscription, however, might furnish a clue to the period of construction. Varuṇaśiva-bhaṭāra's name is inscribed on the south side of the Doḍḍēśvara maṇḍapa. A dated inscription in the year Śaka 858 (936 CE) from Gunimorabagalu also includes Varuṇaśiva. In the former epigraph Varuṇaśiva makes a donation to Māpayya. The object of donation is illegible. If Māpayya and Mārayya are not two individuals but one, the spelling discrepancy due to orthographic error, then Mārayya, the maṇḍapa patron, and Varuṇaśiva are contemporaries, supplying a rough construction date. If Māpayya and Mārayya are not the same, then the record with Varuṇaśiva and Māpayya names could have been incised on the maṇḍapa wall at any time after the maṇḍapa construction: however, a terminus date for the temple construction is Varuṇaśiva's lifetime, assuming the epigraph is not a posthumous record. I surmise that the Doḍḍēśvara inscription antecedes the Gunimorubagalu inscription because Varuṇaśiva is humbly referred to in the former simply as Rudra[śiva]cārya's student but in the latter he has many lofty titles (e.g. mahāsāmatādhipati, paramēśvara, paramabhaṭṭāraka) suggesting the latter record (dated 936) is later in Varuṇaśiva's career.[48]

In addition to the epigraphic consideration, the Doḍḍēśvara temple appears to be posterior to the Siddēśvara, which might be coeval to the only dated monument in central Noḷambavāḍi, the Mahēndrēśvara in Baraguru (dated 878). Unfortunately, the Mahēndrēśvara temple is not a good gauge upon which to formulate a stylistic chronology. The brick Mahēndrēśvara temple has simple architectural elements, including a modest front entrance, and it features mostly śrīkāra (cylindrical) pillars, except for two simplified citrakhaṇḍa pillars in the antarāla, instead of the more typical Noḷamba period citrakhaṇḍa pillars. Hence pillar reliefs, the most prevalent sculptural form in central Noḷambavāḍi monuments, are not available for comparison. Nevertheless, it is my opinion that the Doḍḍēśvara temple can be securely dated posterior to the Mahēndrēśvara (878) and prior to the Varuṇaśiva inscription of 936. I believe the Doḍḍēśvara dates to the first third of the tenth century, possibly *c.* 920-30.

AKKA AND TAṆGI TEMPLES

The Akka and Taṇgi temples are located in the south-west part of Hemavati. These two adjacent dilapidated temples, are similar in appearance and partially buried by depris. The Akka (Kannaḍa: elder sister) temple is slightly larger than the Taṇgi (Kannaḍa: younger sister) temple. The garbhagṛha and antarāla of both survive but the mukhamaṇḍapa has been destroyed, almost without a trace. Both are constructed of granite and axially oriented towards the east.

The Akka temple has bhadra, karṇa and pratikarṇa projections articulated by engaged brahmakānta (rectangular) pilasters. 'Sham-niches', too thin to be intended as dēvakōṣṭhas, are built onto the projecting and receding sections. Above the front south sham-niche sits a two-armed Gaṇeśa with a makara tōraṇa and gaṇas overhead. No other figural sculptures are associated with the temple.[49] Above the walls, a kapōta has relief nāsikās and apex kīrttimukhas. Below the kapōta is a haṁsa/makara mālā. No superstructure survives.

What is now the front of the temple, was originally the antarāla entrance. Two black schist citrakhaṇḍa pillars, lacking figural carvings, are built to the entrance sides. There is not an antarāla doorway and, as is common with Noḷamba period temples, one probably did not exist. Wall extension to the north and to the south of the citrakhaṇḍa pillars indicate that a wider mukhamaṇḍapa originally existed. A structural pillar, about one meter north of the north citrakhaṇḍa pillar, has a corbel extending to the east: the mukhamaṇḍapa interior wall would have attached at this point. This is confirmed by the remains of a small section of exterior wall, in the front of the temple, which projects a meter north from rest of the north wall and then extends eastward. No further information regarding the mukhamaṇḍapa is available.

The garbhagṛha has a pañcaśākhā doorway. The inner śākhā is a kalpavalli bordered by a padma-ratna śākhā, followed by another ratna-padma śākhā, then a stambha-śākhā, a vyāla mālā, and finally a padma-śākhā. At the base are two Śaiva dvārapālas holding triśūla, nāga, gadā, and displaying sūcī-mudrā. The antarāla and garbhagṛha have each a ceiling lotus medallion. Enshrined in the sanctum is a large, black Noḷamba period liṅga.

The more dilapidated Taṇgi temple has the same basic composition as the Akka. The Taṇgi temple walls are three-quarters buried under soil. However, it appears that the wall niches are wider than the ones at the Akka temple; possibly the Taṇgi niches are designed as actual dēvakōṣṭhas. The core of a superstructure, granite slabs surmounting the roof, is on the Taṇgi. The rest of the temple basically resembles the Akka temple, though in greater disrepair.

Admittedly, little evidence remains for a conclusive summary concerning these temples. However, a few speculative observations follow. In spite of their present condition, these two temples probably were important monuments in their time. There are two reasons for suggesting this. One, the names Akka and Taṇgi, elder and younger sisters, though probably not the original names, might derive from the temples original purpose of being commemorative temples for sisters from a wealthy (royal?) family. The fact that the temples are built of granite—the only other granite monument in central Noḷambavāḍi is the Doḍḍēśvara (probably originally named Noṇambēśvara)—demonstrates that construction cost was a secondary concern. If not, the more common and cheaper bricks would have been utilized. Hence, it is reasonable to assume the patrons were wealthy (regardless of whether sisters were actually associated with the temples). Second, the fact that the mukhamaṇḍapas were utterly destroyed, while the remaining portions of the temples were unaltered, suggests a conscious policy by some party to disassemble the maṇḍapas. After their conquest of Noḷambavāḍi, the Cōḷas brought Noḷamba pillars ('war trophies') to Cōḷamaṇḍalam: forty-two Noḷamba pillars were built into the Cōḷa temple at Tiruvaiyur.[50] Indeed it is impossible to determine if the pillars confiscated by the Cōḷas were from the Akka and Taṇgi temples, or from any number of lost monuments. To obtain the pillars, the Cōḷas had to destroy maṇḍapas; maybe this accounts for the condition of the Akka and Taṇgi. The first reason for the temples' importance suggests wealth. The second reason suggests aesthetic importance. However, if the temples had special associations, especially royal, this might add to the reasons a conquering force might what to destroy the monuments.

From the scanty evidence available, I surmise the Akka temple layout was similar to the Mahēndrēśvara temple (without the porch extensions) at Baraguru. The surviving antarāla and garbhagṛha at the Akka temple are approximately the same size as their counterparts at the Mahēndrēśvara temple. Also the mukhamaṇḍapa remnant at the Akka temple indicates the maṇḍapa was about the same width as the one at the Mahēndrēśvara, but, obviously, we cannot determine the Akka's maṇḍapa length. Lacking any definite affirmation, I am, nevertheless, tempted to propose a dating of between the last quarter of the ninth century and the first quarter of the tenth century (that is, sometime between the construction of the Mahēndrēśvara and the Doḍḍēśvara) for the Akka and Taṇgi temples.

VIRŪPĀKṢA TEMPLE

The Virūpākṣa temple, though in disrepair, has some of the most elaborate, at times enigmatic, pillar reliefs in Hemavati. The temple is mentioned in the *Encyclopaedia of Indian Temple Architecture* but the discussion, besides being unduly condensed, is mostly inaccurate.[51] The most blatant and misleading error is that the temple is called 'Mallēśvara'. The Mallēśvara temple in Hemavati is located south-west from the Doḍḍēśvara temple in the same compound. The beautiful Virūpākṣa maṇḍapa doorway has been published by Barrett, also mislabelled 'Malikarjuna' [sic].[52] The inability to cite the temple names correctly is indicative of the casual approach previously applied to the study of Noḷamba monuments.

Exterior

The Virūpākṣa temple faces east and initially had a garbhagṛha, antarāla and mukhamaṇḍapa (fig. 4). The original granite adhiṣṭhāna is intact. However, the vimāna walls are now constructed of rubble and surmounted by a brick Phaṁsanā (tiered) superstructure with circular grīvā-śikhara. The maṇḍapa walls are open. However, the maṇḍapa outer row of pillars were initially embedded into walls, as evidenced by the rough edge on the pillars' outer sides. The adhiṣṭhāna consists of jagatī and tripaṭṭa (three-faced) kumuda, and probably once had a paṭṭika course. Examination of the adhiṣṭhāna outline reveals the original temple design. The vimāna walls had bhadra with subhadra (central offset) and karṇa projections, whereas the maṇḍapa north and south walls had only bhadra projections.

Contiguous to the maṇḍapa front, united by a platform, there is a Nandi maṇḍapa which postdates the temple. The Nandi maṇḍapa adhiṣṭhāna shows jagatī and kapōta, a variant order to the rest of the temple. The Nandi is a late Noḷamba period sculpture (pl. 12). He is heavily embellished with ghaṇṭāmālās at the neck, hanging from behind the hump to below the dewlap, and above the hoofs. Further accessories include a ghaṇṭāmālā around the rear which attaches to an ornate waistband, and additional jewels at the neck and head. Though a majestic Nandi, he is too symmetrical: stylization has overwhelmed the relaxed naturalism featured on the anterior Doḍḍēśvara Nandi.

The temple entrance can be approached by stairs from the north or from the south. The east face of both stairways have exquisite carvings on black schist stone. Both have, at the top of the stairway, a large kīrttimukha spewing a banister and a kalpavalli. Below the banister, the north stairway has a Śaiva guardian in atitribhaṅga pose holding nāga (UR), mālā (UL), kaṭihastamudrā (LR), and gadā (LL). In the centre, a mithuna couple rides upon a lion whose front legs rest above a squatting elephant (pl. 13). The lion's tail emphasizes the intimacy between the embracing couple by forming a tight semi-circle, like a shared halo, around the pair. The south stairway has a more elaborate kalpavalli emitting from the kīrttimukha's mouth (pl. 14). The kalpavalli occupies most of the surface space and forms four spirals which have within them seated gaṇas with especially long curls of hair. A standing mithuna couple is beside the kalpavalli. Truly an elegant, loving couple, the male stands aloof in samabhaṅga pose, while the female in atitribhaṅga posture, with her right foot on top of the male's foot, has her arms wrapped around the male's waist and contently smiles.

Carved in black schist, the maṇḍapa doorway[53] has at its inner śākhā base a pūrṇakumbha (overflowing vase), out of which issues a kalpavalli intertwined with gaṇas who either dance or play instruments. The śākhā is bordered by a ratna-padma band. Next, a stambhaśākhā has the front half of an elephant with Padmanidhi seated above projecting from its south base. The north Śaṅkhanidhi and elephant have been removed. The next śākhā has a kalpavalli with males or females within the lotus stem swirls, followed by a row of large lotus leaves. Above the doorway, there is a kapōta with a meandering lotus relief in the centre and sides, plus four nāsikās with apex kīrttimukhas. Portrayed on the bottom of the kapōta is a delightful bhūtamālā. The auspicious aṣṭa-maṅgalas are in relief on a lintel above the kapōta. Gajalakṣmī is in the centre flanked (from inner to outer) by caurī (fan), dīpa (lamp), pūrṇakumbha (full vase) topped by a śaṅkha (north side) or a cakra (south), darpaṇa (mirror), matsyayugma (pair of fishes), Nidhis (padma to the north and śaṅkha to the south), and vidyādhara.

Interior

The temple interior, as it stands today, has an open maṇḍapa and a garbhagṛha. The maṇḍapa has seventeen free-standing pillars, but originally the temple layout was quite different. The outer row of pillars, which includes four to the north, four to the south, and two to the east, were originally embedded into the temple walls. One pillar is a late addition built for support. The four pillars in the maṇḍapa centre were intended as free-standing pillars and two more pillars towards the west-end were the dividers separating the mukhamaṇḍapa and the antarāla. The four mukhamaṇḍapa pillars and two antarāla pillars are typical Noḷamba period citrakhaṇḍa order with carved caturasra sections. Compared to the Doḍḍēśvara pillars, the Virūpākṣa pillars are more slender.[54] The proportions of the pillar parts are better conceived. The cushion capital and, especially, the dish-shaped abacus sections are slimmer, and consequently the Virūpākṣa pillars have a more balanced appearance. Also the reliefs on the Virūpākṣa pillars are more sophisticated with greater attention to details. The pillars' shape and their sculptural style are major factors in attributing the Virūpākṣa temple to a date later than that of the Doḍḍēśvara temple.

The mukhamaṇḍapa ceiling is divided into nine bays by cross beams which have lotus pendants on the four inner corners. The central bay has a lotus medallion but the other bays are plain. This ceiling type is constructed at other central Noḷambavāḍi temples (e.g. Siddēśvara, Mallēśvara at Hemavati and Mahēndrēśvara at Baraguru). On the floor, directly below the central medallion, a balipīṭha is slightly projected. This is an element rarely seen in earlier or coeval temples, though one is placed in the Noḷamba period Lakṣmaṇēśvara temple at Avani (*c.* 925-40), and becomes popular in later Cālukya (of Kalyana) period temples.

Enshrined in the garbhagṛha is a large black liṅga akin to the one at the Doḍḍēśvara temple. The ceiling has a single lotus medallion relief. As is the case with most Noḷambavāḍi temples, the garbhagṛha doorway is simple. The inner śākhā is plain, followed by a ratna-padmaśākhā. Next, a stambhaśākhā is ornamented with a few four petal lotus flowers, followed by a padmaśākhā. At the base, two Śaiva dvārapālas holding triśūla, vismaya-mudrā, nāga, and gadā, stand in tribhaṅga.

Pillar reliefs

The four mukhamaṇḍapa pillars with caturasra carvings have the same basic format as the Doḍḍēśvara pillars. On the Doḍḍēśvara pillars the area above the kīrttimukha usually have a kalpavalli with frolicking gaṇas, or, occasionally, a deity. The Virūpākṣa pillars utilizes this space with greater skill and imagination: invariably a deity is encircled by a prabhāvalī at the top, with related deities or narrative in a horizontal band below, or some narrative event occupies the entire section. These are among the finest Noḷamba pillars still *in situ*. The workmanship is crisp and detailed, even if the iconographic scheme is occasionally obscure. The two antarāla pillars have the lower two panels divided by jewels, as do the other pillars, but a pūrṇakumbha occupies the upper pillar portion. Similar antarāla pillars are built into the Mahēndrēśvara temple at Baraguru.

Because the Virūpākṣa temple faces the east, the pillar faces will be discussed in east, south, west, north (pradakṣinā) order starting with the first south side mukhamaṇḍapa pillar. The lower left and right panels will be first described. The upper caturasra section will be called 'above', which means the top centre prabhāvalī area, and 'horizontal', which means the band directly below the prabhāvalī portion and discussed from left to right, unless otherwise indicated.

South 1, east face. Left, a male drummer accompanies a female dancer who is in the right panel. Above, Śiva sits at ease holding triśūla (UR), nāga (UL), his lower right arm rests on a cushion, and his lower left arm extends over his left knee. Horizontal band, a mithuna couple, a man bent forward carrying a cane, and two gaṇas. The gaṇas are tilted in awkward angles and the man in the centre is bent over, although he appears to be walking, in order to fit within the limited allotted space: this gives an impression of 'playfulness' on the part of the artist.

South 1, south face (pl. 15). Left, a male warrior stands with his khaḍga (sword) and kheṭaka (shield) held ready for action. Right, a standing Devī holds a triśūla (held in UR and LL), kapāla (UL), and khaḍga (LR). Above, Devī sits holding the same attributes as below but the kapāla is in the lower left hand and an additional ḍamaru is in the upper left hand. In the horizontal band, directly below Devī, a warrior, probably the same man as in the left panel, lies conquered with Devī's left foot on his chest. The side horizontal blocks have female warriors, part of Devī's entourage. I suggest this form of Devī be most appropriately called Caṇḍikā, one of the epithets of Devī in her supreme form. The male might represent the asura Śumbha whom Caṇḍikā annihilated at the climax of the *Devī Māhātmya*.[55] The Hemavati genealogy epigraph dated 942 states that Maṅgaḷa, the first historical Noḷamba king, was a devotee to Caṇḍikā.[56] Her image appears often in Noḷamba period art, and the famous Madras Museum Noḷamba Kālī, originally from Hemavati, might have been understood to be Caṇḍikā at the time of its conception.

South 1, west face. Left, Vṛṣabhāntikamūrti: Śiva stands in samabhaṅga, his lower right arm leans on Nandi, his upper right hand holds a triśūla, and the left hands' attributes are unclear, possibly they are not carved. A small Pārvatī stands to Śiva's left. Right, Gaṅgādhara. Śiva stands on Apasmāra, an unusual addition to this iconography.[57] Gaṅgā is entwined in his jaṭā held outward by his upper right hand, his upper left hand is in āhūyavarada-mudrā(?), his lower right arm is around Pārvatī's shoulders, and his lower left hand is in varada-mudrā(?). Below the left hand stands Bhagīratha performing tapas. Above, Śiva sits in lalitāsana with his pendant right foot resting on Apasmāra or a gaṇa in the horizontal band below. Śiva holds triśūla (UR), nāga (UL), abhaya (LR), and kapāla (LL). Two more gaṇas appear in the band.

South 1, north face. Left, Kaṅkālamūrti, a form of Śiva-Bhairava performing penance after decapitating one of Brahmā's heads, here stands in tribhaṅga holding triśūla (UR), ḍhakkā (?, UL), kaṅkāladaṇḍa (LR), and kapāla (LL). He is joined by a bhūta carrying a bowl on his head to receive alms. Right, two standing females, the larger one holds a bowl. Kaṅkālamūrti is known to inspire lascivious acts among the women from whom he collects alms. Above, Rāvaṇānugrahaṇamūrti: five-headed, ten-armed Rāvaṇa, in the centre of the horizontal band, attempts to move Mt. Kailāsa where Śiva and Pārvatī (above) play.

South 2, east face. Left, Devī sits holding churī (dagger, UR), cakra (?, UL), khaḍga (LR), and kapāla (LL). Right, seated Śiva feeds Nandi (with LL) whose head appears to Śiva's right. Śiva's upper right hand is unclear, his other hands have a triśūla (UL), and mālā (LR). Above, an abstruse scene has delineated in a central circle two males holding padmas worshipping a liṅga by placing a garland around the liṅga. An outer circle has within it six male warriors, each with sword and shield. Below, in the horizontal band, left to right, a six-armed man sits holding a bow and arrow, sword, and cakra(?), (other hands are unclear), followed by two males with a staff(?) in between them sitting with their hands in añjalī, facing the first man. Next, Gaṇeśa, with his head turned in the opposite direction of the first man, looks towards three females.

South 2, south face (pl. 16). Left, a male stands with his hands in añjali before Śiva who holds a nāga (UR), a pāśa (UL, noose), an jambhīra (LR, citron fruit), his lower left hand rests on his hip. Right, a small male carries on his head a liṅga. An animal lies in front of a larger male who carries an axe and has a noose around the liṅga base held by the smaller male. These puzzling scenes might represent an unusual, local rendition of the Kālārimūrti episode. The figure carrying the liṅga might be the boy Mārkaṇḍeya worshipping the liṅga. The larger figure might be Yama, or one of his attendants, trying to bind Mārkaṇḍeya with his noose. (The animal might be a buffalo(?), Yama's vehicle). And the left scene might show Yama, in añjalī, asking Śiva for forgiveness. Above, Yogadakṣiṇamūrti in yogāsana displaying triśūla (UR), mālā (UL), vyākhyāna-mudrā (LR), and varada-mudrā (LL).

South 2, west face (pl. 17). The epiphany of Śiva as a blazing liṅga to demonstrate his ontological superiority is overtly portrayed above as Liṅgodbhava and again implied by the presence of Bhikṣāṭana below. The lower panels amplify the climatic scene above. Left, Brahmā holds akṣamālā (UR), kamaṇḍalu (UL), (LR?), kaṭihastamudrā (LL) and is flanked by two female attendants, possibly his consorts Sarasvatī and Sāvitrī. Right, Viṣṇu holds cakra (UR), śaṅkha (UL), and on his left shoulder sits Bhū Devī. Incongruously, Viṣṇu is portrayed anthropomorphically:[58] it is the Varāha (Boar) avatāra that rescues Bhū, and in the Liṅgodbhava episode it is Varāha that vainly searches for the origin of the liṅga. To Viṣṇu's proper right stands Bhikṣāṭana. In the Pine Forest Śiva as Bhikṣāṭana, a naked ascetic, was cursed by the deluded ṛṣis because they blamed Śiva for the lustful actions of their wives and daughters. To be castrated was the curse and Śiva allowed it to happen: a fiery liṅga created cosmic chaos until it was properly propitiated. Above, Liṅgodbhavamūrti: Śiva reveals himself inside a liṅga flanked by Brahmā and Viṣṇu. At the dissolution of a kalpa Brahmā and Viṣṇu both claimed to be the creator of the universe. During their argument they were bewildered by the manifestation of an infinite blazing liṅga which ultimately proved to be Śiva.

South 2, north face. Left, a large male with a small male behind him sit facing the right scene which has a male carrying a tree (?). Above, within a forest setting there is a battle scene. Horizontal band, with a lion present, a few males are in discussion. Another abstruse pillar relief, these scenes might represent a *Rāmāyaṇa* episode (a *Rāmāyaṇa* scene is depicted on the north 2, north face pillar) or a *Mahābhārata* episode (as shown on north 2, south face pillar).

South 3: Compared to the other pillars, the antarāla pillar is slimmer in width. The south and west sides would have been originally blocked by the antarāla walls, therefore they are not carved. East face: Left, a seated two-armed Gaṇeśa with laḍḍu in his right hand (more commonly sweets are found in his left hand) and an akṣamālā in his left. Right, a two-armed Mahiṣāsuramardinī has in her right hand a triśūla piercing the theriomorphic Mahiṣāsura and the asura's neck is twisted by the other hand. A pūrṇakumbha occupies the section above the panels. The north face is simple: left, a male sits holding padma and fruit; right, a dancing male and, above, a pūrṇakumbha.

North 1, east face. Kirātārjunīyam: Left, Śiva as a Kirāta stands in samabhaṅga holding a bow. To his right Pārvatī, in tribhaṅga pose, displays varada-mudrā (R) and holds a padma. A small Nandi is to Śiva's left. Right, standing in ekapādāsana Arjuna performs tapas. Arrows are beside him and a bow is held in his left hand. Above, an awkward presentation of the fight between Śiva and Arjuna is delineated. The larger figure, identified by his third eye as Śiva, holds a khaḍga (R) and displays sūcī-mudrā. The smaller background figure is not clearly shown, but seems to be Arjuna. Horizontal band, two males, one holds some type of vessel, the other has a padma; a gaṇa playing with a nāga; a vidyādhara showing añjalī-mudrā.

North 1, south face. Left, Gajāsurasaṁhāramūrti: Śiva grips the Gajāsura's hide and dances in a wild celebration in which his upper torso is twisted in the opposite direction from his lower body (pṛṣṭhasvastika pose but his legs do not cross). Right: in the typical Gajāsurasaṁhāra scene Devī (as Pārvatī) with baby Skanda retreats from Śiva's dance, but here an unusual switch occurs; Devī in a fierce 'dark' form joins the dance. She is in catura pose holding triśūla (UR), kapāla (UL), abhaya (LR), and dolahasta (LL). Above, six-armed Naṭēśa in catura pose, dances on top of Apasmāra. Śiva holds mālā (?, UR), abhaya or vyākhyāna-mudrā (main R), triśūla (?, LR), agni (?, UL), gajahasta (main), and nāga (LL). Horizontal band, Gaṇa musicians performing on the flute, drum, and cymbals.

North 1, west face. Possibly a royal couple, sitting in lalitāsana, a female is to the left and a male to the right. Above, a seated mithuna couple with the male having one arm around his partner's shoulders and the other hand touching her breast. Horizontal, mithunas: the first couple sit together but separated; the female in the second couple has her arm on the male's shoulders; lastly, the female actively embraces the male with both arms.

North 1, north face. This pillar has seven avatāras of Viṣṇu distinctly depicted and may be three others represented but, if so, not with distinguishing attributes. The two most popular avatāras, Narasiṁha and Varāha, are portrayed below, and above centre a standing Viṣṇu dominates. The other avatāras appear in the horizontal band. Left (lower), Yoga-Narasiṁha seated wearing a yogapaṭṭa around his waist and left leg, holding cakra (UR), śaṅkha (UL), lower right hand is on his thigh, and a lotus in his lower left hand. Right, Varāha seated on a padmapīṭha displaying cakra (UR), Bhū (UL), LL to his side, and padma (?, LL). Above, Viṣṇu erect in samabhaṅga pose: his upper torso occupies the prabhāvalī section and rest of his body extends into the horizontal area. His attributes are cakra (UR), śaṅkha (UL), gadā (LR), and kaṭihastamudrā (LL). In the horizontal band, to Viṣṇu's proper right, are: Rāma (holds bow and arrow), Paraśurāma (with paraśu), in between the two just a head appears (maybe Vāmana?). To Viṣṇu's left: a seated male holding a gadā (?, Kṛṣṇa?), a small matsya is delineated above a small kūrma, Buddha (in yogāsana, showing dhyāna- and abhaya-mudrās), and another male holding a gadā (?, Kalki?).

North 2, east face (*pl. 18*). Left, Mahiṣāsuramardinī: The most frequent manner in Noḷamba period art of depicting the ultimate defeat of Mahiṣāsura by Durgā is portrayed here: Durgā crushes the theriomorphic asura's back with her foot, one hand twists the asura's neck upward, and a triśūla pierces the asura's body (cakra and śaṅkha in the upper hands). Right, the actual conflict in progress between Durgā and Mahiṣāsura is delineated. Having an anthropomorphic body but a buffalo head, Mahiṣāsura has khaḍga and kheṭaka held for battle but is obviously on the defensive, in a retreating stance. Durgā is bursting forward towards the asura, holding cakra (UR), śaṅkha (UL), khaḍga (LR), and kheṭaka (LL). Above each panel is a vidyādhara. Above, Samudramanthana: Viṣṇu as Kūrmāvatāra supported Mount Mandara which was used as a pestle, Vāsuki as the rope, to churn the ocean of milk in order to produce amṛta and other celestial objects. Here, Viṣṇu stands in the centre as the asuras and dēvas churn the ocean. Below, in the horizontal section, centre, appears to be Garuḍa bearing the upper activity. Indra was a key character in the Samudramanthana; the figure on a horse, to the left of Garuḍa, must be Indra—his horse Ucchaiḥśravas was produced during the churning.

North 2, south face. Mahābhārata battle between Arjuna and Karṇa, a crucial episode in one of the most critical battles at Kurukṣetra. Left, Arjuna stands in his ratha, his charioteer Kṛṣṇa, holds the kapidhvaja (i.e. Arjuna's monkey banner). Right, standing in his ratha, Karṇa holds in his right hand a sarpāstra (snake-weapon) saved specifically in order to destroy Arjuna. Aśvasena, a snake resolved to take Arjuna's life in revenge for his mother's death, had entered the sarpāstra. Śalya, Karṇa's charioteer, warned Karṇa that the aim of his weapon was too high, but Karṇa refused to aim a second time. When the missile was discharged, Kṛṣṇa forced the wheels of his ratha to sink into the earth, consequently the sarpāstra passed Arjuna's head, only damaging his crown's diadem. Karṇa's imminent annihilation is apparent here: Śalya is seen disembarking from the ratha. Six heads portrayed above the scene represent the celestials who witnessed this terrifying encounter. Above, bhūtas with weapons, not associated with the lower narrative. Below the panels, two additional vertical panels provide information relevant to the Arjuna-Karṇa conflict. Lower panel, a female covered with a shawl enters a room and, above, she converses with a male. No doubt the female is Kuntī, mother of the Pāṇḍavas, Yudhiṣṭhira, Bhīma and Arjuna; also of Karṇa who was abandoned at birth. Prior to the war Kuntī secretly approached Karṇa (the male above) to confess that she was his true mother and to request him not to fight against Arjuna, his half brother, whom Karṇa had allied against and vowed to kill.

North 2, west face. Vṛṣabhāntikamūrti: Two-armed Śiva with triśūla (?, R), and mātuluṅga (?, fruit), sits on his vāhana Nandi. A caurī bearer stands to the side. Right, Umāmahēśvara: A particularly intimate Umāmahēśvara, Śiva in one hand grasps a nāga (UR), while his other hands embrace Umā, and his body is tilted towards her. Smiling Umā sits on Śiva's lap, her legs, rather immodestly open, placed to the sides of Śiva. A vidyādhara is above each panel. Above, Dakṣiṇāmūrti: Seated in lalitāsana Śiva holds mṛga (UR), akṣamālā (?, UL), pustaka (LR), and varada-mudrā (LL). Behind him are caurī bearers, lower right, a gaṇa, to the lower left a kneeling male with an unidentified object. Horizontal, a male kneeling, his hands in añjalī; a ṛṣi with a pustaka; a bhūta(?), a gaṇa; another ṛṣi with a pustaka. Because there is a book in Śiva's hand, and ṛṣis and other devotees are included, it seems probable that this is a Dakṣiṇāmūrti .

North 2, north face. Left, Rāma and Lakṣmaṇa stand. Right, with their hands in añjalī, Hanumān and Sugrīva reverently greet Rāma. Above, in Aśokavana Sītā is consoled by Hanumān. On this pillar face the standard corner lions have female riders with wild, flared hair who probably represent the Rākṣasī guardians of Sītā. Horizontal, in the centre, Rāvaṇa abducting Sītā in his ratha; to his right, Jaṭāyu ready to battle. An additional gaṇa is at the other end.

North 3. Same format as for the other antarāla pillar: west and north sides are uncarved, the east face has nidhis below, followed by a pūrṇakumbha with a gaṇa at the pinnacle. South face has the pūrṇakumbha with two male dancers below.

Conclusion

In its current state of dilapidation, at first glance, the Virūpākṣa is an unimposing monument. Yet the miniature reliefs on the pillars and the entrance doorway reflect a sculptural refinement. The stairway panels also are excellent examples of the central Noḷambavāḍi idiom.

At one time, the temple was flanked by two other shrines. About four meters north of the Virūpākṣa, a temple adhiṣṭhāna, with jagatī, tripaṭṭa kumuda, and kapōta, remains. Its vimāna has bhadra and karṇa projections, the antarāla section is recessed and the mukhamaṇḍapa section is wider than the vimāna, without projections. To the south of the Virūpākṣa temple a large, Noḷamba period black liṅga survives. Behind and to the right of the liṅga, granite foundation stones, once part of the vimāna, are noticeable and through excavation more of the temple adhiṣṭhāna would be revealed. The ruins of these two temples not only remind us of the many monuments lost over time in Hemavati; they also indicate that the Virūpākṣa temple and its immediate vicinity was grander than it now appears. Some ceiling panels of outstanding quality, to be discussed later, use to be scattered beside these temples.

Based solely on stylistic considerations, I date the Virūpākṣa temple to the mid-tenth century.[59] Although stylistic chronology is somewhat arbitrary, lacking other evidence it must suffice. Relative to the Doḍḍēśvara temple, which I date *c.* 920-30, the Virūpākṣa displays aspects of later development, the primary determinant being the pillars. Formally Virūpākṣa pillar elements are less bulky, more graceful in comparison to those at Doḍḍēśvara and the reliefs better accommodate their allotted panel space in a detailed, active manner (i.e. the composition is more successful) at Virūpākṣa. It appears that the Virūpākṣa pillars were the work of more experienced sthāpatis (artisans). Another factor to regard in the temple dating is the Nandi. Assuming the Virūpākṣa Nandi is coeval with the temple—he could have been moved from a different, later temple and hence a misleading component. But, if he was originally attached to the Virūpākṣa temple, then his appearance requires consideration. The Nandi is stylized and excessively embellished: superficiality overcomes the form, a tendency exhibited in works too often repeated. Admittedly, the two determinants, the pillars and the Nandi, can seem contradictory. The pillars are later (than Doḍḍēśvara) because of their sleek form and sophisticated reliefs, whereas the Nandi is late for a contrary reason, he lacks elemental harmony and appears stylized. Or, the reasons are the same, except Nandi images developed (and declined) at a different rate as did pillars. The pillars, being *in situ*, are the main criterion of dating, however; I consider the Virūpākṣa to be a temple dating from the mid-tenth century.

MALLĒŚVARA TEMPLE

The Mallēśvara temple (in Hemavati), as it stands today, is mostly rebuilt but has a few noteworthy characteristics. The temple consists of a garbhagṛha, antarāla and mukhamaṇḍapa (fig. 5). In front of the temple, which faces the east, a Nandi pavilion was later constructed. A Noḷamba period Nandi is enclosed by rubble walls on three sides. The temple exterior walls are now entirely composed of bricks (some which appear original) or rubble. A granite adhiṣṭhāna with jagatī, dhārāvṛta-kumuda and paṭṭika mouldings survives. The vimāna adhiṣṭhāna shows karṇa, pratikarṇa, and bhadra projections: the maṇḍapa adhiṣṭhāna is without articulation; a deep recess divides the vimāna and maṇḍapa sections.

The mukhamaṇḍapa doorway is of the caturaśākhā variety. A kalpavalli with gaṇa musicians within the meandering lotus swirls, and bordered by a ratna-padma band forms the inner śākhā. A stambhaśākhā with small Śaiva dvārapālas at the base is next, followed by a kalpavalli and an outer ratna-padmaśākhā. Below the last śākhā, females holding water pots stand. Although the śākhās are clearly delineated, the doorway appears stylized and stifled; the playful vitality infused in the gaṇa musicians, and other figures, at the Doḍḍēśvara and the Virūpākṣa temples is not evident here.

The mukhamaṇḍapa has four proto-śrīkāra pillars (fig. 9). Due to cracks in the ceiling beams, four additional 'generic' square pillars were added later for support. The original pillars, which have a square lower shaft section surmounted by thin octagonal and sixteen-sided bands, a prominent bell-shaped cylindrical shaft, and topped by a cushion capital, are the most 'evolved' of Noḷamba period proto-śrīkāra pillars relative to the succeeding śrīkāra pillars developed during the Cālukya of Kalyana era. The Mahēndēśvara temple, Baraguru, has an agra-maṇḍapa extension, dating later than the original structure, with akin Noḷamba period proto-śrīkāra pillars. These cylindrical, 'proto-lathed-turned' Noḷamba period pillars, along with Rāṣṭrakūṭa period cylindrical pillars, such as those at the Jain temple, Paṭṭadakal,[60] served as convenient harbingers for the developed śrīkāra ('lathed-turned') pillars. Cālukya of Kalyana—the usurpers of Rāṣṭrakūṭa territories and overlords of the Noḷambas after the Cōḷas forced the Noḷambas into the Cālukya camp—chose to incorporate the śrīkāra pillar type as a standard architectural feature in their temples. In the mukha-maṇḍapa of the Kallēśvara temple, Kukkanur,[61] considered an early example of (Later) Cālukya period architecture, the śrīkāra pillars share many characteristics seen in the Noḷamba/Rāṣṭrakūṭa period pillars. This is a prime example of regionally shared traits, unrestricted by political boundaries.

The maṇḍapa ceiling is the same type constructed at the Virūpākṣa temple and earlier at the Siddēśvara temple. Nine bays are divided by beams: a lotus medallion occupies the central bay, the outer sections are plain, and four lotus pendants are placed around the central bay where the beams intersect. The antarāla originally did not have a doorway; however, here, as in the maṇḍapa, the ceiling beam is cracked and a door was built for support. The ceilings in the antarāla and garbhagṛha have a central lotus medallion. A typical Noḷamba period large, black liṅga is enshrined in the garbhagṛha. The sanctum's entrance is modest, having two plain śākhās divided by a ratna-padmaśākhā, and an outer padmaśākhā, along with pūrṇakumbhas at the base.

A mostly dilapidated temple, the walls completely

rebuilt, little evidence remains to date the Mallēśvara temple. As mentioned, the maṇḍapa proto-śrīkāra pillars are the most 'evolved' Noḷamba period pillars of this type. The temple probably dates to the late tenth century, built just prior to Noḷambas' migration to the Bellary district as feudatory to the Cālukya of Kalyana. The Noḷambas continued to administrate substantial portions of Noḷambavāḍi on behalf of the Cālukyas. It is possible that groups of sthāpatis (architects, sculptors, etc.), content with Noḷamba patronage—either directly or by patronage from persons somehow affiliated with the Noḷamba network in central Noḷambavāḍi—also decided to migrate. This direct contact with the Cālukyas, or more importantly with sthāpatis in their employment, might help explain why some features popularly displayed in Noḷambavāḍi (e.g. pillars, doorways, etc.) were absorbed and further developed during the later Cālukya period.

MISCELLANEOUS SHRINES

There are a number of miscellaneous shrines in Hemavati of no great importance, except for an occasional unusual pillar relief. For the sake of completeness, however, I will briefly describe the shrines, with special attention given to pillar reliefs when appropriate.

Basava shrine

The Basava shrine is a one room enclosure which, as its name indicates, houses a bull, Nandi. The walls are built of rubble, but possibly the room was originally a temple garbhagṛha. The simple doorway, similar to the Mallēśvara temple garbhagṛha doorway, consists of a ratna-padmaśākhā, a stambhaśākhā, and a padmastambha, with pūrṇakumbha bases. Two perforated kalpavalli windows are built into the front wall.

The enclosed Nandi is probably slightly posterior to the Doḍḍēśvara temple Nandi. It retains much of the naturalistic ease of the Doḍḍēśvara Nandi but has more ornamentation. A well-preserved black schist Gaṇeśa also is housed in the shrine (pl. 19). The four-armed Gaṇeśa holds in his upper right hand a paraśu, an aṅkuśā in the upper left hand, his broken tusk in the lower right hand and in the lower left hand, laḍḍu (sweets). The sculpture is a fine example of Noḷamba period workmanship, and is probably coeval with the Nandi, maybe dating to the mid-tenth century.

Añjaneya shrine

A small Añjaneya shrine, with Hanumān enclosed, dates considerably later than the period under discussion. However, supporting the front hall are two typical Noḷamba period citrakhaṇḍa pillars with caturasra carvings. Lacking special characteristics, they do not require explication, except for one pillar face. The Gajendramokṣa episode, an iconographic rarity judging from surviving Noḷamba period pillars, is portrayed on the top of a pillar.[62] In the centre, Gajendra, king of the elephants, is held captive by a crocodile. As a symbol of praise directed towards Viṣṇu, a lotus flower is carried in Gajendra's trunk. To the right, Viṣṇu riding on Garuḍa (as Karivarada) approaches to save the elephant. The crocodile was actually a gandharva, named Hūhū, cursed to live a crocodilian existence. A male to the left probably represents Hūhū liberated to his original state after Viṣṇu killed the lower form. Portrayed in the lower left pillar panel is Mahiṣāsuramardinī destroying Mahiṣāsura who has an anthropomorphic body with a buffalo head. Right panel, Durgā stands in samabhaṅga holding the attributes associated with Viṣṇu, the cakra (UR), śaṅkha (UL), abhaya-mudrā (LR) and gadā (LL).

Two pavilions: first one

Two small, open pavilions survive in Hemavati: one at the village west entrance, the other slightly northwest to the Siddēśvara temple prākāra (enclosure walls). Citrakhaṇḍa pillars usually with caturasra reliefs support the roofing. They are standard Noḷamba period pillars but smaller and thinner than the ones in the temples. Unless an unusual feature of a pillar requires elaboration, a cursory description will suffice.

The west pavilion has a finely carved Naṭēśa on its south-east pillar, east face. Instead of being divided into the typical caturasra format of one upper and two lower scenes, this panel is mostly occupied by Naṭēśa. Eight-armed Naṭēśa, depicted in catura pose, dances on the stomach and head of Apasmāra. The main right hand is in abhaya-mudrā, the main left in gajahasta pose, the remaining hands are mostly destroyed except for a sword in the middle right hand and possibly a ḍamaru in the lower right hand. The missing lower left hand must have held the nāga whose outline survives to the side. A gaṇa musician plays the cymbals to Śiva's lower right, and to the left a gaṇa drummer. Overhead are two vidyādharas. At the pillar top is a seated Śiva with a few gaṇas below him. Portrayed in the vertical section below the Naṭēśa scene are four warriors with their weapons held overhead, and mounted on horses. The other sides of the south-east pillar are uncarved.

The south-west pillar has an uncarved east face. The south side has a Bhairava at the top, Gaṅgādhara in the lower left panel, and in the right panel there is a female, which probably is Pārvatī. The west face has Lakṣmī above, and in the lower panels, Manmatha and Ratī. At the top of the north face are frolicking gaṇas, and the lower panels each have a Sūrya. The north-east pillar, east face, has Lakṣmī (above) and seated male and female figures (below). The south face has dancers and musicians; the west face is uncarved; and Nidhis(?) are on the north face. The east and south sides of the north-west pillar are uncarved; the west face has Sūrya with attendants. On top of the north face a seated Ardhanārīśvara—usually this figure is portrayed standing—holds a nāga and abhaya-mudrā on the right, male side, and the female side holds a padma (other hand indistinct). A standing (royal?) couple is below. In proximity of the pavilion a few Noḷamba period liṅgas and Nandis are stored.

Second pavilion

The pavilion near the Siddēśvara temple has on its south-east pillar, east side, Manmatha and Ratī in the lower panels, and gaṇas playing instruments or dancing in the kalpavalli swirls above. The south face also has gaṇa musicians/dancers above, and below, Brahmā in the left panel, a female dancer in the right panel. Gajāsurasaṁhāramūrti is portrayed on the upper section of the west face, and below are two Śaiva guardians. Occupying most of the caturasra section on the north side is Śiva seated at ease, and holding a rope which binds the arm of an unidentified male.

Rendered on the south-west pillar, east face, is one of the few surviving Noḷamba period Andhakāsuravadhamūrti scenes (pl. 20). In the lower, left panel Śiva holds his triśūla with the impaled Andhakāsura overhead, and dances. Śiva's śakti, Yogēśvarī, who along with other Matṛkās drank the blood of Andhaka, dances in the right panel. The quintessential dancer, Naṭēśa, in catura pose dances on top of Apasmāra in the upper section. The south face has a seated Śiva with frolicking gaṇas below him in the upper area; Sūrya is in the lower left panel, and Mahiṣāsuramardinī in the right panel. Nidhis and gaṇas occupy the west face. The lower north face has Ratī and Manmaṭha, and above, a female dancer and gaṇas.

The north-east pillar, east face, in the upper section, has Śiva wearing a yogapaṭṭa, seated above a gaṇa, with a female to his right, a male to the left. Rāma and Viṣṇu are in the lower panels. On the south face, lower left, Vṛṣabhāntikamūrti, Śiva with Nandi is rendered. To the right a bearded ṛṣi sits, and above gaṇas frolic. The south face has a large Viṣṇu encompassing most of the caturasra section. Small figures are to Viṣṇu's sides, possibly representing his avatāras, as are depicted on a Virūpākṣa temple pillar, but only a kūrma (tortoise) is recognizable: the figures are abraded, maybe they were not fully carved. Three abraded figures, the centre one holding a gadā or khaḍga, are seated in the upper section. The north face, upper portion, has an unusual Mahiṣāsuramardinī scene. Six-armed Durgā is on top of her lion, and to her left lies a decapitated buffalo, from which the asura, Mahiṣa, has fully emerge in human (asura) form. In Noḷambavāḍi sculptures Mahiṣāsura is most commonly portrayed in theriomorphic form, or partially theriomorphic with some human features. On this pillar the buffalo carcass is seen discarded and a completely human/asura form continues the battle. Below stands a (royal?) couple.

The north-west pillar, east side, within a flaming Prabhāvalī Devī in an ugra form (Caṇḍikā?) sits on an asura in the upper section, and two females stand below. The south face, above, has Liṅgodbhava flanked by Brahmā and Viṣṇu standing in the lower area. The west face is uncarved. A vidyādhara couple is in the lower portion of the north face, and above sits Śiva.

LOOSE SCULPTURES

Ceiling panels

Five superbly sculpted ceiling panels, now housed in the new site museum, use to lie scattered in front of the Virūpākṣa temple. Sculpturally they exhibit the refinement of the central Noḷambavāḍi idiom at its height. Two panels are part of a set which, accompanied by a missing third panel, would form a typical Naṭēśa and lateral Aṣṭadikpālas group. The other three panels are more enigmatic. Though iconographically identifiable, as ceiling panels they are thematically unique.

The two panels forming the Aṣṭadikpālas and Naṭēśa set are each divided into three scenes. The panel with Indra, Naṭēśa and Varuṇa (pl. 21) would have been the central ceiling panel. The other panel with Īśāna, Kubera and Vāyu (pl. 22) would have been hung to the north. The missing south panel with Nirṛuti, Yama and Agni is now displayed at the Madras Government Museum.[63] That the latter is part of the same group is visually apparent by the stylistic resemblance—though the museum panel appears more glossy black due to polishing—and the fact that the panel has the missing dikpālas required to complete the set.

Standing (dancing) in catura pose on the back of Apasmāra, Naṭēśa holds in his eight hands: āhūyavarada-mudrā (main R), ghaṇṭā (UR), triśūla (mid R), nāga (LR); gajahasta (main L), akṣamālā

(UL), mṛga (deer, mid L), and kapāla (?, LL). Three gaṇa musicians, one playing a drum, another a vīṇā and a third the cymbals, perform for Naṭēśa, and the spectacle is witnessed by a small seated Devī. The Aṣṭadikpāla panels, including the one at the Madras Museum, have the eight dikpālas on their vāhanas along with their consorts. Usually with a cloud formation background, the animated scenes are busy with attendants, vidyādharas and/or gandharva musicians and couples. The scene with Kubera (pl. 23), the guardian of the north, who is generally associated with wealth and sometimes love, has an especially large entourage of eighteen musicians or couples. Typically in ceiling panels the central scene is the most elaborate, yet in this set the Aṣṭadikpāla panels are particularly lively.

This Naṭēśa and Aṣṭadikpāla set is stylistically akin to the other central Noḷambavāḍi sets at the Mailarēśvara temple in Pathasivarama and the Kallēśvara temple in Aralaguppe. Though the sets at each site were sculpted at disparate times, by different hands, they share idiosyncracies which identify them as product of a common school. All the images are graceful, finely proportioned figures ornamented with a diverse array of jewels. The decorative elements do not overwhelm the body form: a delicate harmony between form and embellishment is achieved. Other idioms, of course, can be described similarly. However, even the eastern and southern Noḷambavāḍi works do not exhibit many of the same idiomatic traits encountered in central Noḷambavāḍi sculptures. For instance, ceiling panels in eastern Noḷambavāḍi, and to a lesser extent southern Noḷambavāḍi, are much less ornamented and the figures less animated relative to the panels found in the central Noḷambavāḍi. Generally, central Noḷambavāḍi figures, those that exemplify the idiom at its height, have rounded faces with broad noses, full lips and fleshy cheeks. Bodies are healthily plump, limbs tubular, decorated with the ubiquitous jewels. Again, this description might sound uselessly general as well as applicable to other schools. Nevertheless, the distinctiveness is visually perceptible. These idiomatic traits are amplified in the following panels.

A thematically Vaiṣṇava ceiling panel (pl. 24) has the unusual format of four scenes on one slab, two in a upper register, two in a lower. The upper scenes delineate Viṣṇu in his popular two avatāras of Vāmana and of Narasiṁha; a third celebrated avatāra, Kṛṣṇa, is depicted in the lower scenes destroying asuras. The Vāmana episode in the upper right scene has to one side a royal figure, the asura king Bali, with one hand in varada-mudrā to indicate his approval of Vāmana's request for a boon. The Brahmin boy Vāmana stands to the other side under an umbrella with his hands open, receiving water from a pot poured by a middle figure who, judging by his elegant hairstyle, is an important minister, presumably the rājaguru Śukra. Often Bali is depicted pouring the water to symbolize his respectful acceptance of Vāmana, but in this scene probably Śukra was included to remind viewers of Śukra's recognition of Vāmana as Viṣṇu. The battle between Narasiṁha and Hiraṇyakaśipu is rendered in the upper left scene of the panel. There can be no doubt who the victor will be. Though Hiraṇyakaśipu is charging, he is obviously being restrained by the larger, four-armed Narasiṁha who represses Hiraṇyakaśipu with one hand (the other hands are broken) and has his left leg wrapped around Hiraṇyakaśipu's hip, effectively curbing the assault. The lower scenes have Kṛṣṇa defeating the crane demon Vakāsura (or Bakāsura) in the left square and, in the other scene, Kṛṣṇa destroying Ariṣṭāsura, the bull demon.[64] In both, Kṛṣṇa is four-armed, holding a cakra and a śaṅkha in the upper hands, with the lower hands twisting the necks of the unfortunate animals, and has his right foot on the animals' backs. Though the episodes on this panel are commonly represented in art (and literature), as a ceiling panel these themes are a rarity.

Having three scenes on a horizontal slab, which is the typical ceiling panel format, the next panel depicts Durgā, Viṣṇu and Paraśurāma. In the left scene Durgā sits in (ardha) utkaṭikāsana (as does Viṣṇu and Paraśurāma) on a throne with a lion below. In her upper hands she holds a cakra (UR) and a śaṅkha (UL), her lower hands display abhaya-mudrā (LR) and sūcī-mudrā. In the background there are two female caurī bearers, and two additional females stand beside the throne, one holds a pot. In the central scene Viṣṇu seated on his throne holds cakra (UR), śaṅkha (UL), āhūyavarada-mudrā (?, LL) and abhaya-mudrā (LL). Two male caurī bearers are in the background. Seated on the ground to Viṣṇu's right is Garuḍa. On the opposite side, seated on a throne is Lakṣmī. Paraśurāma, in the left scene, holds a paraśu (axe) in his left hand and his right hand rests on his thigh. He is flanked by two female attendants with caurīs.

The final ceiling panel has rendered in three scenes, Gaṇeśa, Brahmā, and Śiva circumscribed by the Saptamātṛkās and Gaṇeśa (pl. 25). Gaṇeśa in the left panel is seated on a padmapīṭha (lotus throne) in (ardha) utkaṭikāsana with his cognizance the rat below. This majestic Gaṇeśa holds a paraśu (UR), an akṣamālā (UL), a danta (LR, his broken tusk), and laḍḍu (LL). Two male cauri bearers are to the sides in the background and two small monkeys with offerings flank Gaṇeśa. In the central scene Brahmā is seated in padmāsana upon a grand padmapīṭha which has elephants at the base, makara extensions at the throne top, and lions standing in between the animals. (The Gaṇeśa throne has makara extensions as do the thrones in the previous panel.) Below Brahmā is his haṁsavāhana. Three-headed Brahmā holds a pāśa (UR, noose), an akṣamālā (UL) āhūya-mudrā (LR) and a kalaśa (LL, water-pot). He is flanked by two male caurī bearers. In the third scene Śiva is seated in the middle of the panel encircled by Gaṇeśa and the Saptamātṛkās. Śiva grips a triśūla (UL) and displays āhūya-mudrā (UL) and sūcī-mudrā (LR) (fourth hand rests on his thigh). Seated on the inner panel frame, with their heads directed towards Śiva, eight figures circumscribe Śiva: three figures are seated above Śiva, three below him and two to his sides. Brahmāṇī, the standard first mātṛkā in a set, is seated to Śiva's right and in counter-clockwise order next comes presumably Mahēśvarī (no attributes held—each of the mātṛkās are four-armed) followed by Kaumārī, Vaiṣṇavī, Vārahī, Indrāṇī, Cāmuṇḍā and, finally, Gaṇeśa seated to Śiva's upper right.

The rough hewn lower frame of this panel indicates that the slab would have been adjacent to at least one, more likely two, panels hung in the same fashion as were the Aṣṭadikpāla panels. The panel with Durgā, Viṣṇu and Paraśurāma also, as evidenced by the framing, would have been contiguous with other panels. These last two panels probably are from the same set. In addition to the close sculptural style, all the scenes, except for the one with Śiva and the mātṛkās, have the main figure seated on a throne with upper makara extensions, ornamented prabhāvalīs above the figures, and flanking caurī bearers. If the ceiling panels were hung in an identical manner as the Naṭēśa and Aṣṭadikpāla panels, then it is apparent that the panel with Durgā, Viṣṇu and Paraśurāma would have been in the south, the Gaṇeśa, Brahmā and Śiva panel would have been in the north, and the essential middle panel—the required link in solving the iconographic scheme—is now unavailable. If a third, middle panel is missing, then the combined meaning of the panels is lost. In isolation the panels cannot be properly interpreted. As is the case with many sculptures removed from their original setting, their purpose within the context of the total monument often remains enigmatic. Throughout Hemavati many sculptures lie scattered about as testimony to lost Noḷamba period monuments. Although their original temple function might remain a puzzle, the sculptures are identifiable. A brief discussion regarding some of the more important images follows.

The Madras Museum 'Kālī' and Mātṛkās

There are over fifty loose sculptures in Hemavati and more in neighbouring villages. No doubt excavations and an intense survey would reveal others, although even more are lost to time. Some of the aesthetically finer works are housed in the Madras Government Museum and the remaining sculptures in Hemavati are now maintained in a site museum recently constructed by the Archaeological Survey of India. The sculptures exhibit traits not always compatible with each other. Some are less refined with minimal concern for ornamentation and form. However, just the opposite is true for many of the best works, which I consider the 'mature' expressions of central Noḷambavāḍi idiom. The ceiling panels discussed above are examples of this type. The Bhairava enshrined in the Siddēśvara temple is not only a monumental iconographic expression, he is a monumental artistic achievement. Fortunately, he is not an isolated example.

A sculpture comparable to the Bhairava aesthetically and as commanding a spiritual image is the 'Kālī' at the Madras Museum (pl. 26). Sivaramamurti claims this image belonged to a Saptamātṛkā set and in his signature fashion claims elements of Kālī's composition are 'Chalukya' and/or 'Chola'.[65] The sculpture most certainly epitomizes the central Noḷambavāḍi idiom and it is unlikely that the image belonged to a standard Saptamātṛkā group. Like the Bhairava, Kālī is an imposing figure (H: app. 140 cm, her pendant left leg is broken) sculpted in black schist. In her upper right hand she holds a triśūla, a ḍamaru is in her upper left hand (same attributes as Bhairava), and her lower two hands are broken. Her flared jvalitaśikhā ('flaming hair') has an apex muṇḍa (skull) with sarpas (snakes) out of the muṇḍa's mouth. She wears a muṇḍa-yajñopavīta (sacred thread composed of skulls), a sarpabharaṇa (snake breastband), a śavakuṇḍala (an earring with a dangling corpse), a ulūkakuṇḍala (an owl earring), plus some less shocking jewelry. Her youthful face has a third eye, small fangs and a slight grimace which properly conveys her ferocity. Seated in lalitāsana, her left leg is pendant. The Kālī and Bhairava are strikingly alike, possibly sculpted by the same master.

Although a number of mātṛkās survive in Hemavati (and all of Noḷambavāḍi), either as loose sculptures or as panels, none equal the dominating size (or aesthetic brilliancy) of Kālī. Size alone eliminates other known mātṛkās from being part of the same set with Kālī, unless smaller mātṛkās, thus subsidiary, were grouped beside Kālī—a possible arrangement, though none of the known mātṛkās appear as probable mates to Kālī. However, in Hemavati there are six ruined Devī images which are almost equal in size (judging from the remains) to the Kālī and are akin in appearance. Because three are destroyed above the waist level, nothing can be said with certainty regarding their attributes. Among the other three, one, seated like Kālī, has broken arms (pl. 27); the other two are busts (pl. 28).[66] The guise of the latter three is fierce: like Kālī, they have flaming hair with a skull-snake ornament, skull yajñopavītas, snake breastbands, the busts both have a corpse earring and a owl earring (the other figure is unclear), and all have third eyes and fangs.[67] Like Kālī, both of the busts have lost their lower arms. In the upper right hand they have triśūlas. One has a ḍamaru in the upper left hand, as does the Kālī, but the other holds a circular object (possibly a cakra?). As mentioned, the seated Devī is without surviving arms. Though the resemblances between the Kālī and the Devīs are many, they are not intended to duplicate each other. The seated Devī has extra curls of hair at the shoulders. One bust has a pyramid-shaped object behind and above the head, and the circular hand object. Kālī is most bejewelled, the hair most flared and has a halo (śiraścakra) behind the head. These Devīs are not members of a standard Saptamātṛkā set—unless each are variant Cāmuṇḍās which were accompanied by their own set of now missing and presumably smaller mātṛkās. It is possible, however, that Kālī along with these Devīs, and missing images, belonged to one set. These images are fierce aspects of the Goddess; maybe they composed a Navadurga, or a related type of set. This conjecture must await future study: Goddess worship is an immensely complex and intriguing question requiring separate treatment.[68]

Standard Saptamātṛkā sets—that is sets linking Brahmāṇī, Mahēśvarī, Kaumārī, Vaiṣṇavī, Vārahī, Indrāṇī and Cāmuṇḍā—are common in Noḷambavāḍi. In Hemavati, only one panel survives with all the seven mothers intact. Carved in mid-relief on a single slab, the mātṛkās are relatively simple, though attractive, images (H: 51 cm each). With only essential jewellery, such as necklaces, yajñopavītas, earrings, bangles, dhotīs with incised lines, and crowns for most, the figures sit in lalitāsana (their right legs pendant) above their individual vāhanas, which are in low-relief. All have their lower right hand in abhaya-mudrā with the other lower hand resting on their left thigh. The upper hands hold their (and their male counterparts') identifying attributes. Three-headed Brahmāṇī has a pāśa (noose) and a kalaśa (water pot), with her haṁsa vāhana below. Mahēśvarī holds a triśūla and a ḍamaru, and a bull reclines below her. Kaumārī has a śakti (spear) and a pāśa, below her is a peacock. Seated above her Garuḍa vāhana, Vaiṣṇavī holds a cakra and a śaṅkha. Vārahī (whose face is mutilated) has a gadā (club) and a pāśa, below her is a buffalo. Indrāṇī's vāhana is faded, presumably it is an elephant, and she holds a vajra and a pāśa. Finally, Cāmuṇḍā has a triśūla and a ḍamaru, and below her is a jackal. This is the 'standard' type of Saptamātṛkā set in Noḷambavāḍi, and elsewhere, and though occasional variation might occur in attributes held, and the order of figures might be occasionally interchanged—invariably the set commences with Brahmāṇī and ends with Cāmuṇḍā, with Vaiṣṇavī usually the middle (fourth) figure—the group format was codified centuries previous to this panel.[69] Most all standard Saptamātṛkā sets were accompanied by Śiva as Vīrabhadra or Vīṇādhara-Dakṣiṇāmūrti and by Gaṇeśa.

Other Hemavati Saptamātṛkās include six additional panels, each missing a couple mātṛkās, and about ten loose images. The loose mātṛkās tend to be larger than the panels, but none approach the dimensions of the Kālī and Devīs. The largest loose mātṛkā, a Mahēśvarī, is approximately 114 centimeters in height. A Brahmāṇī and a Kaumārī survive from the same set as the Mahēśvarī. These images are sculpted in the round and, though not as elaborate as the Kālī, are fine sculptures. Their vāhanas are not included (or if they are, they are faintly incised below; it is unclear), otherwise the images are similar to the panel mātṛkās described earlier, except their jewels, such as their necklaces and crowns, are more detailed and, because of their size, they are more dominating figures. Most of the mātṛkās are accompanied by their vāhanas. And usually the figures are about fifty to sixty cm in height, including the base. The quality of workmanship varies among the panels and loose mātṛkās: generally the works are not overly elaborate. One panel with three surviving mātṛkās, Vaiṣṇavī, Vārāhī and Indrāṇī (H: 58 cm each; without vāhanas) have breastbands which are uncommon.

Three loose mātṛkās, a Vārāhī, a Indrāṇī and a Cāmuṇḍā (H: 60 cm each), which have their vāhanas—a buffalo, an elephant and a jackal respectively—on their base, are from the same set. Sculpted in high-relief, these images are vigorous, full figures, and, though they lack extensive ornamentation, they are balanced, handsome pieces, representative of the medium in the central Noḷambavāḍi idiom. Another fine example of this sort is a loose Brahmāṇī (pl. 29) (H: 53 cm). Brahmāṇī's three rounded faces are topped by an intricate coiffure (jaṭās) with jewels; remaining ornaments are modest. The figure, though hefty, is a lively, poised composition. Some of the simpler mātṛkās (and other sculptures) are not of great artistic merit; however, most are pleasing images which tend to have robust, slightly stocky bodies. The artistic divergences are reflective of the diversity of individuals at work, and their developed skills, not necessarily to chronology.

More sculptures

There are many more loose sculptures in Hemavati. A listing includes: six Sūryas, five Mahiṣāsuramardinīs, three Viṣṇus, three Vīṇādhara-Dakṣiṇāmūrtis and one Vyākhyāna-Dakṣiṇāmūrti, two Bhairavas (pl. 30), two Umāmahēśvaras and an Āliṅgana-Candraśekhara, a Naṭēśa, a Gaṅgādharamūrti, a Gajāsurasaṁhāramūrti, a Candēśvara, a Kaṅkālamūrti (?), a Kārttikeya, a Vāmana, two Jainas, many Nandis and additional miscellaneous (including two Śaiva guardians, two embracing couples) images. Other Hemavati sculptures are at the Madras Government Museum. In addition to the images at Pathasivarama, Pailabanda and Baraguru (these sites are discussed below), sculptures are scattered in neighboring villages. Among the dispersed figures, at Agali there are a Gaṇeśa and mātṛkā panel with Brahmāṇī, Indrāṇī and Mahēśvarī surviving; at Nidragatta a Gaṇeśa and a Mahiṣāsuramardinī; at Doddabanagere a Gaṇeśa and an Indrāṇī. Between Doddabanagere and Cikkabanagere, at the tank, there is a particularly nice Mahiṣāsuramardinī (pl. 31). In Cikkabanagere, there are two Sūryas, two Cāmuṇḍās, and embedded into the maṇḍapa side walls of a small Īśvara temple, built during the (Later) Cālukya time according to an inscription beside the temple, a Bhairava and a Cāmuṇḍā which appear to be from the Noḷamba period. These surviving loose sculptures suggest a profusion of Noḷamba period temples which are no longer in existence.

Additionally, one stone sculpture and two bronzes have been published as possible 'Noḷamba' images.[70] The stone ('grey-green granite') Yogadakṣiṇamūrti is said to be from Bagli (Bellary district).[71] At Bagli there are a number of temples, none of which have been properly published to date.[72] The best known Bagli temple is the Kallēśvara, acknowledged for its erotic reliefs.[73] The temple has Cālukya (of Kalyana) period additions, but the original shrine (the vimāna and gūḍhamaṇḍapa) appears to have been constructed during the Rāṣṭrakūṭa period.[74] It also is evidenced by epigraphs that the Rāṣṭrakūṭas were active in Bagli ('Balguli'), and the Noḷambas, as feudatory to the Cālukyas, made grants to Bagli temples.[75] Just like the mixed political background of this area, I think the Dakṣiṇāmūrti in question reflects a sharing of features which cannot be associated to a particular dynasty, but is the blending of traits common to styles which are sometimes called Noḷamba, Rāṣṭrakūṭa or Cālukya. There is a definite commingling of elements among some works affiliated with the Noḷamba, Rāṣṭrakūṭa, and Cālukya periods, as I discuss regarding the pillars in the Mallēśvara temple (Hemavati), and further in the Aralaguppe section. Concerning the two bronzes labelled 'Noḷamba', one is an Umāsahita-Candraśekharamūrti set which probably is not from Noḷambavāḍi,[76] and the other, a Somāskandamūrti, might indeed originate from Noḷambavāḍi.[77] Bronzes from Andhra Pradesh and Karnataka have not been thoroughly studied by scholars of Indian art, hence stylistic judgments often are tenuous. The Somāskanda bronze does, however, have many similarities with the Noḷamba period Somāskanda discovered at the Bhōgaṇandiśvara compound at Nandi.[78] Two additional bronzes which have stylistic affinities with the central Noḷambavāḍi school are an Ambikā and a Sarasvatī.[79]

The stylistic generalization I made about the mātṛkās—that is, the images are vigorous, often hefty figures, and, though they lack extensive ornamentation, they are balanced, handsome pieces—is appropriate for the majority of the loose central Noḷambavāḍi sculptures. Among some of the finer works, however, there is a propensity towards heightened elaboration of intricate adornment. Jewels are ornate and hair arrangements, especially, are delicately detailed. Among other illustrations, this propensity is exhibited by the ceiling panels at Hemavati, at Pathasivarama and cumulates with the panels at Aralaguppe.

Another excellent example is the Umāsahita (H: *c.* 60 cm), now displayed in the Madras Government Museum (pl. 32).[80] Sculpted in high-relief, four-armed Śiva holds in his upper right hand a triśūla, an open-hooded cobra is in his upper left hand, a jambhīra (a fruit) in his lower right hand, and his lower left arm is wrapped around Umā's back allowing his fingers to gently touch her breast. His hair strands (jaṭās) are piled high in a manner which resembles an intricate crown (mukuṭa), with additional strands cascading below the shoulders and jewels intertwined throughout. He wears a makarakuṇḍala (a makara-shaped earring) in one ear, the other one is bare. The ratnadāma (necklace), the yajñopavīta, the kaṭibandha (waistband), and anklets are composed of multiple bead strands and other shapes to suggest pearls and additional gems. Umā wears an equally elaborate array of jewels. Her coiffure is composed in a manner particularly favoured by central Noḷambavāḍi sculptors: the hair in front is arranged in tight ringlets with a middle pendant and the hair in back is wrapped by rows of pearls into a sophisticated bun. She wears a dhotī with incised lines which is bound low on the hips by a mekhalā (belt) of pearl strands. In her left hand is held a lotus, in the right hand a mirror(?) and the right arm languorously rests on Śiva's thigh. The intimacy of the couple is emphasized by the plain, black stele backdrop which has a simple bead (pearl) outer border. Behind Śiva's head is a plain śiraścakra ('head-wheel', i.e. halo) also with a bead border. Below Umāsahita is a small recumbent Nandi.[81] This sculpture is indeed a sensitive rendition of the prototypical, quintessential couple (Śiva-Pārvatī), and is representative of a work in the 'mature' central Noḷambavāḍi idiom.[82]

Almost identical to this Umāsahita is another Hemavati Umāsahita, also displayed at Madras (pl. 33). The compositional format is analogous: same attributes are held, the figures are seated in the same manner, and ornamentation is similar though some variant jewels are worn. The stele back is smaller without the bead border on the latter. They share the same idiomatic traits, yet the former has a greater aesthetic refinement than the latter. One of the Umāsahitas might have been a direct copy of the other. However, it cannot be determined if the former is an improvement (i.e. more aesthetically refined) over its predecessor, or conversely, the latter is a degenerate copy of its antecedent. Hence there is no basis for a sequential conclusion. As in all idioms the artistic divergences are attributable to the medley of individuals and their developed skills. Together these two Umāsahitas serve as a reminder of the diversity of talent evident, and why it is difficult to define a particular idiom beyond generalizations which are somewhat applicable to the complete repertoire of available works.

PATHASIVARAMA: MAILARĒŚVARASVĀMĪ TEMPLE

The Mailarēśvarasvāmī temple is in the old Pathasivarama section of Sivaram, a village bordering Hemavati. The unpretentious shrine has a garbhagṛha with a small liṅga enshrined, and a forehall (a maṇḍapa). The maṇḍapa probably was originally hypostyle: it is open in the front, and the side walls are now composed of rubble and rough granite. The shrine has a rare southern axial orientation. Although the temple is architecturally insignificant, the maṇḍapa citrakhaṇḍa pillars and ceiling panels are exquisitely sculpted, exemplifying the refinement of the central Noḷambavāḍi idiom.

The caturasra carved sections of the four free-standing citrakhaṇḍa pillars are equivalent to the standard Hemavati format—the mode resembling the pillars rebuilt into the Siddēśvara temple agramaṇḍapa. Usually deities occupy the left-right panels and the upper portion has either frolicking gaṇas or deities. Because no unique iconographic representations are depicted, a rudimentary pillar description follows.

Front west pillar, south (front) face has Āliṅgaṇamūrti (left) and (right) a dancing female. (Upper portions have gaṇas unless otherwise specified.) West face depicts Manmatha (left) and Ratī (right); north face, Brahmā (left), Viṣṇu (right), and Śiva (above); east face, has embracing couples.

Rear west pillar has on the south face Bhairava accompanied by a dog (left) and (right) Mahiṣā-suramardinī (the defeated Mahiṣāsura is completely anthropomorphic); west face, shows Vīṇādharamūrti (left) and Pārvatī (right); north face, Śaiva guardians; east face, couples and above, Naṭēśa in ūrdhvajānu pose over Apasmāra. This pose is rare, most Noḷambavāḍi Naṭēśas are in lalita or catura pose.

Front east pillar south and north sides have embracing couples. West face has two standing Sūryas; east face, left and right panels both have a royal/aristocratic female with an attendant holding a chattra over her head.

Rear east pillar, south face delineates Brahmā (right) and a dancing female; west face has Śiva (left) and Pārvatī. North face has to the left, a couple transporting baskets on their heads; to the right, two standing females, and above, a Devī holding a cakra and a triśūla. North side is uncarved.

The coffered maṇḍapa ceiling is divided by beams into nine panels, with lotus pendants on the four inner intersecting beam corners. Lateral Aṣṭadikpālas, in their proper directional realms, surround a splendid Naṭēśa (pl. 34). Although the temple is facing the south, the Naṭēśa maintains an east-west axis (the head points east). In lalita pose on top of Apasmāra, Naṭēśa has in his eight hands: vyākhayāna-mudrā (proper right), ḍamaru (UR), ghaṇṭā (mid R), nāga (LR), gajahasta (proper left), mṛga and mālā (UR), triśūla (mid L), and agni (LL). Four gaṇa musicians, two with drums, one with a vīṇā, another with cymbals, perform music for the Lord of Dance (Naṭēśa). The miraculous event is witnessed by two Devī manifestations: to Śiva's upper right sits a four-armed Devī displaying abhaya and varada mudrās, and holds a mālā and a mirror; another two-armed Devī sits to the lower left exhibiting the same mudrās. Riding their vāhanas, the Aṣṭadikpālas are accompanied by their consorts and have an entourage of gandharvas and/or vidyādharas (pl. 35).

The Mailarēśvara ceiling panels are intimately allied to the loose Naṭēśa and dikpāla panels at Hemavati, and the Kallēśvara temple panels at Aralaguppe. They share idiosyncracies which identify them as products of a common school, though the sets are sculpted by different hands, at different times. All are superbly crafted with a harmonized balance between ornament and graceful body form. Sculpted in medium-relief, the Mailarēśvara Naṭēśa has a lithe, elongated body with slightly tubular limbs. Though lovely, the figure does not aesthetically equal the refined Kallēśvara Naṭēśa whose elegant body is articulated with exuberant jewels and sculpted in high-relief, with some limbs in full-relief. The Kallēśvara panels also have full-relief vidyādharas adjoined to the lotus pendants, enhancing the majestic, dramatic three-dimensional presentation. In the Kallēśvara panels stress is placed on the Naṭēśa and Īśāna figures, whereas the Mailarēśvara panels equally distribute sculptural attention to all of the figures. This also is the case in the Hemavati panels which have especially embellished dikpāla panels with large entourages and background cloud formations.

Sculpturally, the Mailarēśvarasvāmī temple typifies a 'mature' and persistent propensity in the central Noḷambavāḍi idiom. The reliefs are detailed sculptures, combining graceful body forms with a balance of embellishments. A loose Gaṇeśa housed in the Mailarēśvara maṇḍapa is in all manners comparable to the many Gaṇeśas at Hemavati. Lacking other evidence upon which to base a dating, the sculptural style is the only available clue. The pillar format and carvings suggest a period coeval or slightly posterior to the Doḍḍēśvara temple (Hemavati), around the second third of the tenth century.

PAILABANDA: RAṄGANĀTHASVĀMĪ TEMPLE

The Raṅganāthasvāmī temple is on the Pailabanda hill outside of the Sivaram village. Although the temple has four Noḷamba citrakhaṇḍa pillars in the maṇḍapa and a jāla-vātāyana in the south maṇḍapa window, there are no further clues indicating the shrine was constructed during the Noḷamba period. The monument probably was built during the Vijayanagara period (by local officials), employing materials from earlier temples. The temple has a Vijayanagara period superstructure and contemporary stucco prastara figures over portions of the walls. The walls are composed of rubble or granite slabs. The agramaṇḍapa or 'yāgaśālā' (sacrificial hall) roof was built by Rāyasam Rāmaṇṇa an officer of Immaḍi Timmaṇa-Nāyaka of Nidugal during the Vijayanagara period.[83] Integrated into the hall are developed śrīkāra pillars dating from the late Noḷamba or, more likely, the succeeding Cālukya (of Kalyana) period. The interior is unusual, certainly atypical for a Noḷamba period monument: a Viṣṇu, probably from the Vijayanagara period, is enshrined in a large garbhagṛha which is flanked in front by two subshrines, followed by a maṇḍapa. The temple layout appears asymmetrical and ill conceived.

The Noḷamba period four free-standing maṇḍapa citrakhaṇḍa pillars have caturasra portions which formally and sculpturally resemble the Virūpākṣa temple (Hemavati) pillars. The front, south pillar is thematically concerned with *Mahābhārata* battle encounters: the four sides have reliefs delineating heroes in rathas confronting each other. The rear, south pillar has in the east, Viṣṇu, Sūrya, and an abraded deity (above); in the south, Śiva, an abraded deity, and Rāvaṇānugrahaṇamūrti (above); in the west, Kirātārjunīyam and Naṭēśa (above); and in the north, Kālī, Narasiṁha and, above, another Kālī.

The front, north pillar has on the east side (pl. 36), lower portion, Ṣaṇmukha (Skanda) on his peacock vāhana (left), and a male warrior (right). In the upper portion, Umāsahita is bordered below by a clash between a female and a male warrior and, to the side, Gaṇeśa. Rarely depicted in Noḷamba art, the Kṣīrodamanthana ('the churning of the ocean of milk') is rendered on the lower portion of the pillar's south side. The upper portion of the pillar has Śiva enthroned above a kīrttimukha with an encircling makara toraṇa and seated below, Brahmā, Gaṇeśa, Lakṣmī and Viṣṇu. The west side has a man in a ratha shooting an arrow upward (left), vidyādharas with one holding a liṅga (right), and, above, temple worship. The north side has Gaṇeśa on Nandi (left), Indra on his vāhana Airavata (right), and Andhakāsuravadhamūrti. Lastly, the rear north pillar has in the east Vāmana with Bali, and Trivikrama; in the south, Yogēśvara(?) and Paraśurāma; in the west, a Rāma-Rāvaṇa confrontation, and, above, Viṣṇu on Garuḍa (possibly as Karivarada, Gajendramokṣa episode might be depicted); and in the north, Narasiṁha, Varāha, and Viṣṇu (above).

The pillar iconography is predominately Vaiṣṇava oriented. Though less common than Śaiva temples, Vaiṣṇava monuments were constructed during the Noḷamba period. Possibly the Raṅganātha maṇḍapa is the remaining portion of a Noḷamba period shrine dedicated to Viṣṇu. All other temple elements are indicative of a later construction date. Built by a local official during the Vijayanagara period, the agramaṇḍapa ceiling has a 'lantern roof' with a central lotus medallion. The identical ceiling type is built into the maṇḍapa, demonstrating a coeval dating. The superstructure also is from the Vijayanagara period, and the rubble-granite walls are a later reconstruction. Only the maṇḍapa citrakhaṇḍa pillars are irrefutably from the Noḷamba period. The agramaṇḍapa śrīkāra pillars might be late Noḷamba period or of the succeeding Cālukya era. Either the maṇḍapa pillars are in their original placement—along with a window, the sole survivors of a Noḷamba shrine—or they were elements of a Noḷamba period Vaiṣṇava temple in the Pailabanda vicinity and, due to their appropriate iconography, were reconstructed into the Raṅganāthasvāmī temple. Because the maṇḍapa pillars closely resemble the Virūpākṣa temple (Hemavati) pillars, I assign them to the mid-tenth century.

BARAGURU: MAHĒNDRĒŚVARA TEMPLE

Baraguru in Tumkur district (Karnataka) is the home of the Mahēndrēśvara temple, royally sponsored by Mahēndrādhirāja in Śaka 800 (878 CE).[84] Two epigraphs, one in Baraguru, another in Hemavati—which are about nine km apart—speak of Mahēndra camped at Baraguru and boast of his exalted status.[85] The inscriptions declare that Mahēndrādhirāja had destroyed the Cōras and other rivals (having the crowns of feudatories rolling before his feet), had increased his kingdom, and was himself a supreme king. Such claims, and more, are substantiated in other records.[86] Executing his royal prerogative, indeed obligation, becoming of his exalted station, Mahēndra patronized religious establishments throughout his 'increased kingdom'.[87] As an offering to Mahādēva (Śiva), Mahēndra had the (god) Mahēndrēśvara and temple erected in Baraguru.[88] Lands were allotted for the temple's maintenance and worship. The grant was entrusted to the chief ascetic priest Dinakarasōma-bhaṭāra, stipulating that the maṭhapati and disciples must be Brahmācarīs. In 920, on the occasion of the solar eclipse, and in honour of his wives Nāgiyabbe and Heleyabbe, Ayyapa, Mahēndra's son and successor, made a grant to the two temples at Baraguru mūlasthāna, and a gift to (the god) Mahēndrēśvara.[89] Special respect ('washing of the feet') was given to Vimalamati-bhaṭāra of the eastern maṭha and the event was witnessed by officials from the five maṭhas of Penjeṟu (Hemavati). Evidently, Baraguru remained a meaningful centre to the Noḷambas: in 977, when Vīramahēndra (II) was re-establishing a hold in central Noḷambavāḍi (after years of insecurity due to the Noḷamba defeat by Gaṅgā Mārasiṁha in *c.* 971), he ruled from Baraguru.[90]

Considering the commanding patronage the temple received, the monument is unassuming. In spite of its modest presentation, the temple was deemed worthy of expansions. The Mahēndrēśvara temple, which faces east, consists of a garbhagṛha, an antarāla, a mukhamaṇḍapa, and an agramaṇḍapa addition divided into two sections, the larger outer hall serving as a Nandi pavilion (fig. 6).[91] The pavilion until recently was a sixteen pillar 'hypostyle' hall; now walls exist covering most of the outer pillars.[92] The complete brick exterior has been renovated and replastered, including its phaṁsanā superstructure. The mukhamaṇḍapa jāla-vātāyanas (windows) with kalpavallis might be original.

Though the mukhamaṇḍapa and the agramaṇḍapa have free-standing śrīkāra order pillars, their divergent forms suggest sequential development. The mukhamaṇḍapa pillar form is simpler, the agramaṇḍapa more 'evolved'; in this case, a passage of time coincides with progress in form. The four mukhamaṇḍapa pillars, though with a slightly more bulbous shaft, are comparable to the Siddēśvara temple (Hemavati) mukhamaṇḍapa śrīkāra pillars. The engaged wall pillars in the mukhamaṇḍapa are the uncarved citrakhaṇḍa type commonly found supporting the walls in all Noḷambavāḍi temples. The front agramaṇḍapa section abutting the mukhamaṇḍapa has four śrīkāra pillars which are not totally consistent in shape among themselves, yet the basic form is akin to the mukhamaṇḍapa pillars (pl. 37). This section probably was built soon after the temple proper. The outer agramaṇḍapa hall is a late Noḷamba expansion. The floor level of the front and outer agramaṇḍapa sections are not horizontally aligned, the latter is a few centimeters lower, and the śrīkāra pillars in the latter are more sophisticated (pl. 38). The pillars have a more developed 'lathe-turned' appearance. The bell shaft is ornamented with thin horizontal bands, some with jewel or lotus petal motifs, and the bell below is sixteen-sided and octagonal rows. Comparable pillars are built into the late tenth century Kallēśvara temple (Aralaguppe), and the form resembles intimately the śrīkāra pillars in the Mallēśvara temple, considered the last Noḷamba monument in Hemavati.

The antarāla two free-standing pillars are a mixed (miśra) order: the shaft has a square base surmounted by octagonal and sixteen-sided sections, a square sculpted portion topped by a pūrṇakumbha, a curved cylindrical section, with a cushion capital and apex corbel. The square sculpted portion resembles the carved caturasra area of the popular citrakhaṇḍa pillars: kīrttimukhas spew jewelled bands which border two figural reliefs. At the Mahēndrēśvara temple the figures are auspicious (e.g. nidhis, females holding padmas, gandharva couples). The upper pūrṇakumbha is an uncommon feature. Pūrṇakumbhas, however, are represented on the Virūpākṣa temple (Hemavati) antarāla pillars, except the Virūpākṣa have deities and the complete shafts are square (citrakhaṇḍa); also a few broken pillars in the Hemavati vicinity display a similar format.

Whereas many central Noḷambavāḍi temple entrances are elaborately decorated with rows of reliefs, the Mahēndrēśvara doorways are modest. The mukhamaṇḍapa triśākhā entrance has two padmaśākhās separated by a stambaśākhā, but no base or lintel figures. The garbhagṛha doorway is plain except for one padmaśākhā. A liṅga is enshrined in the garbhagṛha. Ceilings also are uncomplicated. The mukhamaṇḍapa ceiling is divided into nine parts by cross beams which have lotus pendants on the four inner corners. The inner section has a large lotus medallion, and the outer parts are plain. The same ceiling format is constructed in the Nandi pavilion (outer agramaṇḍapa). This ceiling type is common in central Noḷambavāḍi temples: at Hemavati it can be seen in the Siddēśvara, Virūpākṣa, and Mallēśvara temples.[93]

Seven Noḷamba period sculptures are maintained in the Mahēndrēśvara temple. A Bhairava and a Mahiṣāsuramardinī are in the antarāla, a Viṣṇu and a single mātṛkā (Indrāṇī?) in the mukhamaṇḍapa, a vīṇādhara and a single mātṛkā (too abraded to distinguish) in the front agramaṇḍapa, and Nandi in the outer agramaṇḍapa. Many Hemavati (central Noḷambavāḍi) sculptures display a preponderance of detailed embellishments—jewelled ornaments and costumes are clearly and delicately delineated—though some images are less decorative and have greater emphasis on body mass. The Baraguru images are akin to the latter mode; the slightly bulky bodies are projected forcefully without reliance on adornments. However, centuries of abrading pastes and oils might have hidden once emphatic decorative elements. The images are iconographically standard.

The Mahēndrēśvara temple, built in 878 by Mahēndrādhirāja, is the main surviving monument with an epigraph that unimpeachably states royal construction. The Mallēśvara temple in Chikkamadhure (Chitradurg district) might be the earliest royally patronized Noḷamba shrine. In front of the Mallēśvara temple an inscribed pillar dating to *c.* 805-14, states that Noḷamba Cāruponneṛa's (Paramēśvara Pallavādhirāja) wife Gavagaṇabbe had the Śaiva Gavagaṇēśvara temple built.[94] The brick temple is too dilapidated to study in detail, but judging from the remains and loose sculptures housed in the shrine, the temple is coeval with the epigraph and originally called the Gavagaṇēśvara temple.[95] Another Noḷamba monument which has an epigraph that declares royal sponsorship is in Avani (Kolar district). Queen Dīvambikā had the Noḷamba-Nārāyanēśvara temple constructed, which probably is the shrine currently called the Bhāratēśvara.[96] Also in Avani, the Lakṣmaṇēśvara temple has the king's name Vīra Noḷamba (Aṇṇiga) inscribed on the front temple base, and most likely his portrait is on the south wall, suggesting royal patronage.[97]

Elsewhere in greater Noḷambavāḍi, the Bhōgaṇandīśvara temple at Nandi, and the Kāmākṣamma temple at Dharmapuri, are probable Mahēndrādhirāja-sponsored monuments. Inscriptions testifying to Mahēndra's religious patronage are found in the compounds of both temples, but neither temple has an epigraph recording its construction. Both of these monuments are architecturally impressive, especially relative to the Mahēndrēśvara. Outside of central Noḷambavāḍi, Mahēndra's base, it is possible that as Mahēndra expanded his realm, he felt compelled to state his presence tangibly through traditionally acceptable means, such as grand temple patronage. This dispersion of wealth to regional centres—Nandi is in traditional Gaṅgārusāsira (Gaṅgā 600) region, and Dharmapuri is in the Koṅgu area—could have been a politically advantageous manner of calming the already entrenched dominant personages and alliances within the 'segmentary state' localities.

Though modestly presented, the Mahēndrēśvara temple had a prominent role in Noḷamba history. Royally sponsored and maintained, the temple was considered an extension of the king himself. Its royal status required consistent renewal and purity. Hence the shrine was charged to Dinakarasōma-bhaṭāra, a mahāvrata-pradhāna (chief ascetic priest). It was demanded that he and those of his lineage be ritually pure (celibate). A transgression against this stipulation would tarnish the (god) Mahēndrēśvara, and cause the fall of both the king and kingdom: 'A maṭhapati who is not a Brahmacāri, has ruined the king who rules him, the nāḍ, and the assembly of the village, and is guilty of the five great sins'.[98]

The Mahēndrēśvara temple was constructed in 878 and expanded in two phases. First an agramaṇḍapa was built probably soon after the original structure, and in the later Noḷamba period (mid to late tenth century) a larger agramaṇḍapa extension was added. Both the architecture and sculpture reflect an austere trend in the central Noḷambavāḍi idiom. Restrained, though pleasing, śrīkāra pillars are built into the mukhamaṇḍapa, rather than the more typical Noḷamba period citrakhaṇḍa pillars with their ornate caturasra carvings. Elsewhere in Baraguru village a large (H: 143 cm), loose Viṣṇu demonstrates the more persistent propensity in the central Noḷambavāḍi sculptural style—that of finely ornamented embellishments combined, in this case, with a slender, balanced body. The unassuming presentation of the Mahēndrēśvara temple does not diminish the temple's purpose and must have been intentionally chosen.

ARALAGUPPE: KALLĒŚVARA TEMPLE

The Kallēśvara temple at Aralaguppe, Tumkur district, is justifiably known primarily for its extraordinary Naṭēśa and Aṣṭadikpāla ceiling panels (pls. 39, 41-2). The panels have been published twice in the *Mysore Archaeological Reports*,[99] twice by Seshadri,[100] twice by Sivaramamurti,[101] once by De

Lippe;[102] and the temple has been briefly described by I.K. Sarma[103] and in the *Encylopaedia of Indian Temple Architecture.*[104] Although there is no consensus concerning the date of the temple and its patronage, all agree the panels are superb.[105] An Umāsahita sculpture of comparable aesthetic excellence is preserved in an exterior subshrine (pl. 40).[106]

Consisting of a garbhagṛha, an antarāla and a mukhamaṇḍapa, the Kallēśvara temple faces east.[107] The walls are flat, without projections and recesses, except for the recess at the antarāla dividing the vimāna from the mukhamaṇḍapa, and articulated by plain brahmakānta pilasters. Jāla-vātāyanas, now mostly destroyed, are built into the maṇḍapa and vimāna side walls. The walls and superstructure are constructed of brick; the adhiṣṭhāna and upāna platform are granite. The upāna with its upper kapōta is an unusual feature for Noḷamba period temples. The adhiṣṭhāna is simple, like those at Hemavati, having jagatī, tripaṭṭa-kumuda and paṭṭika mouldings. The brick Phaṁsanā superstructure has a śukhanāsa in front which might be original. The same superstructure arrangement is found on the Siddēśvara temple at Hemavati. The actual śikhara probably is not original. During the summer of 1987 the Department of Archaeology, Karnataka, was in the process of completely rebuilding the exterior walls.

Although the exterior is unimposing, the granite mukhamaṇḍapa entrance is finely sculpted with bands of reliefs, a trait the Kallēśvara shares with other central Noḷambavāḍi monuments (i.e. Siddēśvara, Doḍḍēśvara, Virūpākṣa, and Mallēśvara temples in Hemavati). The inner and outer bands have kalpavallis with females, males or gaṇas within the meandering lotus swirls. Adjoining the inner śākhā is a ratna-padmaśākhā, and the outer śākhā has a vyālamālā-padmaśākhā. In the centre, on each side, is an ornate stambhaśākhā with a female carved three-quarters up the height of the stambha. Padmanidhi and Śaṅkhanidhi sit below the inner śākhās, and dvārapālas stand below the outer śākhās. Portrayed in the centre of the upper horizontal band (lalāṭa) is Gajalakṣmī. Above her, is a kapōta that has two kīrttimukha-nāsikās and lotus design reliefs. The underside of the kapōta has a bhūtamālā with each of the five bhūtas, in varying dance poses, clearly delineated in high relief.

Within the mukhamaṇḍapa are four free-standing proto-śrīkāra ('lathe-turned') pillars, similar to the type at the Siddēśvara temple in Hemavati, and the Mahēndrēśvara temple in Baraguru, except here the bell-shape shaft is more developed. Two more proto-śrīkāra pillars demarcate the antarāla entrance. These pillars have sixteen-sided and octagonal bands under the bell-shaft. At the nearby village of Nonavinakere, the Noḷamba period Noṇabēśvara temple has pillars akin to those of the antarāla, and similarly shaped, though more elaborate, pillars are built into the Mahēndrēśvara temple porch extension, and the Mallēśvara temple in Hemavati. As is commonly found in Noḷamba period temples, the engaged wall pilasters are simple citrakhaṇḍa columns. The antarāla ceiling has a large lotus medallion relief. The simple garbhagṛha doorway has pūrṇakumbhas at the base and three śākhās of lotus and floral motifs. A large, black liṅga is enshrined.

The central black schist coffered portion of the mukhamaṇḍapa ceiling is divided by beams into nine panels. On the beams which circumscribe the central panel there are lotus pendants: attached to each pendant is a garland-bearing vidyādhara. Carved in the round except for the portion of the back attached to the pendant, the graceful, flying vidyādharas are oriented towards the central Naṭēśa panel (pl. 39). Dancing on top of Apasmāra, Naṭēśa is in catura pose[108] with his main right hand in āhūyavarada and his main left arm is extended in gajahasta (pl. 41). His upper two hands hold alternate shaped triśūlas. The vitality and excellence of this sculpture cannot be overstated. Sculpted in high relief, the three-dimensionality of the body is strikingly conveyed. Adorned in various jewels, the makarakuṇḍala in the right ear and the nāgakuṇḍala in the left are especially fine. Intricately depicted, the hair is majestically piled in jaṭās with jewels and the crescent moon affixed in a manner which resembles a mukuṭa (crown). Also intricately rendered is the kaṭibandha (waistband) with its siṁhamukha (lion face) and many tassels. The ornamentation is sensitively delineated. Though exuberant it is not distracting: it supplements, rather than detracts from the beauty of the body form.

The lord of dance, Naṭēśa, is accompanied by three Bhūta musicians. A flutist sits to Naṭēśa's proper right. An elegant open-hooded cobra facing Apasmāra is below the flutist. To the proper left a Bhūta sits playing a three-headed drum (trimukhavādya), and above a Bhūta plays the cymbals.

The Aṣṭadikpālas, the guardians of the eight directions, are portrayed in the surrounding panels. Positioned in their assigned directional realms, each dikpāla is mounted on his vāhana (vehicle) along with his consort.[109] Although in other Noḷamba period panels the guardian of the south-west, Nirṛti, rides a naravāhana (man as his vehicle), here he rides an ass/horse.[110] The other dikpālas are: Indra (N) on an elephant (Airāvata), Agni (SE) on a goat, Yama (S) on a buffalo, Nirṛti (SW), Varuṇa (W) on a makara, Vāyu (NW) on a deer, Kubera (N) on a ram, and Īśāna (NE) on a bull (Nandi). While each panel is sculpted with equal excellence, the north-east Īśāna panel is augmented with subsidiary figures (pl. 42). Īśāna, a form of Śiva, is four-armed (the other dikpālas have two arms), and has an entourage including a flying vidyādhara couple with garlands, two male cymbals players, a female drummer and a female flutist. Gaṇeśa also is included in the panel. All the figures reflect the panel's superb aesthetic quality.

Contiguous to the temple, in the front, is a Nandi platform connected with three lateral subshrines, recently rebuilt. Hoysaḷa period sculptures, a Keśava and a Sūrya, are in the north and east shrines.[111] Housed in the south shrine is a magnificent Noḷamba period Umāsahita (pl. 40).[112] The large stele (H: 150 cm) has a lotus base and a prabhāvallī which has two adjoined flying vidyādharas. The two-armed Śiva holds an akṣamālā in his right hand and his left arm embraces Pārvatī. Like the Naṭēśa panel, the jewelled ornamentation is exceptional. The Umāsahita, a larger, free-standing sculpture, has even more elaborate jewels and dress; however, like Naṭēśa's, the decorative elements blend harmoniously with the image, heightening the elegance of the finely proportioned bodies. This is a central Noḷambavāḍi sculptural idiom trait: the sculptors exploited ornamental embellishment in conjunction with the essential form, achieving a complementary blending. The adornment is not superfluous nor detrimental to the form; rather there is an elemental balance. This is a historical phenomenon, in the following Later Cālukya period, in the same region, the harmony gradually disintegrates and the superficiality dominates. The Umāsahita exemplifies central Noḷambavāḍi idiom sentiment, yet it also anticipates, possibly even serves as a harbinger for the regional aesthetic transformation.

REASONS TO ASSIGN THE KALLĒŚVARA TO THE NOḶAMBA PERIOD

Based on the tenuous support of a Gaṅgā vīrakaḷ in the temple vicinity, Seshadri attributes the Kallēśvara temple to the Gaṅgās during the tenth century.[113] The vīrakaḷ dates *c.* 880 (CE), in the reign of Gaṅgā Satyavākya Rācamalla Permanaḍi, yet Seshadri mistakenly states that Satyavākya reigned during the early years of the second half of the tenth century, which he considers a convenient dating for the temple.[114] The vīrakaḷ, like all vīrakaḷs, commemorates the death of a local hero, in this case a man named Malluga, who protected the village cows from raiders. The memorial stone has absolutely no relevance to the temple, and to use it as evidence of Gaṅgā temple patronage is unwarranted.[115] Seshadri is correct in recognizing that the temple has 'Gaṅgā-Noḷamba' pillars and that the temple 'goes back to the Gaṅgā period' (Gaṅgā and Noḷamba are contemporaneous periods). However, to claim that the temple dates to the reign of Satyavākya—which he misdates by a century—because a vīrakaḷ from Satyavākya's reign is found near the temple, is not adequate evidence to substantiate his observations.

Sarma, too, considers the temple to be 'Gaṅgā'. Although his reasons are not stated, he refers to the temple as a '. . . remarkable example of native Ganga art, influenced by the Chalukya-Noḷamba idioms'.[116] He describes the Umāsahita as '. . . in the typical Ganga style blending with the Pallava-Noḷamba characteristics', and the Naṭēśa '. . . as a unique example of the Ganga-Rashtrakuta vintage. . . '. Sarma's observations are vague and ambiguous, yet at the same time, they are illuminating and helpful. He obviously noticed something 'Noḷamba' (and Cālukya, Pallava, Rāṣṭrakūṭa) in the works. The Gaṅgā, Noḷamba, Rāṣṭrakūṭa (outside of Ellora), and Later Cālukya (of Kalyana) styles lack sufficient analysis and will remain vague attributions until they receive scholarly definition. Where Sarma (and others) see 'influence', I prefer to define it as a regional blending of shared traits and aesthetics. My assertion that the Kallēśvara temple is 'Noḷamba' acknowledges, in fact assumes, a degree of regional artistic sharing. What Sarma sees as 'Pallava' or 'Rāṣṭrakūṭa' is misleading. It implies that particular motifs, or mannerisms can be tangibly associated with the named dynastic styles. If, however, the various dynastic motifs and manners converge on surfaces of independent sculptures—as Sarma states (and as Sivaramamurti repeatedly asserts in regard to Hemavati sculptures and other images)—then the dynastic definitions are not only vague, but deceptive.[117] What actually is being witnessed is an artistic mannerism: one that is regionally based, and which happens to share a few traits that, in past scholarship, have been considered properties of particular dynastic styles. If traits and manners converge on images from outside the stated dynastic territories, then it is not necessarily the result of external 'influences'. Rather, the commingling of these various traits and manners might be best understood as emblematic of idiosyncrasies perpetuated in a given area. This does not imply that all localities have a recognizable, independent idiom. Nor is the opposite true that within regions certain works cannot be differentiated from others. Regional labelling of styles is not without problems. Sthāpatis, trained in one mannerism, or idiom, could be employed in a locality bordering another area which has different sthāpatis, trained in another manner, and both working at approximately the same period. However, a blending, or sharing of manners within a given region is probably most common. The role of royal patron cannot be discounted: and though I believe at times the patron might be an active agent in determining the appearances of monuments, the actual sculptural mannerisms exhibited on temples are the signatures of the sthāpatis. When a dynastic label is utilized as a time definition, limited to specific territories associated to the dynasty, as I use it, it serves as a convenient term.

Aralaguppe was within the Noḷambavāḍi western political boundaries bordering Gaṅgāvāḍi. Besides miscellaneous Noḷamba epigraphs in the area, Noḷamba settlement in the Aralaguppe vicinity is indicated by the nearby village Nonavinakere, called Noṇabanakere in an inscription, which means the tank (kere) built by (or otherwise associated with) the Noḷambas (Noṇaba, a variant spelling).[118] Construction of a tank is evidence of a solid alliance between the Noḷambas and local dominant agrarian powers, suggesting that the Noḷamba political presence was entrenched.[119] However, boundaries were fluid, not fixed: intermittently over the ninth and tenth centuries, according to the flux of power, the area was more in the Gaṅgā, or more in the Noḷamba sphere of jurisdiction. Because of political considerations, and because the sculptural style relates more closely to Hemavati (an indisputable Noḷamba site) than to known Gaṅgā monuments, I consider the Kallēśvara temple part of the Noḷambavāḍi style, intimately related to the central Noḷambavāḍi idiom. The *Encyclopaedia of Indian Temple Architecture*, and De Lippe also assign the Kallēśvara temple to the Noḷamba period, presumably because of style affinity to known Noḷamba sites.[120]

The Pañcakūṭa basti and Śāntinātha basti (Jain temples) at Kambadahalli are generally considered Gaṅgā period temples.[121] In the Śāntinātha basti, east shrine, there are ceiling panels comprising a central Jina Pārśva and lateral Aṣṭadikpālas. Some dissimilarities—as well as sharing of traits—between the Gaṅgāvāḍi and Noḷambavāḍi sculptural styles are illustrated when comparing the Śāntinātha and Kallēśvara panels.[122] Like that of the Kallēśvara temple, the Śāntinātha ceiling, at the corners adjacent to the central panel, has four flying vidyādharas sculpted in the round, except for the back portions attached to the beams. The Aṣṭadikpālas are accompanied by their consorts and ride their vāhanas. The central Jina panel is an exceptional artwork. Carved in medium-relief, the meditating Jina is flanked by a yakṣa, a yakṣī, four caurī attendants and four vidyādharas. Although the central panel is superb and the ceiling format is similar, the style of the Śāntinātha panels, *compared* to that of the Kallēśvara panels is restrained. Whereas the Kallēśvara figures and their jewelled ornaments are exuberantly refined, the Śāntinātha figures, especially the dikpālas and their vāhanas, are slightly clumsy and the ornamentation is simple. The physiques are delineated by different mannerisms. Jain art, in general, tends to be slightly austere; however, the aesthetic discrepancies cannot casually be attributed to religious differences.[123] Relative to Noḷambavāḍi sculptural works, Gaṅgāvāḍi sculptures are inclined to be more austere, yet the distinctions between the two styles are not always readily apparent. The Lakṣmaṇēśvara temple at Avani and the Bhōgaṇandīśvara temple at Nandi, considered Noḷamba period monuments, have plain Umāsahita and Aṣṭadikpāla ceiling panels.[124] Those panels were produced in eastern Noḷambavāḍi by sculptors trained in a local manner. In central Noḷambavāḍi some images tend to be less ornamented than others. However, within central Noḷambavāḍi, at its artistic height, a sophisticated school was cultivated, producing sculptures of refined quality in a distinctive manner. The Kallēśvara Naṭēśa, though in a class by itself, compares well with the loose Naṭēśa ceiling panel at Hemavati and the Naṭēśa ceiling image at Pathasivaram. The Kallēśvara panels and Umāsahita, I believe, are works produced by sculptors trained in the central Noḷambavāḍi sculptural idiom.

Previous dating of the Kallēśvara temple varies from the ninth century, or earlier, to the eleventh century. Though the temple, according to the *Mysore Archaeological Reports*, cannot be dated by epigraphical evidence, '... the typological evidence and sculptural details unmistakably take it back to about the 9th century, if not earlier'.[125] An eleventh century dating is preferred by Sivaramamurti who considers the temple to be a Later Cālukya monument.[126] Although he does not supply explicit reasons, evidently he considered the ceiling panels to be stylistically of the Later Cālukya period: 'From the aesthetic point of view, undoubtedly, the most magnificent late Chalukya carving of Naṭarāja dancing is from the ceiling of the maṇḍapa in the temple of Śiva at Aralaguppe'.[127] The Kallēśvara sculptural style, as discussed above, reflects the manner and sentiment of the central Noḷambavāḍi school. It is a mature work produced during the later phase of the Noḷamba period. It antecedes and anticipates the early sculptural developments in the later Cālukya period.

My study contends that the Kallēśvara is a Noḷamba period temple, probably constructed in the mid to late tenth century. Because of the overwhelming style affinity between the Naṭēśa-Aṣṭadikpāla ceiling panels and the Umāsahita sculpture to the sculptures produced in Hemavati and Pathasivaram, it seems likely that the Aralaguppe sculptures were produced by sculptors trained in the central Noḷambavāḍi idiom.

NOTES

1. The Siddēśvara, Mallēśvara and Doḍḍēśvara are in adjoining compounds represented in fig. 1.
2. One popular pillar type—called proto-śrīkāra pillar to distinguish it from the later, more complex śrīkāra pillars developed during the (Later) Cālukya and Hoysaḷa periods—is uncarved, except for a few decorative adornments, and cylindrical with a bulbous bell-shaft (fig. 9).
3. Even the eastern and southern Noḷambavāḍi subregions had a greater flux of stylistic interactions with neighbouring regions, resulting in amalgamated sculptural styles, which are less recognizable as independent 'idioms', in comparison to central Noḷambavāḍi.
4. In Śaka 800 (878) Mahēndrādhirāja had the first brick of the Mahēndrēśvara temple laid (*EC,* 12: Si 38). The temple received further royal support in 920 by Ayyapa (*EC,* 12: Si 39).
5. This temple is too dilapidated to discuss separately. I make further note of it in the Baraguru section.
6. *EITA,* 2: 213, gives a six-sentence description of the Siddēśvara temple but even this brief mention is inaccurate; the published pillar, no. 634, is not located in the mukhamaṇḍapa as stated, but in the front open porch (agramaṇḍapa). *EITA* did not propose a dating for the Siddēśvara (nor has anyone else).
7. To simplify explanation of deities' attributes, 'UR' means the proper right upper hand, 'UL' upper proper left hand, 'LR' lower proper right hand, and so forth. Because using the Sanskrit term for attributes usually is more accurate and often less wordy, I follow this convention. Some readers might feel inconvenienced by this but a glossary is supplied and most terms are repeated enough that they should become recognizable.
8. Minor damage to the nose recently was repaired.
9. During one of my stays in Hemavati, an extended family from Bangalore, about 140 km away, came for their annual worship to Heñjerappa—their ancestoral deity, as they told me—at which time they performed a goat-sacrifice.
10. Some Pāśupata rituals can be gleamed from H. Chakraborti (tr. and intro.), *Pasupata Sutram with Panchartha-Bhasya of Kaundinya.* (Calcutta: Academic Pub., 1970). For a detailed study of Śaiva Siddhānta temple rituals during the Cōḷa period see Richard Davis, *Ritual in an Oscillating Universe* (Princeton: Princeton University Press, 1992).
11. *EC,* 12: Si 28.
12. Deities enshrined in royal monuments commonly were named the lord of (iśvara) the king-patron. For another example of a son maintaining the king-deity after the king's death, see Baraguru discussion.
13. See Inden, *Imagining,* pp. 253-6 especially.
14. *SP,* 3.8.47 (Śiva said:) 'You are called Bhairava because you are of terrifying features and you are capable of supporting the universe. Since even Kāla is afraid of you, you are called Kālabhairava.'
15. *MAR,* 1928, p. 28; *EC,* 7: Sk 123; also see D. Lorenzen, *The Kapalikas and Kalamukhas* (New Delhi: Thomson Press, 1972.)
16. K.K. Handiqui, *Yasastilaka and Indian Culture* (Sholapur: Jaina Samskrti Samrakshaka Sangha, 1968), p. 198.
17. R. Nandi, *Religious Institutions and Cults in the Deccan* (Delhi: Motilal Banarsidass, 1973), p. 83. Possibly Cilluka was a Kālāmukha and possibly Hemavati was a Kālāmukha centre as suggested by K.R. Basavaraju, 'Noḷambara dharmika parampare', in *Noḷamba Itihasa Darshana* (Tiptur: Nolamba Itihasa Parishath, 1976), p. 132, in Kannada.
18. For more on the Nandi epigraphs, see my Nandi section. Tandikonda grant, *EI,* 23: 161-6. Noḷamba temple grant in 1054, EC, 11: Jl 10.
19. The best discussion on the Kālāmukhas is Lorenzen, *The Kapalikas and Kalamukhas.* No Kālāmukha affiliated text survives; limited information regarding Kālāmukha rituals can be obtained by reading inscriptions. Lorenzen concentrates on inscriptions during the eleventh-twelfth centuries, which state definite Kālāmukha affiliation. I have read the same epigraphs, and ones dating earlier. He concludes, and I concur, that the Kālāmukha and Pāśupata rituals were closely related. Also see Handiqui, *Yasastilaka* regarding the Pāśupatas, the Kālāmukhas and other religious (and socio-political) conditions of tenth century Karnataka.
20. Lorenzen, *The Kapalikas and Kalamukhas,* pp. 4, 83-4.
21. A. Sundara, 'A unique Virabhadra image from Mulgund', in *Srinidhi,* ed. by K.V. Raman, *et al.* (Madras: New Era Pub., 1983), pp. 151-4; plate 37, unfortunately the plate is unclear and too dark to study properly.
22. Ibid., pp. 153-4.
23. Stella Kramrisch, *The Presence of Śiva* (Princeton: Princeton University Press, 1981), p. 332: 'Although the Pāśupata doctrine may appear to be grafted onto the myth of Dakṣa's sacrifice, the two are intrinsically connected. They stem from the primordial scene and preserve its metaphysical ontology in terms of myth and religion. At the time of the Purāṇas, the Pāśupata doctrine had long been established.'
24. For example, 'Lord [Vīra]Bhadra surrounded by the Bhadras shone like Kālabhairava surrounded by hundreds of deadly fires at the time of dissolution'. *Śiva Purāṇa (SP)* 7.19.56; or, '(Vīrabhadra said)... I have assumed the form of Bhairava'. *Liṅga Purāṇa (LP)* 1.96.42. Usually Vīrabhadra is considered an emanation from Śiva's hair.
25. Paramasivayya, 'Noḷambara Heṁjeru Mahāphaṭikasthana' in *Nolamba Itihasa Darshana,* p. 68. (in Kannada). His reasons for citing Heñjerappa as Yajñarīśvara are not supplied.
26. This observation was confirmed by Dr. C.S. Patil, Dept. of Archaeology and Museums, Karnataka.
27. The west and east sides of this pillar are published in M.S. Nagaraja Rao, *Kiratarjuniyam in Indian Art*

(Delhi: Agam Kala Prakashan, 1979), pp. 69-70. On Hemavati pillars other representations of Kirātārjunīyam are depicted at Virūpakṣa temple, north 1 pillar, and Doḍḍēśvara temple, south 2 and 5 pillars, which are not mentioned by Rao.

28. M.S. Krishna Murthy, 'The First Nolamba Coin', *Journal of the Numismatic Society of India* 62 (1980): 130-2. Prof. A.V. Narasimha Murthy informed me (in personal conversation) that two more Noḷamba coins are in private collections, but I cannot verify their whereabouts.
29. Nagaraja Rao, *Kiratarjuniyam*, pp. 69-70, identifies this figure as Arjuna with a boar on his back. However, the object on the back does not resemble a boar. Rao makes the dubious suggestion that the upper scene shows Śiva presenting the *pāśupatāstra* to Arjuna.
30. *EITA*, 2: 210, pls. 627-31; M.S. Krishna Murthy, *Nolambas*, pp. 166-8, pls. 1, 17-18; Soundara Rajan, *Temple Styles*, p. 130, mentions the Doḍḍēśvara, Siddēśvara and Mallēśvara(?) in one paragraph. Also temple windows are published in Barrett, *Hemavati*, pls. 8-12 and Sivaramamurti, *Nolamba*, pls. 28, 32, 35 (incorrectly labelled).
31. *ARE*, 1917, no. 14 (app. B), summarizes the inscription but does not actually publish the epigraph. With the help of N. Swamy, Epigraphy (ASI), Mysore, we read a rubbing of the inscription. The epigraph is on the window, under the mithuna couple, not on the wall.
32. *EITA*, 2: 210, mistakenly assumes that Yamunā does in fact accompany Gaṅgā in their description of the Doḍḍēśvara temple. *EITA* also incorrectly labelled the front wall as east.
33. *EC*, 12: Si 23. The epigraph is dated 1167 (CE), during the Cālukya period. Evidently the god of Noḷamba (Noṇambēśvara) maintained beyond the Noḷamba period.
34. *ARE*, 1917, app. B, no. 13. *ARE*, reads Mādayya the recipient of the grant. The abraded inscription is difficult to see but with the aid of N. Swamy, Epigraphy (ASI), Mysore, we deciphered the name as Māpayya, or possibly as Māḷayya, but not as Mādayya. The object of donation is illegible.
35. *ARE*, 1916, no. 959 (app. B), published in *SII*, 9 (pt. 1): 24, and discussed in K.V. Ramesh, 'Two Noḷamba Inscriptions', *EI*, 39: 27-34.
36. Possibly the Noḷambēśvara temple that Varuṇaśiva is the administrator over is the (current) Doḍḍēśvara.
37. *SII*, 6: 559. The epigraph is published in Kannaḍa without English translation, my reading is tentative.
38. See *EITA*, 2: pl. 627 for exterior photograph. Since their visit the adhiṣṭhāna has been cleared.
39. Sivaramamurti, *Nolamba*, pl. 35, published this Brahma but mistakenly labelled it as at Siddēśvara temple.
40. Sivaramamurti, *Nolamba*, fig. 1, pl. 33.
41. *EITA*, 2: pl. 623, published this window but wrongly labelled it as 'mukhamaṇḍapa, south wall'.
42. *ARE*, 1917, no. 14 (app. B).
43. Devangana Desai, *Erotic Sculpture of India* (New Delhi: Tata McGraw-Hill Pub., 1975), p. 82.
44. Ibid., p. 35, fig. 13, and photo 34. For photo of erotic scene on a lintel at Badami Cave 1, R.D. Banerji, 'Basreliefs of Badami', *MASI*, 25 (1925): pl. 4.
45. Desai, *Erotic*, p. 31.
46. Ibid., fig. 10.
47. Arthur Ryder, tr., *Gold's Gloom, Tales from the Panchatantra* (Chicago: University of Chicago Press, 1925), pp. 48-52. An old, lazy heron tricked some gullible fishes into believing that fishermen were about to cast their nets into the pond. The fishes accepted the heron's offer to carry them to safety, unaware that the heron ate each fish when a small distance away. One day the heron carried a crab who, upon seeing the fish skeletons, clawed the bird's neck and exposed the bird to the remaining fishes. If what appears on the pillar as a tortoise actually is a crab, possibly this story is meant to be conveyed.
48. Because Varuṇaśiva's name is on the temple wall and in a dated epigraph, *EITA*, 2: 213 dates the Doḍḍēśvara to the second quarter of the tenth century. Krishna Murthy, *Nolambas*, p. 168 dates the temple to the time of the dated inscription, i.e., *c.* 936.
49. Krishna Murthy, *Nolambas*, p. 168, briefly mentions this temple and reports that a Durgā is on the north side of the temple. Due to debris and overgrowth I was unable to view this portion, so unable to verify Durgā's existence.
50. Sivaramamurti, *Nolamba*, p. 3 and pl. 25. Additionally, deities—some of which are in worship today—were confiscated by the Cōḷas from Noḷambavāḍi. A Śiva-Pārvatī, an Umāmahēśvara, and two Mahiṣāsuramardinīs (and the perforated window discussed in Doḍḍēśvara section) are reported by D. Dayalan, 'The Role of War-Trophies in Cultural Contact', *Tamil Civilization* 3 (1985): 135-6; cf., K. Kulandaivelan, 'Chalukya and Nolamba Sculptures from Trailoka', in *South Indian Studies*, ed. by R. Nagaswamy (Madras: Society for Archaeological, Historical and Epigraphical Research, 1978), pp. 176-7. The two Mahiṣāsuramardinīs are published in R. Nagaswamy, *Tantric Cult of South India* (Delhi: Agam Kala Prakashan, 1982), pls. 75 and 76.
51. *EITA*, 2: 213 and they do not offer a suggested dating for the temple.
52. Douglas Barrett, *Hemavati* (Bombay: Bhulabhai Memorial Institute, 1958), pl. 20. Doorway also is in *EITA*, 2: Pl. 635 and called Mallēśvara.
53. See *EITA*, 2: pl. 635 for photograph (which is incorrectly labelled as Mallēśvara doorway).
54. Compare Doḍḍēśvara pillar drawing (fig. 7) with Virūpākṣa pillar (fig. 8).
55. *Mārkaṇḍeya Purāṇa*, 91.7-28. Not to suggest this is the actual text followed, but to call attention to the tradition.
56. *EC*, 12: Si 28.
57. Rarely does Apasmāra appear in the Gaṅgādhara scene; however, there are a few examples in Tamil Nadu, probably the best known one is at the Pallava cave temple at Trichinopoly, west wall, where Śiva

has his right foot raised on top of a gaṇa or Apasmāra who is seated in an upright position. Also to be noted, contrary to standard iconography, Pārvatī stands to Śiva's right on the Virūpākṣa pillar.

58. Extremely faint protrusions seem to extend from Viṣṇu's mouth which indicate the tusks of a boar; however, the face is carved as distinctly human not boar-like.
59. Prior to my discussion, a dating for the Virūpākṣa has not been suggested, nor have the pillar reliefs been identified.
60. *EITA*, 2: pl. 461.
61. H. Cousens, *The Chalukyan Architecture of the Kanarese Districts* (Calcutta: ASI, 1926), pl. LVI.
62. An unclear scene on a pillar at Pailabunda might be the only other Gajendramokṣa depiction from the Noḷamba period.
63. Published in Sivaramamurti, *Nolamba*, pls. 11a-14.
64. These Kṛṣṇa episodes are encountered one other time in Noḷambavāḍi; they are rendered together on a pillar in the Bhōgaṇandīśvara temple at Nandi.
65. Sivaramamurti, *Nolamba*, pp. 17-18; pls. 8 and 9. It is unclear if he is claiming the Kālī comes from the same Saptamātṛkā set as the Vīṇādhara-Dakṣināmūrti which he describes preceding Kālī. The Kālī is substantially larger than the Vīnādhara. Also unclear is why he labels the image Kālī instead of Cāmuṇḍā if he considers her a Saptamātṛkā.
66. Of the two busts, one is published in Sivaramamurti, *Nolamba*, pl. 30; though not discussed, the image is labelled Cāmuṇḍā and said to be from Hemavati. I did not see this image in Hemavati (possibly an example of how easily sculptures disappear); however, she is almost identical to the other bust (my pl. 28). Possibly the two bust were originally attached to two of the images broken above the waist. If so, there are at least four Devīs at Hemavati similar to the Madras Museum Kālī; or, if each piece is remains of independent pieces, than there are six figures (plus Madras Kālī equals seven).
67. The seated figure has an abraded face. The outline of a third eye is visible, however the mouth and fangs are not.
68. In reference to Devī worship by kings, see Avani discussion. For a recent study regarding some problems on identification of Devī forms see: David Kinsley, *Hindu Goddesses* (Berkeley: University of California Press, 1986).
69. Katherine Harper, 'An Iconological Study on the Origins and Development of the Saptamātṛkās' (Ph.D dissertation, University of California, Los Angeles, 1977) pp. 163, 191.
70. S. Kramrisch, *Manifestations of Shiva* (Philadelphia: Philadelphia Museum of Art, 1981), pp. 22, 124, 135.
71. Ibid., p. 22, in the collection of Mr. and Mrs. John Gilmore Ford.
72. See A. Rea, *Chalukyan Architecture* (Madras: Government Press, 1896), pp. 6-9, pls., 1-8; and *EITA*, 2: 159-60, pls., 509-15.
73. See Desai, *Erotic*, pls., 101-5, 124, 136, 150: cf. E.N. Katkar, 'The Enigma of Bagali', in *The Chalukyas of Kalyana*, ed. by M.S. Nagaraja Rao (Bangalore: Mythic Society, 1983), pp. 191-93.
74. *EITA*, 2: 159-60. They note that 'the bhadra having upabhadra-projection and the presence of pratirathas is typical of both late Rāṣṭrakūṭā and Noḷamba conventions'. Also note the citrakhaṇḍa antarāla pillar (their pl. 513); although the caturasra format varies from those in Noḷambavāḍi, the basic pillar composition between the two are strikingly similar. The Kallēśvara gūḍhamaṇḍapa pillar (pl. 512) is a type not common in Noḷambavāḍi.
75. For Rāṣṭrakūṭa inscriptions, *SII*, 9 (pt. 1): 59, 66, 71: Noḷamba, ibid., nos. 80-1.
76. Kramrisch, *Manifestations of Shiva*, p. 124 (from the British Museum). These images do have facial types which might be associated with some central Noḷambavāḍi sculptures. The general ornamentation of the images does not appear to be idiomatic of the central (or eastern and southern) Noḷambavāḍi school. The suggested dating of eleventh-twelfth century (at which time the Noḷambas had migrated to Bellary district), and Andhra Pradesh location seem correct.
77. Ibid., p. 109 (from the Norton Simon Foundation).
78. A Somāskanda and Candraśekhara bronze images were discovered at the Bhōganaṇḍīśvara compound and removed to the Government Museum, Bangalore. They are published by K. Khandalavala, 'Two Bronze from Karnataka', in Madhu, ed. by M. S. Nagaraja Rao (Delhi: Agam Kala Prakashan, 1981), pp. 239-41, pls. 89-90. He assigns the Somāskanda to early eleventh century, and the Candraśekhara to *c.* 1050-75. I suggest both images might be about a half century earlier.
79. The Ambikā (from the L.A. County Museum) is published in P. Pal, *Indian Sculpture*, 2 vols. (Los Angeles: Los Angeles County Museum of Art, 1988), 2: 245. The Sarasvatī (British Museum) in A. Ghosh (ed.), *Jaina Art and Architecture*, 3 vols. (New Delhi: Bharatiya Jnanpith, 1975), 3: pl. 319. These two bronzes are closely akin to each other and display traits, especially the coiffure, common to many Hemavati female images (as Pal rightly observes; however, he considers it a Late Cālukya product, of the tenth century). The Jains were patronized in Hemavati and, although only two Jainas survive today in Hemavati, possibly portable images like these bronzes were once commonly produced.
80. Published in Sivaramamurti, *Nolamba*, pl. 1, and Huntington, *Ancient India*, fig. 15.26.
81. Inscribed on the base is 'svastiśrī Pasanabbe'. I am unaware of this name in other inscriptions, though an effaced epigraph during Iriva's reign (*c.* 940-68) mentions Ponnabbe (*EC*, 12: Si 14); the latter rough record could be misread, the *sa* and *na* in Haḷe-Kannaḍa are not too different in appearance.
82. I disagree with Huntington's assertion, which follows Sivaramamurti's method, that 'Śiva's taut torso and high headdress bespeak the southern tradition, while the full-bodied Umā is tied to western Deccan styles... '. I consider it difficult to believe an artist in

Hemavati was attempting to juxtapose figural types from disparate traditions. Further, I cannot believe, as Huntington does, that the bead motif border above the stele is indicative of 'influence' by 'Pala-period art'. Huntington *Ancient India*, p. 340. Sivaramamurti and Huntington consider Umāsahita a ninth century piece, whereas I suggest the second third of the tenth century.

83. *ARE*, 1917, no. 6 also see nos. 1-5, and *EC*, 12: Si 31 which give coeval temple maintenance epigraphs.
84. *EC*, 12: Si 38. The shrine is now called the Īśvara temple.
85. Ibid., and *EC*, 12: Si 24.
86. For instance: *EI*, 10: 65, 68, states that besides having crowns of prostrating feudatories (sāmantas) at his feet, he had destroyed the Bāṇa race (Mahābalikulavidhvaṃśa).
87. Grants to temples or religious personage include: Hemavati, *SII*, 9 (pt. 1): 19; Kambaduru (A.P.), ibid., no. 18; Baraguru, *EC*, 12: Si 38; Nandi, *EC*, 10: CB 26 (and my appendix one); Dharmapuri, *EI*, 10: 54-70 (includes *ARE*, 1901, no. 304, 348); Tayalur (deep in Gaṅgavādi, Mandya district) *EC*, 14: Md 13 (rev.).
88. *EC*, 12: Si 38.
89. *EC*, 12: Si 39.
90. *SII*, 9 (pt. 1): 40.
91. The temple is discussed in Krishna Murthy, *Nolambas*, pp. 170-2, and limitedly mentioned by Sarma, *Indian Archaeology 1980-81—A Review*, p. 122. Ignoring the epigraph which states Mahēndra erected the temple, Sarma calls the monument 'Gaṅga' (as he does the Kallēśvara temple at Aralaguppe). His role in an A.S.I. survey charged with locating Gaṅga sites might be the cause of his Gaṅgaphilia.
92. Krishna Murthy, *Nolambas*, p. 170, reports the hall to be hypostyle. He does not distinguish a dating discrepancy between the temple proper and the agramaṇḍapa (Nandi pavilion).
93. The other popular ceiling format is the more ornate Śiva with Aṣṭadikpāla ceiling panels. These are built in central Noḷambavāḍi temples at Pathasivarama, Hemavati (loose panels), Aralaguppe, and are common at eastern and southern Noḷambavāḍi monuments.
94. *EC*, 11: Cl 33-4. Another Noḷamba inscription, dating *c.* 970, is beside the temple, published in *MAR*, 1947-56, pp. 72-4 (no. 10).
95. I inspected the temple in late 1986. About ten loose sculptures are stored in the hall. They lack much ornamentation and have stocky bodies, not too different from some simpler central Noḷambavāḍi images.
96. *EC*, 10: Mb 38 and 50.
97. *EC*, 10: Mb 293 (see Avani discussion).
98. *EC*, 12: Si 38.
99. *MAR*, 1935, pl. 2, and pp. 11-12; *MAR*, 1947-56, pls. 53-4, pp. 56-7.
100. M. Seshadri, 'Sandhyā Tāṇḍava', *Artibus Asiae* 18 (1955): 117-20. 'Aṣṭadikpāla Figures from Aralaguppe, Mysore State', *Journal of the Mysore University* 23 (1967): 70-1.
101. Sivaramamurti, *Nataraja in Art*, fig. 128, and *Panorama of Jain Art*, fig. 211.
102. De Lippe, *Indian Mediaeval Sculpture*, pls. 291-3.
103. *Indian Archaeology 1980-81—A Review*, p. 122.
104. *EITA*, 2: 213.
105. 'There is hardly anything worth comparing in figure sculpture with it [Naṭēśa] in the entire Mysore State and South India', *MAR*, 1947-56, p. 46.
106. Published once in *MAR*, 1935, pl. 3.
107. See *EITA*, 2: pl. 632.
108. Seshadri identifies the dance mode as Sandhyā Tāṇḍava, the 'evening dance'. In his 'Aṣṭadikpāla Figures', Śiva and all the dikpālas are illustrated, plus the mukhamaṇḍapa doorway and interior pillars. Other published photographs of the ceiling panels are listed in the beginning of this section.
109. All other Noḷamba period ceiling panels have the Aṣṭadikpālas positioned with their heads towards the central (Śiva) panel (their feet towards the outer frame), yet here the Aṣṭadikpālas' feet are directed towards the centre.
110. Sarma, *Indian Archaeology*, p. 122, states that Nirṛti rides a ram; apparently he confused Nirṛti (SW) with Kubera (N), possibly the reason why he considers the dikpālas in placements differing from textual descriptions.
111. These sculptures might have been taken from the Hoysaḷa period Cennakēśvara temple in Aralaguppe. The temple is described in *MAR*, 1935, pp. 3-10.
112. *MAR*, 1935, p. 12, pl. 3, and Sarma, *Indian Archaeology*, p. 122, call the image an Umāmahēśvara but Umā does not sit on Śiva's left leg, she sits to his left side, thus the image is properly called an Umāsahita.
113. Seshadri, 'Sandhyā Tāṇḍava', p. 117 and 'Astadikpala Figures', p. 70.
114. Ibid. He does not cite the vīrakaḷ, presumably he is referring to *EC*, 12: Tp 55. *EC* dates the vīrakaḷ *c.* 880. Ramesh, *Inscriptions of the Western Gangas*, p. 293 dates it second half of the ninth century. Sheik Ali, *History of the Western Gangas* (Mysore: Mysore University, 1976) considers Satyavākya's reign to be 817-53.
115. Other inscriptions in the temple vicinity, but unrelated to the temple, include: a vīrakaḷ dated 961, without acknowledgment to a king (*EC*, 12: Tp 56); an epigraph dated 1091, during the Later Cālukya period, recording the construction of a tank (*EC*, 12: Tp 57), as well as other unpublished vīrakals. A vīrakaḷ in the nearby Kurugallu village commemorates a fallen hero during a skirmish between Gaṅga Satyavākya and Noḷamba Poḷalcōra (EC, 12: Tp 47).
116. Sarma, *Indian Archaeology*, p. 122.
117. As one of the chief advocates for regional style labels observes: 'It is becoming abundantly clear that the style of Indian art is determined by conditions prevalent during a period of time in a particular cultural and territorial unit, and not by any dynastic patronage or ethos.' Chandra, *On the Study of Indian Art*, pp. 71-2. Although I am in basic agreement, I believe, however, Chandra understates the role of

patron as a determinant in the prevalent local conditions.

118. *EC*, 12: Tp 61.

119. This idea is borrowed from Stein's 'segmentary state' model. In the village two renovated, adjacent coeval shrines, the Noṇambēśvara and Gaṅgēśvara, were built possibly to commemorate a marriage alliance. The temples are nearly identical: they both have rebuilt exteriors, their interiors consisting of garbhagṛha, antarāla and mukhamaṇḍapa. Śrīkāra free-standing pillars are in the antarāla and mukhamaṇḍapa, and the ubiquitous Noḷamba period engaged pilasters are to the sides. They have a lotus relief on the antarāla ceiling (like at the Kallēśvara temple) and the mukhamaṇḍapa in the Noṇabēśvara has a ceiling divided into nine sections by cross beams with lotus pendants on the inner corners and a lotus relief in the central square. A Śiva and four loose Mātṛkās (Mahēśvarī, Indrāṇī, Brahmāṇī and Vaiṣṇavī) were taken from Nonavinakere to the Bangalore Museum. The sculptures are stylistically akin to the images in central Noḷambavāḍi which exhibit the propensity towards less ornamented, stocky (though handsome) figures and date anterior to the Kallēśvara images. A Cāmuṇḍā and Kālabhairava in Nonavinakere (at the Police station) and a Mahiṣāsuramardinī (in the Colēśvara temple) are also from the Noḷamba period.

120. *EITA*, 2: 213; De Lippe, *Mediaeval*, p. 182.

121. *MAR*, 1939, pp. 44-9. *EITA*, 2: 202.

122. Geographically, Kambadahalli, Nagamangala taluk, Mandya district, is the closest Gaṅga site to Aralaguppe with ceiling panels (Sravanabelgola is of comparable distance but without panels). Because the Kallēśvara temple architectural features are rudimentary, and now altered, it is necessary that the sculptural style serves as the comparative focus.

123. The Ganga period Śaiva temples at Begur have ceiling panels (unpublished) which are austere and less refined than the Śāntinātha panels.

124. Though the Bhōgaṇandīśvara ceiling panels are simple, the exterior sculptures are not. Eastern Noḷambavāḍi sculptures share more mannerisms with the Gaṅgavāḍi style than does the central Noḷambavāḍi idiom. See chapter four.

125. *MAR*, 1947-56, p. 46. *MAR*, 1935, p. 11, adds to the ninth century date 'Pallava period'. It is unclear if the Report was referring to the Pallavas of Kancipuram, which seems unlikely, or the Noḷamba-Pallavas.

126. Sivaramamurti, *Nataraja*, p. 265.

127. Ibid.

CHAPTER FOUR

Eastern Noḷambavāḍi Monuments

INTRODUCTION

The monuments of eastern Noḷambavāḍi—located in modern-day Kolar district, Karṇataka—include the Bhōgaṇandīśvara and Aruṇācalēśvara temples at Nandi, and the Lakṣmaṇēśvara, Bharatēśvara, Śatrughnēśvara, and Añjanēśvara temples at Avani. The most elegant and best preserved Noḷamba period temple is the Bhōgaṇandīśvara, which also serves as the matrix for the eastern Noḷambavāḍi artistic repertoire. Although the monuments at Nandi and Avani are morphologically and stylistically akin, none of the other temples approach the sculptural sophistication which is exhibited by the images on the exterior of the Bhōgaṇandīśvara. Iconographically, no other Noḷamba temple approaches the innovative, but anomalous, scheme displayed on the exterior walls of the Lakṣmaṇēśvara temple at Avani. The eastern Noḷambavāḍi works share some characteristics with central Noḷambavāḍi monuments, and even more traits with the southern Noḷambavāḍi temples, yet enough stylistic disparities exist between the three divisions of Noḷambavāḍi to demand separate discussions.

NANDI

Introduction

The Noḷamba period Bhōgaṇandīśvara and Aruṇācalēśvara temples are located in Nandi village (Kolar district), at the north-east base of Nandi hill (Nandidurg), once a major military fortification and today a popular religious and tourist site, about forty-eight km north of Bangalore. The Jains had a centre on Nandi hill and the Gaṅgas, active supporters of Jainism, often referred to themselves as 'lords of Nandagiri' ('Nandagiri-nātha');[1] it was a traditional title the Gaṅgas retained, even after their presence in this portion of Gaṅgarusāsira (Gaṅga 6000, a territorial name) became negligible. It remained an epithet of symbolic weight, much like the Noḷamba's fond claim to be the 'lords of Kāñcī'. However, no Gaṅga epigraphs have been found on Nandi hill nor in the village.

Two sets of copper-plates dating from the reign of Rāṣṭrakūṭa Gōvinda III—one dated 806, the other 810—include information about the Gaṅgas, the Bāṇas, and grants made to the Kālāmukha preceptor Īśvaradāsa, the overseer of the maṭha (or sthāna) on Nandi hill.[2] Because of the numerous orthographical and grammatical errors, as well as unjustifiable genealogical inaccuracies, both sets of plates are considered spurious.[3] Although the plates are not legitimate Rāṣṭrakūṭa records, the Haḷe-Kannaḍa script, as sloppy as it might be, is paleographically ninth-tenth century. It is possible that Īśvaradāsa had the plates forged in order to receive the income (lands) specified in the grants for the maṭha's maintenance.[4] According to one set of plates, the Bāṇa queen Ratnāvalī instigated the grant and was responsible for the construction of a Śaiva temple. How much information in the spurious plates is factual cannot be validated. Most likely a Kālāmukha maṭha administrated by Īśvaradāsa, student of Kāḷaśakti, existed on the hill, and possibly Ratnāvalī built a temple which also could have been on the hill. It has been proposed in *Mysore Archaeological Reports* 1914 and 1932 that the temple associated with Ratnāvalī is the Bhōgaṇandīśvara temple, dating the temple to *c.* 800—a dubious suggestion.

Within the Bhōgaṇandīśvara compound there are no Rāṣṭrakūṭa, Gaṅga, nor Bāṇa records. The earliest lithic epigraph is a land grant to Divyaśakti-paṇḍita, presumably for temple maintenance, issued during the reign of Noḷambādhirāja.[5] Poḷalcōra and, at times, his son Mahēndra employed the title Noḷambādhirāja. During Poḷalcōra's reign and the early part of Mahēndra's reign, the Noḷambas and Gaṅgas were intimately allied, sanctified by marriage—Poḷalcōra's wife (Mahēndra's mother) was a Gaṅga princess, as was Mahēndra's wife. During the alliance years, Gaṅga Nītimārga and his successor Rācamalla II placed Gaṅgarusāsira, composing most of present-day Kolar district, under Noḷamba control.[6] Judging from the extensive remains of Noḷamba epigraphs, opposed to the insignificant amount of Gaṅga records in Kolar following *c.* 870, after Mahēndra disavowed Gaṅga suzerainty, the Kolar region was permanently affixed to the greater

Noḷamba sphere. Noḷamba epigraphs subsequently are sovereign records. The grant inscription in the Bhōgaṇandīśvara compound does not acknowledge Gaṅga affiliation, which probably places the epigraph in Mahēndra's reign.

The grant has been published and translated in different ways. One translation reads '. . . Paḷiyaṇa having built a tower to the temple of Nandi, he received lands. . . '.[7] However, the actual inscription does not mention the construction of a tower. A paraphrase of a more accurate translation runs as follows: while Noḷambādhirāja was ruling over the earth, local leaders granted to Divyaśakti-paṇḍita lands purchased from Puḷiyaṇṇa.[8] Unfortunately, the inscription does not furnish temple construction information. Land, purchased by gold, given to the Śaiva teacher Divyaśakti, implies the existence of a religious establishment, probably the Bhōgaṇandīśvara temple. Other epigraphs in the compound are Cōḷa period or later and note grants to the existing temple 'Nandīśvara-Mahādēva'.[9] During the Cōḷa and subsequent periods (Hoysaḷa, Vijayanagara and Pallegar), extensions were built to the original Bhōgaṇandīśvara and Aruṇācalēśvara temples.[10] One additional inscription, incised on the Aruṇācalēśvara temple, south maṇḍapa window, below Naṭēśa, has been assigned to the Noḷamba period (tenth century) by paleography.[11]

Generally the Bhōgaṇandīśvara and Aruṇācalēśvara temples are recognized as Noḷamba period temples. The *Mysore Archaeological Reports* consider the Aruṇācalēśvara temple to be Noḷamba period, but, as already mentioned, because of the (spurious) plates they suggest that the Bhōgaṇandīśvara might be the temple built by queen Ratnāvalī. However, the information in the plates is unreliable and the location of the alleged temple could have been anywhere on Nandi hill. (No traces of a *c.* 800 shrine are on the hill.) The Bhōgaṇandīśvara and Aruṇācalēśvara are called Noḷamba temples in the *Encyclopaedia of Indian Temple Architecture*,[12] by Krishna Murthy,[13] Krishna Sastri,[14] and others.[15] Soundara Rajan and De Lippe call the temples 'Gaṅga-Noḷamba'.[16]

BHŌGAṆANDĪŚVARA TEMPLE

The Bhōgaṇandīśvara temple is the most architecturally impressive and best preserved Noḷamba period monument (fig. 10, pl. 43) Sculptures on the vimāna superstructure and hāra (cloistered parapet) level throughout the temple are exquisitely carved and feature an encyclopedic iconographic scheme. Facing east, the temple consists of a garbhagṛha, antarāla and mukhamaṇḍapa. Whereas in central Noḷambavāḍi simple adhiṣṭhāna mouldings are common, in eastern Noḷambavāḍi the base mouldings are complex. The Bhōgaṇandīśvara adhiṣṭhāna has a jagatī, a tripaṭṭa-kumuda, a kaṇṭha with mostly makaras and some vyāla and bhūta reliefs, a gala, and a lotus leaf band surmounted by a paṭṭika moulding. Protruding from the north vimāna adhiṣṭhāna, the praṇāla (ablution drain) is shaped into a squatting, pudgy gaṇa from whose large mouth the sanctum's abhiṣeka water drains.

The vimāna walls slightly project into bhadra, pratikarṇa and karṇa sections and are articulated by engaged brahmakānta (rectangular) pilasters. The mukhamaṇḍapa walls have the same format along with additional projections flanking the bhadra. Wider than the other sections, the mukhamaṇḍapa bhadras (central projection) have jāla-vātāyanas (perforated windows) which also are placed in the antarāla recess. Portrayed in the north antarāla window is Durgā holding cakra (UR), śaṅkha (UL), abhaya-mudrā (LR), and kaṭihastamudrā (LL), standing in samabhaṅga pose on top of a buffalo head. This sort of Mahiṣāsuramardinī is not represented in central Noḷambavāḍi, standing on the severed head of Mahiṣāsura is more of a lower Drāviḍadēśa design. Deities are not depicted in the other windows: the north mukhamaṇḍapa window has three horizontal rows of gaṇa dancer/musicians,[17] the south mukhamaṇḍapa and antarāla have kalpavallis with dancers and musicians within the lotus stem swirls. The vimāna bhadras have two central engaged pilasters forming a 'sham-niche', too shallow and slender to be authentic dēvakōṣṭhas.

Above the walls, elaborate prastara (entablature) and hāra levels are featured at the Bhōgaṇandīśvara temple. These are unique components, not encountered on any other Noḷamba period monument. Immediately above the walls is an exuberant bhūtamālā which has interspersed vyāla, haṁsa, and other animal reliefs. A kapōta tops the bhūtamālā. Delineated on the kapōta are kīrttimukhas spewing nāsikās which encircle human (i.e. celestial) faces or other designs. Over the kapōta is an ornate moulding, looking much like the kaṇṭha and gala mouldings of the adhiṣṭhāna, but with even more animal reliefs, especially lions. Corresponding to the wall projections, the maṇḍapa hāra level has a large central śālā (wagon-vault aedicula), flanked by two pañjara (vaulted apsidal aedicula) and outer kūṭas (square aedicula). The vimāna śālā has one pañjara, not two, on each side. Carved on the front of the aediculas are figural sculptures, usually deities, which have large, decorative nāsī motifs overhead. Subsidiary figures, usually seated males holding lotus or with their hands in añjalī-mudrā, are within nāsīs bordering the hāra architectural elements.

Today, due to a maṇḍapa extension to the temple's

east and a shrine to the south, the east and south mukhamaṇḍapa hāra sculptures cannot be viewed unless one stands on the roof of the structural additions. Some vimāna hāra figures are identified in the *Encyclopaedia of Indian Temple Architecture* Bhōgaṇandīśvara temple summary.[18] I will discuss all the hāra figures and include the vimāna second tala and śikhara sculptures. To avoid tedious descriptions, I will present the scheme in a table form, identifying the figures and their main attributes, and commenting when appropriate.

The corner kūṭa figures (pls. 44, 46, 48) are portrayed as chubby seated males, except three times when they are females. Possibly the males are Bhūtanāyakas, leaders of the elemental powers made manifest by Śiva.

In south Indian temples bhūtas and gaṇas are frequently featured on adhiṣṭhānas, prastaras and upper stories of vimānas.[19] Usually pot-bellied and dwarfish, sometimes grotesque or terrifying, others times attractively jolly, bhūtas and gaṇas are rendered in a multitude of forms, as are seen in the bhūtamālās on the Bhōgaṇandīśvara temple's prastara and vimāna levels. The kūṭa figures are dignified, though pudgy, human figures. Similar figures at Kalagumalai, Tamil Nadu (Pāṇḍināḍu, *c.* 800), on the second story vimāna corners have been identified as Bhūta-nāyakas.[20] Bhūtanāyakas are personifications of the primal elements of nature and have directional realms.[21] Facing the four directions, the Bhogaṇand-īśvara temple kūṭa figures might appropriately be Bhūtanāyakas (or regular bhūtas). The three-eyed, four-armed south-east kūṭa figure might be the creator and lord of the bhūtas, Śiva as Bhūtanātha or Bhūtēśvara (pl. 44).

A unique portrayal of the Kirātārjunīyam episode is delineated on the south antarāla pañjara (pl. 45).[22] Seated in the centre are Śiva and Pārvatī disguised as kirātas (hunters). Kneeling below them is a small male in añjalī. Identified by the bow to the side, the lower male is Arjuna receiving grace by Śiva, whose foot touches Arjuna's head. Two semi-circles of figures surround Śiva-Pārvatī. The inner circle has gaṇas and vidyādharas, the outer circle narrates portions of the Kirātārjunīyam. In the lower left, Arjuna in ekapādāsana (standing on one foot) performs tapas and a liṅga is depicted over his head. A boar pierced by two arrows is rendered in the upper right of the outer circle. Below the boar, two small figures, Śiva (kirāta) and Arjuna fight. Exhausted by his futile attempt to defeat the kirāta, Arjuna realizes the hunter is Śiva and requests the boon of receiving from Śiva the pāśupatāstra (weapon). The climactic central scene shows Śiva bestowing grace. Unrelated to the scene, an unusual subsidiary figure sits to the left. With his face in profile, the male has his back towards the viewer, a playful placement not encountered in other images.

A finely carved Bhairava stands in the north antarāla pañjara (pl. 49). Holding khaṭvāṅga, ḍamaru, nāga, kapāla, and feeding Nandi (one hand not identified), he stands in atitribhaṅga pose. He wears a long ghaṇṭāmālā, typical for Bhairava images, but it is not common for Bhairava to be accompanied by Nandi, usually a dog is his companion. The khaṭvāṅga (staff with a skull at the top) might actually be a kaṅkāladaṇḍa (skeleton broken and bound to the top of a staff), identifying the Śiva-Bhairava image as Kaṅkālamūrti.[23] Kaṅkālamūrti often feeds a deer, not Nandi, however. The small female touching Bhairava/Kaṅkālamūrti's foot, with pots to her side, is probably one of the women from whom alms were collected. Sivaramamurti mistakenly identifies the image as Naṭarāja.[24] He also mistakenly writes that the Bhōgaṇandīśvara temple is in Andhra Pradesh, and, without historical support, calls the temple 'early Chola with traces of Rāṣṭrakūṭa influence'.[25] This misinformation is repeated by Filippi who traces the first example of a Cōḷa Naṭarāja to the Bhōga-ṇandīśvara temple (which he, too, thinks is in Andhra Pradesh).[26]

The vimāna second story (tala) has a format similar to the hāra, except it has a central pañjara flanked by śālās and corner kuṭas (hāra has central śālā bordered by pañjaras). Only the pañjara images are of iconographic interest, the other aedicula figures are subordinate males or females and more attendants flank the sides. Seated in the vimāna south pañjara is an ascetic or ṛṣi. His hair is in long straight jaṭās which flare-out around his head, a style which is repeated on the attendant to his right while the left attendant's hair is piled upward, strangely shaped like a triśūla. Vṛṣabhārūḍhamūrti, Śiva seated on Nandi, is the west pañjara image; in the north pañjara Yogamūrti Viṣṇu is seated wearing a yogapaṭṭa; and an unidentified four-armed male is seated in the east pañjara.

The otherwise granite temple has eight exquisite black schist sculptures placed at the grīvā-śikhara level.[27] The kalaśa at the temple's apex also is black stone (as are the interior pillars). Facing the four directions, four couchant Nandis are in the corners of the grīvā platform. The other four sculptures are standing deities: Śiva in the south, three-headed Brahmā in the west, the north image is of Viṣṇu flanked by Garuḍa and Gadādēvī, and the most important front (east) figure is of Śiva leaning on Nandi as Vṛṣabhāntikamūrti (pl. 50).[28]

The Bhōgaṇandīśvara temple mukhamaṇḍapa entrance is a relatively simple triśākhā doorway consisting of an inner padmaśākhā, an outer kalpavalli, and a middle śākhā having musicians

TABLE 1: IDENTIFICATION OF BHŌGAṆANDĪŚVARA HĀRA FIGURES

Position	*ID*	*Attributes*	*Comments*
South (E>W) Mukha-kūṭa (pl. 44)	Śiva (as Bhūtanātha or Bhūtēśvara ?)	UR padma (?) UL mālā, LR abhaya LL fruit (?)	Identified as Śiva because of third eye. Sits in yogāsana. See text discussion.
pañjara (a) (pl. 44)	Viṣṇu on Garuḍa	UR śaṅkha UL cakra LR khaḍga LL shield	Overhead on nāsī Gajalakṣmī sits.
pañjara (b)	female deity	UR kalaśa (?) UL ? LR and LL garland	A row of haṁsas are on the nāsī.
śālā	Dakṣiṇāmūrti	UR ? UL mṛga LR ? LL pustaka	Flanked by ṛṣis, vidyādharas and on the śālā a kinnara couple.
pañjara (c)	Manmatha	R lotus arrow L sugar cane bow	
pañjara (d)	Ratī	R mirror (?) L holds tree	
kūṭa	liṅga worship		Two monkeys worship a liṅga.
kūṭa (west)	male/Bhūta-nāyaka (?)	R ?, L on knee	see Bhūtanāyaka comment in text.
pañjara (west)	Gajāsurasaṁ-hāramūrti and Andhakāsura-vadhamūrti	8-armed all holding gajāsura's hide, but one has triśūla	Impaled by triśūla, on top of nāsī is Andhaka.
pañjara (south, antarāla) (pl. 45)	Kirātārjuniyam		see discussion in text.
kūṭa (vimāna)	male/Bhūta-nāyaka (?)	R padma L on knee	
pañjara (pl. 46)	Gaṅgādhara	UR on jaṭā which holds Gaṅgā, UL nāga, LR varada, LL on thigh	Flanking Śiva are Devī and Bhagīratha, adoring figures in nāsī.
śālā (pl. 46)	Dakṣiṇāmūrti	UR paraśu UL mṛga LR abhaya LL on leg	Śiva sits on Nandi with his pendant foot on Apasmāra who holds a nāga.
pañjara (pl. 46)	Kārttikeya	UR śakti, UL mālā LR abhaya LL āhūyavarada	Sits on peacock. Two Kinnarīs in nāsī.

Position	ID	Attributes	Comments
kūṭa (pl. 46)	male/Bhūta- nāyaka (?)	R paraśu L bowl (?)	
west (S>N) vimāna, kūṭa	male/Bhūta- nāyaka (?)	R śaṅkha (?) L on knee	
pañjara (pl. 47)	Narasiṁha	UR cakra, UL śaṅkha, LR & L Hiraṇyakaśipu	Apsarāsas in nāsī.
śālā (pl. 47)	Yogamūrti (Viṣṇu)	UR cakra, UL śaṅkha, LR mālā LL on thigh	Sits in yogāsana.
pañjara (pl. 47)	Sūrya	R & L padmas	In ratha drawn by horses.
kūṭa	male/Bhūta- nāyaka (?)	R on thigh L over knee	Wears yogapaṭṭa.
north (W>E) kūṭa	male/Bhūta- nāyaka (?)	R padma L on knee	
pañjara (pl. 48)	Vṛṣabhāntika	UR paraśu, UL mṛga LR on Nandi LL on hip	
śālā (pl. 48)	Liṅgodbhava	UR mālā UL mṛga LR abhaya LL on hip	To Śiva's right Brahmā and a haṁsa; left, Viṣṇu and a boar.
pañjara (pl. 48)	Umāmahēśvara		Nandi below, but carving is not finished or badly abraded.
kūṭa (pl. 48)	female	R & L padmas	In yogāsana.
pañjara (antarāla) (pl. 49)	Śiva-Bhairava	UR ?, main R khaṭvāṅga (?), LR feeding Nandi, UL ḍamaru, main L kapāla, LL nāga	A small female sits at, and touches, Śiva's foot. In nāsī are vidyādharas, gandharvas and apsarās. See text discussion.
pañjara (west, mukha)	Vaiṣṇavī (?)	UR cakra (?) UL śaṅkha (?) LR abhaya LL kapāla	Two ascetics (?) pour water over her head.
kūṭa	female	R padma, L knee	
kūṭa (north mukha.)	male/Bhūta- nāyaka (?)	R ?, L on thigh	

Position	*ID*	*Attributes*	*Comments*
pañjara (a)	Mahiṣāsura-mardinī	UR cakra UL śaṅkha LR triśūla LL on āsura	Theriomorphic Mahiṣāsura. Dancing gaṇas in nāsī.
pañjara (b)	male	R padma L thigh	
śālā	Devī	R khaḍga L kapāla	
pañjara (d)	Viṣṇu	UR cakra UL śaṅkha LR gadā LL on hip	
pañjara (d)	Mahēśvarī	UR mālā UL triśūla LR padma, LL thigh	Faded Nandi reclines below her pendant leg.
kūṭa	female	R abhaya, L thigh	
East (N>S) mukha-kūṭa	male/Bhūta-nāyaka (?)	4-armed, only LR abhaya is clear	Figure displays a big smile. Sits in yogāsana.
pañjara (a)	Indra		Sits on his vāhana Airāvata.
pañjara (b)	Naṭēśa	UR triśūla UL nāga LR gajahasta LL āhūya-varada	In lalita pose. Gaṇa musicians in nāsī.
śālā	Candēśvara	UR paraśu UR nāga, LR abhaya LL on thigh	
pañjara (c)	Tripurāntaka	8-armed, bow is main attribute	Brahmā and Viṣṇu (?) in ratha. Three cities represented by 3 buildings in nāsī.
pañjara (d)	Gaṇeśa	UR mālā UL paraśu, LR tusk	Two caurīs overhead. Vidyādharas in nāsī.
kūṭa	female	R knee, L padma ?	

and dancers contained within rectangular blocks. Above the door, the middle band (lalāṭa) becomes a panel of 'auspicious signs' ['maṅgala', i.e. śaṅkha, pūrṇakumbha, darpaṇa (mirror), dīpa (lamp) and Nandi] with Gajalakṣmī in the centre and standing females at the outer sides. Below, Padmanidhi and Śāṅkhanidhi sit at the base. Stylistically, the doorway is inconsistent with the temple and probably is a replacement.

Interior

The interior pillars are of the citrakhaṇḍa order.[29] The four free-standing mukhamaṇḍapa pillars have caturasra carvings parallel to those at Hemavati (central Noḷambavāḍi temples) but more rudimentary in design. As at Hemavati, central and side kīrttimukhas spew jewel bands which outline left and right panels occupied by figural sculptures.

Below the panels, gaṇas in kalpavallis usually are rendered, occasionally other figures. At Hemavati, but not at Nandi, the portion above the kīrttimukhas is utilized for additional carvings—which at the Virūpākṣa temple becomes quite elaborate—and invariably small lions are included at the top corners. The Nandi pillars are simpler not only in format and mannerism but also iconographically, as the following list indicates.

South 1. East face has a man with a club (left) and Durgā; south side has a female (left) and unidentified four-armed male deity; Nidhis are to the west; and the north has a female dancer and male drummer.

South 2. East side depicts Sūrya (left), a gaṇa (right) and a Naṭēśa below; south face has two gaṇas; west and north sides have male dancers and a drummer.

North 1. The east and north sides narrate the Vāmana episode. East face has, to the left, Vāmana under a chattra, who talks to (right) the āsura king Bali. Inexplicably depicted below is (a) four females: one dominant lady leans on the head of another while a third lady, on her knees, pleas to the main lady; (b) a kneeling elephant. North face has, left, Bali, with his wife behind him, pouring water for Vāmana. To the right a male is on the ground with one hand in vismaya (astonishment), another male stands over the first, and a female stands to the side with her hands in añjalī. Probably this represents Garuḍa (standing male, even if wings are not visible) seizing Bali's guru Śukra. The female might be Bali's wife acquiesce to Viṣṇu's (Vāmana) superiority. West face has Varāha (left) and Trivikrama; on the south face is Śiva (left) and Viṣṇu.

North 2. East face has Kṛṣṇa killing Arṣṭāsura (bull demon) and, to the right, Kṛṣṇa killing Bakāsura (or Vaka, the crane demon). The only other time Kṛṣṇa is seen performing these duties in Noḷambavāḍi is on a ceiling panel from Hemavati. South face has two Sūryas; two gaṇas are on the west side with a four-armed male deity below; and two gaṇas dance on the north face.

The caturasra sections of the antarāla pillars are uncarved and have sixteen-sided lower shafts. The north pillar, south face is the exception: it has an anthropomorphic Nandi with a theriomorphic (bull) head seated with a yogapaṭṭa around his legs, lecturing to a male standing to the side.

The garbhagṛha doorway is triśākhā: the inner śākhā is plain, followed by a stambhaśākhā and a padmaśākhā. Female attendants with caurīs stand at the base. Above the door is a lintel with shrine motifs (i.e. central śālā flanked by pañjaras). A large black liṅga is enshrined in the garbhagṛha. On the ceiling is a central lotus medallion.

The coffered mukhamaṇḍapa ceiling has Aṣṭadikpālas, in their proper directional spaces, encircling a central Umāsahita. The sculptor has reversed vehicles for Śiva and Pārvatī: below Pārvatī is Nandi and below Śiva is a lion. Sculpturally, these images are much simpler than ceiling panels in central Noḷambavāḍi.

Conclusion

Within the artistic repertoire of greater Noḷambavāḍi, the Bhōgaṇandīśvara temple forms the matrix of an eastern regional subschool, which includes the adjacent Aruṇācalēśvara and the temples at Avani. The temples at Nandi and Avani are morphologically and stylistically analogous.

Traits present at the Bhōgaṇandīśvara and central Noḷambavāḍi temples include the citrakhaṇḍa pillars with caturasra reliefs, Aṣṭadikpāla ceiling panels with a central Śiva, and perforated windows (jālavātāyanas). The pillar and ceiling panels are less conspicuous than their counterparts in central Noḷambavāḍi monuments. Generally, central Noḷambavāḍi sculptures are more intricately detailed. Most central Noḷambavāḍi temples have renovated exteriors; hence a taxonomic comparison of architecture between the central and eastern temples remains inconclusive. The fact that most of the central Noḷambavāḍi temple walls are remodelled, suggests that brick construction was popular, whereas in eastern Noḷambavāḍi the monuments are granite.

The harbingers for the eastern Noḷambavāḍi subschool, beginning with the Bhōgaṇandīśvara, are unclear. The Bhōgaṇandīśvara temple probably dates to the last quarter of the ninth century, during Mahēndra's reign, or possibly to his predecessor, Poḷalcōra.[30] The only temple definitely assignable to Mahēndra's reign is the Mahēndrēśvara temple at Baragur in central Noḷambavāḍi. The Mahēndrēśvara has a renovated exterior. The mukhamaṇḍapa has śrīkāra (proto 'lathe-turned') pillars, while Bhōgaṇandīśvara has citrakhaṇḍa pillars. The antarāla pillars in the two temples are akin: basically they are square (citrakhaṇḍa) pillars, except with sixteen-sided shafts between upper and lower square portions. The Mahēndrēśvara pillars (but not the Bhōgaṇandīśvara) have an octagonal band below the sixteen-sided area and above it a sculpted portion with gaṇas within jewelled borders and surmounted by pūrṇakumbhas. Besides the antarāla pillars and the temple layout, before the additions to both, the two temples do not have many parallels. Most likely the Kāmākṣamma temple at Dharmapuri, forming a southern Noḷambavāḍi subschool, is datable to Mahēndra's reign. Some characteristics at the Bhōgaṇandīśvara and Kāmākṣamma temples are allied (see southern Noḷambavāḍi). However, the Kāmākṣamma has idiosyncracies of a local tradition, one which has affinity with the lower Drāviḍadēśa culture.

The lower Drāviḍadēśa tradition, especially the Pāṇḍināḍu, is a likely contributor to the amalgamated style of the Bhōgaṇandīśvara temple. For example, the hāra level sculptures on the Bhōgaṇandīśvara are comparable to the Pāṇḍya period (*c.* 800) Kalagumalai shrine in Pāṇḍināḍu. The same feature on the Vijayālaya Cōḷīśvarman temple at Narttamalai (in Cōḷanāḍu)—probably built in the Muttaraiyar period (*c.* mid-ninth century)—is considered by some as a borrowing from the Pāṇḍya artistic tradition.[31] Another source, and probably a greater contributor to the eastern Noḷambavāḍi development, comes from a closer neighbour (geographically and politically), the Rāṣṭrakūṭas and the monuments associated with their period. In particular, some features encountered on the Bhōgaṇandīśvara are exhibited on the antecedent temples at Bhavanasi Sangam[32] in present-day Kurnool district (Andhra Pradesh), which is a contiguous district north of central Noḷambavāḍi (i.e. Hemavati, Anantapur district, A.P.). To complicate matters, Bhavanasi Sangam is in an area associated with the Eastern Cālukyas, Vēṅgīdēśa, and the Bhavanasi Sangam temples reflect a subregional school of the Rāṣṭrakūṭa artistic tradition.[33] Features the Bhōgaṇandīśvara shares with central Noḷambavāḍi temples are also found in some Rāṣṭrakūṭa monuments (e.g. citrakhaṇḍa pillars, jāla-vātāyanas, sometimes Aṣṭadikpāla and Śiva ceiling panels), though in a variant form and manner. Many of the same features are shared in Gaṅgavāḍi monuments (e.g. at Begur, Narasmangala, Hale-Alur). The adjoining eastern Noḷambavāḍi and western Gaṅgavāḍi did not have unalterable boundaries; at times the penumbra territories merged and artistic ideas, probably the artisans themselves, freely moved throughout. The Gaṅgavāḍi sites that have comparable traits, however, postdate the Bhōgaṇandīśvara temple.

At Nandi, the assimilation and reordering of divergent artistic sources, by whoever the arbiters were—be it the patron and/or the sthāpatis (chief architects)—resulted in the production of the elegant Bhōgaṇandīśvara temple. The temple composition served as the harbinger for subsequent eastern Noḷambavāḍi temples, although the hāra section on the Avani temples is abandoned. As the only Noḷamba period temple with all its architectural features unaltered, the Bhōgaṇandīśvara temple is one of the most aesthetically pleasing monuments in greater Noḷambavāḍi.

ARUṆĀCALĒŚVARA TEMPLE

The adjacent Aruṇācalēśvara temple is similar to the Bhōgaṇandīśvara temple but with some notable variations and later alterations. The Aruṇācalēśvara temple has not been properly analyzed, possibly because of the alterations, and because at first glance the two adjacent temples appear almost identical. After describing the Bhōgaṇandīśvara temple, the *Mysore Archaeological Reports* (1932) listed a few deviations found on, or in, the Aruṇācalēśvara temple, at times incorrectly. Unfortunately, Krishna Murthy repeated *Mysore Archaeological Reports*' method and mistakes,[34] and the *Encyclopaedia of Indian Temple Architecture* six sentence description also has mistakes.[35] It was correctly noted in the *Mysore Archaeological Reports* that the mukhamaṇḍapa pillars were replaced in the Vijayanagara period and that the maṇḍapa hāra and śikhara stucco figures also were added probably at the same time.[36] However, previous scholars have failed to notice that the complete granite superstructure[37] was rebuilt, probably in the Vijayanagara period; that the iconographic scheme identically copies the format of the Bhōgaṇandīśvara superstructure, and that an archaizing style seems to have been attempted.

Like the Bhōgaṇandīśvara, the Aruṇācalēśvara has a garbhagṛha, antarāla and mukhamaṇḍapa, and is approximately the same size (fig. 10, pl. 51). The adhiṣṭhāna and wall elements on the Aruṇācalēśvara are more elaborate, however. The adhiṣṭhāna mouldings are a jagatī, a kapōta with nāsikās, a kaṇṭha with lions, elephants and makaras reliefs, a gala, and a padma-paṭṭika. The praṇāla (ablution drain) is makara shaped with a man/bhūta standing in the open mouth.

Articulated with brahmakānta pilasters, the bhadra, pratikarṇa and karṇa wall projections at the Aruṇācalēśvara are more pronounced than their counterparts at the Bhōgaṇandīśvara. Though the Aruṇācalēśvara's vimāna bhadras have an additional central projection bordered by engaged pilasters, these niches (bhadrakoṣṭhas) are empty, not intended to serve as dēvakoṣṭhas. Inside the vimāna karṇa and pratikarṇa projections two small engaged pilasters support a vimāna superstructure motif (i.e. pañjarakōṣṭha), or a nāsī with kīrttimukha motif (i.e. nāsīkōṣṭha), usually with a female standing in between the pilasters.

The mukhamaṇḍapa bhadrakōṣṭhas are actually jāla-vātāyanas (perforated windows) with a Naṭēśa in the south window, and in the north window, a kalpavalli with dancers and musicians in its three swirls.[38] The south Naṭēśa (pl. 52) is in lalita pose on top of Apasmāra, displaying in his eight hands: (main R) gajahasta, (UR) ḍamaru, (mid R) triśūla, (LR) pustaka, (main L) abhaya, (UL) nāga, (mid L) ghaṇṭā, (LL) kapāla. A drummer and a cymbals player sit to the lower sides. Flanking the niche are elephants, yāḷis and, above, makaras ridden by gaṇas and a central kīrttimukha. In relief on the walls are two male ascetics. To their proper right sits Dakṣiṇāmūrti; to the left, Indra and consort on his elephant. An unpublished inscription is incised on the window which Mysore Archaeological Reports (1914) assigns to the tenth century on the basis of paleography.[39] Jālavātāyanas also are placed in the antarāla recess. Three frolicking gaṇas within kalpavalli swirls are depicted in the south window; in the north one sits a three-headed Kārttikeya with his peacock vāhana below.[40]

Above the wall level, the temple has been rebuilt. The mukhamaṇḍapa and antarāla have prastara and hāra levels constructed of brick and mortar. The stucco hāra images are mostly unidentifiable due to disrepair The vimāna upper stories are assembled in granite, except the apex śikhara which is brick and mortal. Structurally and iconographically the reconstructed vimāna portions repeat the format of the Bhōgaṇandīśvara temple.[41]

That the Bhōgaṇandīśvara superstructure (pls. 44-50) is an earlier construction than the Aruṇācalēśvara tower is evident upon close inspection (pls. 51-5).[42] The Aruṇācalēśvara images tend to be stiffer, less fluid, more stylized, and some of the ornamental motifs are variants of earlier forms.[43] The original Aruṇācalēśvara temple dates slightly later than the Bhōgaṇandīśvara, as is evident in the advanced articulation of the adhiṣṭhāna and walls. However, the stylistic affinity of the windows and other sculptural motifs indicates the edifices were constructed at close to the same time.[44] The paleographically assigned tenth-century inscription on the Aruṇācalēśvara south mukhamaṇḍapa window also indicates temporal proximity. The style discrepancy between the Aruṇācalēśvara superstructure and its lower portions (adhiṣṭhāna and walls) demonstrates that some time separates the sculpting of the two. The extent of the time interval becomes clearer when comparing the disparities between the Aruṇācalēśvara and Bhōgaṇandīśvara superstructures; though, the disparities, occasionally, are somewhat obscured by the archaizing attempt of the later sculptors to duplicate many earlier motifs. Nevertheless, the later sculptors manneristic approach and own preference for some motifs reveals the disjunction between the styles.

Certain characteristics which are peculiar to the Vijayanagara period are present on the Aruṇācalēśvara superstructure.[45] An Umāmahēśvara shrine constructed in between the Bhōgaṇandīśvara and Aruṇācalēśvara temples during the Vijayanagara period, coeval, or slightly after the Aruṇācalēśvara superstructure, exhibits the same traits (pl. 56). Lions (siṁha), or variant forms of lions (e.g. vyāḷis or yāḷis), are ubiquitous decorative motifs in Indian art. However, during the Vijayanagara period a particular manner of representing lions seated frontally became popular.[46] This lion type is seen on the Aruṇācalēśvara superstructure in the bhūtamālā and gala moulding sections (pls. 53-5). The lion's face has large rounded, bulging eyes, a partially open (smiling?) mouth, and a mane which resembles a beard forming a circle around the face. The lion's folded rear legs extend outward beyond the front legs. The same facial features also are seen on lions seated, or standing, in profile with the faces usually frontally oriented. The identical lion type is rendered on the Umāmahēśvara shrine (pl. 56) and numerous other Vijayanagara period monuments.[47] A cursory comparison with the lions on the Bhōgaṇandīśvara tower (pls. 46-8) reveals the disparities between the earlier and later styles. The physiognomies are distinctive: the Bhōgaṇandīśvara lions have longer manes flowing downwards (not forming a circular beard as in the Vijayanagara type), and the bodies are more gracefully delineated.

Other motifs indicate that the Aruṇācalēśvara superstructure is from the Vijayanagara period. Females often wear long, stiff lower garments (e.g. north pañjara Umāmahēśvara image); crowns are shaped by rows of spirals (as also commonly seen on the Umāmahēśvara shrine); and diamond-shape or floral designs face the squares in the jāla mouldings (not rendered on the earlier period mouldings). The Aruṇācalēśvara hāra aediculas have more attendant figures which, compared to the Bhōgaṇandīśvara, are rigid and stylized.[48]

Close inspection of the superstructures exposes the stylistic (and temporal) distance between the two. However, as stated earlier, possibly the later sculptors were aspiring to archaize the Aruṇācalēśvara tower in order to heighten the similarity. In addition to the facts that the iconographic scheme and the basic structural format are copied, other minor elements seem to have been duplicated. Most importantly, or most readily visible, the nāsikā reliefs on the kapōtas are strikingly akin. The Aruṇācalēśvara nāsikā, with its apex kīrttimukha and its inner space occupied by a human face or ornamentation, repeats the Bhōgaṇandīśvara model. Occasionally the inner nāsikā motif is exactly duplicated. Over the Bhōgaṇandīśvara west śālā of Yogamūrti (pl. 47) the nāsikās exhibit, in one, an open hood of a nāga (cobra) and, in the second, the upper torso and head of a female holding a staff. Curiously, the identical subjects are copied at the same location on the Aruṇācalēśvara temple (pl. 54), though the female lacks the sensuality evoked in her prototype. The inner portions of other nāsikās do not necessarily repeat exactly from one temple to the other, but the general design does.

The nāsikās on the Vijayanagara period Umāmahēśvara shrine are variantly shaped. The nāsikā vegetative-motif borders are not confined to the basic U-shape (an upside down U) depicted on the superstructures; rather the vegetation randomly radiates to the sides (pl. 56). Also the nāsikā inner faces are rounded and project beyond the nāsikā plane, whereas the superstructure faces are flatter, squared and restricted to the nāsikā interior. Intent on conforming to the anterior iconography and format of the Bhōgaṇandīśvara temple, the Vijayanagara period sculptors apparently abandoned their more familiar nāsikā form, as seen on the Umāmahēśvara shrine. In addition, the bhūtamālās on the Aruṇācalēśvara and Bhōgaṇandīśvara temples are remarkably similar; however, the later lion shape, discussed earlier, and other minor deviations, distinguish the two.

Interior

The Aruṇācalēśvara temple interior is considerably remodelled and of little importance. The mukhamaṇḍapa entrance is similar to the Bhōgaṇandīśvara entrance: both probably were later renovations to the temples. The four free-standing mukhamaṇḍapa pillars are distinctly Vijayanagara period replacements. It is difficult to ascertain if the temple ceiling is original or if it was rebuilt at the same time as the exterior prastara and tower. The latter option seems most likely.[49] The workmanship is crude, not displaying features distinctive of any particular period. The mukhamaṇḍapa and garbhagṛha have 'lantern roofs' (or 'square and diamond system') with a central lotus medallion. This ceiling type is built into the central Noḷambavāḍi Siddēśvara temple at Hemavati; however, at that temple too, the ceiling appears to be a later replacement. Possibly a feeble attempt was made to imitate the Bhōgaṇandīśvara mukhamaṇḍapa ceiling: two dikpālas, Indra (E) and Īśāna (NE), are roughly carved in low relief. The inappropriateness of Aruṇācalēśvara 'lantern roof' shape for dikpāla images might have been the cause of abandoning the work.

Entrance to the antarāla originally was open, as was the Bhōgaṇandīśvara antarāla, but during renovations a doorway was added for structural support. Only the west antarāla pillars and the modest triśākhā garbhagṛha doorway have Noḷamba period characteristics. The pillars are plain citrakhaṇḍa type with small lions carved in the lower caturasra corners. Though simplistic, the pillar design is indicative of its tenth century origin.

Conclusion

The Aruṇācalēśvara temple is a tenth century structure, but only the adhiṣṭhāna, walls, including the window carvings, and limited interior portions are original. Because of structural advancements at the Lakṣmaṇēśvara temple at Avani, which dates *c.* 920-40 (see Avani), the likely dating of the Aruṇācalēśvara is the first quarter of the tenth century. During the Vijayanagara period the temple received extensive renovations, including a rebuilt superstructure. The later sculptors copied from the Bhōgaṇandīśvara temple the structural and iconographic format for the tower. As a result, the appearance of the monuments—except for the obvious brick and mortar sections, and interior pillar replacements—is consistent in both. However, as I argued earlier, definite disparities between the structures are discernable, indicating that the Aruṇācalēśvara tower is not just slightly later than the Bhōgaṇandīśvara, as previous scholars presumed, but approximately six centuries later.

AVANI

Introduction

Avani in Kolar district is traditionally known as Avantikakṣētra and is famed for its *Rāmāyaṇa* connection. Here Rāma lodged during his return from Laṅka, and after her expulsion by Rāma, Sītā lived with Vālmīki on Avani hill (Vālmīki Parvata) and gave birth to her twin sons, Lava and Kuśa. Scattered over the hill are numerous rocks and caves associated with Sītā's, Rāma's and Vālmīki's stay.[50] In the village, at the south-west lower corner of the hill, a group of temples collectively called Rāmēśvara are within a walled compound. A thirteenth-century Pārvatī temple, facing south, was erected in between a group of earlier temples named after *Rāmāyaṇa* heroes. The temples, however, are dedicated to Śiva. Looking from the south to north, to the west of the Pārvatī temple (the temples face east), are the Lakṣmaṇēśvara, Rāmēśvara, and Śatrughnēśvara temples. To the east (facing west) are the Bharatēśvara and Añjanēśvara temples.[51] Beyond the Añjanēśvara is a Noḷamba mānastambha (large free-standing inscribed pillar).[52] Another important inscribed Noḷamba pillar is by the Rāmēśvara compound entrance.[53] Additional temples, dating to later periods, are also in the compound.

The Lakṣmaṇēśvara, Bharatēśvara and Śatrughnēśvara temples have Noḷamba epigraphs on their adhiṣṭhānas and the structures date from the Noḷamba period. The Añjanēśvara has interior pillars and an adhiṣṭhāna closely related to those of the Bharatēśvara and probably is coeval, though renovations to both obscure their origins. The Rāmēśvara is attached to the thirteenth-century Pārvatī temple. Possibly the former was constructed before the latter, but if so, it was remodelled to resemble the Pārvatī temple. Except for the Lakṣmaṇēśvara, the temples are relatively simple and their exterior walls are renovated.

LAKṢMAṆĒŚVARA TEMPLE[54]

The Lakṣmaṇēśvara temple's morphology and style relates to the eastern Noḷambavāḍi temples at Nandi, especially the Aruṇācalēśvara temple. The iconographic scheme of the exterior walls of the Lakṣmaṇēśvara is anomalous. Devī (Goddess) manifestations predominate: there are five major manifestations of her with four arms, and five two-armed forms intended as minor manifestations or attendants. Śiva is depicted twice as Naṭēśa and twice in a raudra (fierce) form. Viṣṇu, Gaṇeśa and Sūrya are each rendered once. A portrait of Tribhuvanakaratabhaṭāra, the religious overseer of Avani, identified by an inscription,[55] is on the north vimāna wall. A figure on the south vimāna probably portrays the Noḷamba King Vīra Noḷamba (Aṇṇiga). On the front (east) adhiṣṭhāna, to the south of the stairs, is inscribed 'Śrī Vīra Noḷamba' and to the stairs' north 'Śrī Tribhuvanadēvam'.[56] Tribhuvanadēvam appears as Tribhuvanakarata on the north vimāna wall. He 'ruled the Āvaniya sthāna' during the reigns of two Noḷamba kings, Aṇṇiga and Iṛiva, and during his forty years of control is reputed to have built two tanks and fifty temples.[57] Evidently he was an important Śaiva teacher called the 'Kālī-yuga Rudra'.[58]

The Lakṣmaṇēśvara temple, with a mukhamaṇḍapa, antarāla and garbhagṛha, faces east (fig. 11). Like the Bhōgaṇandīśvara and Aruṇācalēśvara temples, this eastern Noḷambavāḍi temple has an elaborate adhiṣṭhāna. Built on a low upāna platform the adhiṣṭhāna mouldings consist of a jagatī, a tripaṭṭa-kumuda, a kapōta with kīrttimukha-nāsikās, a kaṇṭha with vyāla, elephant, and makara carvings, and a lotus leaf band topped by the paṭṭika moulding. The praṇāla (ablution drain) protruding from the north vimāna adhiṣṭhāna is shaped into a makara with a man/bhūta in its mouth. The identical praṇāla form is built into the Aruṇācalēśvara temple.

The walls clearly project into bhadra, pratikarṇa and karṇa sections. Brahmakānta (rectangular) pilasters border the sections, and two half brahmakānta pilasters within the sections flank further wall projections. These inner projections are extended into the adhiṣṭhāna which has the same projection-recession format. The bhadra and karṇa projections serve as authentic dēvakoṣṭhas, except the antarāla and mukhamaṇḍapa bhadras are actually jālavātāyanas with deities.[59] Above the wall level, the complete brick superstructure is a later period reconstruction, probably from Vijayanagara times.

The temple triśākhā entrance and the stairway leading to it also are Vijayanagara period replacements. To the south of the doorway a Śaiva dvārapāla and a Śaṅkhanidhi have been built into the temple wall. The images conform stylistically with the other temple wall sculptures. Presumably the dvārapāla and nidhi were preserved from the original doorway and integrated into the temple. Ruined stucco dvārapāla and nidhi images are added on to the wall north of the doorway.

Interior

In the temple mukhamaṇḍapa interior there are four typical Noḷamba period free-standing citrakhaṇḍa pillars with sculpted caturasra sections.[60] Less intricate than the caturasra carvings produced in central Noḷambavāḍi, these pillars are akin to the ones at the Bhōgaṇandīśvara temple at Nandi. The figures were cut in low relief and have not aged well. Iconographically, the works are relatively simple: mostly dancers and musicians are rendered, and infrequently deities.

On the front south pillar, east face, the asura king Bali and his wife who washes the feet of Vāmana are to the left. To the right, the episode's climax is indicated by Trivikrama with his leg raised. Naṭēśa on the front north pillar, south face, dances accompanied by a male drummer. The rear north pillar, east face, has two effaced images, one a seated Devī (right) the other a naked female (left). On the same pillar, north face, there are (left) Vṛṣabhāntika (Śiva with Nandi) and (right) an ascetic with wild hair stands with one arm extended upwards with a bag, like the one Tribhuvanakarata has, over his shoulder.

The two free-standing pillars at the antarāla entrance have cylindrical shafts with square lower sections. The side engaged pillars throughout the temple are the ubiquitous Noḷamba period plain citrakhaṇḍa pillars. Like other eastern Noḷambavāḍi temples, the garbhagṛha doorway is relatively simple. The inner śākhā has a pot at the base from which a kalpavalli issues. The middle stambhaśākhā is plain, and the outer śākhā has small squares with lotus flowers at regular intervals bordered by a padmaśākhā and a female at the base. A Gajalakṣmī is above the door. In the garbhagṛha a large black liṅga is enshrined.

A Mātṛkā set, lacking Cāmuṇḍā, is housed in the antarāla. The sculptures might be from the Noḷamba period but are aesthetically of low quality. A better quality Noḷamba period Sūrya stands in front of the west wall, north side.

The coffered ceiling in the mukhamaṇḍapa has a central Umāsahita with lateral Aṣṭadikpālas in their proper directional realms. As is the case with the ceiling panels at Bhōgaṇandīśvara temple, Nandi, the Lakṣmaṇēśvara temple panels are not sculpted with the refined skill and intricate detail that is characteristic of central Noḷambavāḍi panels, as demonstrated at the Kallēśvara temple, Aralaguppe, for instance. On the floor, below the panels, a Nandi is placed upon a circular balipīṭha. The antarāla ceiling has a large lotus medallion.

Exterior deities and suggested function

The figural sculptures on the karṇa and bhadra projections, starting with the front (east) south karṇa and proceeding clockwise (pradakṣiṇā) order, are as follows:

East maṇḍapa, south karṇa (pl. 57). A major form of Devī, four-armed holding ḍamaru (UR), triśūla (UL), khaḍga (sword, LR), and kapāla (LL), sits in lalitāsana with her right leg pendant resting on a corpse from whose body a human (asura) upper torso and head projects (seen below the sword).

South maṇḍapa, east karṇa (pl. 58). Śiva/Bhairava, maybe Kṣetrapāla, holding ḍamaru (UR), triśūla (?, UL), churī (knife, LR), and kapāla (LL), with an open-hooded cobra below the kapāla, stands naked except for a ghaṇṭā-kaṇṭibandha (bell waistband), yajñopavīta (sacred thread), kuṇḍalas (earrings) and a muṇḍa (skull) on the top of his head. This is the only niche with figural reliefs above. A seated Śiva, probably Dakṣiṇāmūrti—attributes are unclear, he seems to hold a nāga and a pustaka (book, a common attribute of Dakṣiṇāmūrti)—is flanked by Nandi and a Bhūta.

South maṇḍapa, bhadra (jāla-vātāyana) (pl. 59). In lalita pose with his left foot on Apasmāra and the right foot on another demon, Naṭēśa has his main right hand in abhaya-mudrā, a ḍamaru in the upper right hand, the main left arm is in gajahasta and the upper left hand holds a nāga. Musicians and vidhyādaras are to the sides. Barrett suggested that this image might be the harbinger of comparable Cōḷa bronze Naṭēśas, especially the 'Kuram Naṭarāja', and his suggestion received support by Schwindler.[61]

South maṇḍapa, west karṇa (pl. 60). A two-armed Devī/attendant stands in samabhaṅga posture holding a churī (dagger) and a padma(?). Her jvalitaśikhā ('flaming hair'), nakedness and attribute (knife) suggests she is a minor Devī manifestation, or an intimately associated attendant (e.g. yoginī, ḍakinī, etc.,) as are the other two-armed females around the temple.

South antarāla, jāla-vātāyana (pl. 61). Viṣṇu,[62] in samabhaṅga pose, has his main right hand in abhaya-mudrā and next to the main left hand, which rests on his hip, is a gadā. A padma(?) is held in the upper left hand, and the upper right attribute is unclear. Two protrusions at the neck's sides, though not distinct, appear to be animal heads. Viṣṇu as Vaikuṇṭha has a lion (Narasiṁha) head and a boar (Varāha) head to the sides (and the head of fierce Kapila or a woman behind), and though the heads here are not differentiated, probably this Viṣṇu is a locally misunderstood version of Vaikuṇṭha. The inclusion of Vaikuṇṭha, the supreme deity of Pañcarātra Vaiṣṇavism, heightens the temple's anomalous iconographic scheme; however, in Śaiva context Viṣṇu is often praised for his devotion to Śiva.

South vimāna, east karṇa. A seated Gaṇeśa holds danta (broken tusk) and laḍḍu (sweets).

South vimāna, bhadra. A two-armed Devī/attendant might hold a type of plant(?) in the left hand, and the right arm is held downwards, the hand open.

South vimāna, west karṇa (pl. 62). Wearing a crown and other jewels, a male holds a wreath. This royal figure probably represents the Noḷamba king Vīra-Noḷamba (Aṇṇiga) whose name is inscribed on the front, south side, adhiṣṭhāna.

West vimāna, south karṇa (pl. 63). A major Devī manifestation tramples on a defeated male asura. Her main right hand holds a khaḍga and a kapāla is held in the main left hand. The other right hand has a triśūla impaled into the asura, and a nāga is held in her remaining left hand.

West vimāna, bhadra. Similar to the south maṇḍapa, west karṇa image, except without a skull on top of the head, this Śiva/Bhairava's attributes are a ḍamaru (UR), a nāga (UL), a churī (LR) and a kapāla (LL).

West vimāna, north karṇa (pl. 64). Beautifully executed, this four-armed Devī stands firmly above a defeated male asura with a jackal to the side. She holds a ḍamaru (UR), a nāga (UL), a triśūla (LR) and a kapāla (LL). Like the Devī on the opposite side of the same wall, she wears a sacred thread composed of skulls and a skull at the head's apex.

North vimāna, west karṇa. A Devī/attendant stands in tribhaṅga pose with a churī (R) and a kapāla (L).

North vimāna, bhadra (pl. 65). Tribhuvanakaratabhaṭāra, identified by the inscription to his right, sits in yogāsana upon a padmapīṭha (lotus throne). He wears a yajñopavīta, a rudrākṣa-mālā and has a small bag hanging from his left shoulder.

North vimāna, east karṇa. A Devī/attendant has her left hand on her hip and the right hand holds a flower(?).

North antarāla, jāla-vātāyana. Mahiṣāsuramardinī has her right foot on the ground and her left foot on top of the buffalo-headed, otherwise anthropomorphic, Mahiṣāsura. She holds a cakra (UR), śaṅkha (UL), a triśūla impaled into the asura's neck (LR) and the remaining hand touches the asura's head.

North antarāla, west wall, karṇa (the corresponding south antarāla placement does not have an image). A naked Devī/attendant holds a vajra(?) and a kapāla.

North maṇḍapa, west karṇa. Sūrya in samabhaṅga pose holding two padmas.

North maṇḍapa, bhadra (jāla-vātāyana). A three swirl kalpavalli has dancers and musicians within the circles.

North maṇḍapa, east karṇa (pl. 66). A major Devī manifestation stands in tribhaṅga, without an asura below her (the other four-armed Devīs are accompanied by defeated asuras), holding a triśūla (UR), a ḍamaru (LR), a khaḍga (LR) and kheṭaka (shield).

East maṇḍapa, north karṇa. Naṭēśa, in catura pose, displays the same attributes as the Naṭēśa in the south maṇḍapa window [i.e ḍamaru (UR), nāga (UL), abhaya-mudrā (main R) and (main left) gajahasta].

One can only speculate on the intended meaning of this iconographic scheme. The repeated representations of victorious four-armed Devīs over fallen asuras and additional, usually fierce, female attendants, suggest an emphasis on the supremacy of the Goddess. The Goddess is manifest in myriad forms: her 'dark' destructive nature predominates at the Lakṣmaṇēśvara temple. Always her powers are superior to the haughty asuras who, in their best moments, taunt the harried Dēvas (gods) and disharmonious the cosmic order. She conquers enemies and hence is revered (or feared) for her martial prowess. Yet, the Goddess is an inherent, integral part of Śiva in Pāśupata (and other) Śaiva schools. The Lakṣmaṇēśvara temple is dedicated to Śiva and his presence is not neglected on the temple walls. Twice he is in raudra form and twice more he performs his dance of destruction/creation (Naṭēśa). It is the terrific forms of Śiva and Devī which dominate the temple walls.

I suggest the primary purpose of the Lakṣmaṇēśvara iconographic scheme is to laud the combined destructive (subsequently beneficial) supremacy of Śiva and Devī. It is well-known from the Purāṇas, and other sources, that Śiva and Pārvatī (Devī), in one or many of her 'dark' manifestations, were required to silence disruptive asuras or other opponents. Such episodes are numerous in the *Śiva Purāṇa*, for instance, a text known to have had Pāśupata input.[63] Śiva creates Vīrabhadra and Bhadrakālī (at another time Mahākālī) with entourage to destroy Dakṣa's sacrifice;[64] Vīrabhadra, Bhadrakālī and entourage also battle the Dānava Śaṅkhacūḍa.[65] A terrible Kṛtyā (a horrific female) was created by Śiva in the battle against Jalandhara[66] and Pārvatī with the Śaktīs of other gods and Śiva combat Andhaka.[67] Kālī, or Kauśikī, created from Pārvatī's discarded dark outer skin, annihilates Śumbha, Niśumbha and their asura armies.[68]

The destruction of Dakṣa's sacrifice is repeated in many sources and had special philosophical significance to the Pāśupatas.[69] This episode, as well as any number of related events in which Śiva and Devī dominate over oppositions, might be simultaneously implied by the temple imagery. The vimāna west wall has a central fierce Śiva/Bhairava (who might be Vīrabhadra) flanked by two victorious Devīs (who might be Bhadrakālī and Mahākālī). The various two-armed Devī/attendants probably represent the host of yoginīs, ḍākinīs, śākinīs, etc., who accompany the Goddess into battle and who often drink the blood and eat the flesh of fallen victims. Specific events are rendered on the walls: the Mahiṣāsuramardinī in the north antarāla window obviously depicts Durgā's victory over Mahiṣāsura. The west vimāna Devīs might also represent specific images and their conquest over specific enemies, although their iconography does not differentiate them from numerous possibilities. Nevertheless, the scheme in totality seems to suggest the combined benign (to their allies) destructive potentiality of Śiva and Devī.

It is the benevolent grace of Śiva and Devī, their protection against enemies, that might explain the inclusion of Tribhuvanakarata and Vīra Noḷamba among the wall images. They identify with Śiva's and

Devī's triumphs and, as temple patrons and devotees, hope to reap the benefits of the deities' compassion. The iconographic penchant for violent domination seems to indicate the patrons' desire for martial strength. Like Vīrabhadra and Bhadrakālī who destroy the enemies of Śiva, Tribhuvanakarata and Aṇṇiga (Vīra Noḷamba), hopefully, conquer their foes and, by extension, the opponents of Śiva. Kings worshipped Kālī/Durgā for success in warfare.[70] That Devī and entourage are repeated most on the walls is probably due to the Goddess's (and her hosts') relentless ferociousness.

Through rituals and seasonal festivals a king's authority was constituted and sustained. The king's priests often performed rituals intended to protect and aid the king in his military campaigns. The Lakṣmaṇēśvara scheme might be an experiment or variation on invoking divine aid, especially from the Goddess. The temple may represent a bold ritualistic attempt to perpetuate Vīra Noḷamba's martial success.[71]

Conclusion

The Lakṣmaṇēśvara temple is a Noḷamba monument derived from the eastern Noḷambavāḍi regional development, exemplified at Nandi by the Bhōgaṇandīśvara and Aruṇācalēśvara temples. Though the exterior wall projections are more pronounced and the adhiṣṭhāna is slightly more ornate, the morphology of Lakṣmaṇēśvara temple is based on the Aruṇācalēśvara prototype. The Lakṣmaṇēśvara iconographic scheme is unique: a regional antecedent for its format remains unknown. The religious leader Tribhuvanakarata-bhaṭāra's image is incorporated on the temple, at the important placement above the praṇāla (north vimāna bhadra), suggesting his sacerdotal power, patronage, and direct supervision of the iconography. Control would have been shared by, and beneficial to, the Noḷamba king Aṇṇiga. The name Vīra-Noḷamba's (Aṇṇiga) is inscribed on the temple[72] and the royal figure bearing a wreath on the vimāna south (west karṇa) wall is probably intended as his portrait. The preponderance of Devī imagery, within a Śaiva context, probably reflects Tribhuvanakarata's teachings, which were presumably based on a sanctioned, contemporaneous school of thought, most likely, Pāśupata or Kālāmukha. Because of her relentless ferocity, the Goddess, in her 'dark' manifestations, was important to kings seeking strength, guidance and protection in warfare.[73] This aspect of Devī, combined with the destructive, yet compassionate, potency of Śiva, appears to be the cause of the enigmatic Lakṣmaṇēśvara wall scheme.

Tribhuvanakarata, after controlling Avani and its religious establishments for forty years, died in 961.[74] Aṇṇiga began his reign in *c.* 924[75] and his last known inscriptions are from 938.[76] The first known record of his successor Iṛiva is dated 942.[77] The Lakṣmaṇēśvara temple must date within Tribhuvanakarata's lifetime and during Aṇṇiga's reign, assigning the temple construction to *c.* 925-40.[78] The Lakṣmaṇēśvara temple scheme is an example of specific agents—King Vīra Noḷamba, the religious leader Tribhuvanakarata, active deities (especially 'the Goddess') (also remembering the artisans)—formulating a specific monument that was intended to function within the dialectics of Noḷamba polity.

BHARATĒŚVARA AND AÑJANĒŚVARA TEMPLES

The Bharatēśvara temple, opposite the Lakṣmaṇēśvara temple, and the Añjanēśvara temple, adjacent to the Bharatēśvara, are both architecturally unimpressive. Because the buildings are analogous, I will summarize their features together. The brick walls have been renovated. The Bharatēśvara has a Vijayanagara period superstructure like the one on the Lakṣmaṇēśvara, but the Añjanēśvara is without a tower. The granite adhiṣṭhānas are original. Built on a low upana the adhiṣṭhāna mouldings are a jagatī, a rounded kumuda, a kaṇṭha with mostly vyāla carvings on the Bharatēśvara and elephants on the Añjanēśvara, and a padma-paṭṭika. On the Bharatēśvara's south adhiṣṭhāna, an inscription records that Dīvāmbikā (a Noḷamba queen) had the Noḷamba-Nārāyaṇēśvara temple built.[79] Dedicated to Mahēśvara (Śiva),[80] the Noḷamba-Nārāyaṇēśvara is the likely original name of the Bharatēśvara. The Bharatēśvara has a perforated window with dancers and musicians on the south maṇḍapa wall, and the Añjanēśvara has one with dancers on the north maṇḍapa wall. The Añjanēśvara has a rebuilt entrance, similar to Lakṣmaṇēśvara, but the Bharatēśvara has a black schist pañcaśākhā doorway that probably is original.

The interior pillars of these temples are of some importance. The ubiquitous Noḷamba period plain citrakhaṇḍa engaged pillars are once again embedded into the side walls. However, except for the two cylindrical pillars at the Bharatēśvara antarāla entrance, the free-standing pillars are not the citrakhaṇḍa type or the cylindrical pillars (śrīkāra) commonly placed in Noḷamba period temples. Rather, they are square at the base with a shaft that is sixteen-sided below, octagonal in the middle and cylindrical above with a cushion capital and a dish-shaped abacus. The middle octagonal bands have low relief figural sculptures, mostly dancers and musicians with an occasional deity. One of the

Añjanēśvara pillars has a Naṭēśa on one side and the Saptamātṛkās on the encircling sides. These pillars are akin to the Noḷamba inscribed manastambha to Añjanēśvara's north, in that the manastambha has the identical format but is elongated, especially at the sixteen-sided portion. The Śatrughnēśvara temple has related, yet simplified pillars; the complete shafts are octagonal with a square base.[81]

The Bharatēśvara mukhamaṇḍapa ceiling has Aṣṭadikpāla panels with an Umāsahita central panel that includes a small Gaṇeśa. The panels appear better sculpted than the Lakṣmaṇēśvara panels, though this might be due to better preservation. The Añjanēśvara mukhamaṇḍapa has a central lotus medallion encompassed by eight smaller lotuses. The size of the Añjanēśvara mukhamaṇḍapa was reduced when the thirteenth-century Pārvatī temple was constructed. The front Añjanēśvara pillars, originally free-standing, are embedded into the front wall. The Pārvatī temple east side wall is about a meter in front of the Añjanēśvara temple. For whatever reason, the selected site of the Pārvatī temple required the builders to restructure the Añjanēśvara.

The Noḷamba inscription, dating *c.* 980, on the Bharatēśvara temple probably is the construction time of the Bharatēśvara and Añjanēśvara temples. These are the last Noḷamba temples in eastern Noḷambavāḍi. As attested by the many Cōḷa epigraphs on the Bharatēśvara temple, this area, especially the present-day Kolar district area, became colonized by Cōḷa forces.[82] The interior pillars, though definitely associated with the Noḷambas—the maṇastambha is Noḷamba inscribed—are more accurately considered a popular regional pillar type, rather than an idiosyncrasy of a dynastic idiom. Similarly shaped pillars are built into the Gaṅga associated temples at Begur (Bangalore district) and a variant form is found in the Noḷamba associated temples at Dharmapuri (Dharmapuri district, Tamil Nadu).

THE MUTYĀLAMMA DEVĪ

Now at the Bangalore Museum, but originally enshrined in a small sanctum in the Rāmēśvara compound by the Śeṣatīrtha and Giṇḍitīrtha tanks,[83] is an impressive Devī sculpture (H: 130 cm) (pl. 67). The tanks are probably the two tanks that Tribhuvanakarata had built.[84] Judging by the style, the Devī sculpture is coeval with the Lakṣmaṇēśvara temple.[85] Holding a ḍamaru (UR), a triśūla (UL), abhaya-mudrā (LR) and a kapāla (LL), she sits in the same position as the Devī on the east wall, south karṇa of the Lakṣmaṇēśvara, that is, in lalitāsana with her pendant right foot on a defeated asura. The asura is male, and if he is Mahiṣāsura, which would identify the image as Durgā, there is no sign of his bovine nature. Devī has a śavakuṇḍala (corpse earring) dangling from her ear, a muṇḍa (skull) with nāgas at the summit of her jvalitaśikhā ('flaming hair'), a muṇḍa-yajñopavīta (sacred thread composed of skulls) and a sarpābharaṇa (snake breastband). In spite of her horrific presentation, her youthful body and face are pleasant and she displays abhaya-mudrā. According to H. Krishna Sastri, she was locally called Mutyālamma, 'the pearl-like mother'.[86] This image might be an example of a local deity given the shape of a pan-Indian goddess and, hence, elevated into an expanded context.[87] Her local tutelary function is maintained, yet she has the appearance of the paramount Goddess and is therefore the Purāṇic Devī who conquers all opponents.

About twenty km from Avani, another vital Devī centre during the tenth-eleventh centuries and later, is in Kolar (Kolar district capital) at the Kōlāramma temple. The temple received extensive Cōḷa-associated patronage, and the temple epigraphs suggest the process of a local goddess assimilated into the Purāṇic Devī.[88] In 1033 a Cōḷa general Uttamaśōḷa Brahmamārāyan had the formerly brick temple of 'Piḍāri' rebuilt in stone.[89] The grants suggest that worship to 'Piḍāriyar of Kuvaḷālam' (Kolar) 'in Nigarilisōḷamaṇḍalam, alias Nuḷamba-pāḍi'[90] was popular prior to the Cōḷa area control. Piḍāri is Tamil for (village) goddess similar to the Sanskrit gramādēvatā. Krishna Sastri describes Piḍāri 'as a seated goddess with fire issuing from her whole body to indicate her great wrath. . . . Piḍāri is said to be the chastiser of all evil spirits because those who hang or poison themselves, or die any violent death, are turned into malignant demons who would destroy [the] human race if not kept in check by Piḍāri.'[91] Piḍāri is a local, or 'folk', guardian, yet Kōlāramma was patronize by outsiders (Cōḷas—who probably hoped to pacify her). She is considered Cāmuṇḍā and surrounded by Purāṇic deities. The Kōlāramma inscriptions give detailed information regarding the temple finances, wages and functions of temple employees, even food allotments to the deities. One epigraph reads: 'To each of the deities—Vīrabhadra, Brahmāṇī, Īśvarī, Kaumārī, Vaiṣṇavī, Vārāhī, Indrāṇī, Śrī-Camuṇḍēśvarī, Gaṇapati, Camuṇḍēśvarī of Mūlasthāna, Yōgēśvarī, Kṣētrapāla-dēva, Mahā-śāsta and Sūrya-dēva—4 naḷi of rice, 2 dishes of curry, 2 areca-nuts and 4 betel-leaves for each offering'.[92] The epigraph continues to describe the amount of cloth and other necessities required, including the 'intoxicating drink required for Yoginī-Yogēśvara-pūjai' and the required meat (amount of sheep).[93] In spite of this non-Brāhmanical means of worship, orthodox Brahmān employees included one Ṛgvēdī, a Sāmavēdī, a Yajurvēdī and others.[94]

The Kōlāramma image is a large (app. H: 120 cm), fierce, eight-armed Cāmuṇḍā housed in a temple with smaller Saptamātṛkās, including Vīrabhadra.[95] She is a local Devī and simultaneously she is the Purāṇic Goddess. The actual Kōlāramma image probably dates to the Noḷamba period, prior to Cōḷa occupation of 'Nuḷambapāḍi'.[96] Regardless, Kōlāramma should be recognized as a locally produced and revered Devī from the tenth or early eleventh century. She represents a local goddess elevated is status—a function she currently maintains.

Like Kōlāramma, the Mutyālamma image from Avani probably functioned in a similar, though perhaps humbler, manner. Mutyālamma is contemporary with the Lakṣmaṇēśvara temple. Devī imagery is stressed on the temple because of the Goddess's ferocity. Yet, the Goddess protects and aids her devotees.

NOTES

1. *EC*, 10: CB 29, *c.* 750 is the earliest Jain record. The hill was called Nanda (pleasure) prior to the eleventh century.
2. *MAR*, 1914, pp. 35-7; 39-41 = *EC*, 17: CB 66, 106.
3. This is the opinion of Dr. K.V. Ramesh, Director (retired) of Epigraphy, ASI, in personal conversation, Nov. 1986. *MAR*, 1914 recognized mistakes ('The grant is rendered unintelligible in some portions owing to the omission of letters and the occurrence of a large number of orthographical and grammatical errors'.—p. 40), yet did not declare the plates spurious. The 'unique' Gaṅga genealogy was considered possibly a '. . . collateral branch of the Gaṅgas not hitherto known' (p. 37).
4. Dr. K.V. Ramesh concurs with this suggestion.
5. *MAR*, 1914, p. 42 = *EC*, 10: CB 26 = *EC*, 17: CB 26 (rev)= my appendix one.
6. *EC*, 10: Kl 79 and Bp 64; *EC*, 9: Ht 9.
7. *EC*, 10: CB 26.
8. I am grateful to Dr. K.V. Ramesh, who agreed to have a new rubbing of the epigraph made and supplied me with a transliteration and translation. The information, exactly as I received it, is included as appendix one.
9. Tamil (Cōḷa) inscriptions in Nandi pavilion facing the Bhōgaṇandīśvara temple, *ARE*, 1911, nos. 180-1.
10. Information regarding expansions see *MAR*, 1914, pp. 12-15, and *MAR*, 1932, pp. 71-5.
11. *MAR*, 1914, p. 15.
12. *EITA*, 2: 208-10.
13. Krishna Murthy, *Noḷambas*, pp. 179-81. The temple descriptions are essentially the same as in *MAR*, 1932.
14. Krishna Sastri in *ARE*, 1910, p. 62 does not discuss the temples but compares the Mallikārjuna complex at Dharmapuri with the Bhōgaṇandīśvara temple as coeval (late ninth century) Noḷamba monuments.
15. The Bhōgaṇandīśvara temple has been mentioned, because of its beauty, in passing by many. For instance, D. Barrett, *Hemavati*, p. 3, 'There the Bhoganadisvara [*sic*] shrine, which with the neighbouring Arunachalēśvara forms perhaps the loveliest group in the old Mysore State, gives a good idea of the beauty of a Noḷamba temple when clean and complete'. The most lengthy, though incomplete, descriptions are in *MAR*, 1914, pp. 12-15 and *MAR*, 1932, pp. 65-71. *MAR*, 1940, pl. 23 gives the Bhōgaṇandīśvara compound groundplan as it stands today (my fig. 10).
16. Soundara Rajan, *Indian*, pp. 144-5. De Lippe, *Mediaeval*, pp. 182-3.
17. Illustrated in *EITA*, 2: pl. 621.
18. *EITA*, 2: 209. A few other hāra figures are mentioned but the entire scheme is not identified.
19. M.A. Dhaky, 'Bhūtas and Bhūtanāyakas: Elementals and Their Captains', in *Discourses on Siva*, ed. by M. Meister (Philadelphia: University of Pennsylvania Press, 1984), p. 253.
20. Ibid., p. 253, pls. 217-19.
21. Ibid., pp. 243-5.
22. *EITA*, 2: 209, suggests the identification to be Ratī-Manmatha or Umā-Mahēśvara.
23. *EITA*, 2: 209, calls the image Bhairava. Kaṅkālamūrti and Bhairava are essentially the same. When Śiva-Bhairava killed Viṣṇu's doorkeeper, Visvaksena, he placed the skeleton on his triśūla (kaṅkāladaṇḍa) and performed penance. Kaṅkālamūrti without clothes is Bhikṣāṭana.
24. Sivaramamurti, *Nataraja*, p. 225 and fig. 76.
25. Ibid.
26. Gian Filippi, *Some Iconographic Aspects of Siva as 'King of Dances' In Early Cōḷa Art* (New Delhi: Star Pub., 1972), p. 13.
27. Because the sculptures are carved in a different stone than the actual temple, Soundara Rajan, *Indian Temple Styles*, p. 145, thought the sculptures were later dated replacements. *EITA*, 2: 210, (written by Soundara Rajan) says the vṛṣa (Nandi) images are original. All the sculptures are coeval with the temple in my opinion. The more pliable black stone was chosen to give the sculptors flexibility and to accentuate the elevated iconographic import of the placement.
28. All four images are wrongly identified as Śiva by *MAR*, 1932, p. 69. This mistake is repeated by Krishna Murthy, *Noḷambas*, p. 180.
29. For illustration see *EITA*, 2: pl. 622.
30. *MAR*, 1932, p. 66 dates the temple to *c.* 800, because they identify this temple with the one mentioned in the spurious plates dated 810 (and they date the Aruṇācalēśvara from late ninth century). With the

plates in consideration, Soundara Rajan, *Indian*, pp. 144-5 dates the Bhōgaṇandīśvara and Aruṇācalēśvara to '*c.* 800 A.D. and after'; and Krishna Murthy, *Noḷambas*, p. 180 dates them (early?) ninth century. Although *EITA*, does not discuss dating in the text, they label a photo of the Bhōgaṇandīśvara (pl. 620) and one of the Aruṇācalēśvara (pl. 623) both as 860-900. Krishna Sastry in *ARE*, 1910, p. 62 calls the Bhōgaṇandīśvara a late ninth century temple, as does De Lippe, *Mediaeval*, pp. 182-3 (and the Aruṇācalēśvara as an early tenth century temple).

31. For temple description, *EITA*, 1: 133-5. The temple, once considered a Cōḷa monument, has been reassigned to the Muttaraiyars by Soundara Rajan, 'Early Pāṇḍya, Muttaraiyar and Irrukuvēḷ Architecture', in *Studies of Indian Temple Architecture*, ed. by Pramod Chandra (New Delhi: AIIS, 1975), p. 284; and his *Indian Temple Styles*, pp. 111-12. Also M.A. Dhaky, 'Cōḷa Sculpture', in *Chhavi* (Banaras: Bharat Kala Bhavan, 1971), pp. 272-3, and followed in *EITA*. There is not a consensus on the attribution of this temple and related monuments. A 1981 dissertation, G. Hoekveld-Meijer, *Koyils in the Cōḷamandalam* (Amsterdam: Vrije Universiteit ti Amsterdam, 1981) pp. 280-1 calls the Narttamalai temple 'Pallava' *c.* 860-70, and refutes most of Soundara Rajan's points, pp. 48-58.
32. De Lippe, *Mediaeval*, p. 183, and *EITA*, 2: 210 also note similarities between the Bhavanasi Sangam and Nandi monuments.
33. For description: *EITA*, 2: 130-4, which gives a second quarter of ninth century date, and B. Rajendra Prasad, 'Rāṣṭrakūṭa Temples at Bhavanasi Sangam', *Artibus Asiae* 34 (1972): 211-16, who gives a early ninth century date. It is temples such as these which gives credence to the advocacy of regional names of styles, rather than dynastic.
34. Krishna Murthy, *Noḷambas*, p. 181.
35. *EITA*, 2: 210. Soundara Rajan, *Indian Temple Styles*, p. 145, noted briefly the Bhōgaṇandīśvara temple but ignores Aruṇācalēśvara.
36. *MAR*, 1932, pp. 70-1. The report does not specify when the śikhara images were added.
37. *EITA*, 2: 210, inexcusably states that 'images on the superstructure of the vimāna are made of *brick and mortar* and are perhaps later additions'. (emphasis mine)
38. See *EITA*, 2: pl. 624.
39. *MAR*, 1914, p. 15, reports that possibly the sculptor's name 'Keśava' is written, unfortunately, the complete inscription is not given.
40. Presumably another three heads are implicitly present in the back of the head, identifying this Karttikeya in his Sanmukha form.
41. See Bhōgaṇandīśvara section for iconographic identification.
42. Compare pl. 53 south Aruṇācalēśvara vimāna to pl. 46 south Bhōgaṇandīśvara vimāna; pls. 54 and 47 west vimāna of both temples, and pls. 55 and 48 north vimānas.
43. *MAR*, 1932, p. 71, considers the Aruṇācalēśvara images 'less handsome'.
44. The antarāla pillars also are closely related.
45. Vijayanagara royal patronage is not implied. Though their participation is a possibility, no concrete evidence (epigraph) is available.
46. Huntington, *The Art of Ancient India*, p. 581, fig. 23.10. 'Another common pillar decoration is a forward-facing squatting lion (Fig. 23.10), which is seen virtually without variation on pillars throughout the Vijayanagar territories'. This form is known as 'Kunda-siṁham'.
47. Ibid. Also see Rajasekhara, *Masterpieces of Vijayanagara Art* (Bombay: Taraporvala, 1983), pls. 15, 27. This type of lion is delineated on the adhiṣṭhāna and bhūtamālā of the Umāmahēśvara shrine.
48. For example, compare the west śālā Yogamūrti images (pl. 54 to pl. 47): more peripheral figures surround the Aruṇācalēśvara Yogamurti and his clothing, crown and attributes are obviously more manneristic.
49. *MAR*, 1932, p. 71 agrees.
50. *MAR*, 1930, pp. 10-13.
51. There is some confusion concerning the proper appellation of the temple built opposite the Lakṣmaṇēśvara. *MAR*, 1935, p. 51, and the *Mysore State Gazetteer, Kolar District*, p. 77, identifies the temple as the Śatrughnēśvara, as did a temple attendant during my visit in 1986. However, the temple in question has many Tamil (Cōḷa) inscriptions which *EC*, 10: Mb 47 through 49c records are on the Bharatēśvara shrine. Also the village chairman, Naguraja Sastry, during my 1987 visit called the temple Bharatēśvara, and this study will follow his usage.
52. *EC*, 10: Mb 59.
53. *EC*, 10: Mb 38. Other important Noḷamba epigraphs include: *EC*, 10: Mb 43, 50, 51; *EC*, 17: Mb 293 and 294 (all temple inscriptions); and less important (vīrakaḷs, etc.) records: *EC*, 10: Mb 65, 91, 93, 94, 264; *MAR*, 1923, p. 54 nos. 33, 34, and *MAR*, 1927, p. 90 no. 96.
54. I discuss this temple and illustrate all of the exterior images in my 'The King and the Goddess: The Noḷamba Period Lakṣmaṇēśvara Temple at Avani', *Artibus Asiae* 52 (1992): 7-24. This temple was briefly reported in *MAR*, 1935, pp. 50-1 and the information supplied in the account repeated by Krishna Murthy, *Noḷambas*, pp. 172-5, and *EITA*, 2: 210. Soundara Rajan, *Indian Temple Styles*, pp. 143-4, supplies a mostly inaccurate description: he dates the temple from the mid-ninth century, at the time of Mahēndrādhirāja, for no apparent reason other than he was a great king. And wrongly claims that 'tāṇḍava Śiva' is the centre mukhamaṇḍapa ceiling panel (when, in fact, it is Umāsahita).
55. *EC*, 10: Mb 43. The image is described below.
56. *EC*, 17: Mb 293 and 294.
57. *EC*, 10: Mb 65.
58. *EC*, 10: Mb 65 and 67.
59. The Aruṇācalēśvara vimāna has projections similar to the Lakṣmaṇēśvara which are not dēvakōṣṭhas. Some have female attendants (harbingers for the

evolved attendant/Devīs on the Lakṣmaṇēśvara ?) and there are jāla-vātāyanas in the mukhamaṇḍapa and antarāla.

60. See *EITA*, 2: pl. 626 for illustration of the mukhamaṇḍapa and antarāla pillars.
61. D. Barrett, *Early Cōḷa Bronzes* (Bombay: Bhulabhai Memorial Institute, 1965), p. 40; G. Schwindler, 'The Dating of South Indian Metal Sculpture', Ph.D dissertation, University of California, Los Angeles, 1975, pp. 102-3. Schwindler acknowledges that the Lakṣmaṇēśvara temple is 'Noḷamba' (although he misdates the temple to *c.* 895-900, p. 48). He believes the Kuram bronze could have been made in Avani, modelled on the Lakṣmaṇēśvara Naṭēśa prototype, and transported to Kuram (less than a hundred miles away) by the artisan workshop operating within that region (which implies, accurately, workshops are not bound by political borders) p. 103; fn 6, p. 220.
62. *EITA*, 2: 210 wrongly identifies the image as Sūrya.
63. The *Śiva Purāṇa* varies in date between individual *Khaṇḍas.* Different sections discuss Pāśupata views and Dasgupta considers the Vāyavīyasāṁhitā completely Pāśupata, S. Dasgupta, *A History of Indian Philosophy* (Cambridge University Press, 1962) p. 97.
64. *SP*, 2.2.32-7; 7.1.19-23. For a lengthy list of sources for the Dakṣa sacrifice see: Wendy O'Flaherty, *Hindu Myths*, (Middlesex: Penguin Books, 1975) p. 324.
65. *SP*, 2.5.33-40.
66. *SP*, 2.5.20.52.
67. *SP*, 2.5.45-6. In the *Vamāna Purāṇa* the Śaktīs are other forms of Parvati.
68. *SP*, 7.1.25. *SP*, 5.46-8 gives a variant version in which the Goddess is created from the combined force (light) of the gods. It is in this form that the famous Devīmāhātmyam of the *Mārkaṇḍeya Purāṇa* reveres the Goddess. But, the Goddess and her many manifestations are considered intrinsically part of Pārvatī in Pāśupata Saiva context which is different from the Devīmāhātmyam goddess tradition.
69. Stella Kramrisch, *The Presence of Siva* (Princeton: Princeton University Press, 1981), p. 332. See my Siddēśvara temple discussion regarding Bhairava/Vīrabhadra.
70. There was a tradition in the south in which warriors offered parts of their flesh, even their own heads, in exchange for protection by the Goddess: 'This kind of vow was taken by the warrior class when they desired victory for their king in battles or even in their cattle raiding expeditions and hunts. The goddess is believed to have gone always in front of them assuring protection and victory.' K.R. Srinivasan, *Some Aspects of Religion as Revealed by Early Monuments and Literature of the South* (Madras: University of Madras, 1960), p. 30: cf., R. Nagaswamy, *Tantric Cult of South India,* (Delhi: Agam Kala Prakashan, 1982), pp. 6-7 and passim.
71. Possibly the temple was composed to aid Vīra Noḷamba during his fierce campaign into bordering Gaṅgavāḍi against his former ally Gaṅga Rācamalla III.
72. *EC* 17 Mb 294.
73. During the early years of Cōḷa ascendancy, when Vijayālaya captured Tanjore (*c.* 850), he celebrated by dedicating a temple to Niśumbhasūdinī (Durgā) Also, Noḷamba Mangaḷa, the first recorded Noḷamba king, is remembered for his victories and dedication to Caṇḍikā (*EC*, 12: Si 28).
74. *EC*, 10: Mb 65.
75. *EI*, 39: 14.
76. *EI*, 39: 13-16; *ARE*, 1972-3, nos. 277-8.
77. *EC*, 12: Si 28. This epigraph records the grant in Hemavati to Cilluka-bhaṭāra, the reincarnation of Lakulīśa, indicating that the Pāśupatas, possibly the Kālāmukhas, received Noḷamba royal patronage.
78. Disregarding the inscriptions, *MAR*, 1935, p. 50 gives a ninth century date for the temple, as does Soundara Rajan, *Indian*, p. 143. Krishna Murthy, *Noḷambas*, p. 174 notes the Tribhuvanakarata epigraph (but not the Vīra Noḷamba one) and dates the temple to the tenth century. *EITA*, does not discuss the date in the text, but pl. 625 labels the temple as 919-40—a correct terminus date.
79. *EC*, 10: Mb 50. Epigraph dates *c.* 980, see history section for information regarding Dīvāmbikā.
80. *EC*, 10: Mb 38 repeats that Dīvāmbikā had the Noḷamba-Nārāyaṇēśvara temple built, which was dedicated to Mahēśvara.
81. The Śatrughnēśvara has no other noteworthy features (walls are plain). On its adhiṣṭhāna there is a Noḷamba epigraph dating from Iṛiva's reign, *c.* 940-67 (*EC*, 10: Mb 51). According to *EC*,10: Mb 263, there is a Gaṅga adhiṣṭhāna inscription which they tentatively date '? about 400 A.D'. Certainly this date cannot be associated with the temple and its construction.
82. See Stein, *Peasant State*, pp. 191-6.
83. *MAR*, 1935, p. 53; pl. 18, no. 2.
84. *EC*, 10: Mb 65. Inscription is located next to the Giṇḍitīrtha, also where the Devī shrine was located.
85. Next to the Giṇḍitīrtha an epigraph, *EC*, 10: Mb 76, dating to *c.* 920 states 'Mahendra-bhaṭṭa made for Kali-yuga Rudra the smaller temple'. If this record refers to the Devī shrine, it dates the image coeval with the Lakṣmaṇēśvara temple and heightens the shrines importance by its association with Tribhuvanakarata (i.e. Kali-yuga Rudra).
86. H. Krishna Sastri, *South-Indian Images of Gods and Goddesses* (New Delhi: Asian Educational Services, 1986 reprint), p. 224, pl. 138. First published in 1916.
87. For examples of this in Tamil Nadu see, David Shulman, *Tamil Temple Myths* (Princeton: Princeton University Press, 1980).
88. *EC* 10: Kl 106a to 112g.
89. *EC*, 10 Kl: 109a. Earlier Cōḷa temple epigraphs which refer to 'Piḍāriyār of Kuvaḷālam' start at 1006 (Kl 106b).
90. *EC*, 10: Kl 106a.

91. Krishna Sastri, *South-Indian Images*, p. 224, who quotes *SII*, 2: 41 (intro.).
92. *EC*, 10: Kl 108. The Cāmuṇḍēśvari of the Mūlasthāna is Kōlāramma and, presumably, the 'Pīḍari' for whom the temple was rebuilt in stone.
93. Ibid. The Yoginīs and Yogēśvaras were actual people, there were four of each mentioned in the list of employees during 1071 (*EC*, 10: Kl 106d). Also Kanyāpūja, virgin worship, is mentioned and the clothing, jewels, required by the virgin (Kl 108).
94. *EC*, 10: Kl 108.
95. Kōlāramma is published in *MAR*, 1935, pl. 18, no. 3.
96. The epigraphs indicate that the 'Pīḍari' brick temple was popular before the Cōḷa expansion. During my visit to the Kōlāramma temple in 1987, Kōlāramma was extensively dressed and ornamented. Judging from the exposed portions of the image and from the published photograph in *MAR*, 1935, a tenth or early eleventh century dating seems likely.

CHAPTER FIVE

Southern Noḷambavāḍi Monuments

INTRODUCTION

The Mallikārjuna temple complex is in the old 'fort' section of Dharmapuri, Dharmapuri district (Tamil Nadu), known in medieval inscriptions as Tagaḍūru, or Tagaḍanāḍu. The larger, more important temple of the complex now enshrines Kāmākṣi; hence it is called the Kāmākṣamma temple, though this does not seem to be its original deity or name. The smaller Mallikārjuna temple has a number of alterations and expansions; however, the original shrine and the Kāmākṣamma temple are morphologically related, the Kāmākṣamma the antecedent. For convenience, the two temples are collectively called the Mallikārjuna complex.

Noḷamba Mahēndrādhirāja, 'the destroyer of the Mahābali [Bāṇa] race (Mahābalikulavisvaṁśa)',[1] seized the northern portion (i.e. Tagaḍūru and vicinity) of the traditional region of Koṅgu country, formally Bāṇa territory, in *c.* 878[2] and the Noḷambas controlled the territory until *c.* 940.[3] Arokiaswami, following the conventional historiographic assumption that dominating, major dynasties had centralized control over vast regions, acknowledges Bāṇa and Noḷamba settlements in the Koṅgu country, but considers their presence as weakly ineffective, and he concludes that the region was ripe for conquest and unification by the powerful Cōḷas in the late ninth century—hence, he is dismissive of any meaningful contributions by the Noḷambas.[4] More recently, an article by Murton studies north Koṅgu according to Stein's 'segmentary state' model with emphasis on the agrarian system and its complex relationship with other groups of peoples.[5] Murton argues that until the late ninth century the region was used primarily by pastoralists and shifting cultivators, with sacred places/temples and tribal settlements, or warrior-agriculturalist settlements, as local centres.[6] During the tenth to thirteenth centuries the region was settled by a new influx of Brahmins, peasants and merchants who, with local leaders, established a complicated balance of self-rule.[7] According to Murton's and Stein's model, the 'segmentary state' is an intricate balance of rule in which local leaders, including Brahmins and peasants, cooperate among themselves and with royalty. The king serves as patron and mostly symbolic suzerain. In this role, royalty upholds their traditional hierarchic function of protector and provider. Hence, temple patronage is a vital duty. The Noḷambas had longstanding, legitimate roots in other portions of Noḷambavāḍi, but in southern Noḷambavāḍi their presence was intrusive. In order to fit harmoniously into the north Koṅgu (southern Noḷambavāḍi) balance of power, already locally intact, I suggest Mahēndra and succeeding Noḷamba kings might have had strong motivations to announce their presence in a traditionally acceptable manner. For example, Mahēndra established Mahēndramaṅgalam, now a village called Adhamankottai near Dharmapuri,[8] and, as the suffix maṅgalam suggests, this was a centre supported by royalty (Mahēndra) for the emerging agrarian-Brahman alliance.[9] Presumably the Mallikārjuna complex is another Noḷamba sponsored monument which ensconced their royal role within the regional dialectics.

The most notable discussion regarding Noḷamba settlement in the Dharmapuri area is written by Krishna Sastri.[10] Focusing on two Noḷamba inscriptions—both of which pronounce kingly patronage to Jain temples—one from the reign of Mahēndra, the other from the succeeding reign of Ayyapa, Krishna Sastri incorporates other epigraphs into his study in order to demonstrate the Noḷamba expulsion of the Bāṇas in Dharmapuri and their own settlement in Dharmapuri and greater Noḷambavāḍi in general. Although the Mallikārjuna complex was not seriously considered, he did state that the 'unique architecture [of the Mallikārjuna complex] is undoubtedly to be attributed to the Noḷambas of the 9th century A.D.'.[11]

The Mallikārjuna complex received limited attention in the *Encyclopaedia of Indian Temple Architecture.* Soundara Rajan described, in turgid terms, some of the temple features and assigned the complex to the second quarter of the ninth century or a little later, during the Bāṇa period—the sole surviving Bāṇa monument.[12] The temples are without dedicatory inscriptions to aid our understanding of their origin. Pillars with epigraphs declaring Noḷamba temple patronage were found built into the Mallikārjuna temple and other pillars lying in the vicinity state the same. *No* Bāṇa temple inscriptions are found in the area. The temples' 'unique architecture'—to use Krishna Sastri's words—does confuse matters; however, some features shared in the Mallikārjuna complex and in eastern Noḷambavāḍi temples (Nandi and Avani), which geographically are not too distant, suggest that the Kāmākṣamma and the Mallikārjuna temples were built during the Noḷamba period. No scholar has suggested that the temples are posterior to the Noḷamba period; the question remains if the monuments were constructed between *c.* 878, the year of Mahēndra's ascendancy in the area, and *c.* 940—after which Noḷamba presence in southern Noḷambavāḍi is minimal—or constructed earlier. The question of whether the monument is 'Bāṇa' or 'Noḷamba' is not the primary issue. It is more meaningful to situate the monument in its proper context, demonstrating its shared characteristics with other temples, in this case with temples in eastern Noḷambavāḍi (and Gaṅgavāḍi), and to acknowledge the local traditions and their affinity with the lower Drāviḍadēśa culture. In reference to the local tradition, it should be noted that prior to the ninth-century Tagaḍūru (Dharmapuri) was the centre of the Atiya (Adiyanman or Adigaman) chieftains—an example of Murton's 'warrior-agriculturalists' of pre-tenth century—who patronized the little-known yet exquisite eighth century Vaiṣṇava cave temples at Namakkal.[13]

The Mallikārjuna complex received mention by Krishna Murthy who considers the monument to be of the Noḷamba period.[14] Sanford is also of the opinion that the temples are Noḷamba, built in the late ninth to early tenth centuries. In his study on early Cōḷa *Rāmāyaṇa* reliefs, he discusses for comparative purposes the Kāmākṣamma *Rāmāyaṇa* cycle, though not in detail, as an example of reliefs outside of Cōḷanāḍu proper.[15] A rudimentary listing of the panels, occasionally inaccurate, is supplied and Sanford indicates that the frieze format on the upapīṭha is closer to the Cālukya tradition, perpetuated in the art of the Noḷambas, than to the Cōḷa tradition.[16] I will first discuss the Kāmākṣamma temple at some length, then summarize the relevant features of the Mallikārjuna temple.

THE KĀMĀKṢAMMA TEMPLE

The Kāmākṣamma temple consists of a mukhamaṇḍapa, an antarāla and a garbhagṛha, and is oriented towards the east (fig. 12).[17] The temple is constructed on an upapīṭha which has panels depicting the *Rāmāyaṇa*. Superbly rendered couchant elephants 'support' the monument at the temple corners and projected bhadra sides. Alternating mouldings form the bhadra, pratikarṇa, and karṇa adhiṣṭhāna (fig. 13).[18] The bhadra lowest moulding is curved like an inverted lotus with some foliage-motif reliefs, whereas the pratikarṇa has a plain jagatī, and the karṇa has an inverted lotus moulding carved with lotus leaves. Next, the bhadra has a kumuda decorated with a kalpavalli having frolicking gaṇas in the meandering swirls. The pratikarṇa and karṇa kumuda is bordered at the top and bottom with lotus leaves and the karṇa has additional central ridges. The bhadra and pratikarṇa kaṇṭha have interspersed vyāḷis, the karṇa does not. Next the karṇa has a kapōta surmounted by vyāḷis, the bhadra and pratikarṇa are plain except they have makaras at the sides, and all are topped by a thin paṭṭika. A vedī moulding cuts across the walls a small distance above the adhiṣṭhāna.

The wall projection-recession format is similar to the Lakṣmaṇēśvara temple at Avani; however, the Kāmākṣamma recesses which divide the bhadra, pratikarṇa, and karṇa sections are much deeper than on eastern Noḷambavāḍi temples.[19] The karṇas and pratikarṇas have flanking brahmakānta (rectangular) engaged pilasters. The pratikarṇa pilasters support a pañjara (vaulted apsidal shrine) motif, making the section a 'pañjarakōṣṭha'. The Aruṇācalēśvara temple at Nandi has small pañjarakōṣṭhas within the vimāna pratikarṇa sections, while at the Kāmākṣamma temple the pañjarakōṣṭhas encompass the complete pratikarṇa section. Emphatically presented, the bhadras are wide and project the furthest. Viṣṇukānta (octagonal) engaged pilasters flank the bhadras and inner rectangular pilasters border slender niches which are without images. They are not dēvakōṣṭhas. The mukhamaṇḍapa and antarāla bhadras have plain pierced windows, though perhaps more typical Noḷamba-type jāla-vātāyanas once were in place. The bhadras and karṇas are surmounted by a kapōta with rafters, rather than a bhūtamālā, underneath it. The superstructure is decorated with modern stucco figures and the complete tower appears to be a later addition.

The *Rāmāyaṇa* panels are a set of continuous friezes, unbroken by moulding sections except for thin vertical scene dividers, carved around the complete temple upapīṭha.[20] The narration does not begin at the front of the temple but starts on the west (back) wall, to the south of the bhadra, and the friezes proceed in apradakṣiṇā (counter-clockwise) order. However, the north and north-west vimāna panels do not seem to relate to the *Rāmāyaṇa*; instead they depict non-specific court scenes, mostly music and dancing.[21] The following is a list of episodes starting at the beginning of the narration (west wall, south). Numbers correspond to panels in sequential order, letters divide the frieze events into the order in which they appear.

1. a. male (guardian?).
   b. Daśaratha's three wives: Kauśalyā, Sumitrā, Kaikeyī (latter one is around the corner on panel 2).
2. a. Daśaratha in discussion with a minister (decides to perform a horse sacrifice in order to have progeny).
   b. Ṛṣi Ṛśyaśṛṅga (to perform and protect the sacrifice).
   c. Daśaratha's sacrifice: Ṛśyaśṛṅga pours ghee into the fire and out of the sacrifice, Agni appears and presents pāyasam to Daśaratha (which will impregnate his wives).
   d. Daśaratha distributes pāyasam to wives, attendants in witness.

3.a.b.c. Pregnant wives sit with attendants present.
d.e.f. Reclining wives nurse their new-born sons: d. Kaikeyī with Bharata; e. Kauśalyā with Rāma (most attendants present here); f. Sumitrā with twins, Lakṣmaṇa and Śatrughna.
   g. Two youths (Rāma and Lakṣmaṇa) led by maid to school.
   h. Rāma and Lakṣmaṇa tutored by a seated teacher.
   i. Rāma instructed in archery.

4. a. More archery instructions for Rāma.
   b. Male (Rāma?) stands holding a bow.

5.a.b.c. Viśvāmitra ask Daśaratha for Rāma's assistance: a. Rāma and Lakṣmaṇa standing; b. Daśaratha seated with minister (? or youth=Rāma?) beside him; c. Viśvāmitra standing (request that Rāma be allowed to come with him and protect his sacrifice).
   d. Viśvāmitra, Rāma and Lakṣmaṇa depart.
e.f.g. Bharata and Śatrughna comfort Daśaratha: e. Female attendant fans (Daśaratha in f.); f. Daśaratha sitting flanked by Bharata and Śatrughna; g. Daśaratha standing supported by Bharata and Śatrughna.

6. a. Lakṣmaṇa and Rāma led by Viśvāmitra.
   b. Standing female (represents crossing of river Gaṅga and worship to her?)

7.a.b.c. Rāma defeats Tāṭaka: a. Viśvāmitra and Lakṣmaṇa behind Rāma; b. Rāma shoots arrow at charging Tāṭaka; c. Fallen Tāṭaka is defeated; to her side, an unidentified dancing figure (=celebration of Tāṭaka's death?).
   d. Viśvāmitra blesses Rāma, by pouring water on Rāma's hands, Lakṣmaṇa to side.
   e. Lakṣmaṇa, Viśvāmitra and Rāma standing, followed by a male with drawn bow (=Rāma protecting Viśvāmitra's sacrifice?).
   f. Same three with smaller male walking (to Mithilā).

8. (Abraded) Same figures as 7f(?) and drummer.

9. (Some of the panels, especially this one, have lower portions buried) a. Two ṛṣis greet Viśvāmitra, Lakṣmaṇa and Rāma.
   b. In Mithilā, at Janaka's palace, dancers-musicians (?, left) and (right) Sītā in chambers with attendants.
c.d. Rāma-Sītā's wedding: c. Lakṣmaṇa and Rāma stand; d. Lakṣmaṇa beside Rāma, Sītā (marriage) and, probably, Janaka and wife.

10. a. Ṛṣi (or Paraśurāma?) blesses Rāma and Sītā, Lakṣmaṇa to side.
   b. (at Ayodhyā, Daśaratha's palace) Kaikeyī sits alone.
   c. Lakṣmaṇa, Rāma and Sītā standing.
   d. Kaikeyī talks to hunchback maid Mantharā.
   e. Kaikeyī before Daśaratha (obtaining the two boons previously promised to her; she demands that Rāma is banished for 14 years, and that Bharata is installed to the throne).

11. a. Kaikeyī, seated, tells Rāma of his exile (he is in attitude of acceptance). Figure beside Rāma probably is Lakṣmaṇa who is outraged.
   b. Rāma before grieving Daśaratha.
   c. Lakṣmaṇa, Sītā and Rāma with male in añjalī (probably Sumantra, charioteer, at departure).
   d. Lakṣmaṇa, Sītā and Rāma walking in forest.
   e. Śūrpaṇakhā conversing with (trying to entice) Rāma.
   f. Lakṣmaṇa maims Śūrpaṇakhā (Rāvaṇa's sister).

12. a. Śūrpaṇakhā complains to the rākṣasas Khara and Dūṣaṇa.
   b. Rāma slays Khara and Dūṣaṇa, shown topsy-turvy.
   c. Śurpaṇakhā before seated Rāvaṇa calling for revenge. (Rāvaṇa is not multi-headed).

13. a. Rāvaṇa in counsel, possibly with his brothers Vibhīṣana and Kumbhakarṇa, plus a female (Śūrpaṇakhā or Rāvaṇa's wife, Mandodarī). To the side, Rāvaṇa's puṣpaka vimāna (chariot).
   b. Rāma shoots the golden deer.
   c. Rāma shoots at the deer's true form, the rākṣasa Mārīca.
   d. Rāma and Lakṣmaṇa in discussion (about abduction of Sītā).
   e. Rāma and Lakṣmaṇa walk (in search for Sītā).

14. a. Rāma proves his strength to Sugrīva, Hanumān, and other monkeys by shooting an arrow through seven śāla trees.[22]

b. Rāma and Lakṣmaṇa consult with Sugrīva and monkeys.

15. a. Rāma gives his ring to Hanumān (in order to prove to Sītā that Hanumān is Rāma's messenger).
    b. Hanumān leaps across the ocean to Laṅkā, in route resisting the demonesses Surasā and Singhikā.
    c. Hanumān seated on the Laṅkā fort, surveys the city.
16. a. (After visiting Sītā at Aśokavana) Hanumān is surrounded by, and battling, six rākṣasas.
    b. Sugrīva, Rāma, Lakṣmaṇa, and Hanumān walking.
    c. (pl. 68) Rāma and Lakṣmaṇa watch as the monkeys help Nala build the bridge to Laṅkā.
17. a. With Rāma present, Vibhīṣana (Rāvaṇa's brother who allied himself with Rāma) conversing with Hanumān.
    b. Rāma battles four rākṣasas, one has fallen, two charge, one retreats.
    c. A monkey, probably Aṅgada as Rāma's envoy, before Rāvaṇa who sits in his puṣpaka vimāna, a building—his palace—to the side.
18. a. Hanumān carries Lakṣmaṇa who battles Indrajit (or Rāvaṇa?), two additional rākṣasas to the side.
    b. Hanumān carries unconscious Lakṣmaṇa back to Rāma.
    c. Two figures converse (maybe Susena describing the medicinal herbs available at Mahodaya mountain).
    d. Hanumān carries Mahodaya mountain (?)
    e. Revived Lakṣmaṇa and Rāma standing.
    f. Large rākṣasa, possibly Kumbhakarṇa, battles Rāma; witnessed by Lakṣmaṇa, Hanumān and Vibhīṣana(?).
19. a. Rāvaṇa, the only time depicted multi-armed, with two attendants.
    b. Rāma, Lakṣmaṇa, Hanumān, and Vibhīṣana (?) standing.
    c. Four rākṣasas stand with swords.
20. a. Death of Rāvaṇa(?): a large rākṣasa maimed (part of leg and arm missing) presumably represents defeated Rāvaṇa.
    b. Lakṣmaṇa, Sugrīva, Sītā, and Rāma with Vibhīṣana(?) on knees in añjalī (receiving Rāma's blessing).
    c. Male and female sits on dais (Rāma and Sītā? or coronation of Vibhīṣana?) flanked by attendants and unidentified large figure sits cross-legged to the side.
    d. Maid, carrying a caurī, Sītā, Rāma, Lakṣmaṇa, and two monkeys (Sugrīva and Hanumān?) standing.

Here ends the *Rāmāyaṇa* sequence. The remaining panels depict court scenes (non-specific scenes of Rāma and Sītā enjoying courtly life?): mostly dancers, musicians, and sometimes couples, often embracing, seated together. The last scene on the west bhadra might represent Rāma and Sītā seated together with two males, their sons Kuśa and Lava, to the side reciting the *Rāmāyaṇa*.

Rāmāyaṇa episodes from the first six sections (kāṇḍa)—Bāla, Ayodhyā, Araṇya, Kiṣkindhā, Sundara, and Yuddha kāṇḍas—are delineated on the friezes, but the final seventh Uttara kāṇḍa (in Vālmīki's version) is not. Although the narration appears closely allied to Vālmīki's *Rāmāyaṇa*, Sanford, in reference to all the *Rāmāyaṇa* cycles he studied, concludes that a multiplicity of literary sources existed and suggests that court plays/epics might have been the most important source for the renditions.[23] Kingship ideals were personified by the perfect hero-king Rāma: temple *Rāmāyaṇa* panels, I suggest, might have been intended to heighten the king's (patron's) identification with Rāma, also to liken his accomplishments to those of Rāma.[24]

Due to the considerable height of the upapīṭha and adhiṣṭhāna, the temple entrance is almost two meters above ground level, approached by modern stairs. The doorway has an inner padmaśākhā and an outer śākhā with dancers and musicians, mostly females. Above the door, heavily whitewashed, is Gajalakṣmī flanked by auspicious signs (aṣṭamaṅgalas). Gajalakṣmī and aṣṭamaṅgalas are also present on top of the otherwise plain garbhagṛha doorway.

Interior

The interior eight free-standing pillars, four in each the mukhamaṇḍapa and the antarāla, are a variation, or combination, of two pillar types built within other Noḷambavāḍi temples. The shaft is mostly octagonal, including the cushion capital, with a lower square section. This is comparable to the pillars at Avani (Bharatēśvara, Añjanēśvara, the maṇastambha, and Śatrughnēśvara) and in the adjacent Mallikārjuna temple, though the Kāmākṣamma pillars have an additional square portion two-thirds up the shaft with relief carvings of deities or some Purāṇic/epic scenes, resembling the typical Noḷamba period citrakhaṇḍa pillars.[25] Central Noḷambavāḍi citrakhaṇḍa pillars have lions carved above the main square sculpted (caturasra) portions; here the lions surmount the lower square section.[26] The octagonal shaft between the two square sections is decorated with vertical kalpavallis which have mostly frolicking gaṇas or dancers and musicians within the swirls.

The following listing is an identification of scenes delineated on the square carved portions of the mukhamaṇḍapa pillars (1 and 2) and the antarāla pillars (3 and 4):

South 1, east face. Śiva seated and a male with wild, flared hair, who appears to be fleeing from Śiva.

South face. A kneeling male, possibly Arjuna (Kirātārjunīyam is on the next pillar), worshipping a liṅga.

West face. Seated Śiva and beside him a male in añjalī.

North face. Naṭēśa holding a huge triśūla (other hands empty) dances accompanied by a drummer.

South 2, east face. Kirātārjunīyam: A kirāta (Śiva, identified by the dog below him) and Arjuna face each other with drawn bows, a boar in between them.

South face. Vāli, with bound Rāvaṇa (without extra heads or arms), worshipping a liṅga.

West face. Arjuna kneels before seated Śiva.

North face. Seated Gaṇeśa flanked by jackfruits.

South 3, east face (pl. 69). Seated Āliṅgamūrti (Śiva embracing Pārvatī), female attendant to the side.

South face. Gajāsurasaṁhāramūrti: Śiva's ugra dance holding Gajāsura's hide and Pārvatī absconding with Kārttikeya.

West face. Jñana-Dakṣiṇāmūrti teaching two ṛṣis under a banyan tree.

North face. Bhikṣāṭanamūrti attended by a gaṇa with a bowl on his head, receives alms from a woman.

South 4, east face. Gajendramokṣa (this and a Kṛṣṇa are the only Vaiṣṇava-associated pillar reliefs).

South face. (Unidentified, pillar face is too close to south wall to properly view.)

West face. Female dancer and male drummer.

North face. Seated Umāsahita.

North 1, east face. Naṭēśa dancing within a large meandering lotus swirl.

South face. Bhikṣāṭanamūrti (like south 3, north face, but by different sculptor).

West face. Yoga-Dakṣiṇāmūrti with two students.

North face (pl. 70). Kālaharamūrti (Śiva as the conqueror of time/death): Śiva kicks the fallen Yama; above him, Mārkaṇḍeya embraces a liṅga.

North 2, east face. Gajāsurasaṁhāramūrti (similar to south 3, south face).

South face. Kālī on dais with left pendant foot on defeated āsura and emaciated female attendant/ yoginī dancing to the side.

West face. Valī and Sugrīva fighting.

North face. Rāvaṇānugrahamūrti: Śiva and Pārvatī seated together. A small figure below Śiva might be Rāvaṇa caught under the mountain, and the larger, fleeing figure Rāvaṇa liberated.

North 3, east face. Female dancer and male drummer.

South face. Unfinished.

West face. Navanīta-nartana Kṛṣṇa: Kṛṣṇa dancing with a pot of butter balanced on his arm.

North face. Mahiṣāsuramardinī.

North 4, east face. Gajāsurasaṁhāramūrti (more exuberant than previous examples).

South face. Female dancer and male drummer.

West face. Somaskanda.

North face. Umāsahita.

Though Kāmākṣī is enshrined in the garbhagṛha, the temple's original dedication to Śiva is suggested by the overwhelming Śaiva pillar iconography. Pārvatī (i.e. Kāmākṣī) does play a substantial role in the reliefs: four times Śiva and Pārvatī sit together—Umāsahita twice, Aliṅgaṇamūrti once, and Somāskanda once—and in a subsidiary position Pārvatī is present four further times. The most repeated image is Śiva in a destructive form: Gajāsurasaṁharamūrti three times, and once as Kālaharamūrti. Additionally, Śiva grants grace (to Arjuna and Rāvaṇa), bestows knowledge (Dakṣiṇāmūrti twice), appears as an naked ascetic (Bhikṣāṭana twice), the supreme dancer (Naṭēśa twice) and in a few miscellaneous roles. Viṣṇu's presence is subordinate, he saves the elephant king (Gajendramokṣa) and dances as Kṛṣṇa. This negligible inclusion of Vaiṣṇava iconography substantiates my suggestion that the exterior

Rāmāyaṇa friezes are an affirmation of kingship identification, ideals and role, rather than a religious proclamation.

The mukhamaṇḍapa's coffered ceiling (pl. 71) has a central Umāsahita with Nandi panel circumscribed by panels of the Aṣṭadikpālas in their proper directional realms. Small lotus medallions are on the corners and middles of the beams dividing the panels. Aesthetically, the panels are comparable to those at Avani (Lakṣmaṇēśvara and Bharatēśvara temples) and Nandi (Bhōgaṇandīśvara temple), though the style is not completely analogous. The carving, though adequate, is not of superior quality. For the most part this also is true for the pillar and *Rāmāyaṇa* reliefs. Although many images are lively and graceful (e.g. Āliṅganamūrti, Yoga-Dakṣiṇāmūrti, etc., some *Rāmāyaṇa* scenes), the quality of workmanship fluctuates. This is not the case in the adjacent Mallikārjuna temple. The Mallikārjuna might be architecturally simple, but the interior ceiling panels and pillars are testimony to the artisans' cultivated skills.

THE MALLIKĀRJUNA TEMPLE

The Mallikārjuna temple has mukhamaṇḍapa ceiling panels with Naṭēśa in the centre and lateral Aṣṭadikpālas (pl. 72).[27] The reliefs in the Mallikārjuna are generally more refined than the Kāmākṣamma images. There is not a style disjunction: the temples are closely related temporally and stylistically. However, for whatever reason—perhaps the sculptors fine-tuned their skills first on the Kāmākṣamma temple—the Mallikārjuna temple images are more engaging. The ceiling panels and pillars are lightly painted, a reminder how the works were intended to be viewed. The central panel Naṭēśa has his right leg raised, knee bent, in ūrdhvajānu pose, the left foot is on Apasmāra. In his four right hands Śiva has gajahasta (across the chest, main R), ḍamaru (UR), triśūla (mid R), and abhaya (LR); in his left hands, gajahasta (extended upwards, main L), agni (UL), nāga (mid L), LL uncertain. Gaṇa musicians, a drummer and cymbals player, accompany Śiva. There is a spirited elegance conveyed in the well-proportioned body and dance movement. The exuberant ornateness of the Aralaguppe, Kallēśvara temple, Naṭēśa is not present; nevertheless, the Mallikārjuna figure is gracefully dignified, as are the surrounding Aṣṭadikpālas. A comparison of the dikpālas and their vāhanas to their counterparts at the Kāmākṣamma reveal the more comfortable control the sculptors had in defining the body forms at Mallikārjuna. Also the lotus medallions on the beams dividing the panels are more developed, and supplementary lotus petals encompass the panels' inner borders at the Mallikārjuna temple.

Aesthetically, the most extraordinary sculpture at Dharmapuri is the antarāla ceiling panel (pl. 73). A large, single panel has a central female dancer, flanked by a female playing the cymbals, and a male drummer. They are encircled by a lotus stalk and peripheral lotus flowers. The outer beams have lotus designs and small dancers at the centres. The figures exude understated refinement through their finely-proportioned youthful bodies and postures. The unpretentious relief is a harmonious blend of decorative (lotus motifs) and content.

The four free-standing mukhamaṇḍapa pillars retain the shaft octagonal and lower square format as at Kāmākṣamma, except the upper square shaft position is rejected.[28] Though the Mallikārjuna pillar shape is basic, its presentation is spectacular. The complete shaft is finely sculpted: the lower square sections have deities or narratives with the ubiquitous lions above the panels, while the octagonal portions have figural images in vertical bands which invariably are topped by a row of musicians and dancers bordered by jewels spewed from small kīrttimukhas, and surmounted by a row of vidyādharas. The cushion (ghaṭa) capitals and the apex pōṭikā capitals have decorative lotus designs. The octagonal shafts usually have on the main axes (N-S, E-W) scenes within small blocks built one upon another, and on the other four sides the pillars have dancers within kalpavalli swirls, with one exception (south-east pillar). The iconography has anomalies; a number of scenes not readily identifiable might have been inspired by a contemporaneous local tradition which is no longer popular. To demonstrate the pillar composition and, at times, peculiar themes, the south-east pillar is described in its entirety, followed by a briefer description of the remaining pillars.

On the lower panel of the south-east pillar, east side, standing Viṣṇu and Brahmā flank Śiva who sits on a padmapīṭha, with an asura and a nāga below. The vertical band in the octagonal section directly above the panel has three blocks with a male seated in each and an upper scene with a guru teaching a student. Moving clockwise, the corner vertical band has at the bottom a lion, as do all the corners. Seated upon the lion is a goddess, Dūrgā, holding Viṣṇu's typical attributes, a cakra and a śaṅkha in her upper hands. Above her is a male sitting upon a flying male (lacking identifying attributes, it is not necessarily Viṣṇu on Garuḍa).

The south side's lower panel is divided into two registers: in the upper register two males in a forest (trees shown), one maybe an ascetic (has flared hair), presumably are watching the activity in the lower register which has a reclining female attended by three maids, one of whom appears to be pouring water from a pot onto the dominant woman. The vertical band has, lower block to upper, an embracing couple, a female, a male, a ṛṣi. Generally the vertical bands do not seem to interconnect directly with the panels, and if here the band contributes clues to the panel activity, it remains unclear. If the relief is a self-contained narrative, one that a tenth-century observer would recognize, that, too, cannot be determined. The corner band has a male holding a sword sitting on the corner lion, and above, a male seated on a flying male.

West side, lower panel, has a male riding an elephant. In the vertical band: a male with a sword in its sleeve, talking to a female who is in añjalī; a guru teaching a student; a solitary male with a sword in his sleeve. The corner vertical band has in one block a female standing with her arm extended over a large triśūla placed upright. Above the triśūla is a male falling head first. Perhaps this represents a self-sacrifice. The upper block has a solitary seated male.

The north panel (pl. 74) repeats the format of the south panel (possibly the stories are related): the upper panel register has a female seated on a dais with many females seated to one side, and a male, with sword in sleeve, standing before the dominant woman. Lower register has three standing females (gender of one unclear) to the left, and to the right in another setting, a male (with sword) worshipping a liṅga. The vertical band has a seated embracing couple with a female attendant aside touching the main female, an embracing couple, a female seated beside a lamp, and in the top block, a male with a dog and a flying vidyādhara. The final vertical corner band has an embracing couple, a female seated on a flying male, a male standing beside a building.

The south-west pillar, east side, has Kālahāramūrti in the lower panel, and in the upper band, a seated Ardhanārīśvara followed by dancers. On the south panel, Sūrya is flanked by a male (with sword in sleeve) and a female, both in añjalī. The upper band has a male (in añjalī) on a horse, Lakṣmī, Viṣṇu, and Brahmā. The west panel has a novel representation of Caṇḍeśānugrahamūrti: both displaying vismaya-mudrā (wonderment), Pārvatī and Śiva are seated on a dais, and the latter presents a wreath to Vicāraśarman (Caṇḍēśa) seated below. The male in the background probably is Yajñadatta whose leg was chopped off by his son Vicāraśarman for disturbing a sand liṅga. In the upper band a male worships a liṅga, Gaṇeśa, Śiva, and Aiyaṇār(?). North panel (pl. 75) has a female attended by a maid, offering alms to Bhikṣāṭana with a gaṇa. In the band above is a seated Bhairava instructing a ṛṣi and, occupying most of the band, a beautiful rendition of Liṅgodbhavamūrti.

The north-east pillar is the most problematic: each panel depicts an unrecognized narrative. The east panel has in two registers: two figures on an elephant approaching a seated (ascetic?) male in the upper section, below, two males holding staffs with double-prong tips before a seated, bearded ṛṣi. The band above has a drummer, a man on a horse, two males wrestling, two males conversing. The south panel has females attending a royal female and a chubby male. The upper band might be related: a female presents a boy to a guru; the guru talks to the boy; both standing, the guru instructs the boy in wrestling(?); the guru is seated (knocked-down?) and the boy has arm raised (victoriously?). West panel has a standing male (sword in sleeve) and beside him three males—or one male in motion—falling topsy-turvy. In the upper band there is a ṛṣi conversing with a male, a small male beside a benign goddess, a larger male beside a ugra goddess/Kālī, and a male beside a liṅga. East panel, upper register, has a reclining couple and to the side, a gandharva(?) (allusion to a passionate 'gandharva wedding'?); the lower register has two males playing the conch and a male before a seated male (ascetic?). The band has two males talking, a couple conversing, a male with a nāga, and another male.

The final north-west pillar has on the east panel an exuberant Naṭēśa with gaṇa musicians. The upper band has Somāskanda, Vṛṣabhāntika (Śiva standing with Nandi), Viṣṇu, and a standing Ardhanārīśvara. The south panel has Bhikṣāṭana, this time accompanied by Nandi instead on a gaṇa. The band has Dakṣiṇāmūrti with a ṛṣi, and three representations of seated Śiva. West panel shows Gajāsurā-saṁharamūrti. The band has Gaṇeśa and assorted seated Śivas. The north panel has a liṅga flanked by two males. One male, with sword in sleeve, possibly represents the king/patron of the temple, and the other male a minister (pl. 76).[29] Upper band has forms of seated Śiva and a Naṭēśa.

Śaiva iconography dominates the Mallikārjuna pillars, as also is the case in the Kāmākṣamma temple. A more incongruous scheme is present at the Mallikārjuna due to the aberrant narratives. In the Arkēśvara temple at Hale-Alur (Mysore district)—which is a shrine mostly rebuilt—there are eight free-standing pillars, four in the Nandi pavilion and four in the mukhamaṇḍapa, which have cylindrical shafts and lower square portions all completely sculpted with images divided into horizontal bands. Mostly scenes from the *Mahābhārata* are delineated on the Nandi pavilion pillars. Depicted on the mukha-maṇḍapa pillars are many royal scenes, usually court narratives, sometimes military episodes. It has been suggested that the Arkēśvara temple dates from the period of Rajēndra Cōḷa, *c.* 1020, and the pillars chronicle exploits of Rajēndra.[30] An alternative suggestion is that the scenes depict Gaṅga Būtuga II's victorious contributions at the battle of Takkolam, and that the pillars date to *c*. 935-60.[31] Regardless of whose adventures are shown, it does seem likely the royal scenes represent a historical narrative. The resemblances between the Arkēśvara and Mallikārjuna pillars are striking—unusual narratives sculpted on comparably shaped pillars (and the sites are relatively proximate, though the latter antecedes the former)—possibly offering a clue to the purpose of the Mallikārjuna narratives. Yet, although a number of the Mallikārjuna scenes show royal personages, it does not seem likely that the anomalous reliefs can be attributed to historical events, though statements about the concerns of royalty probably are intended, comparable to the *Rāmāyaṇa* frieze on the Kāmākṣamma. Most likely stories and myths with a localized popularity are the topics.[32]

In contrast to the ostentatious mukhamaṇḍapa pillars, the two antarāla free-standing pillars are pleasantly rudimentary: the shafts are cylindrical with lower square sections and a plain cushion capital.[33] Above the unsculpted square panels the ubiquitous lions sit at the corners and in between them usually small dancers are carved. The south pillar, north side has Yoga-Narasiṁha, the north pillar, east side has a man worshipping a liṅga. Like the mukhamaṇḍapa pillars, these have a row of dancers and musicians within jewelled borders emitted from kīrttimukhas three-quarters up the shafts. The doorways duplicate the Kāmākṣamma doors: Gajalakṣmī flanked by Aṣṭamaṅgalas are on the garbhagṛha and mukhamaṇḍapa entrance lintels, the latter has an inner kalpavalli śākhā and an outer row of dancers and musicians. Enshrined in the garbhagṛha is a liṅga.

Conclusion

Morphologically the Mallikārjuna complex has parallels with temples in eastern Noḷambavāḍi (at Nandi and Avani) and Gaṅgavāḍi (at Begur, Narasmangala, and limitedly Hale-Alur), which is not surprising considering that the macroregions border Koṅgu country, and, at intermittent times prior to the Cōḷas, both the Gaṅgas and the Noḷambas had territorial control over portions of Koṅgu country. The projection-recession wall articulation at the south shrine at Begur, the Rāmaliṅgēśvara temple at Narasmangala, and to a lesser extent, the Lakṣmaṇēśvara temple at Avani, and the Bhōgaṇandīśvara and the Aruṇācalēśvara temples at Nandi resemble the Mallikārjuna complex. The Lakṣmaṇēśvara and Bharatēśvara temples at Avani, Bhōgaṇandīśvara temple at Nandi, the south shrine at Begur, and the Kāmākṣamma temple all have mukhamaṇḍapa ceiling panels with central Umāsahita and lateral Aṣṭadikpālas (Mallikārjuna has a central Naṭēśa),[34] and they all have related, slightly variant, pillars. The Mallikārjuna complex antecedes the others, except the temples at Nandi which might be contemporary.

Contact between the regions, exchange of ideas (religious and artistic) and goods are obvious reasons for the shared architectural (sculptural and iconographic) traits. A pillar found in the Mallikārjuna complex was donated during the time of Noḷamba Mahēndra by Bhairava-bhaṭāra of Nandi,[35] testimony to the religious (Śaiva, the name might suggest Kālāmukha affiliation) flow between Nandi and Dharmapuri. Another epigraph mentions a Śaiva teacher Vidderāśi which Krishna Sastri suggests might be a Kālāmukha preceptor from Madurai known through an inscription at Kodumbalur.[36] Part of the Tamil-speaking culture, Tagaḍūru (Dharmapuri) had steady contact with its southern neighbours and, as the last inscription suggests, especially with Pāṇḍināḍu, the region of the Pāṇḍyas which also had intermittent control in parts of Koṅgu country. The Caṇḍēśānugrahamūrti and Kālāharamūrti images are especially popular in lower Drāviḍadēśa,[37] and their presence at the Mallikārjuna complex is indicative of the cultural identification.

During the last quarter of the ninth century through the first four decades of the tenth century Tagaḍūru (Dharmapuri) was within the southern parameters of greater Noḷambavāḍi. Mahēndrādhirāja, after ousting the Bāṇas from the area, established a Noḷamba presence and fulfilled the obligatory kingship role of temple patron. Epigraphs in Dharmapuri attest to Mahēndra's (and his successors') patronage of the Jains and the Śaivas.[38] The Kāmākṣamma was patronized by a king intent on declaring his identification with kingship ideals and accomplishments, hence the *Rāmāyaṇa* friezes on the upapīṭha. It is possible that Mahēndra, the Mahābalikulavisvaṁśa, the destroyer of the Bāṇas, and of the Cōras, whose '. . . lotus feet [were] resplendent from crowns on the heads of feudatories rolling on the ground before him, . . '.[39] was responsible for the Kāmākṣamma temple construction in the late ninth century.[40] Probably during the first third of the tenth century one of Mahēndra's successors was responsible for the Mallikārjuna temple. The Noḷamba period Kāmākṣamma and Mallikārjuna temples have idiosyncrasies of a local tradition—one that has affinity with the lower Drāviḍadēśa culture—and some shared characteristics with eastern Noḷambavāḍi monuments. The temples are a southern expression in the greater Noḷambavāḍi artistic repertoire.

NOTES

1. Mahābalikulavisvaṁśa is an epithet employed by Mahēndra, *EI*, 10: 65, 68. See history section concerning Noḷamba-Bāṇa hostilities.
2. *EI*, 10: 63. Bāṇa territory was referred to as Pulināḍu or Perumbāṇavāḍi.
3. Last dated Noḷamba record from Dharmapuri district, in Harur taluk, is dated the fifteenth regnal year (938-9 CE) of Vīra-Noḷamba (Aṇṇiga), *EI*, 39: 15.
4. A. Arokiaswami, *Kongu Country* (Madras: Madras University, 1956) pp. 172-3.
5. Brian Murton, 'The Evolution of the Settlement in Northern Kongu to 1800 A.D.', in *Perspectives on a Regional Culture*, ed. by Brenda Beck (New Delhi: Vikas Pub., 1979), pp. 1-33. Also see M. Kitti, 'Gaṅgas, Noḷambas and Bāṇas in Kongu Country', in *Srinidhi*, ed. by K.V. Raman, *et al.* (Madras: New Era Pub., 1983), pp. 329-32 for a more traditional study, yet one that acknowledges Noḷamba (Gaṅga and Bāṇa) contributions in Koṅgu country.
6. Murton, 'Evolution', p. 9.
7. Ibid., pp. 9, 13, 25, 32.
8. *ARE*, 1910, p. 62.
9. Murton, 'Evolution', p. 7, explains that maṅgalams were places founded mostly between the tenth and thirteenth centuries, donated by kings, chiefs, or regional assemblies, to Brahmans for the purpose of promoting Brahmanical culture. Their existence in an area is indicative of established peasant agriculture and a settled way of life.
10. H. Krishna Sastri, 'Two Noḷamba Inscriptions from Dharmapuri of the 9th Century A.D.', *EI*, 10: pp. 54-70. Also his comments in *ARE*, 1901, p. 5; *ARE*, 1910, pp. 61-2.
11. *ARE*, 1910, p. 62.
12. *EITA*, 1: 109.
13. P. R. Srinivasan, 'Sculptures in the two Rock-cut Vaisnava Cave Temples in Namakkal', *Artibus Asiae* 24: 107-16. Vidya Dehejia, *Namakkal Caves* (Tamil Nadu State Dept. of Archaeology, 1977).
14. Krishna Murthy, *Nolambas*, pp. 176-9.
15. David Sanford, 'Early temples bearing Rāmāyaṇa relief cycles in the Chola area' (Ph.D dissertation, University of California, Los Angeles, 1974).
16. Ibid., p. 145; panel listing pp. 105-8.
17. For illustrations, see *EITA*, 1: pls. 89-98.
18. See *EITA*, 1: pls. 91-3.
19. In Gaṅgavāḍi, at Begur (Bangalore district), the southern shrine of the twin temples has a wall format akin to the Kāmākṣamma temple, including similar pañjarakōṣṭhas and wide bhadras with fake dēvakōṣṭhas. Also similar is the Rāmāliṅgēśvara temple vimāna at Narasmangala (Mysore district). For temple descriptions, *EITA*, 2: 200-2.
20. Sanford, 'Early temples', p. 146, states that this is in contrast to the Cōḷa preference for non-continuous panels separated by stretches of plain moulding surface. This is the main reason, he believes, the panels relate closer to the Cālukya rather than the Cōḷa tradition.
21. *EITA*, 1: 109, incorrectly states that *Mahābhārata* scenes as well as *Rāmāyaṇa* are present.
22. Panels 14 and 15 on the front (east) upapīṭha, were covered by rubble during my visit (July 1987). Because I was unable to view the panels myself, the listing for panels 14 and 15 is the result of consultation with the temple priest and Sanford, 'Early temples', p. 107. In between these two panels an additional panel, hidden by stairs, might show Sugrīva fighting and defeating Vāli—the priest was uncertain.
23. Sanford, 'Early temples', p. 250.
24. Ibid., pp. 16-18, 250, 264. A study on south Indian kingship by David Shulman, *The King and the Clown South Indian Myths and Poetry* (Princeton: Princeton Univ. Press, 1985) discusses ideals and dilemmas of kings. For images of royalty in Kamban's *Rāmāyaṇa*, pp. 42-3, 50-7, 63-4, and passim.
25. See *EITA*, 1: pl. 95. The Bharatēśvara, Añjanēśvara temples and maṇastambha at Avani have an extra sixteen-sided band on the shaft, the Śatrughnēśvara does not. Relief figures are carved midway up the octagonal shaft. Akin to the Śatrughnēśvara pillars are ones built into a maṇḍapa extension at the Mallikārjuna temple.
26. At Nandi, the Aruṇācalēśvara temple antarāla pillars have lions similarly placed.
27. The Mallikārjuna exterior has alterations and does not require detailed description. The walls have bhadra and karṇa projections topped by a kapōta as at the Kāmākṣamma; the adhiṣṭhāna is simpler, without decoration, shows jagati, kaṇṭha, paṭṭa, kumuda, and there is an upper vēdī moulding.
28. See *EITA*, 1: pl. 96-7.
29. If this suggestion is correct then the couple flanking Sūrya (south-west pillar, east) which has a similar male (with sword in sleeve) might also be the (Noḷamba) king/patron and wife.
30. *MAR*, 1937, pp. 45-53; *MAR*, 1947-56, pp. 41-2.
31. K.K. Ramamurthy, 'Narrative sculptures from Arkēśvara Temple at Alur', in *Srinidhi*, pp. 187-9. Both of the suggested temple dates are posterior to the Mallikārjuna complex.
32. The unidentified friezes do not seem to represent historical events or stories from the *Periyapurāṇam*, activities associated with the Tamil Śaiva saints.
33. *EITA*, 1: pl. 98.
34. Elsewhere in Noḷambavadi, refined Naṭēśa panels are at Aralaguppe, Pathasivarama, and Hemavati (loose). An awkward central Naṭēśa panel is at Hale-Alur (Gaṅgavāḍi).
35. *ARE*, 1901, no. 306; *EI*, 10: 63.
36. *EI*, 10: 64. The Kannada record is paleographically assigned to the Noḷamba period.
37. Concerning the popularity of the Kālahāramūrti see: David Shulman, 'Notes on the Kālāntaka myth at Tirukkandavur', in *Srinidhi*, pp. 267-74.

38. The only Jain remains are a couple Jainas in the Dharmapuri Museum and a loose standing Paśvanātha in a field at Adhamankottai, a definite Noḷamba period sculpture. (Same period, a loose standing Bhairava is next to the Mariyamma temple, Dharmapuri.)

39. *EC*, 12: Si 24; Si 38 (both from central Noḷambavāḍi); *EI*, 10: 65.

40. Sanford, 'Early temples', p. 173, suggests that Mahēndra erected the Kāmākṣamma and his son, Ayyapa, built the 'more refined' Mallikārjuna temple.

Conclusion

This study offers the first comprehensive documentation of monuments from Noḷambavāḍi constructed during the Noḷamba period, mostly from the ninth and tenth centuries. Because the Noḷambavāḍi 'style' lacks homogeneity, I have not attempted to make generalizations applicable to the whole region. I divide Noḷambavāḍi into three smaller subregions, central Noḷambavāḍi, eastern Noḷambavāḍi, and southern Noḷambavāḍi, which conform roughly to traditional territorial groupings. Central Noḷambavāḍi corresponds approximately to Noḷambaḷige, the earliest locality associated with the Noḷamba dynasty. Eastern Noḷambavāḍi is often called Gaṅgarusāsira (or Gaṅga 6000) in inscriptions. Although this area had historic affiliation with the Gaṅga dynasty, sometime prior to the mid-ninth century they entrusted the vicinity to Noḷamba control, and by the late ninth century the territory was ceded into greater Noḷambavāḍi. Southern Noḷambavāḍi corresponds to north Koṅgu region. In this locality Noḷamba presence was more intrusive: seized *c.* 878, north Koṅgu, especially around Dharmapuri, remained within the Noḷamba realm until about mid-tenth century. Reflecting the political fluidity of eastern and southern Noḷambavāḍi, these subregions had a flux of artistic interactions resulting in amalgamated styles, exhibiting traits shared with neighbouring regions. With a blending of eastern Noḷambavāḍi and Gaṅgavāḍi traits, southern Noḷambavāḍi monuments additionally exhibit an affinity with lower Drāviḍadēśa works, especially with Pāṇḍināḍu. Eastern Noḷambavāḍi monuments share less characteristics with the lower Drāviḍadēśa traditions, and more features with central Noḷambavāḍi, Gaṅgavāḍi, and neighbouring Rāṣṭrakūṭa period monuments. The central Noḷambavāḍi locality also appears to have been subject to regional sharing, yet for whatever reason, possibly because the area was traditionally a secure Noḷamba base, it remained more artistically insulated than the other portions of Noḷambavāḍi, and consequentially developed a more identifiable 'idiom'.

Because the central Noḷambavāḍi 'idiom' is the most recognizable of the Noḷambavāḍi 'style', in Chapter three I supplied a lengthy description of the temples and sculptures in Hemavati and neighbouring Noḷamba period monuments in central Noḷambavāḍi. Hemavati, or Heñjeru as it is called in medieval epigraphs, was a Noḷamba capital. The architectural and sculptural remains are irrefutably representative of the central Noḷambavāḍi idiom. This does not imply, however, that the works are consistently homogeneous. As should be expected, fluctuations in the sculptural style are distinguishable. This is attributable to the diversity of individuals at work and their varying skills. A few manneristic propensities are recognizable none the less. A representative median sculpture appears robust, even slightly hefty, without being overly embellished. There are other sculptures, however, which I have repeatedly called 'mature' examples of the central Noḷambavāḍi refinement, which show a greater concern for harmonized elemental forms. This mature trend blends essential form—the body of a deity, for example—with a balanced supplement of adornments (i.e. jewels, hair styles, etc.), in order to give the sculpture an aesthetic appeal. This description of course is applicable to most 'idioms'; Indian aesthetic ideals require temples and sculptures to be properly decorated. Yet, certain repeated mannerisms characterize this group of central Noḷambavāḍi works which distinguish them from others, including eastern Noḷambavāḍi sculptures. For example, certain facial and body types are repeatedly portrayed. In specific manners jewels and especially hair arrangements duplicate. The repetition of certain decorative elements common on reliefs, such as the kalpavallis, kīrttimukhas, gaṇas, lions, etc., is distinctive. These elements are singled out for mention—others are available—to indicate that idiosyncracies are perceptible.

By detailing idiomatic attributes my look at central Noḷambavāḍi monuments tries to explain the internal manifestation of the style—I acknowledge sharing with other regional styles, but emphasize the localized artisan traditions. We are reminded that people make monuments (not style influencing style) and complex agencies are involved in the process of building and maintenance of temples. This is different from the approach of Sivaramamurti (and other scholars) who identifies elements in order to claim proof of influences from external sources. He assumes that particular motifs or manners are identifiable with certain dynasties (large, better-studied dynasties). I maintain that if various traits and manners commingle, then the resulting products are symptomatic of idiosyncrasies of the locality. This then minimizes the distortion caused by the over emphasis on 'influences' and allows lesser-studied artistic periods to be appreciated for what they are. It also acknowledges that temples are complex monuments in form and function, having a role within regional dialectics.

The problems inherent in a regional artistic discussion are multifarious and many issues remain unresolved. The role of royalty, not only as patron but as sovereign and his functions throughout his realm is a question yet to be fully understood. Also in question is the role of sthāpatis and the various artisans: are they passive agents in their construction of temples and sculpting of deities, responding to demands of a patron (and, again, is the king, as patron, attempting to shape a 'style' reflective of his power?), or are the sthāpatis, who are responsible for the outcome of their work, initiating the temples' appearances. Also, how restricted are artisans to localities, or how freely do they travel according to their own needs? These are issues that require more research and debate by scholars of Indian art. No doubt answers to these issues vary from region to region and over time. In a region where a substantial number of relatively well-preserved monuments survive, and where many epigraphs survive which identify patrons and provide other relevant information, the questions are less open to speculation. But in an area such as Noḷambavāḍi, where inscriptional information concerning temple construction is minimal, and the actual monuments are in varying states of disrepair, with some notable exceptions, the questions are more subject to conjecture. The political climate from region to region, and over time, changes, and generalizations appropriate for Cōḷamaṇḍalam, are not necessarily helpful for Kaliṅga, or Mālavā, for instance. Judging from the proclivity for temple inscriptions during the Cōḷa and Later Cālukya periods, from eleventh century onwards—whereas epigraphs furnishing temple records are less common prior to this time—I suggest caution in assuming inscriptions have a timelessness (i.e. that we can use a Cōḷa inscription, for example, to explain patronage and maintenance of monuments in earlier periods or distant localities). Once other lesser known, contemporaneous periods of art in regions contiguous to Noḷambavāḍi, especially the Gaṅga period, and the Rāṣṭrakūṭa monuments in present-day Karṇataka, and early monuments of the (Later) Cālukya, are better studied and published, the monuments of Noḷambavāḍi and their shared traits with other regional styles might be better understood.

I do not discount the role of the king as patron and as a contributing determinant in regional temple growth. All evidence I have studied from the Noḷamba period indicates that the king, or other allied members of the aristocracy, or elite sacerdocy, were substantial sponsors of temples. A patron gains 'merit', which remains the patron's property transcending time (i.e. the merit is beneficial to future lifetimes). More concretely, however, temples are obvious statements of wealth and power.

'Style', on the other hand, is not restricted exclusively to the dominion of any particular king, because, after all, it is the artisans who compose the temples and sculpt the images. *Rāmāyaṇa* panels, for instance, at the Kāmākṣamma temple in Dharmapuri (southern Noḷambavāḍi), or the exterior wall reliefs of deities on the Lakṣmaṇēśvara temple at Avani (eastern Noḷambavāḍi)—including a portrait of Noḷamba king Aṇṇiga—or the enshrined Bhairava at the Siddēśvara temple, Hemavati (central Noḷambavāḍi), might serve as emphatic kingly statements, yet the manner in which the images are carved is idiomatic of the sculptors.

APPENDIX ONE

Inscription from the Bhōgaṇandīśvara Compound, Nandi

This inscription has been published differently in *Mysore Archaeological Reports,* 1914, p. 42; *Epigraphica Carnatica,* 10: CB 26, and *Epigraphica Carnatica,* 17: CB 26 (rev.). Because of confusion caused by the alternative readings, Dr. K.V. Ramesh, Director of Epigraphy, Archaeological Survey of India, agreed to have a new study of the inscription made. I am including the following new transliteration and summary of the inscription exactly as I received it from Dr. Ramesh.

TRANSLITERATION OF THE TEXT

1. Svasti [|*] samata (dhi)gata-pañcha-
2. mahāśabda Pallav-ānvaya śrī-pṛi-
3. thivī-vallabha Pallava-kulatala(tila)-
4. ka śrīmat Noḷambādhirājar pṛ-
5. thivīrājya[ṁ] geyuttumire śrīma-
6. d-Divyaśakti-paṇḍita[dēva]rike Mayda-gā-
7. muṇḍanu[ṁ] pādamūlamu[ṁ] [pa]nn[e]raḍaṟu-
8. gāmuṇḍa[r]kkaḷum-iḻdu Janyavvāchāriya
9. maga Puḷiyaṇṇa Nandiyāvaraṇada bā-
10. ḷge mūligan-āge po[ṁ]koṭṭu paḍeda sthiti
11. khaṇḍuga-kaḷaniyuḷ-eḷkaṇḍuga[muṁ] To-
12. ṇḍapaṭṭūṟu[ṁ] koḷamuṁ śāśa[sa]namāge ko-
13. ḍaṁge paḍadō[ṁ] [|*] idan-aḻidō[ṁ] Vāraṇāśi(si)
14. yuma kapil[e]yunam-aḻidōr[|*]

TRANSLATION

Be it well. While the illustrious Noḷambādhirāja who had obtained the five great sounds, who was of Pallava descent, who was the favourite of the goddesses of wealth and earth and who was the fore-head mark of the Pallava family, was ruling over the earth, Mayda-gāmuṇḍa, the pādamūla and the twelve gāmuṇḍas having met, made a grant to Divyaśakti-paṇḍitadēva. The grants consisted of seven khaṇḍugas of paddy-field, purchased by payment of gold, for the holdings of the original tenant Puḷiyaṇṇa in Nandiyāvaraṇa, the village Toṇḍapaṭṭūṟu and a tank. The record ends with the imprecatory statement that those who flout the grant would have committed the sin of destroying Vārāṇaṣī and tawny cows.

APPENDIX TWO

Genealogical Chart of the Noḷambas

Trinayana Pallava of the Īśvara vaṁśa

Maṅgaḷa Noḷambādhirāja

Siṁhapōta (Kali Noḷambādhirāja Kolliarasa), *c.* 775-805

Cāruponneṟa (Paramēśvara Pallavādhirāja), *c.* 805-30

Poḷalcōra Noḷambādhirāja (Pallavamalla), *c.* 830-70

Mahēndrādhirāja (Noḷambādhirāja), *c.* 870-95

Ayyapadēva, *c.* 895-923

Aṇṇiga Vīra Noḷamba, *c.* 923-40 | Iṟiva Noḷamba (Diliparasa), *c.* 940-69

Nanni Noḷamba (Chaladaṅkakāṟa), *c.* 969-75

[Poḷalcōra (II), ?-*c.* 975]

Vīra Mahēndra (II), *c.* 975-81

Ekavākyadēva, *c.* 981-1000 | Iṟiva Noḷamba (II) (Gaṭeyaṅkakāṟa), *c.* 1000-18

Jagadēkamalla Noḷamba Pallava Permāṇḍi Udayāditya, *c.* 1018-37

Jagadēkamalla Iramḍi Noḷamba, *c.* 1037-44 | Trailōkyamalla Nanni Noḷamba (II) Pallava Permāṇḍi, *c.* 1044-52

Illustrations

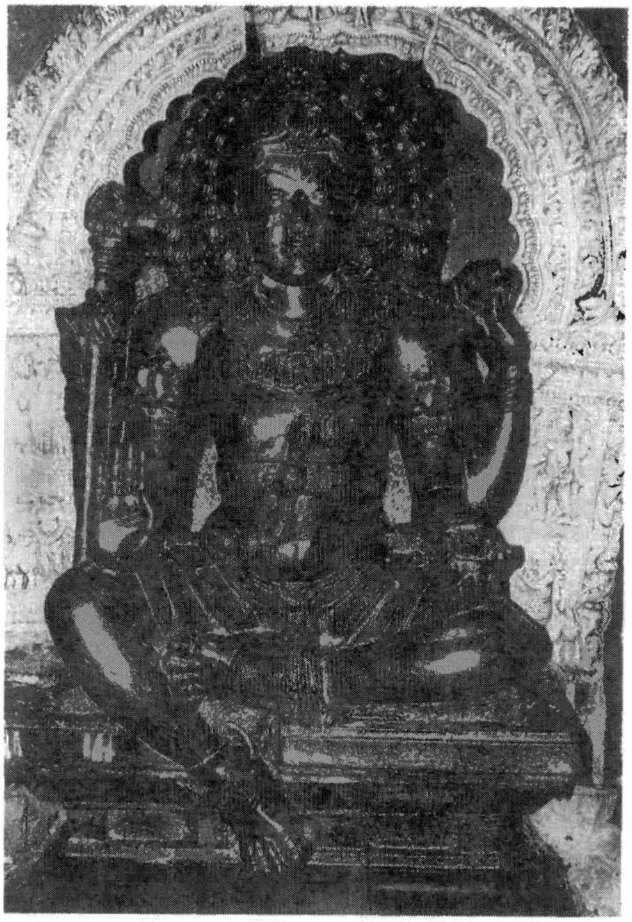

Plate 1. Hemavati, Siddēśvara temple, Bhairava (enshrined).

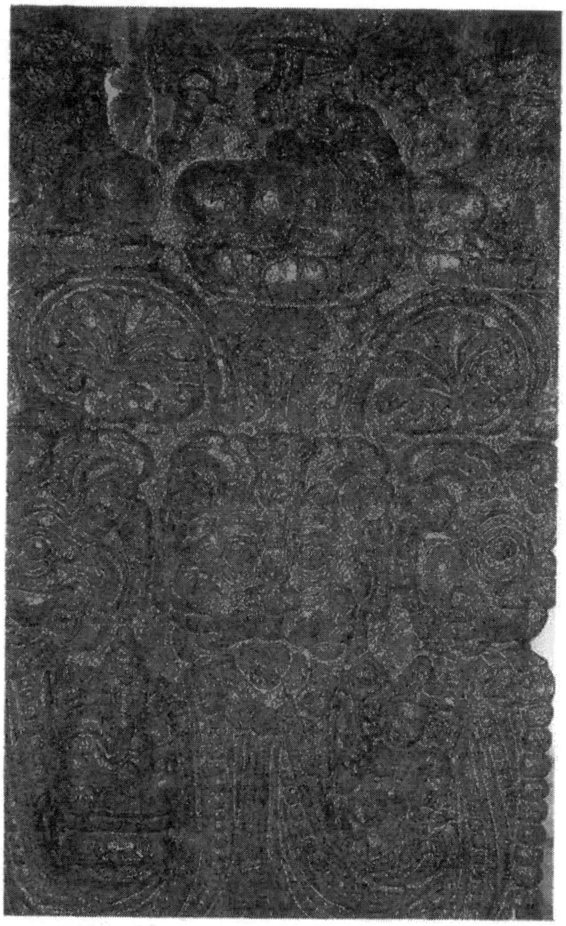

Plate 2. Hemavati, Siddēśvara temple, detail of agra-maṇḍapa pillar.

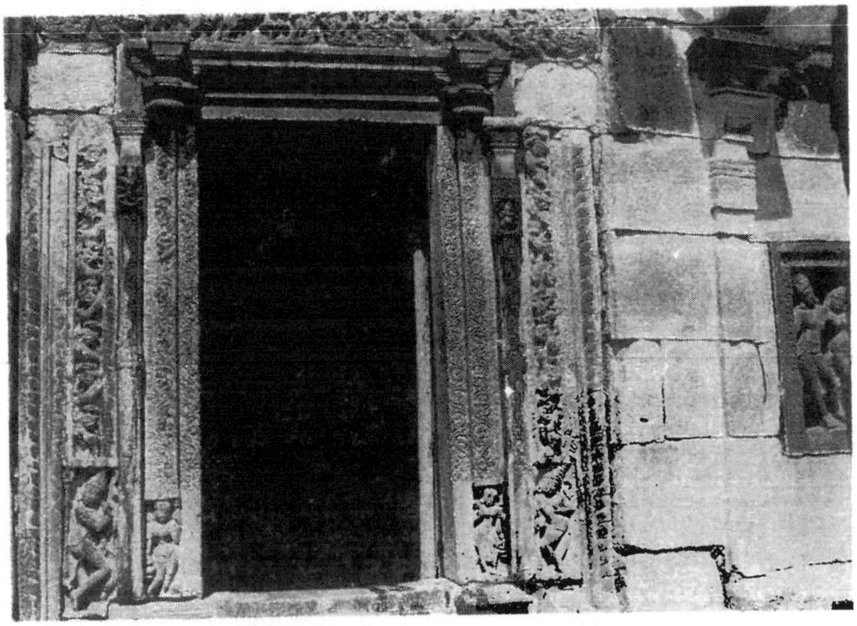

Plate 3. Hemavati, Doḍḍēśvara temple, mukhamaṇḍapa entrance.

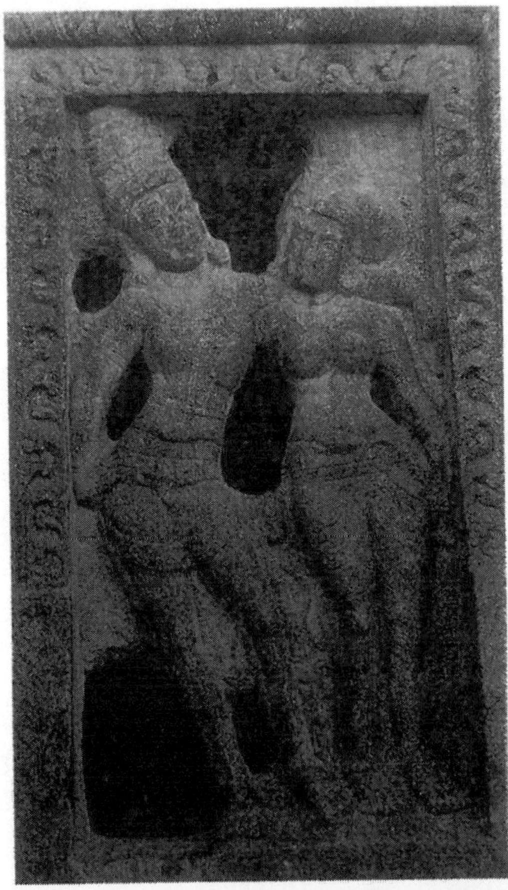

Plate 4. Hemavati, Doḍḍēśvara temple, west wall, possibly Mārayya and wife in window.

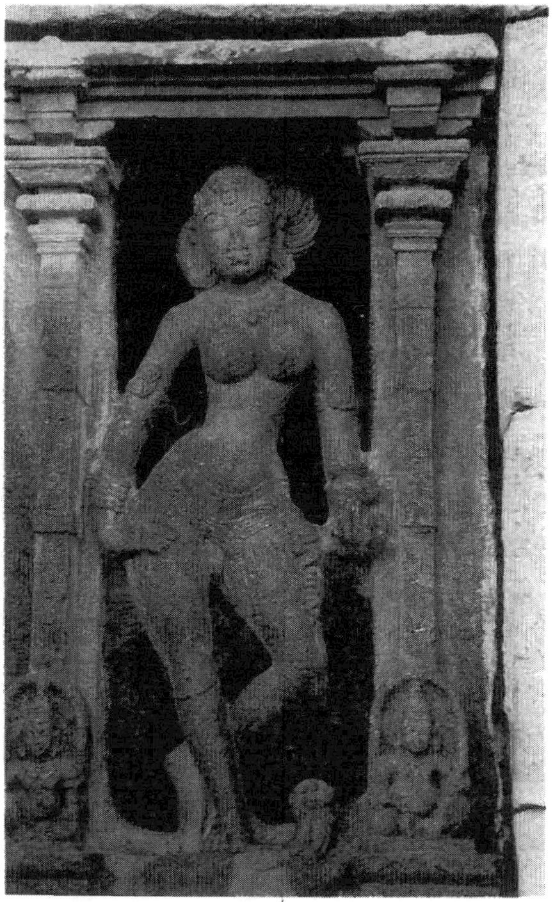

Plate 5. Hemavati, Doḍḍēśvara temple, west wall, Gaṅgā in window.

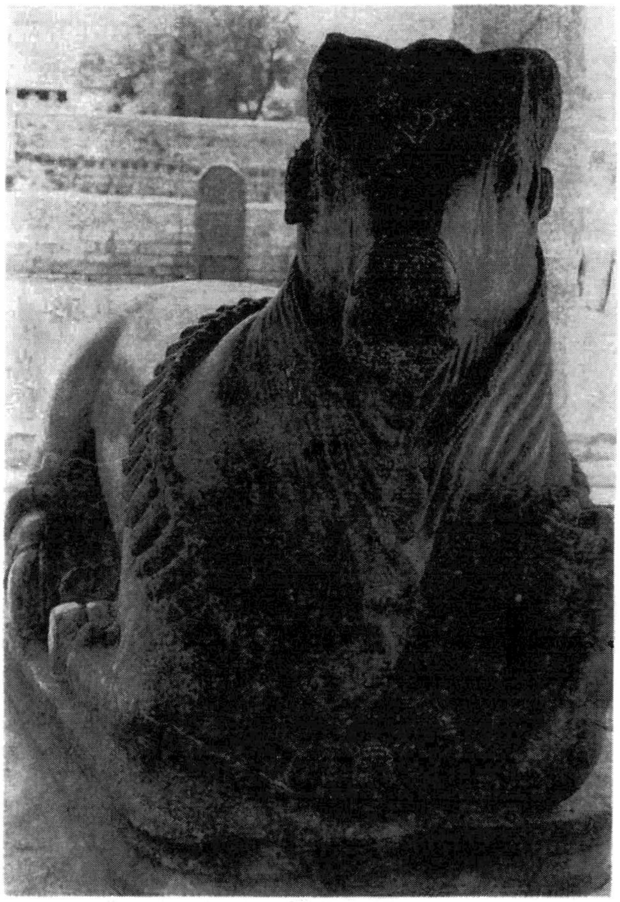

Plate 6. Hemavati, Doḍḍēśvara temple, Nandi.

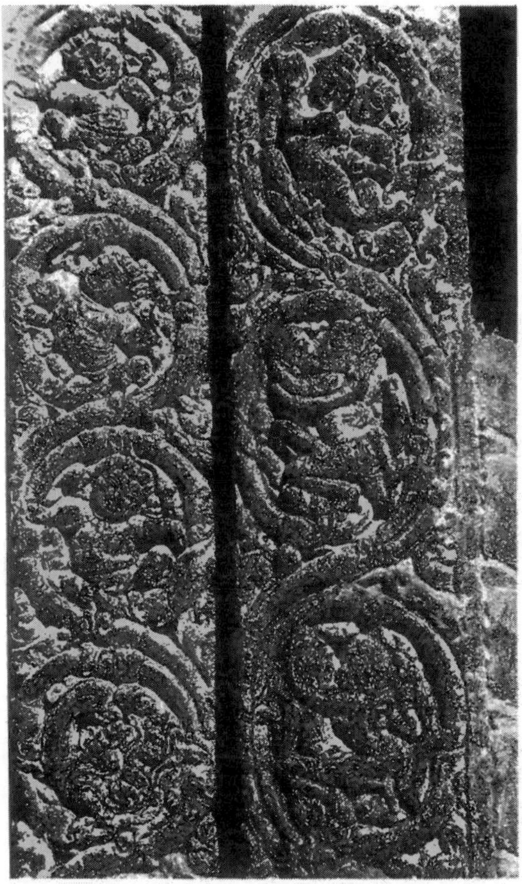

Plate 7. Hemavati, Doḍḍēśvara temple, detail of mukhamaṇḍapa entrance.

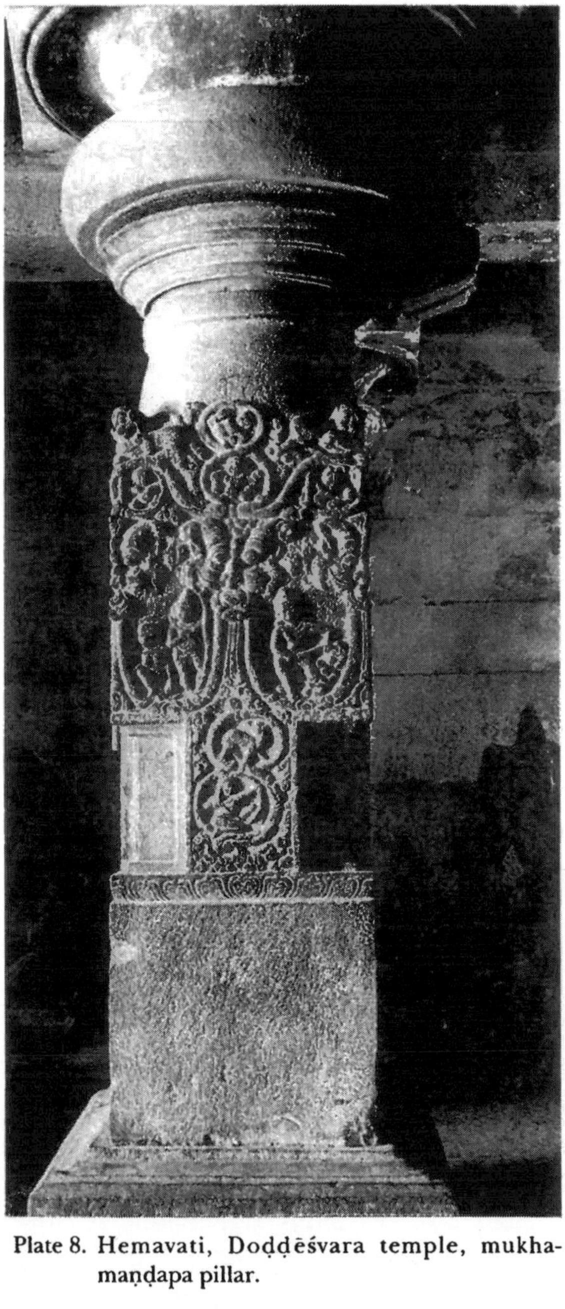

Plate 8. Hemavati, Doḍḍēśvara temple, mukhamaṇḍapa pillar.

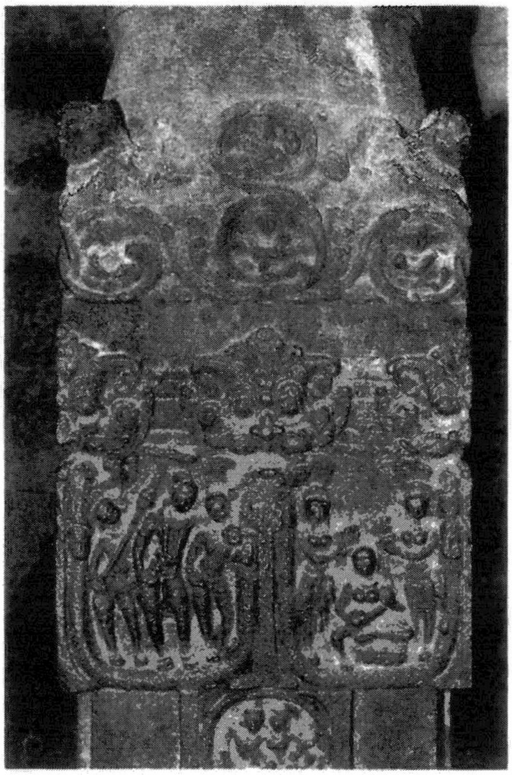

Plate 9. Hemavati, Doḍḍēśvara temple, detail of ardhamaṇḍapa pillar.

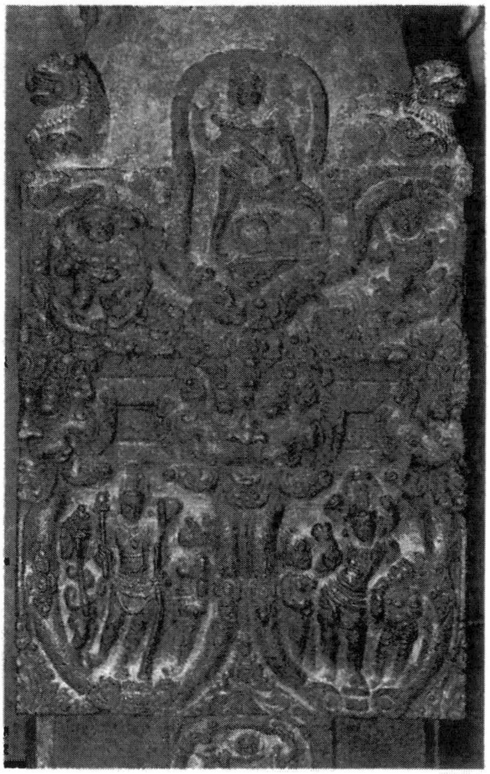

Plate 10. Hemavati, Doḍḍēśvara temple, detail of ardhamaṇḍapa pillar.

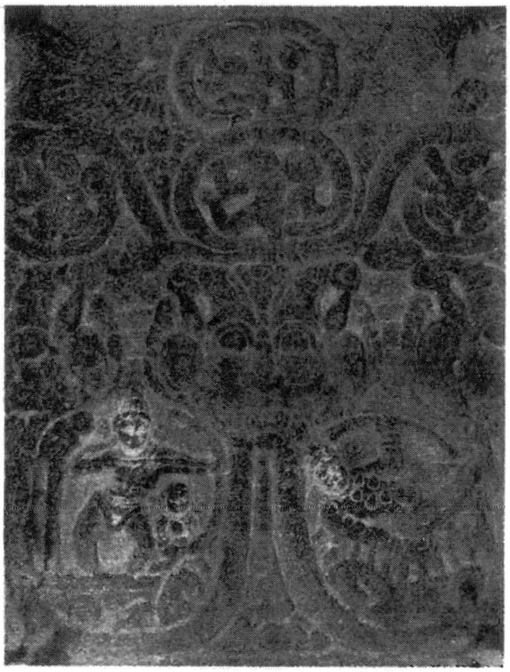

Plate 11. Hemavati, Doḍḍēśvara temple, detail of mukhamaṇḍapa pillar.

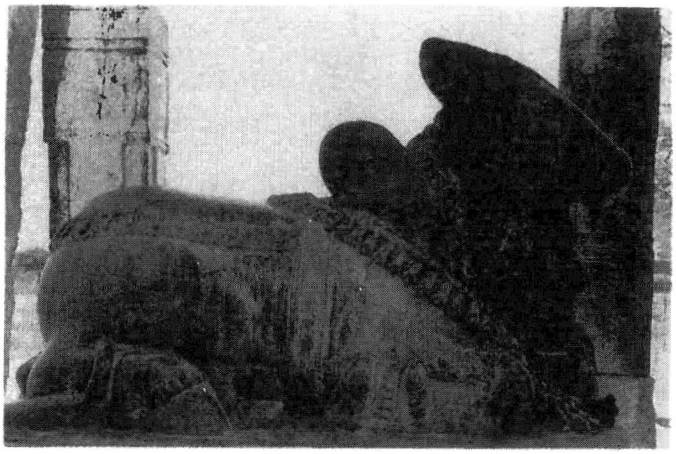

Plate 12. Hemavati, Virūpākṣa temple, Nandi.

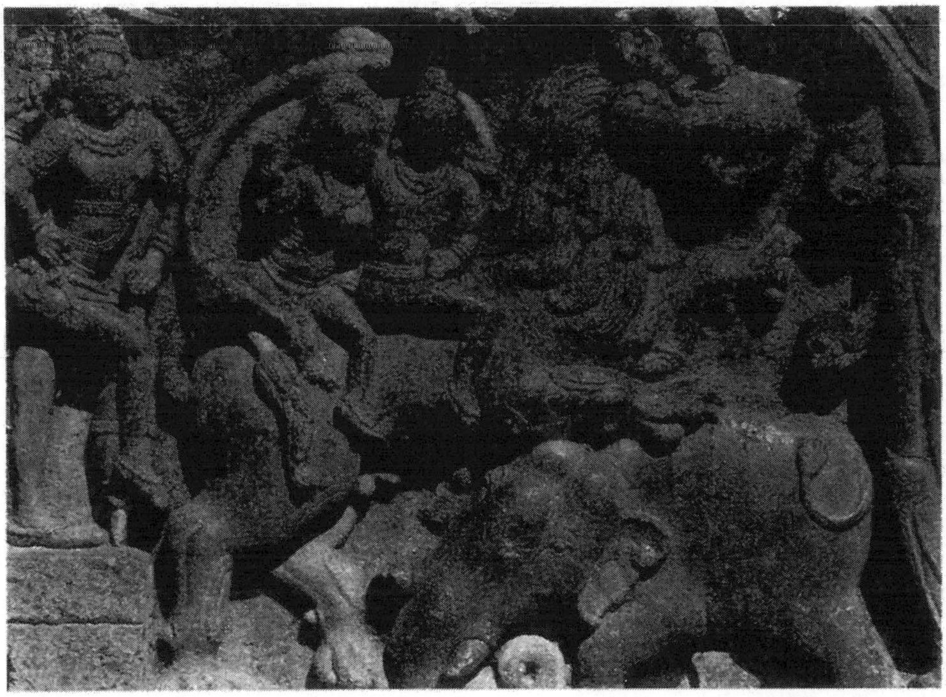

Plate 13. Hemavati, Virūpākṣa temple, north staircase.

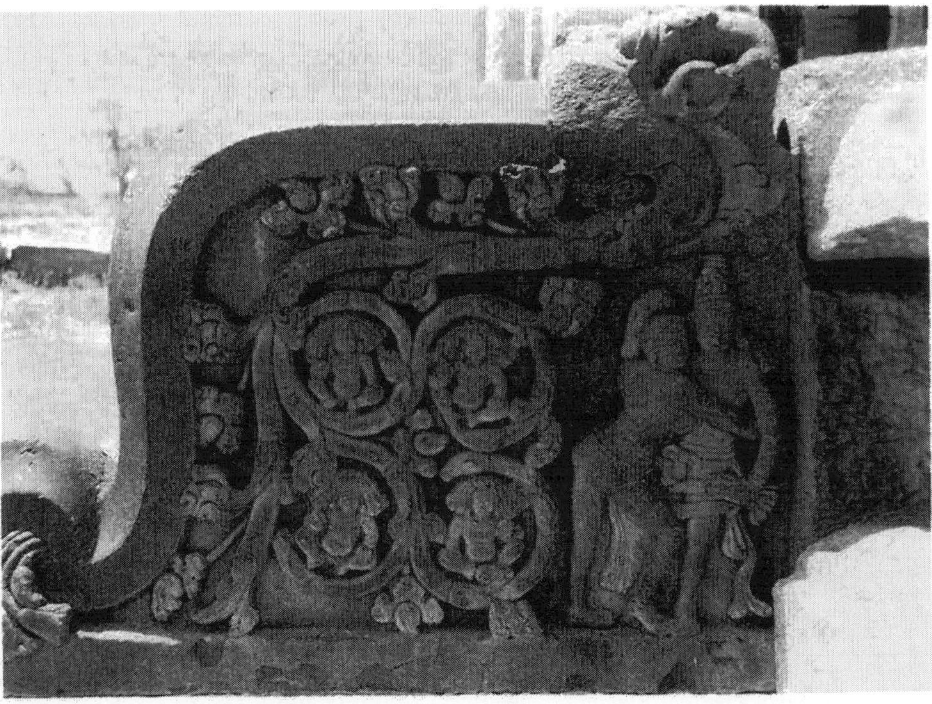

Plate 14. Hemavati, Virūpākṣa temple, south staircase.

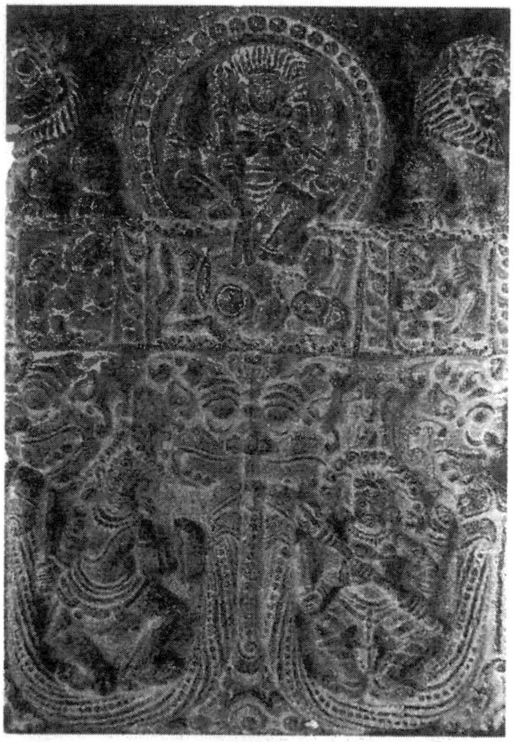

Plate 15. Hemavati, Virūpākṣa temple, detail of mukhamaṇḍapa pillar.

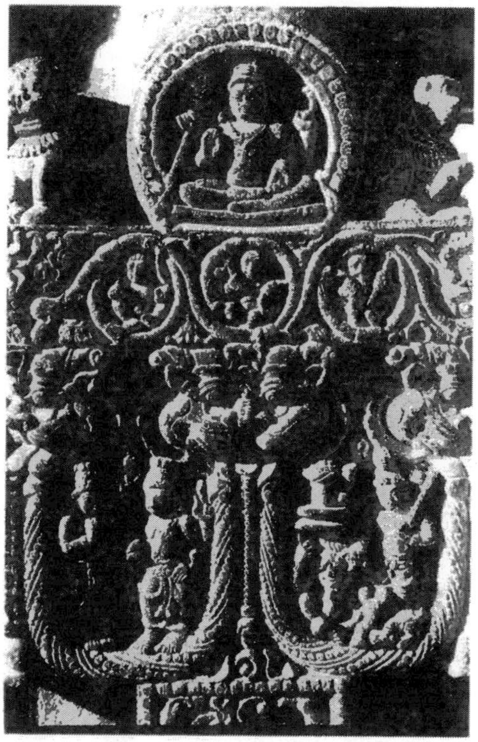

Plate 16. Hemavati, Virūpākṣa temple, detail of mukhamaṇḍapa pillar.

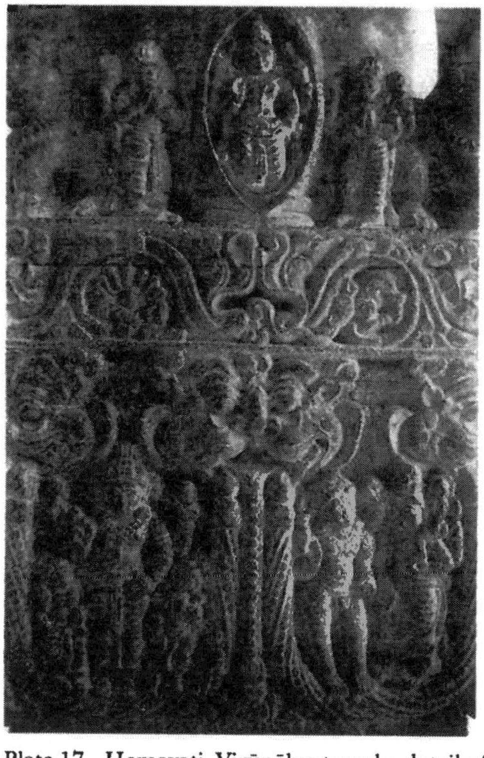

Plate 17. Hemavati, Virūpākṣa temple, detail of mukhamaṇḍapa pillar.

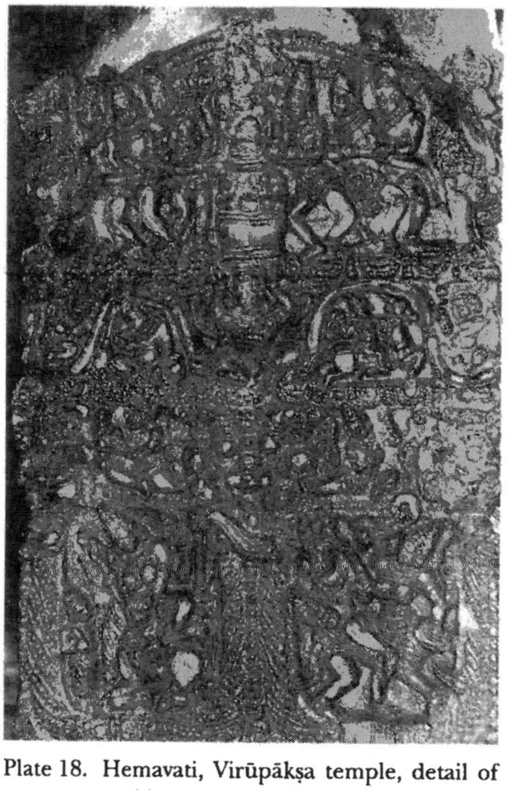

Plate 18. Hemavati, Virūpākṣa temple, detail of mukhamaṇḍapa pillar.

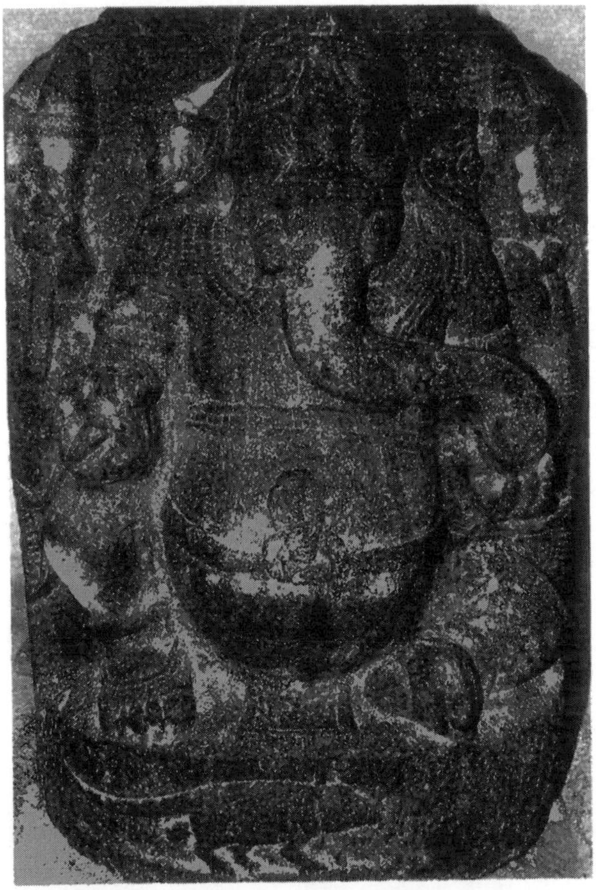

Plate 19. Hemavati, Basava shrine, Gaṇeśa.

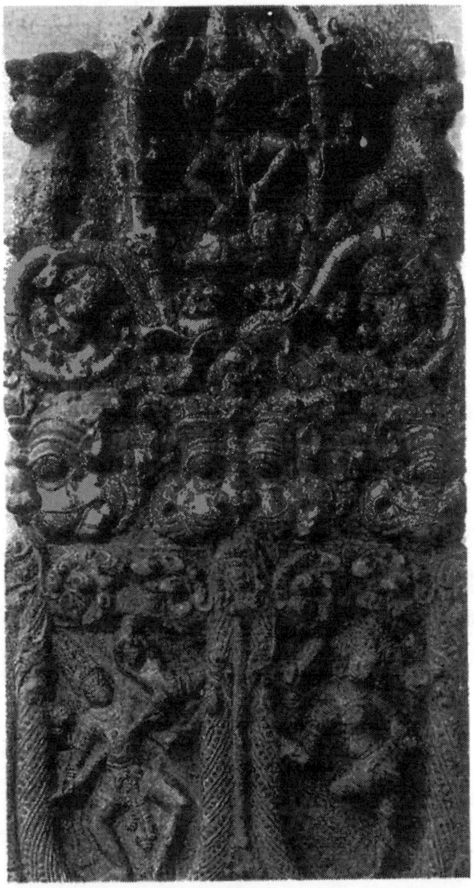

Plate 20. Hemavati, 'Shrine two', detail of pillar.

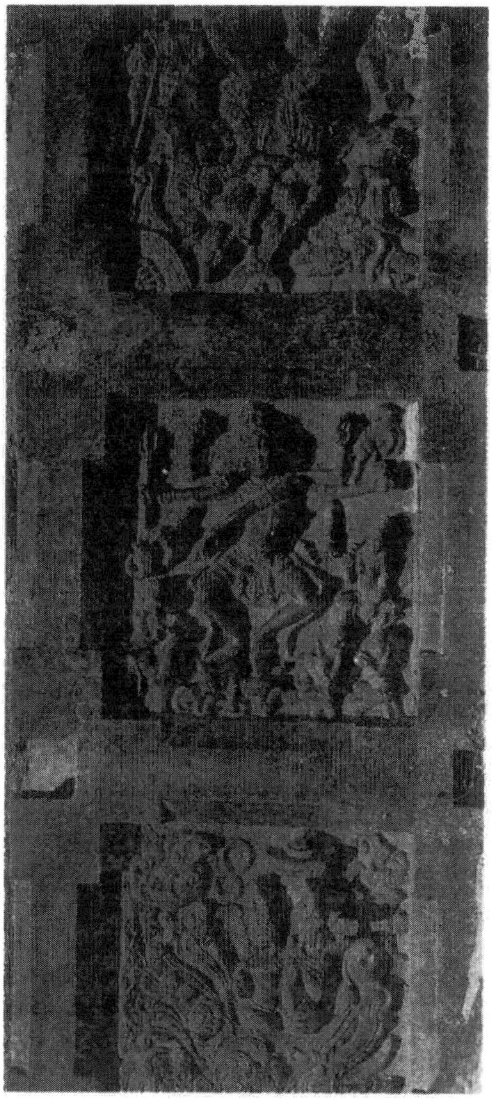

Plate 21. Hemavati, loose ceiling panel—Indra, Naṭēśa Varuṇa.

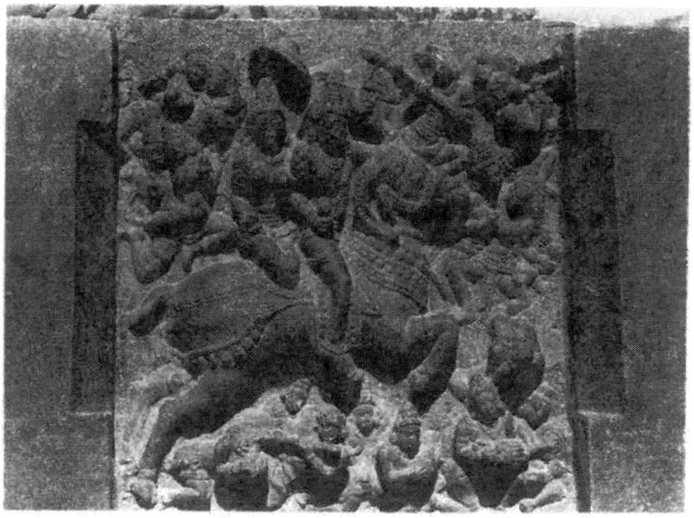

Plate 23. Hemavati, detail of Kubera in plate 22.

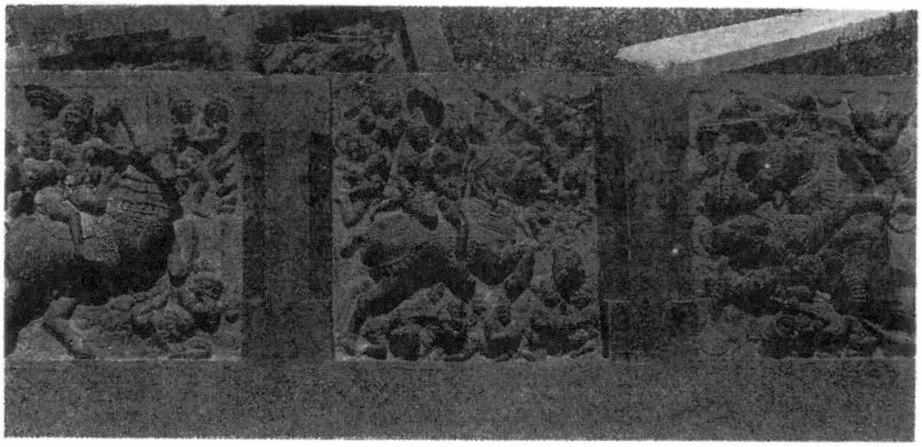

Plate 22. Hemavati, loose ceiling panel—Vāyu, Kubera, Īśāna.

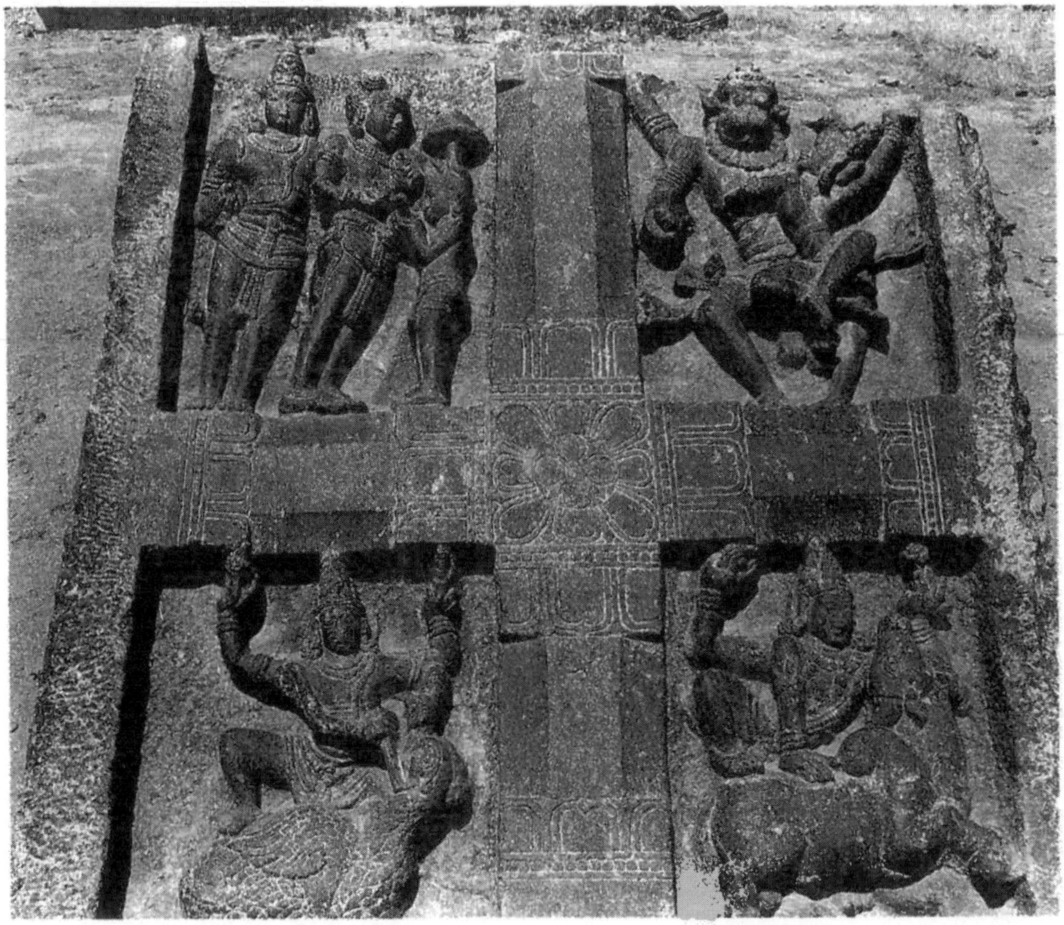

Plate 24. Hemavati, loose ceiling panel—Vāmana, Narasiṁha, and two Kṛṣṇas.

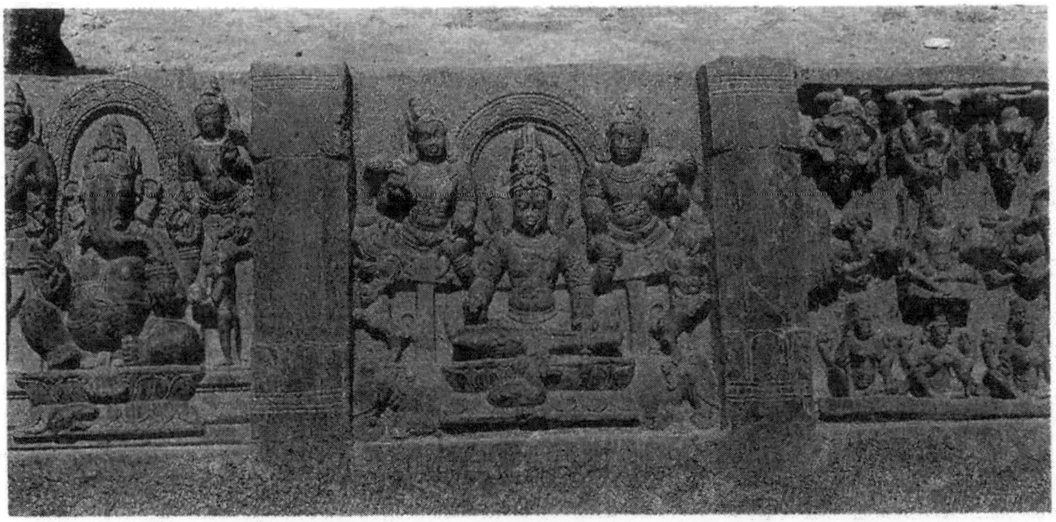

Plate 25. Hemavati, loose ceiling panel—Gaṇeśa, Brahmā, Śiva with Mātṛkās.

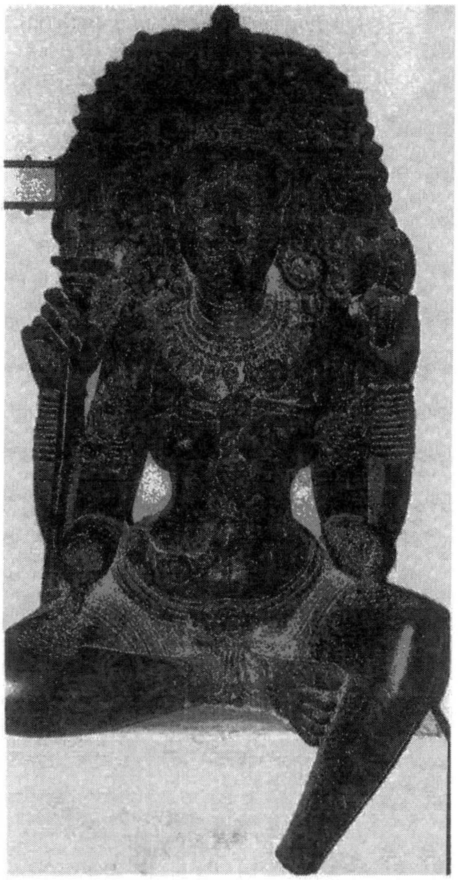

Plate 26. Hemavati (now at Madras Government Museum), 'Kālī'.

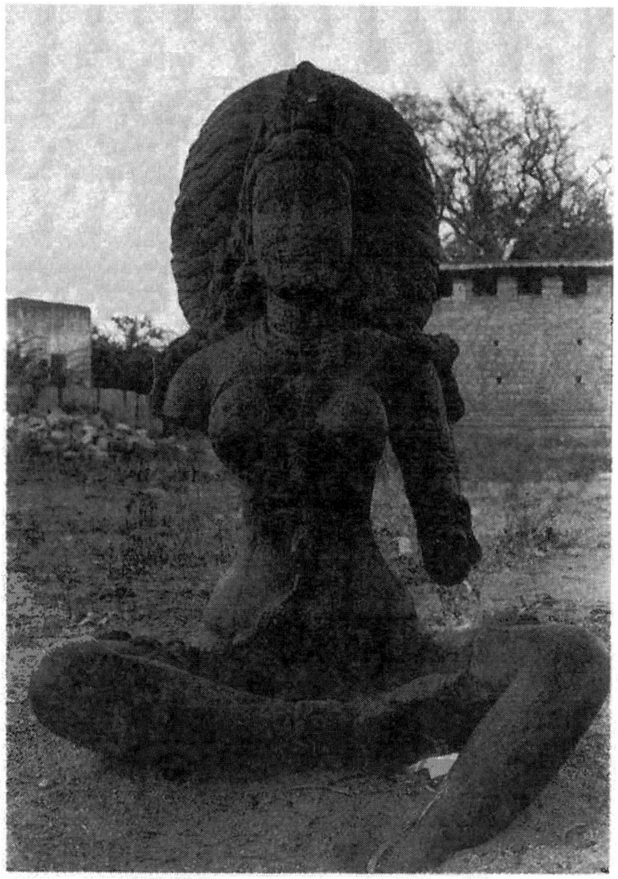

Plate 27. Hemavati, 'Kālī'.

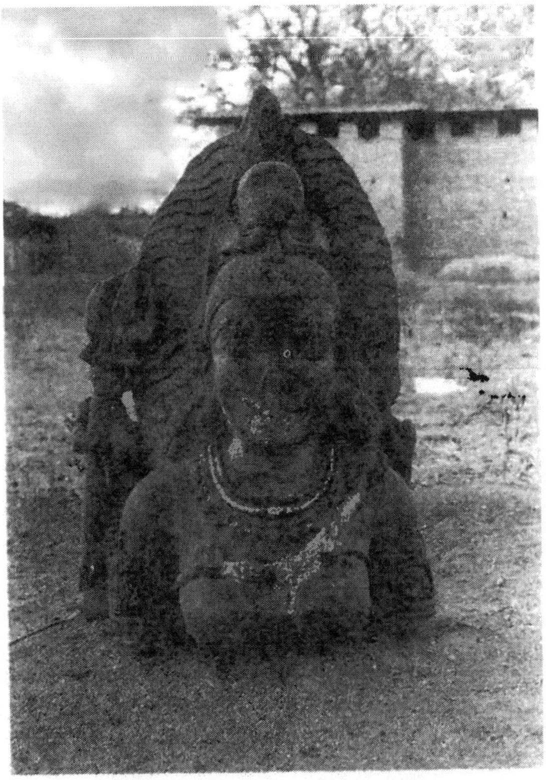

Plate 28. Hemavati, a 'Kālī' bust.

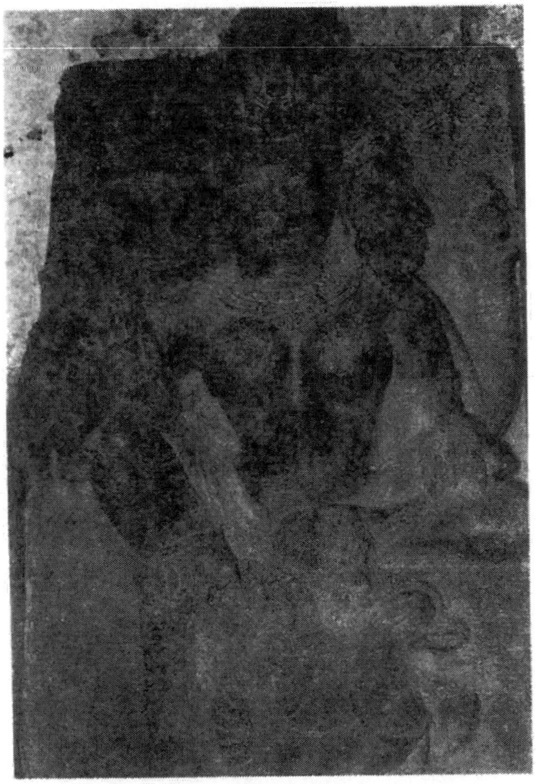

Plate 29. Hemavati, Brahmāṇī.

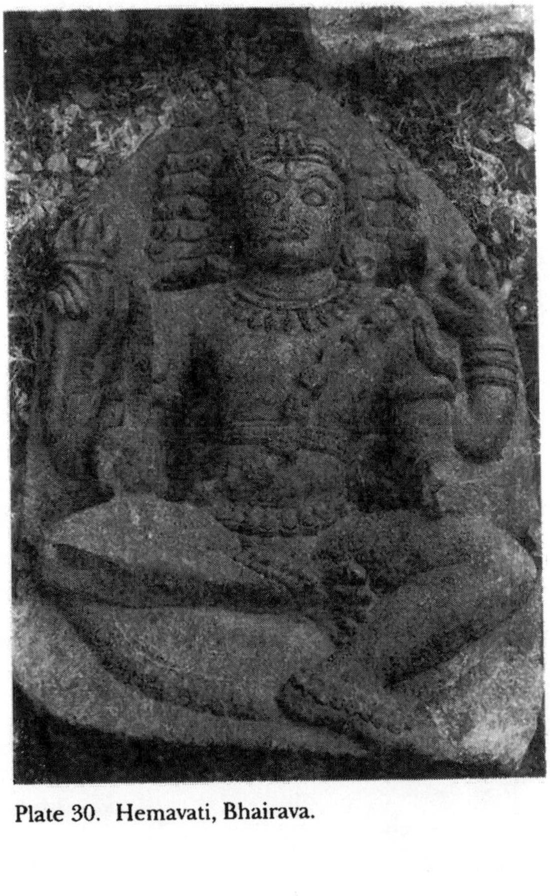

Plate 30. Hemavati, Bhairava.

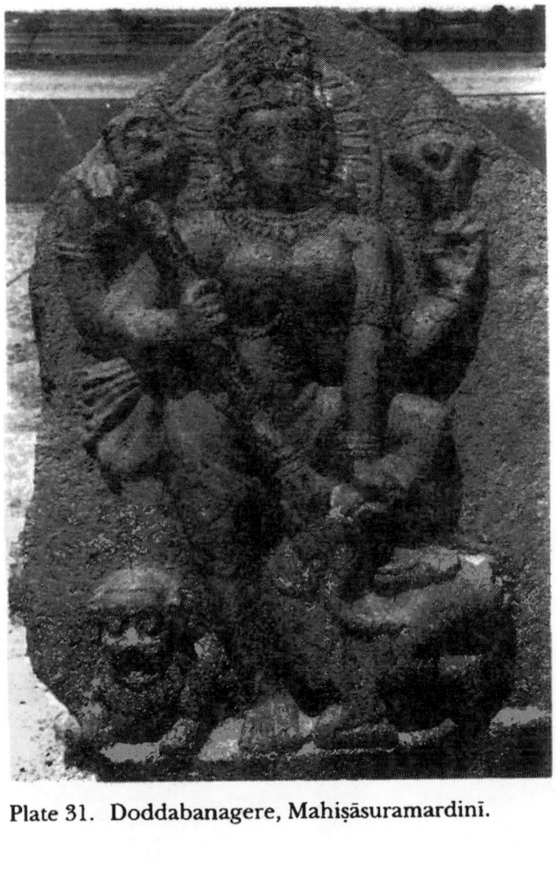

Plate 31. Doddabanagere, Mahiṣāsuramardinī.

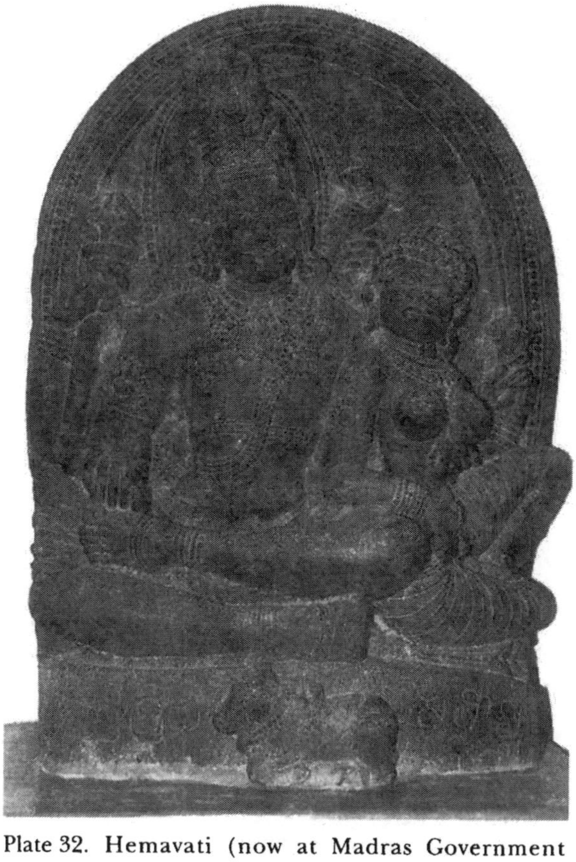

Plate 32. Hemavati (now at Madras Government Museum)—Umāsahita.

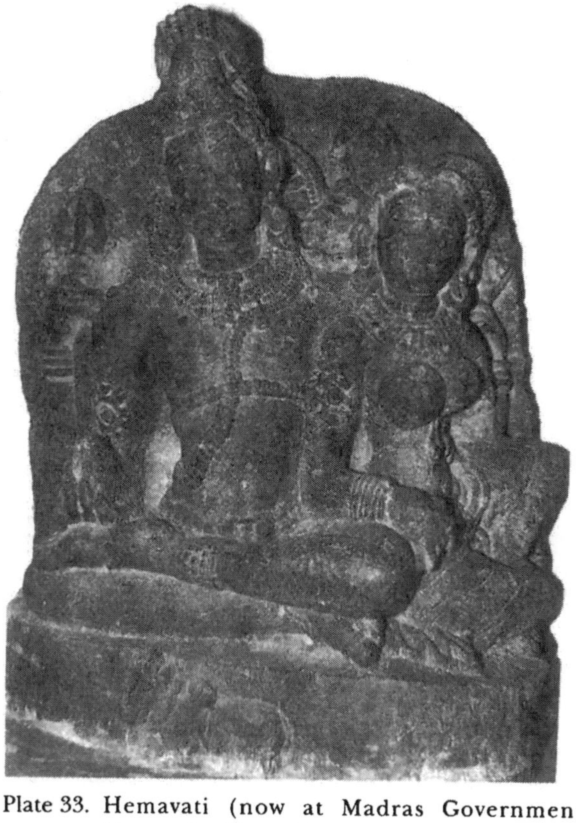

Plate 33. Hemavati (now at Madras Government Museum)—Umāsahita.

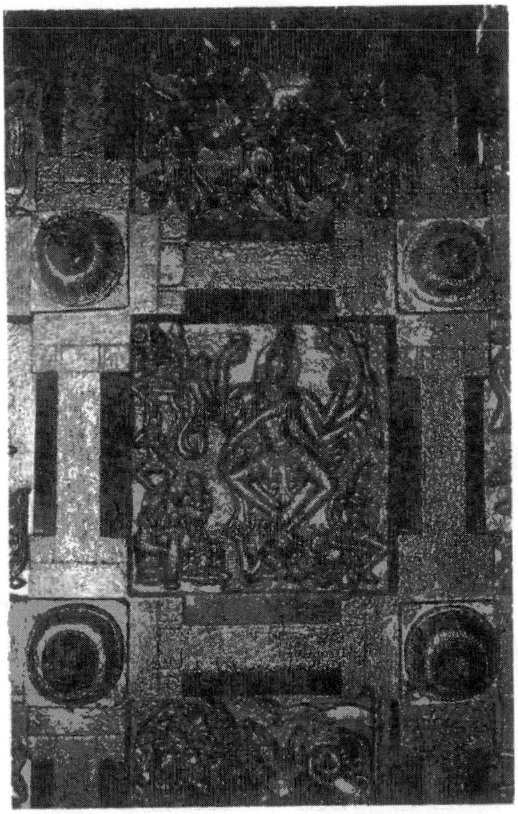

Plate 34. Pathasivarama, Mailarēśvara temple, mukhamaṇḍapa ceiling panels.

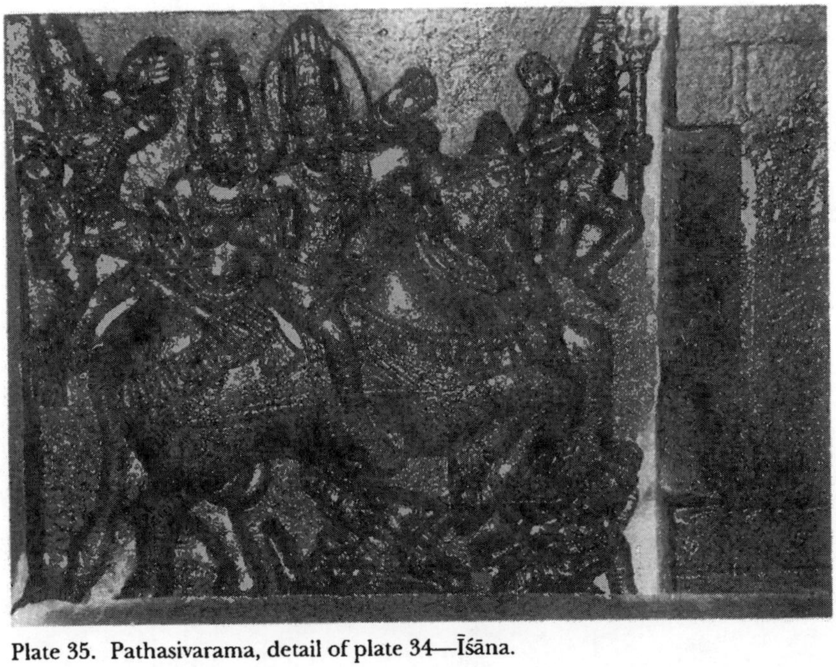

Plate 35. Pathasivarama, detail of plate 34—Īśāna.

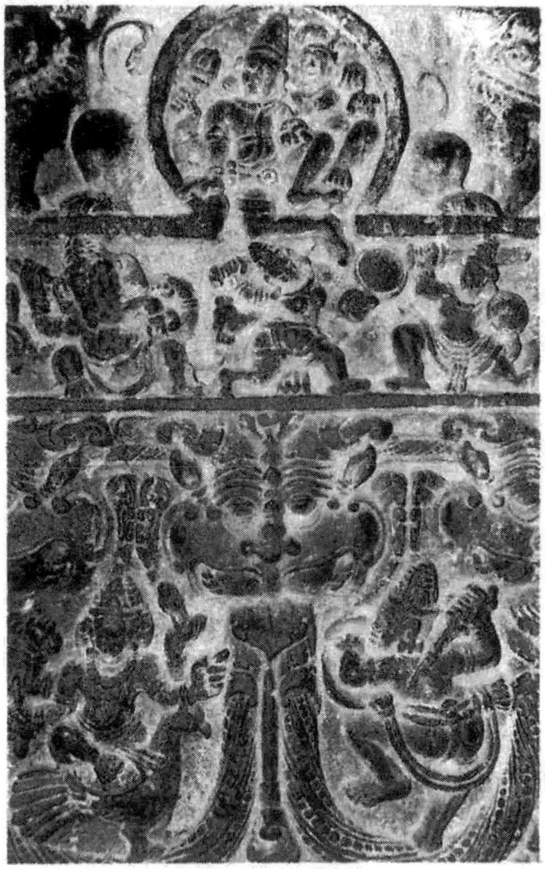

Plate 36. Pailabanda, Raṅganāthasvāmī temple, detail of mukhamaṇḍapa pillar.

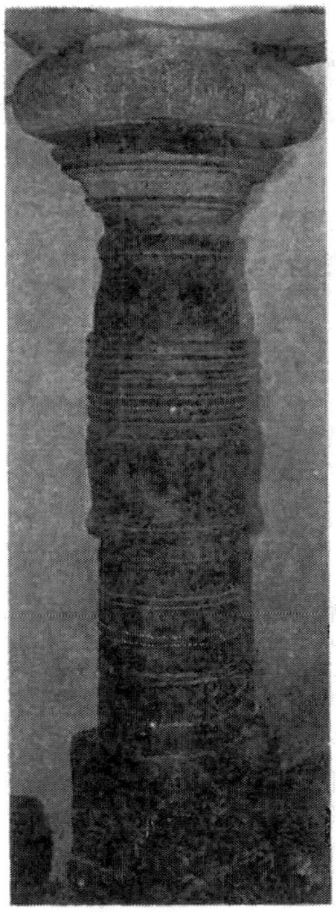

Plate 37. Baraguru, Mahēndrēśvara temple, inner agramaṇḍapa pillar.

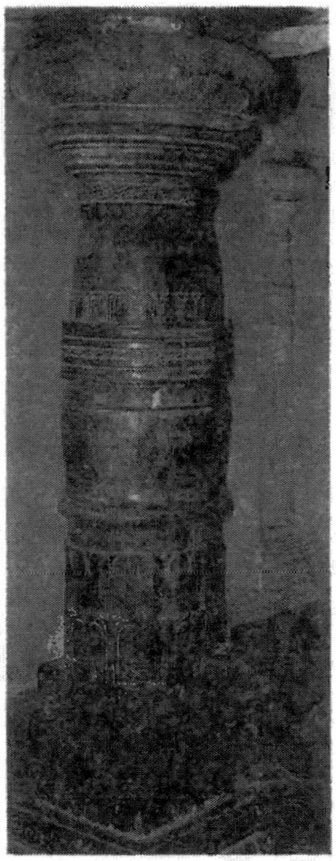

Plate 38. Baraguru, Mahēndrēśvara temple, outer agramaṇḍapa pillar.

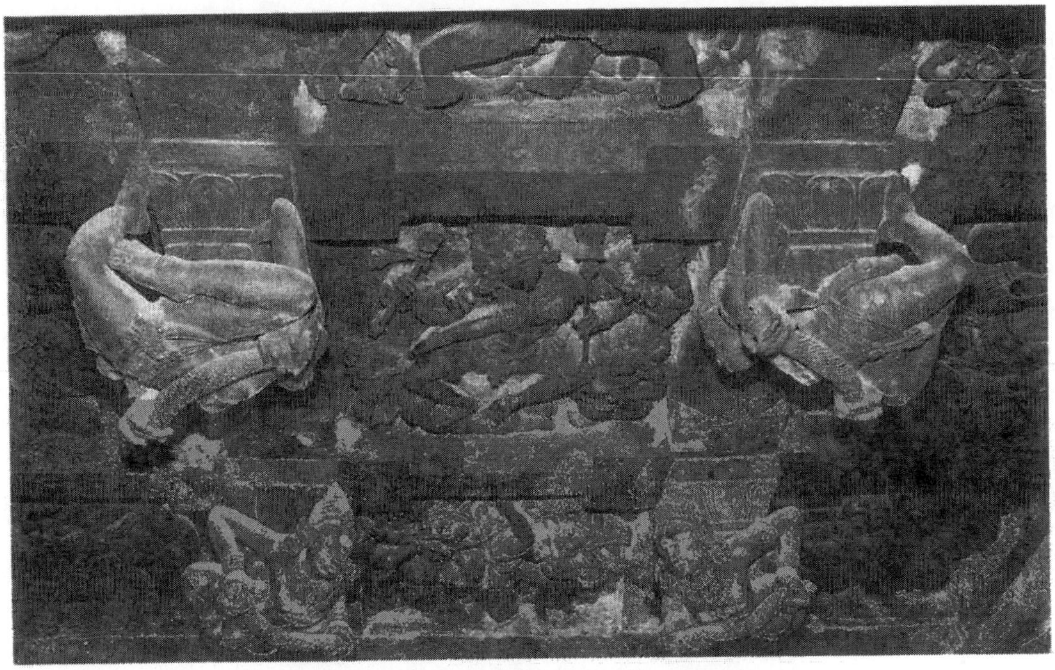

Plate 39. Aralaguppe, Kallēśvara temple, mukhamaṇḍapa ceiling panels.

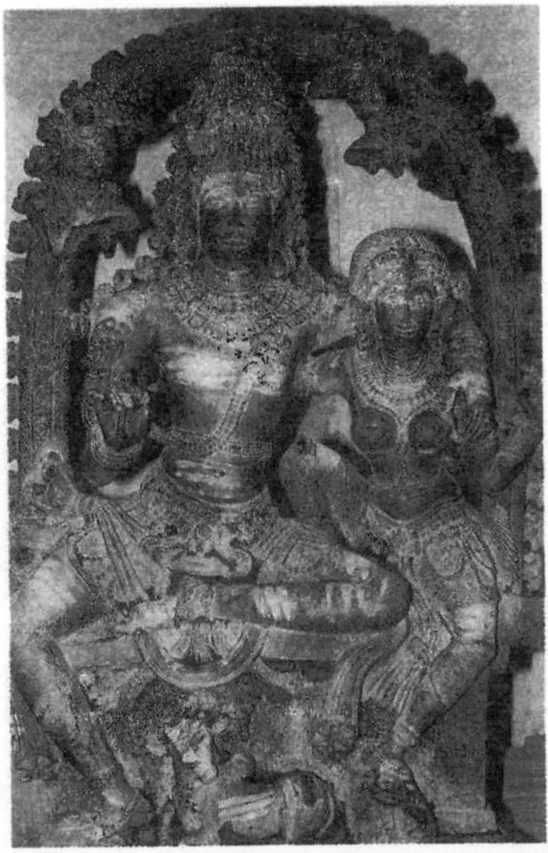

Plate 40. Aralaguppe, Kallēśvara temple, Umāsahita.

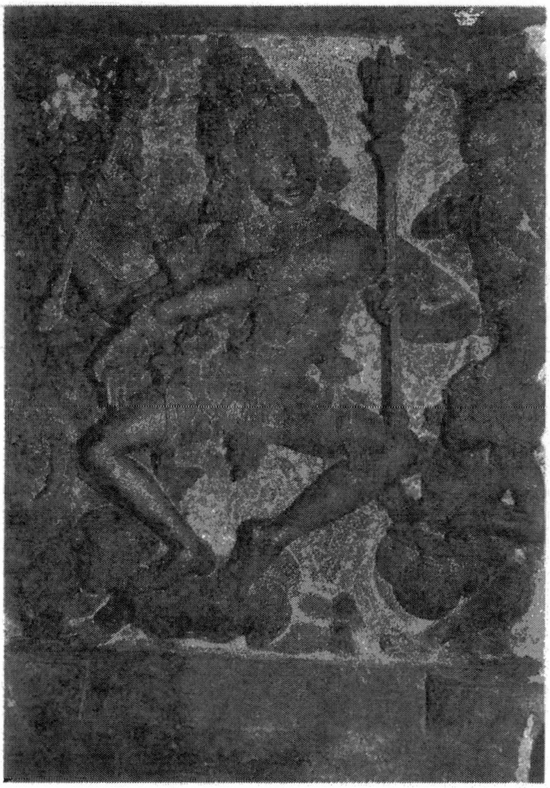

Plate 41. Aralaguppe, Kallēśvara temple, detail of plate 39, Naṭēśa.

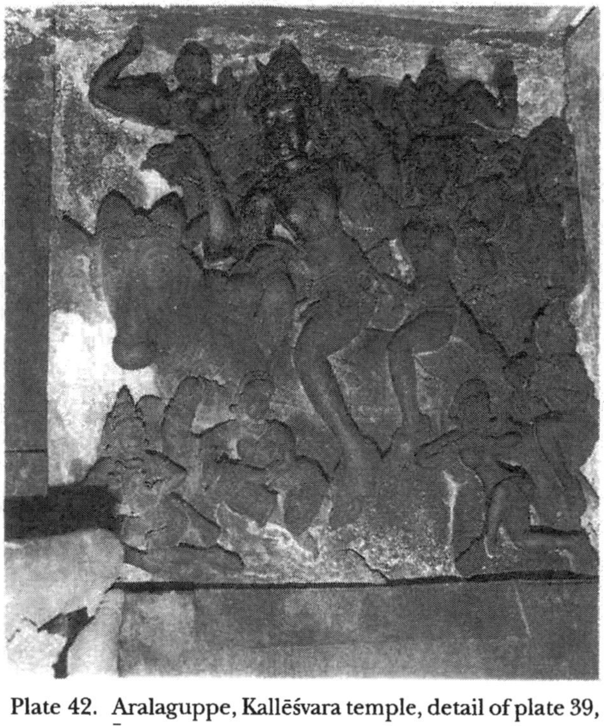

Plate 42. Aralaguppe, Kallēśvara temple, detail of plate 39, Īśana.

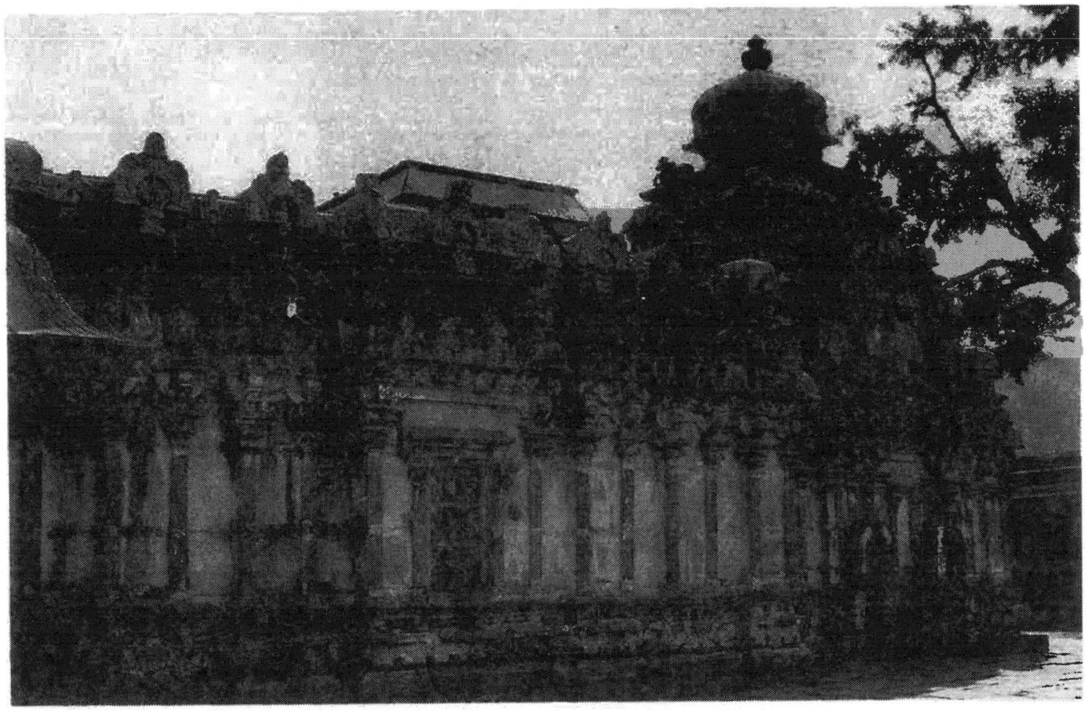

Plate 43. Nandi, Bhōgaṇandīśvara temple.

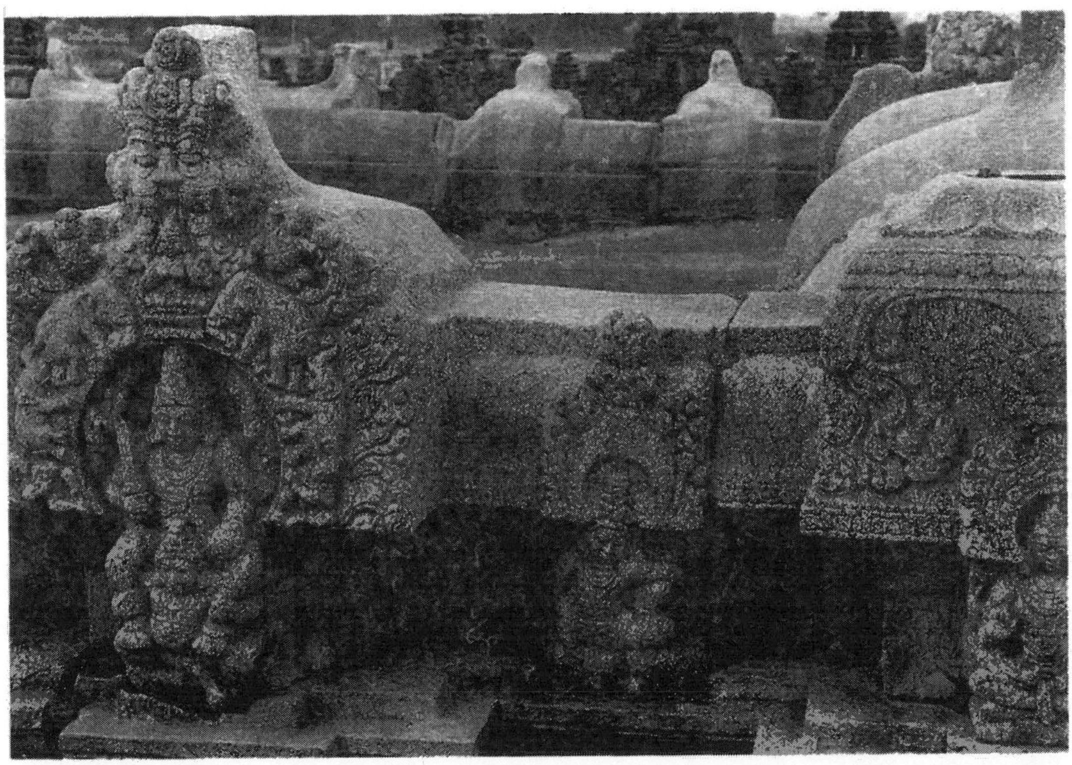

Plate 44. Nandi, Bhōgaṇandīśvara temple, south maṇḍapa, hāra detail—Bhutēśvara (right) and Viṣṇu (left).

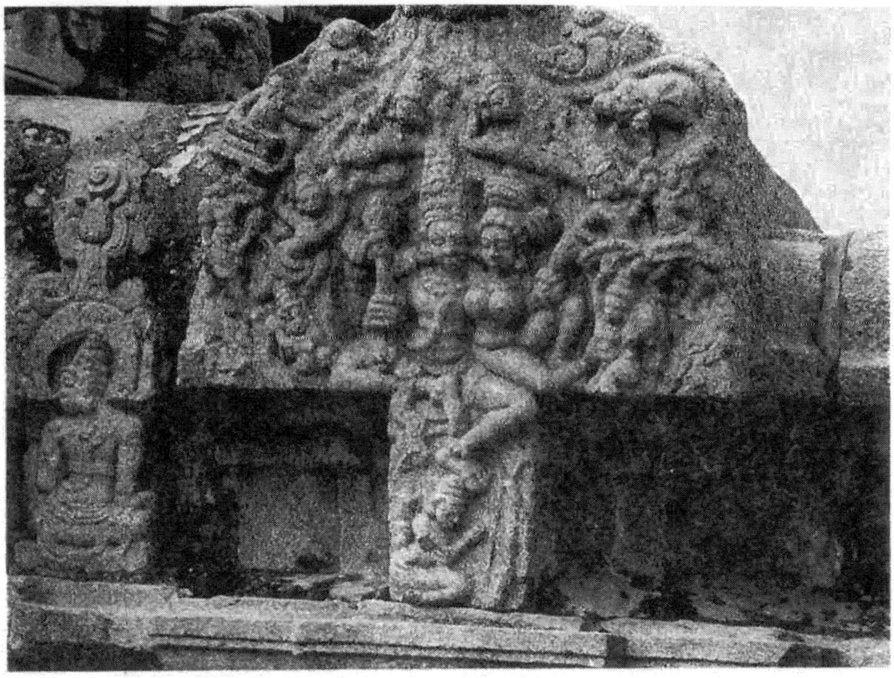

Plate 45. Nandi, Bhōgaṇandīśvara temple, south antarāla, hāra detail—Kirātārjuniyam.

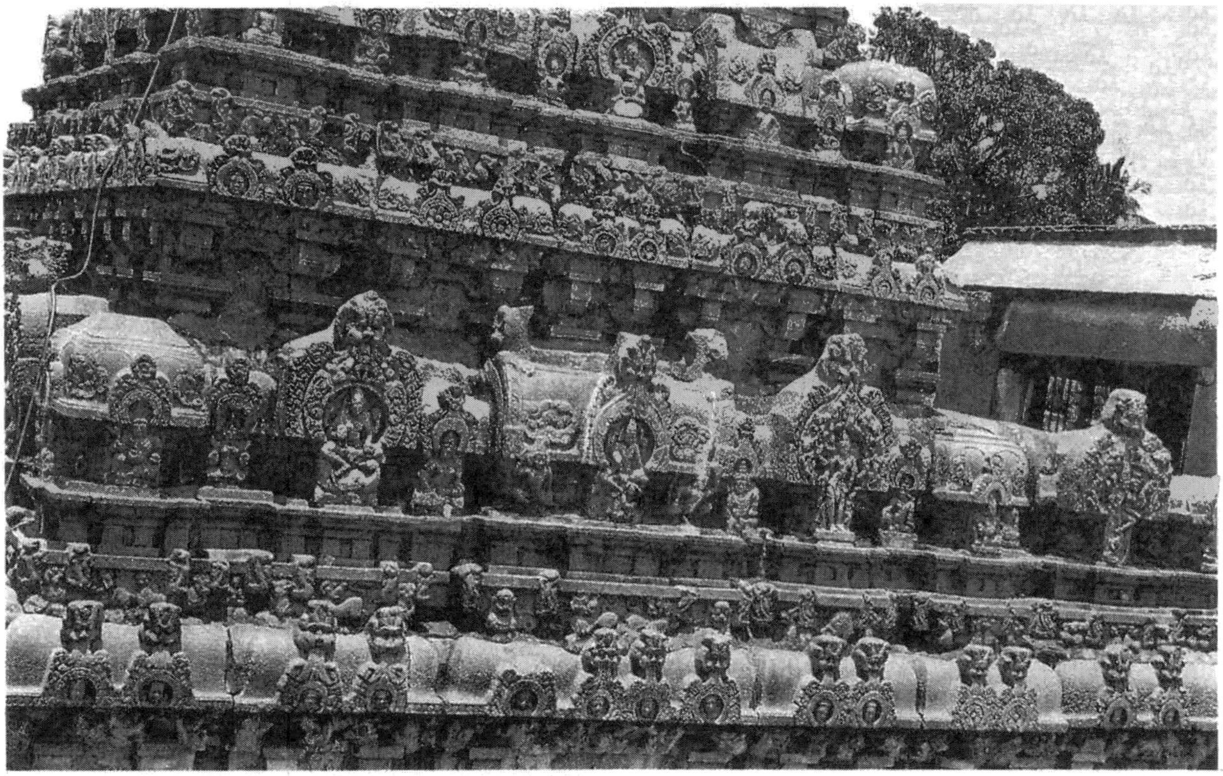

Plate 46. Nandi, Bhōgaṇandīśvara temple, south vimāna.

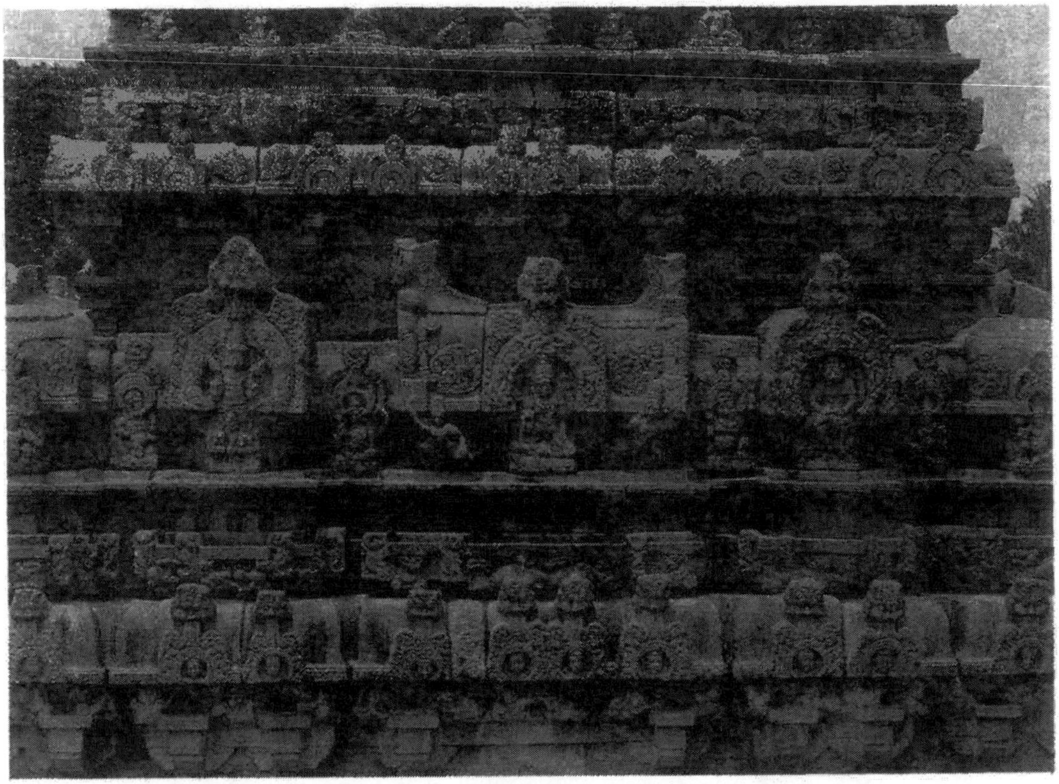

Plate 47. Nandi, Bhōgaṇandīśvara temple, west vimāna.

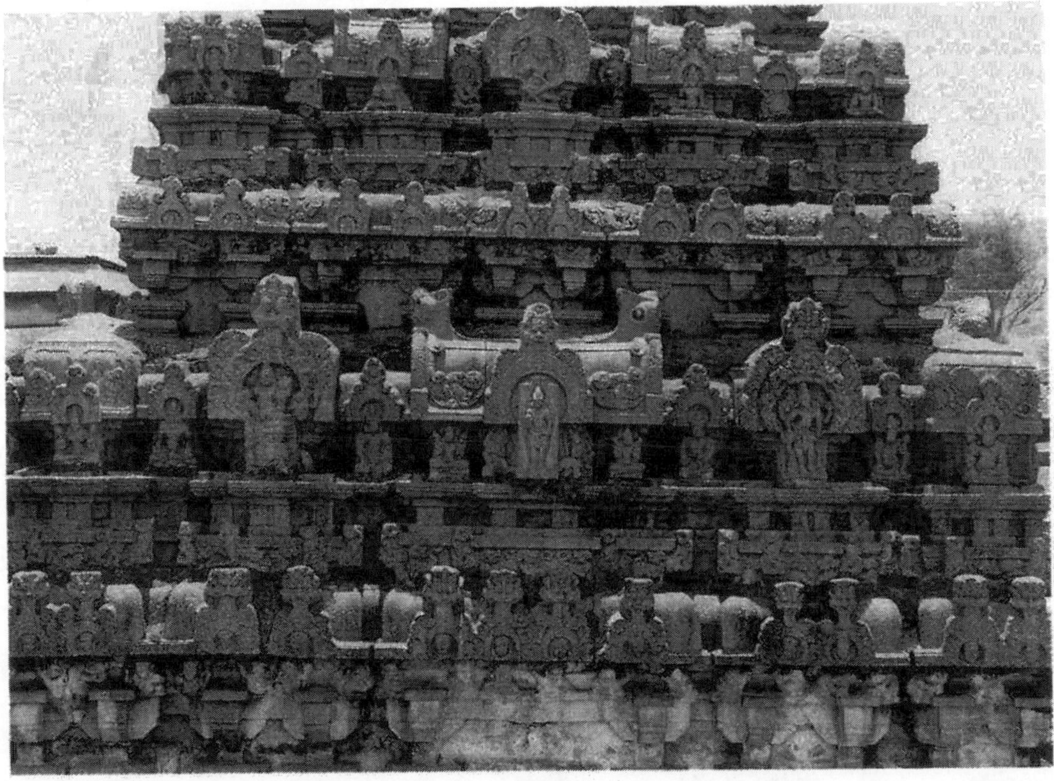

Plate 48. Nandi, Bhōgaṇandīśvara temple, north vimāna.

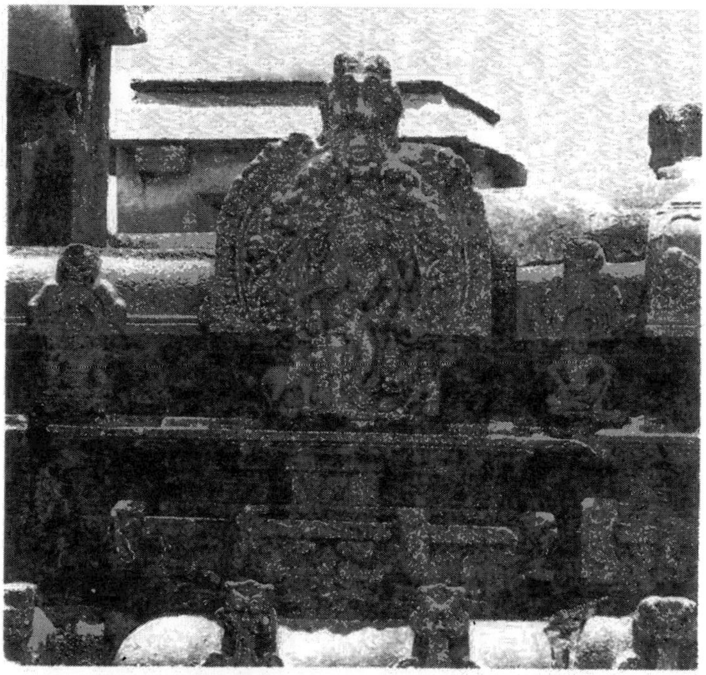

Plate 49. Nandi, Bhōgaṇandīśvara temple, north antarāla, hāra detail—Śiva/Bhairava.

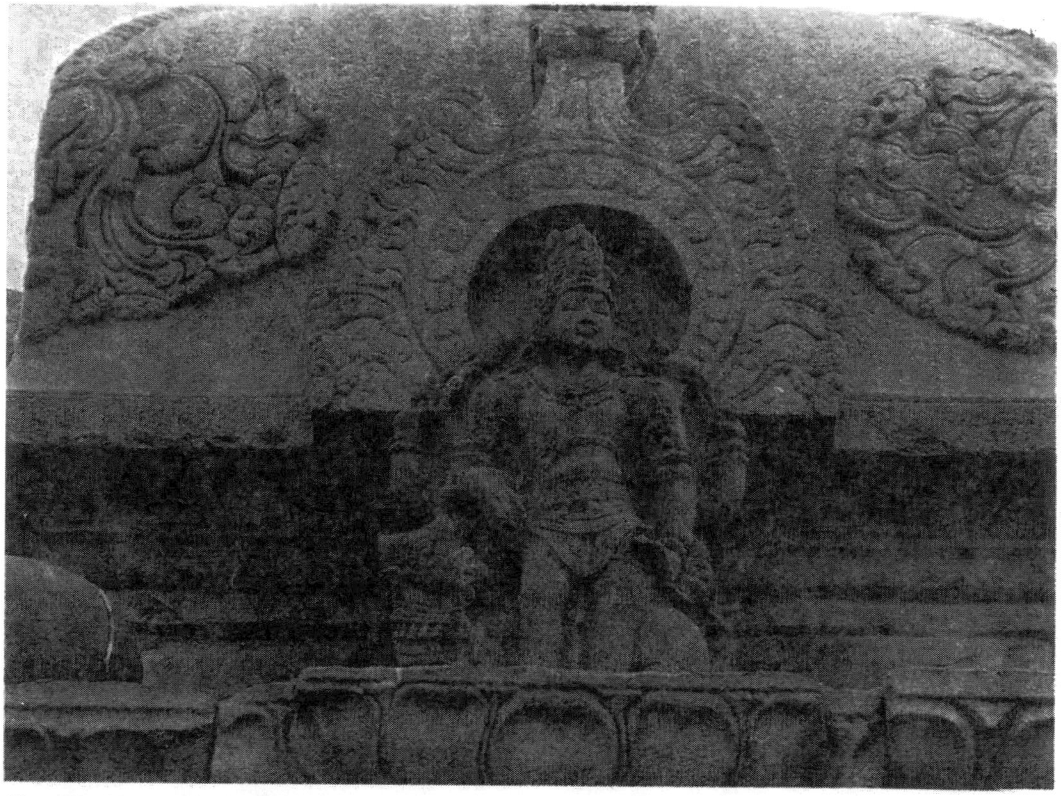

Plate 50. Nandi, Bhōgaṇandīśvara temple, east vimāna (top) detail—Śiva.

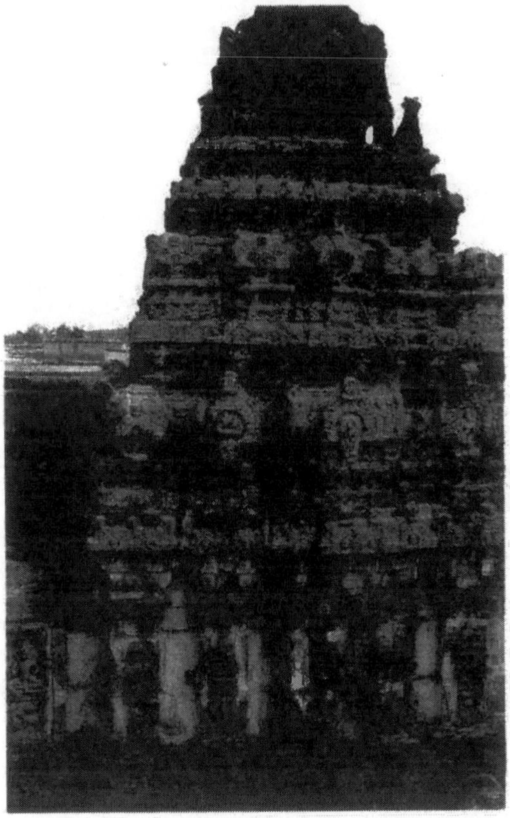

Plate 51. Nandi, Aruṇācalēśvara temple, from the south.

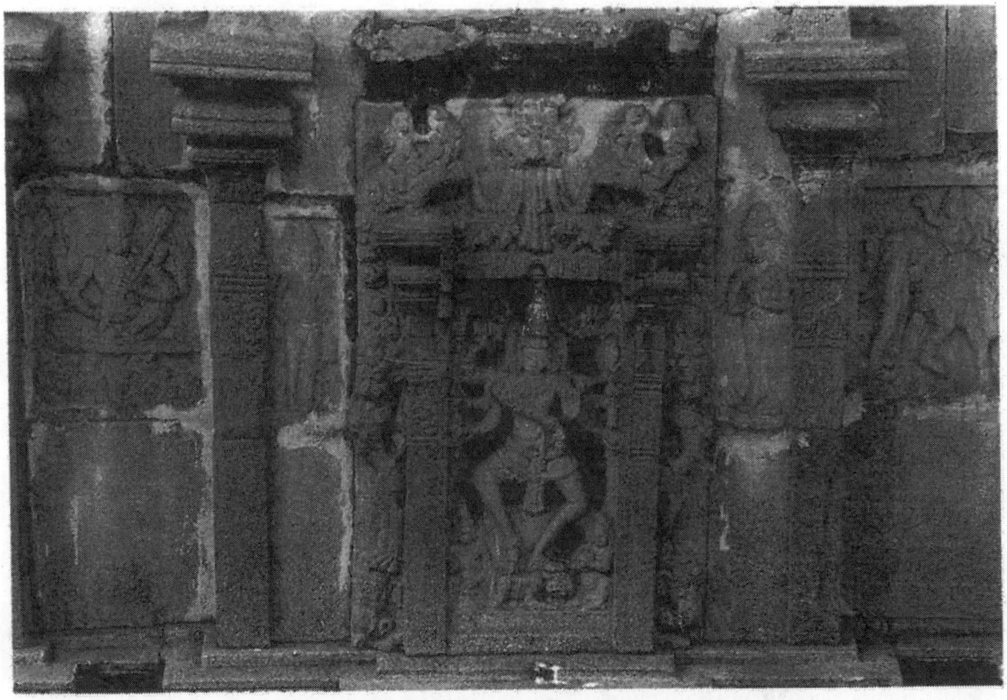

Plate 52. Nandi, Aruṇācalēśvara temple, south maṇḍapa window—Naṭēśa.

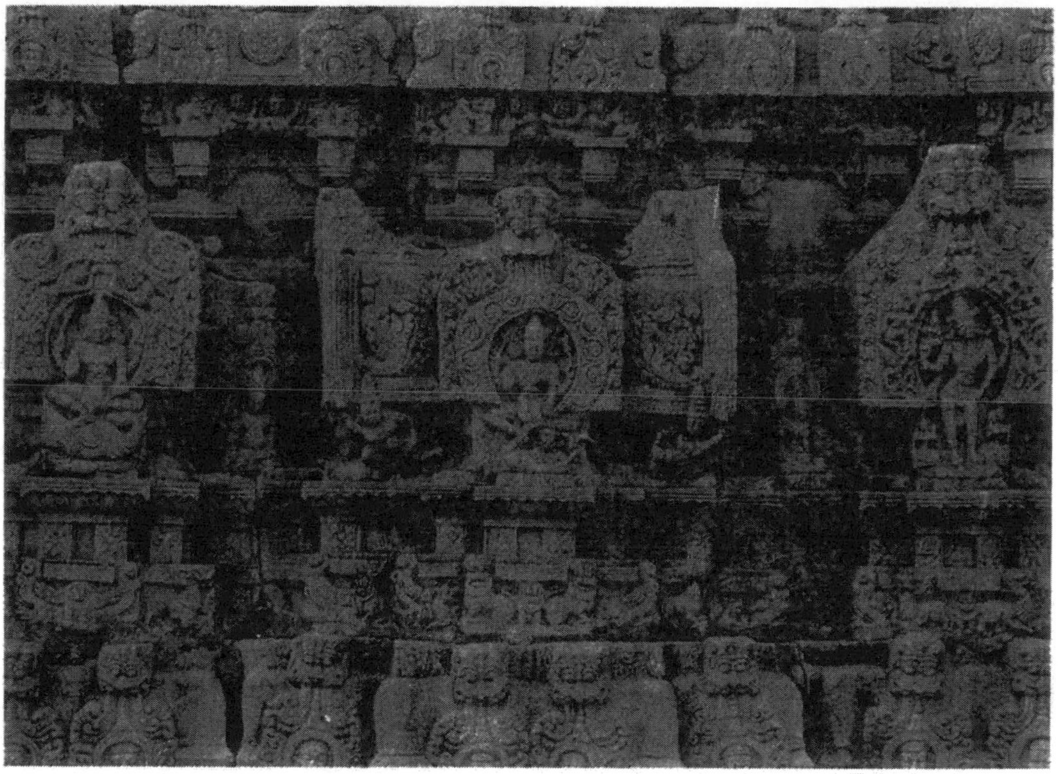

Plate 53. Nandi, Aruṇācalēśvara temple, south vimāna.

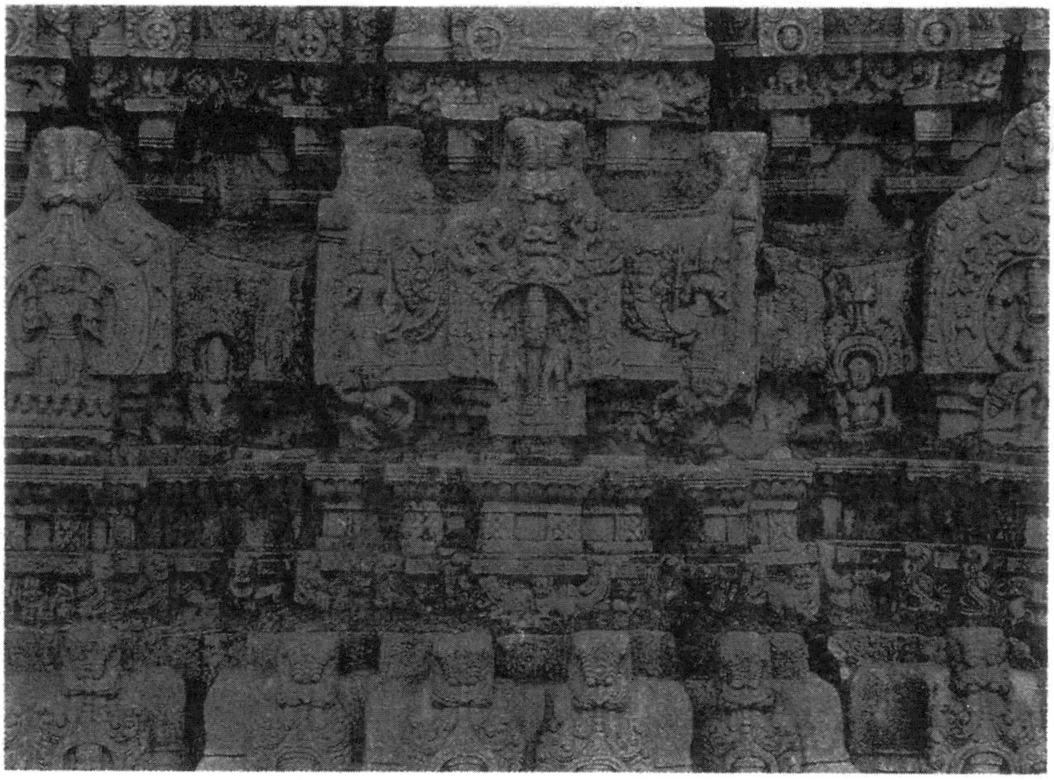

Plate 54. Nandi, Aruṇācalēśvara temple, west vimāna.

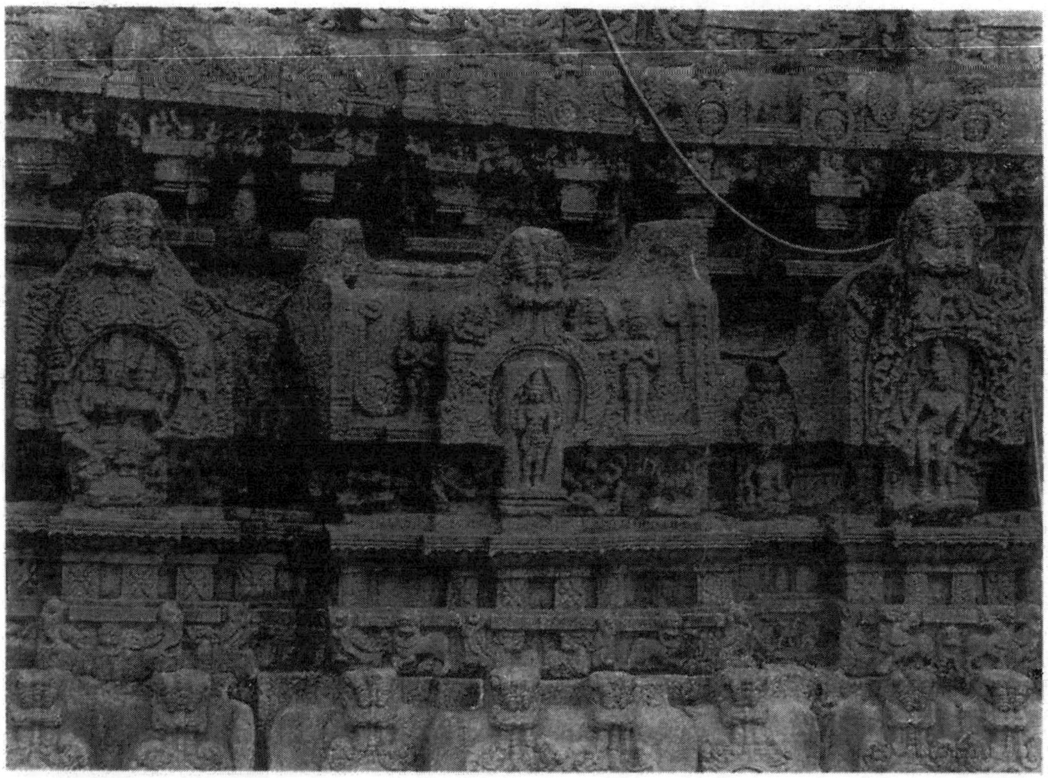

Plate 55. Nandi, Aruṇācalrēśvara temple, north vimāna.

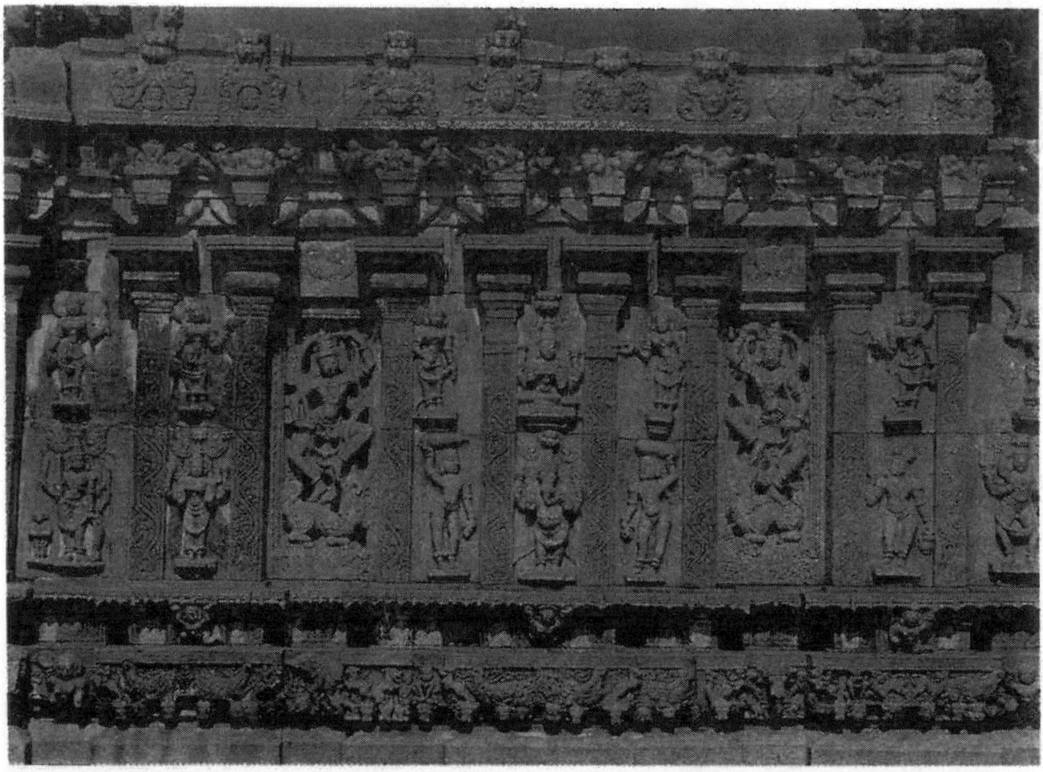

Plate 56. Nandi, Umāmahēśvara shrine from the west.

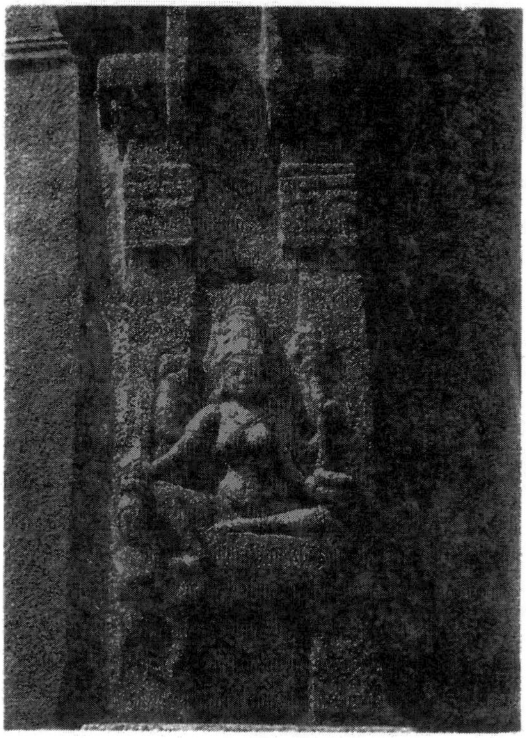

Plate 57. Avani, Lakṣmaṇēśvara temple, east maṇḍapa—Devī.

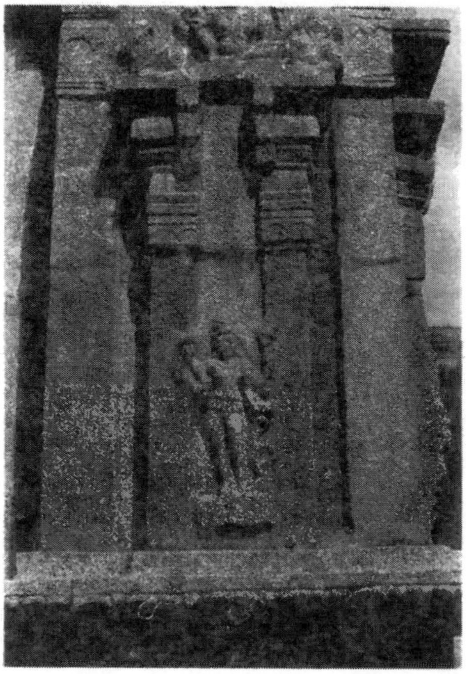

Plate 58. Avani, Lakṣmaṇēśvara temple, south maṇḍapa—Śiva/Bhairava.

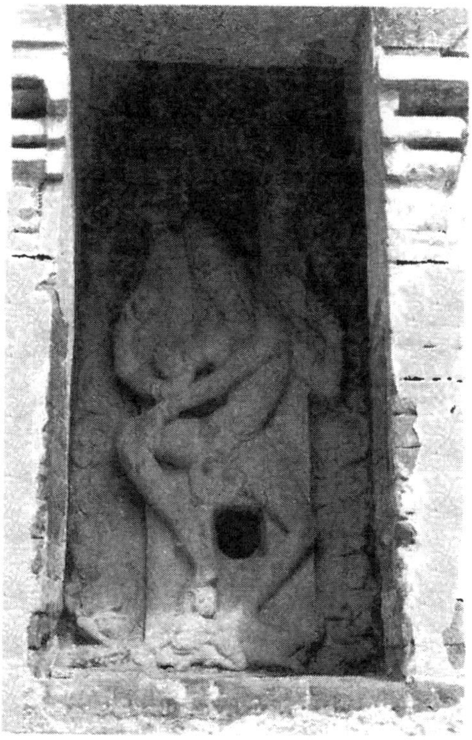

Plate 59. Avani, Lakṣmaṇēśvara temple, south maṇḍapa window—Naṭēśa.

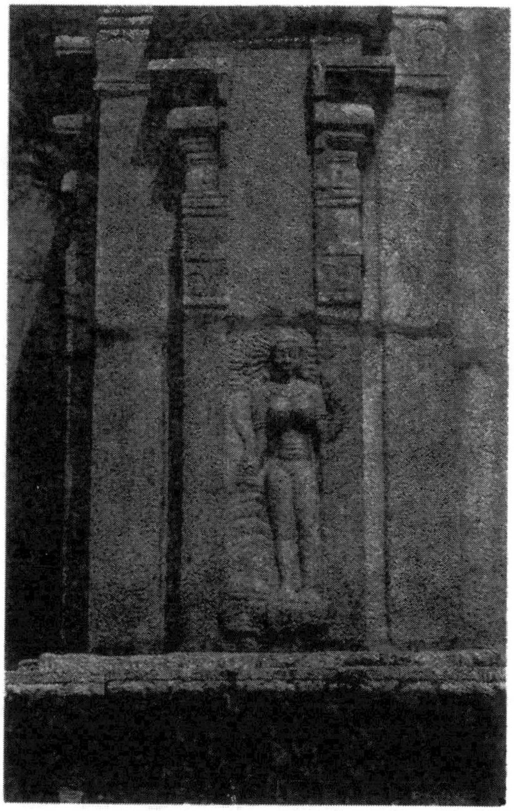

Plate 60. Avani, Lakṣmaṇēśvara temple, south maṇḍapa—attendant/yoginī.

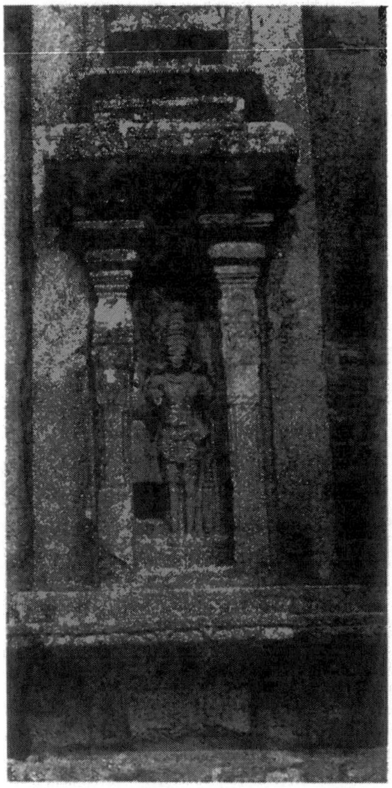

Plate 61. Avani, Lakṣmaṇēśvara temple, south antarāla window—Viṣṇu.

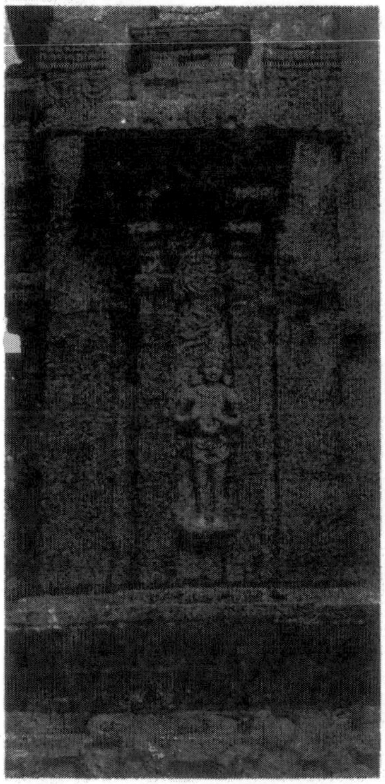

Plate 62. Avani, Lakṣmaṇēśvara temple, south vimāna—King Vīra-Noḷamba.

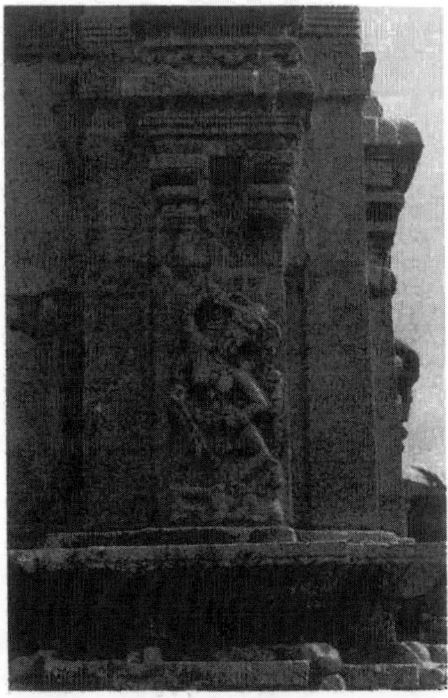

Plate 63. Avani, Lakṣmaṇēśvara temple, west vimāna—Devī.

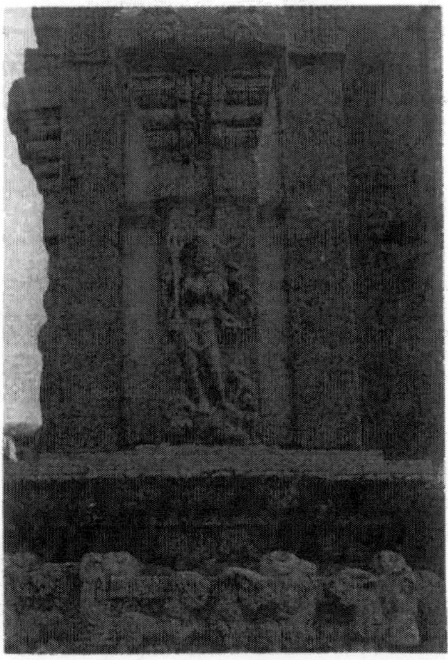

Plate 64. Avani, Lakṣmaṇēśvara temple, west vimāna—Devī.

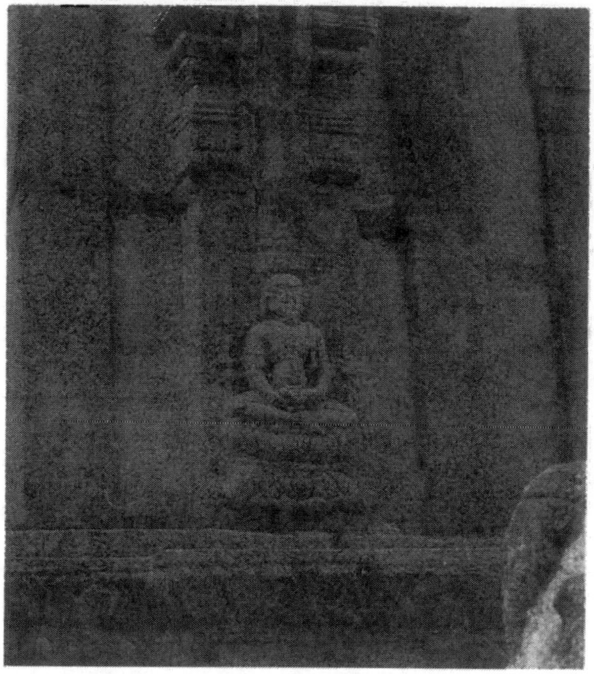

Plate 65. Avani, Lakṣmaṇēśvara temple, north vimāna—Tribhuvanakarata.

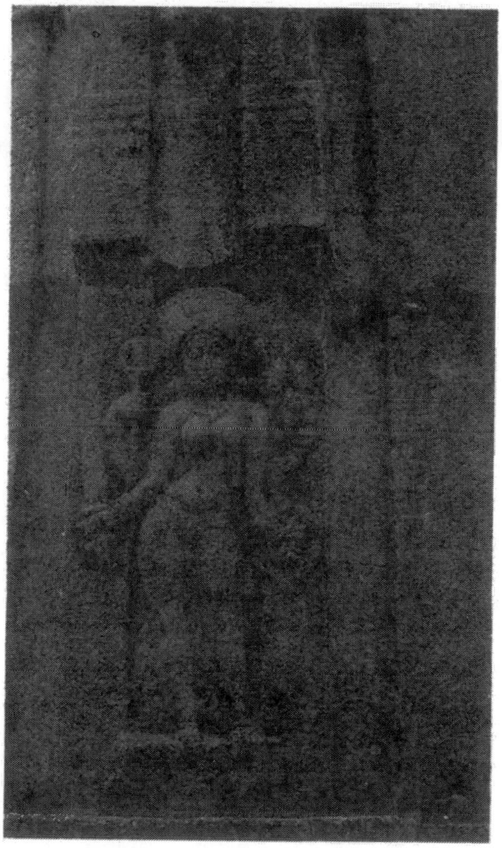

Plate 66. Avani, Lakṣmaṇēśvara temple, north maṇḍapa—Devī.

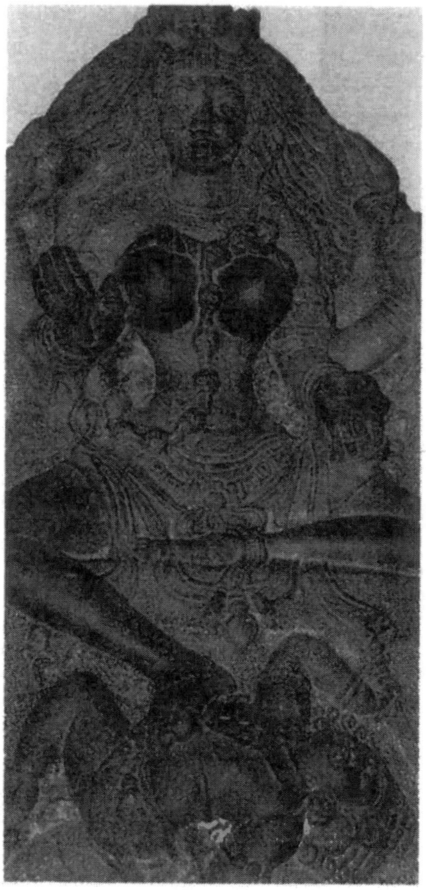

Plate 67. Avani (now at Government Museum, Bangalore), Devī.

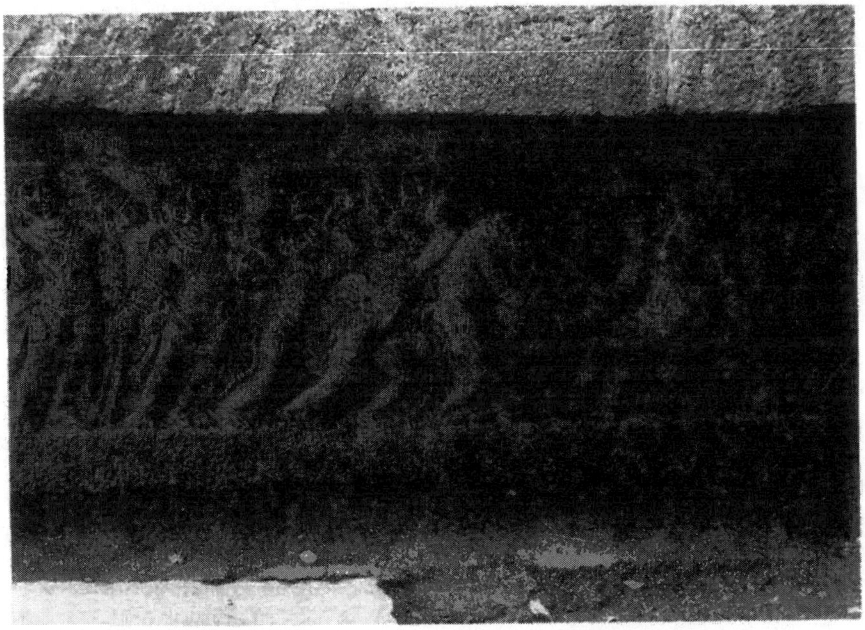

Plate 68. Dharmapuri, Kāmākṣamma temple, upapīṭha *Rāmāyaṇa* panel.

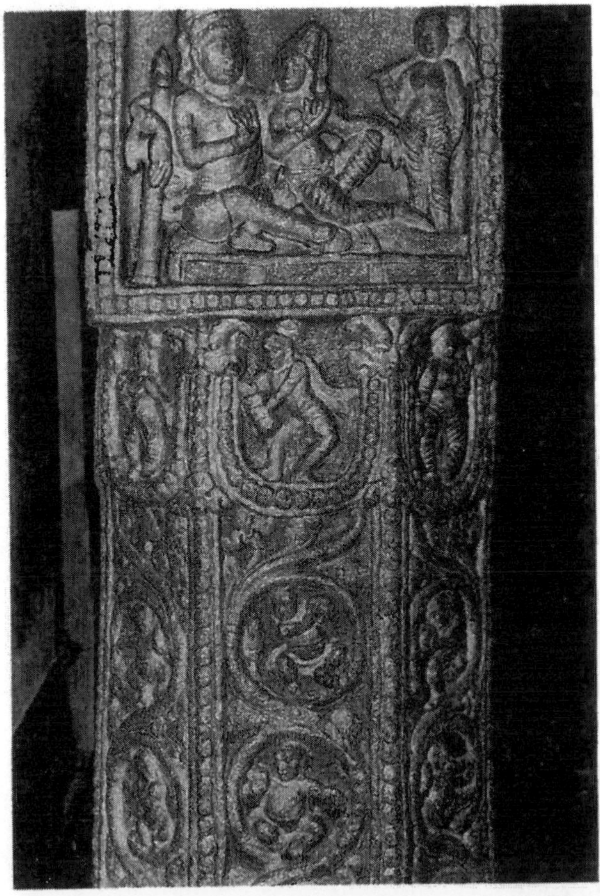

Plate 69. Dharmapuri, Kāmākṣamma temple, detail of mukhamaṇḍapa pillar—Āliṅgamūrti.

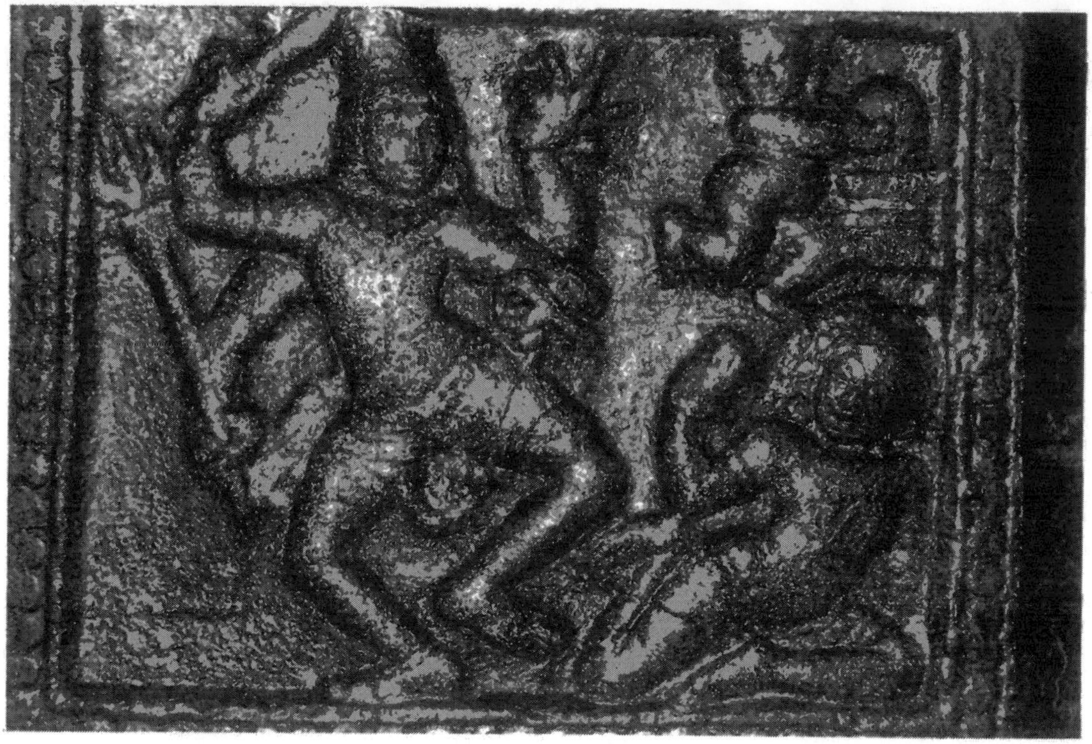

Plate 70. Dharmapuri, Kāmākṣamma temple, detail of mukhamaṇḍapa pillar—Kālaharamūrti.

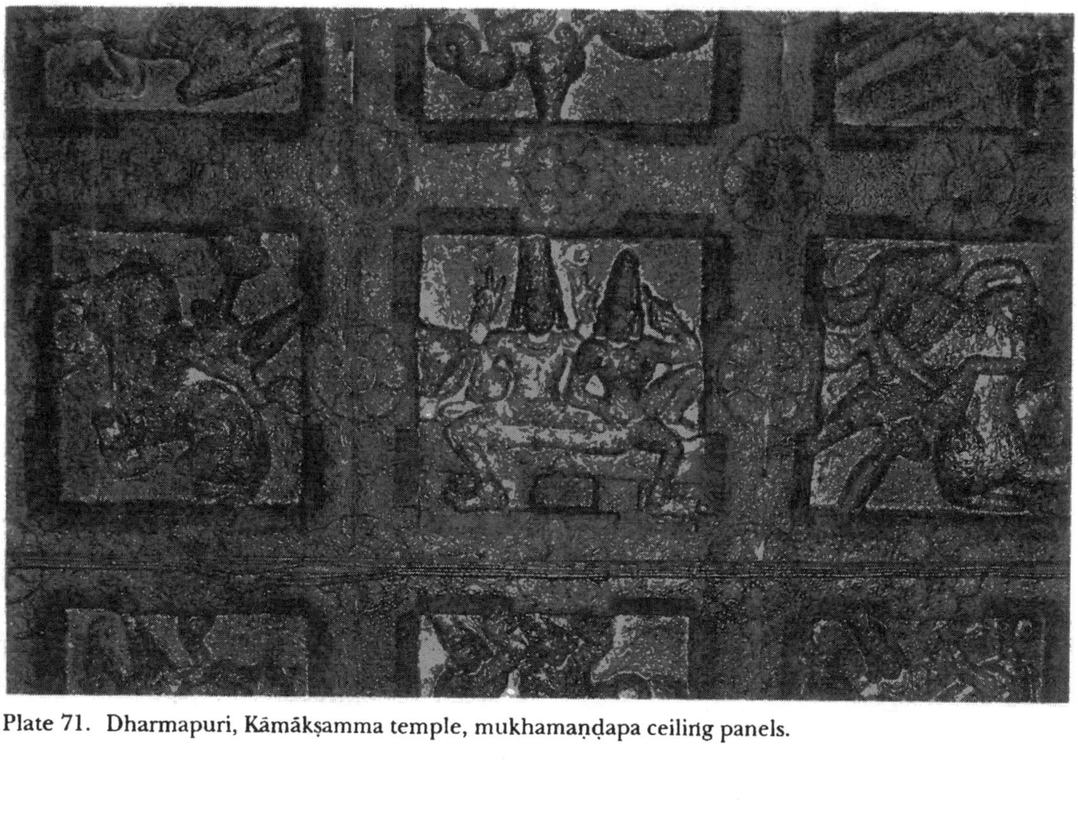

Plate 71. Dharmapuri, Kāmākṣamma temple, mukhamaṇḍapa ceiling panels.

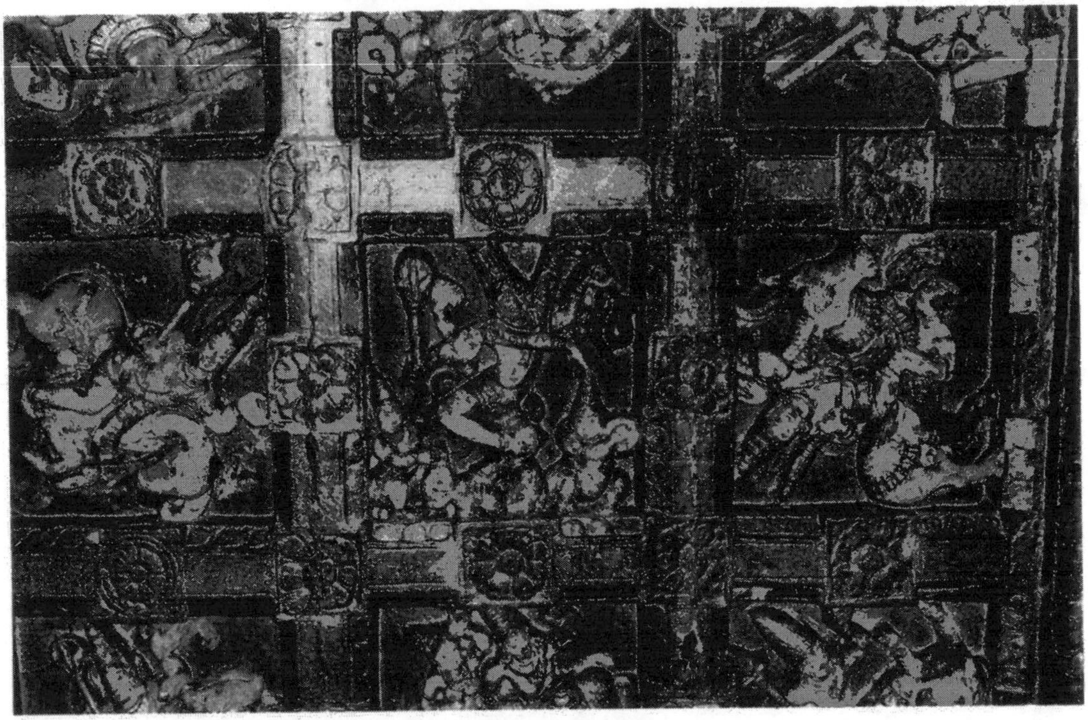

Plate 72. Dharmapuri, Mallikārjuna temple, mukhamaṇḍapa ceiling panel.

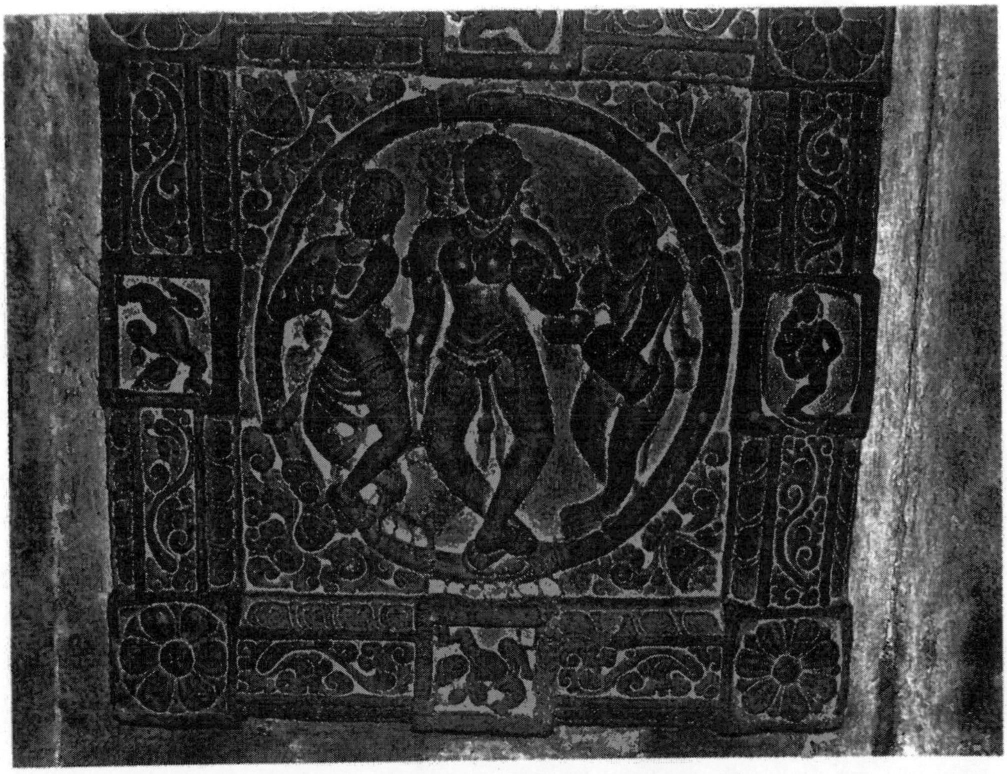

Plate 73. Dharmapuri, Mallikārjuna temple, antarāla ceiling panel.

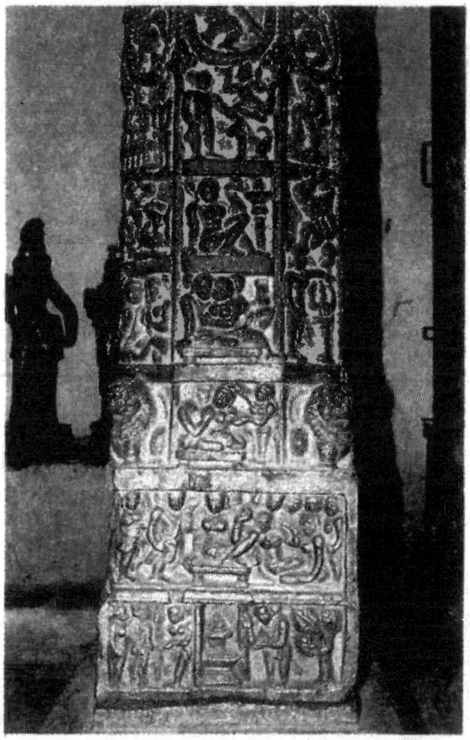

Plate 74. Dharmapuri, Mallikārjuna temple, detail of mukhamaṇḍapa pillar.

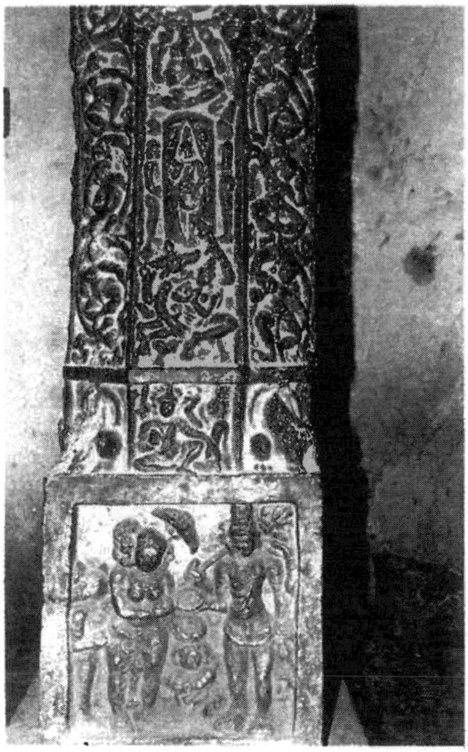

Plate 75. Dharmapuri, Mallikārjuna temple, detail of mukhamaṇḍapa pillar.

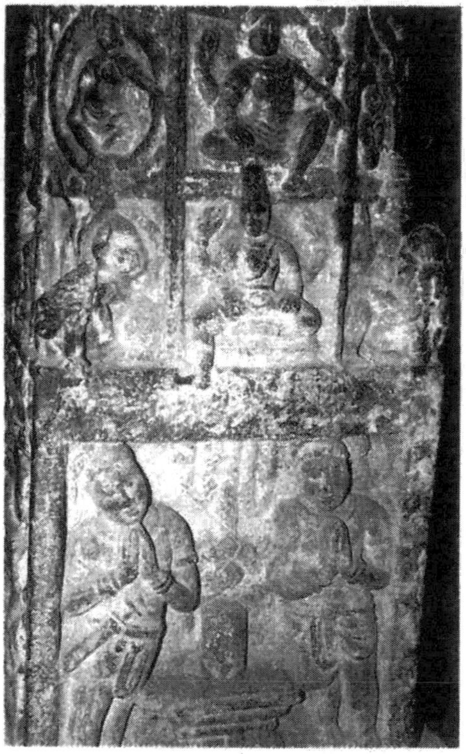

Plate 76. Dharmapuri, Mallikārjuna temple, detail of mukhamaṇḍapa pillar.

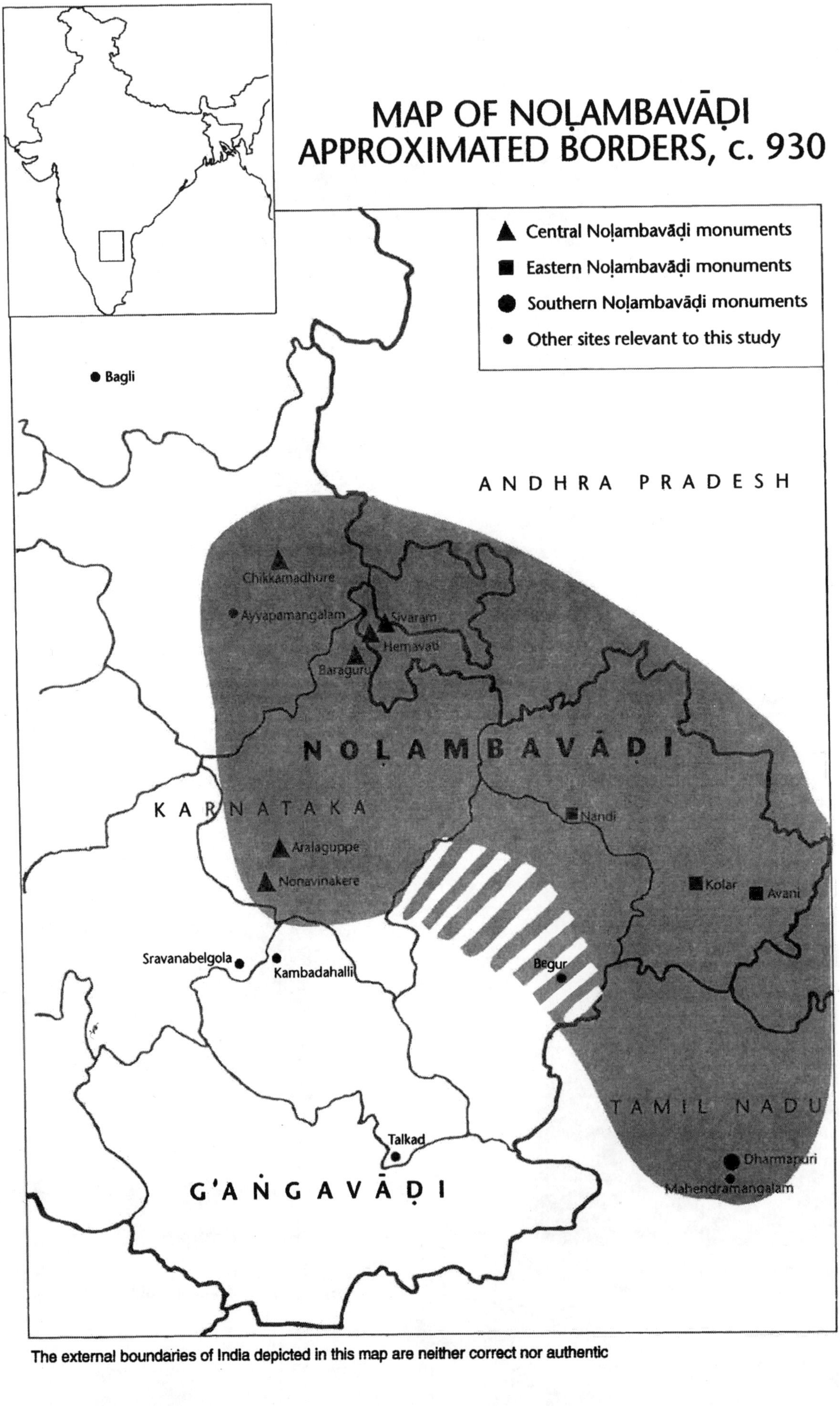

The external boundaries of India depicted in this map are neither correct nor authentic

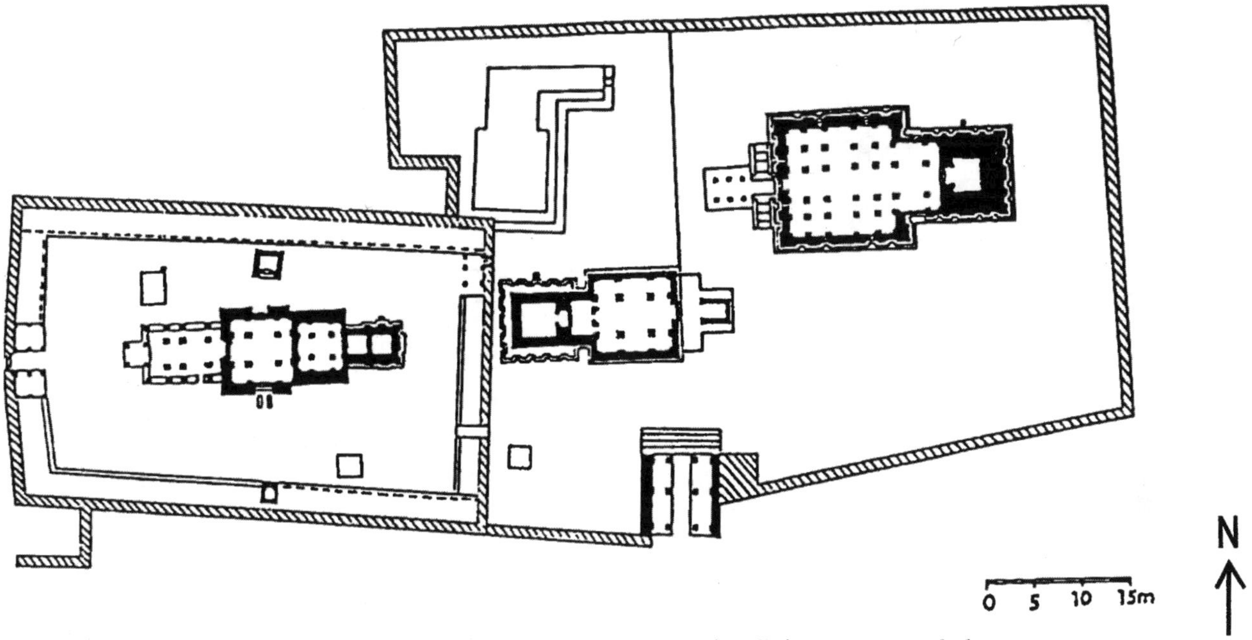

Figure 1. Hemavati, Siddēśvara, Doddēśvara, and Mallēśvara compound plan

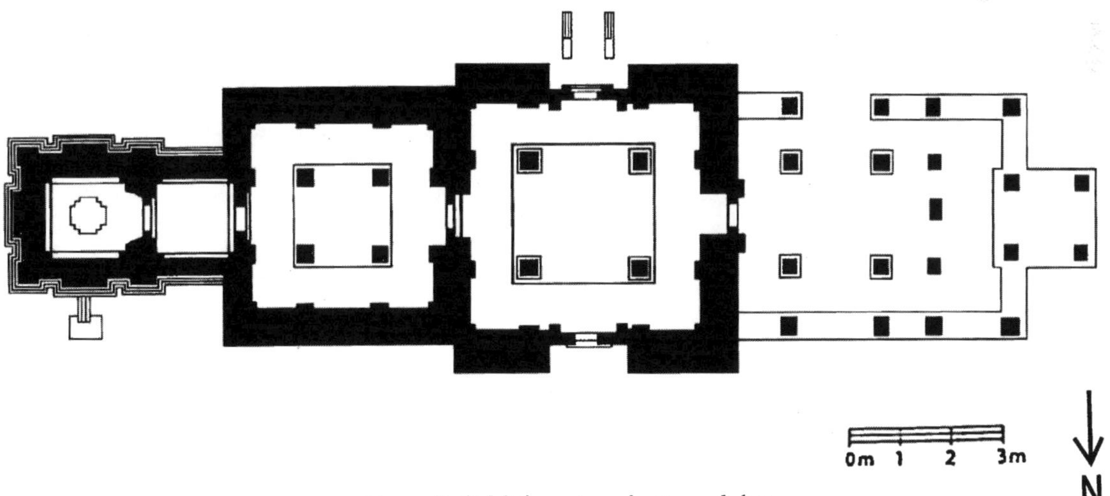

Figure 2. Siddēśvara temple groundplan

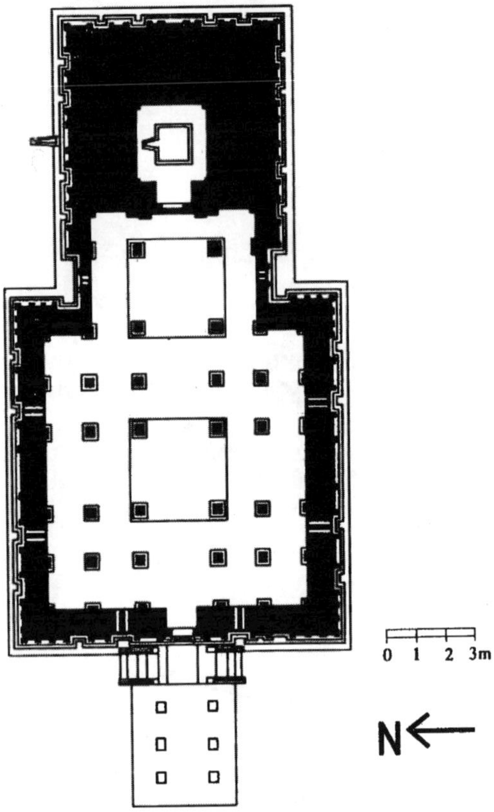

Figure 3. Doḍḍēśvara temple groundplan

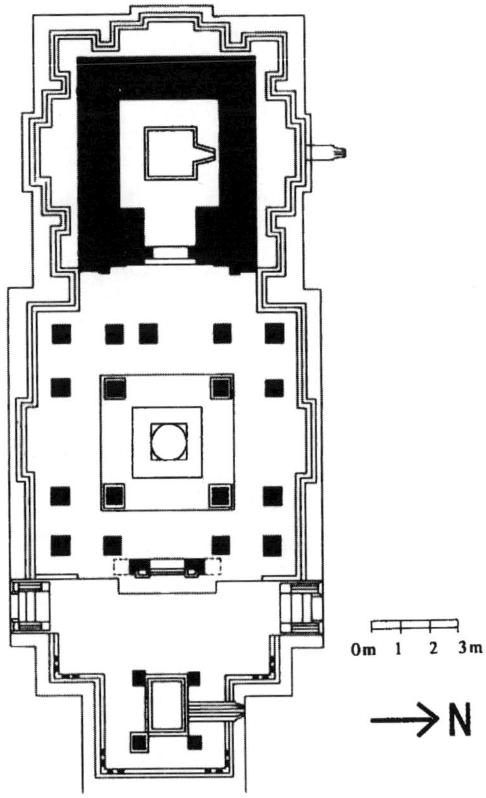

Figure 4. Virupaksa temple groundplan

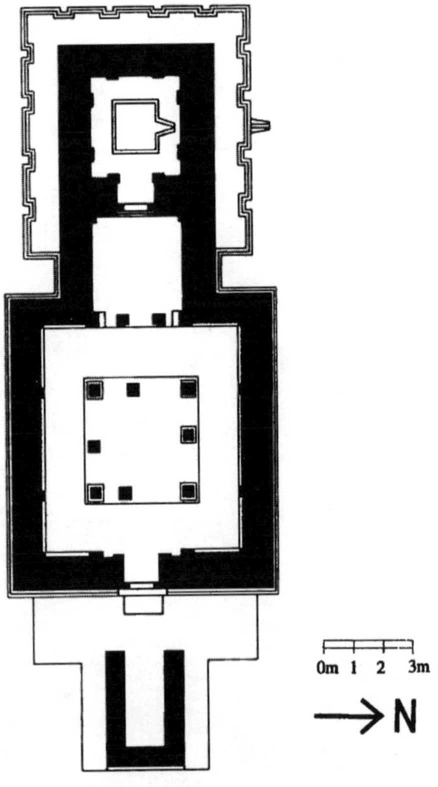

Figure 5. Mallēśvara temple groundplan

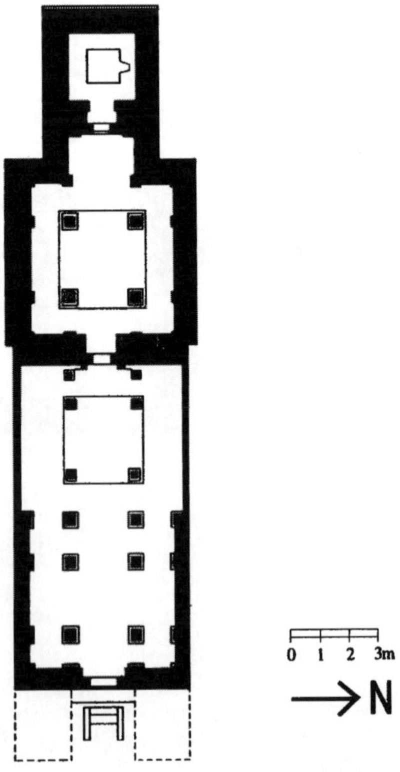

Figure 6. Mahendrēśvara temple groundplan

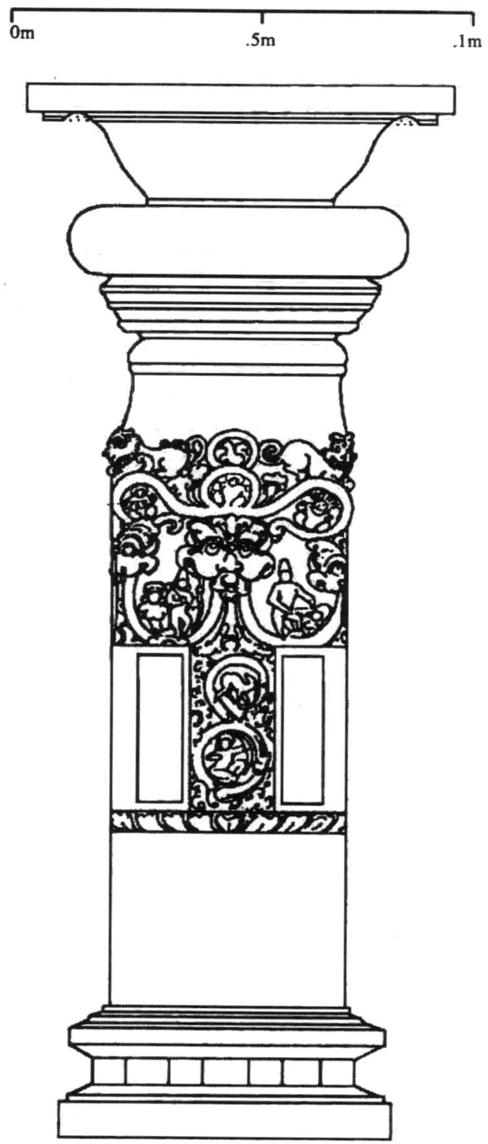

Figure 7. Doddēśvara mukhamaṇḍapa pillar

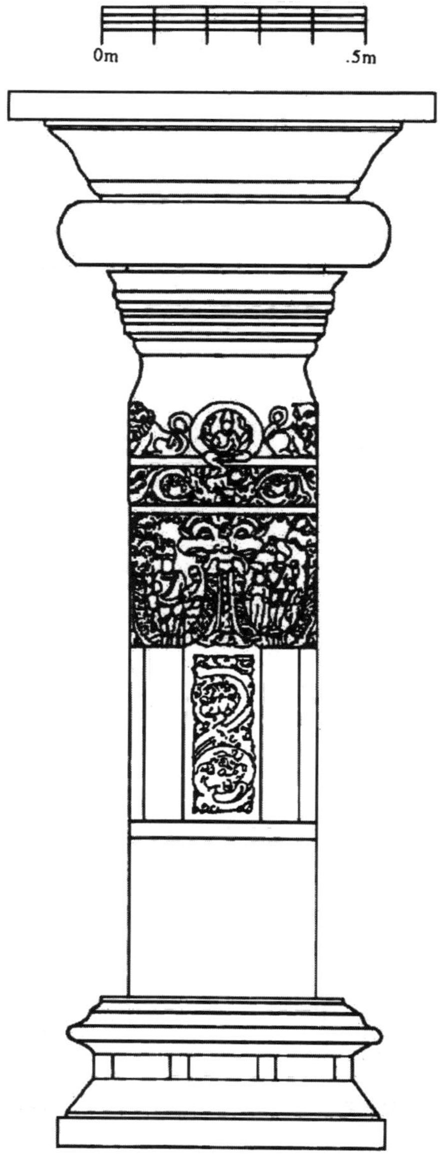

Figure 8. Virupaksa mukhamaṇḍapa pillar

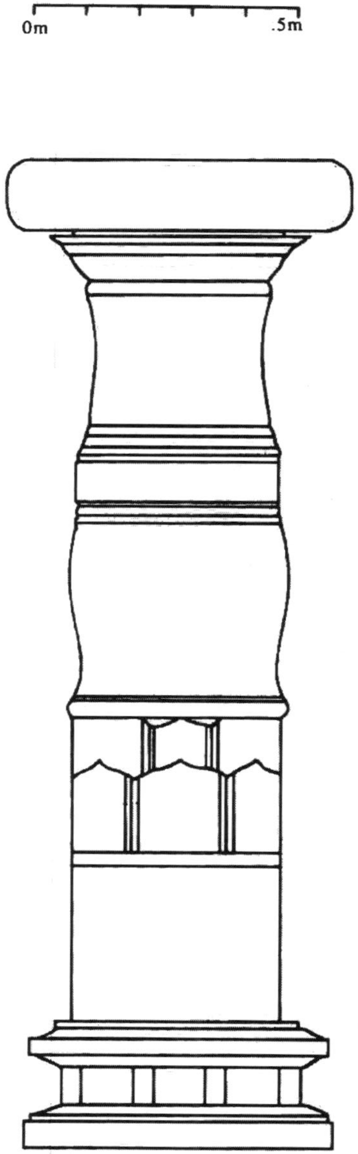

Figure 9. Mallēśvara mukhamaṇḍapa pillar

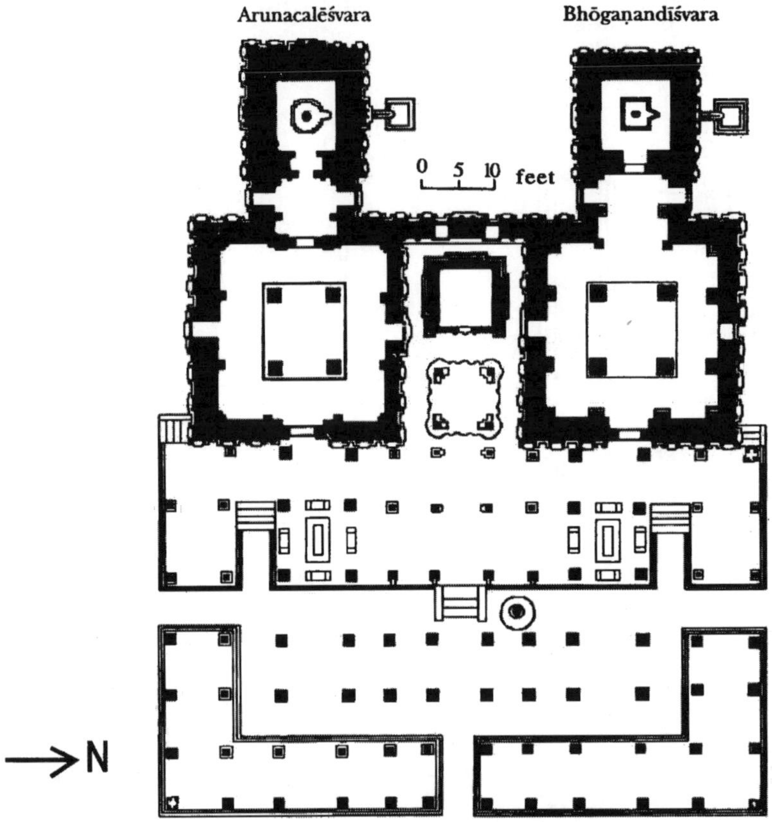

Figure 10. Bhōgaṇandīśvara compound groundplan (from *Mysore Archaeological Report*, 1940, pl. 23)

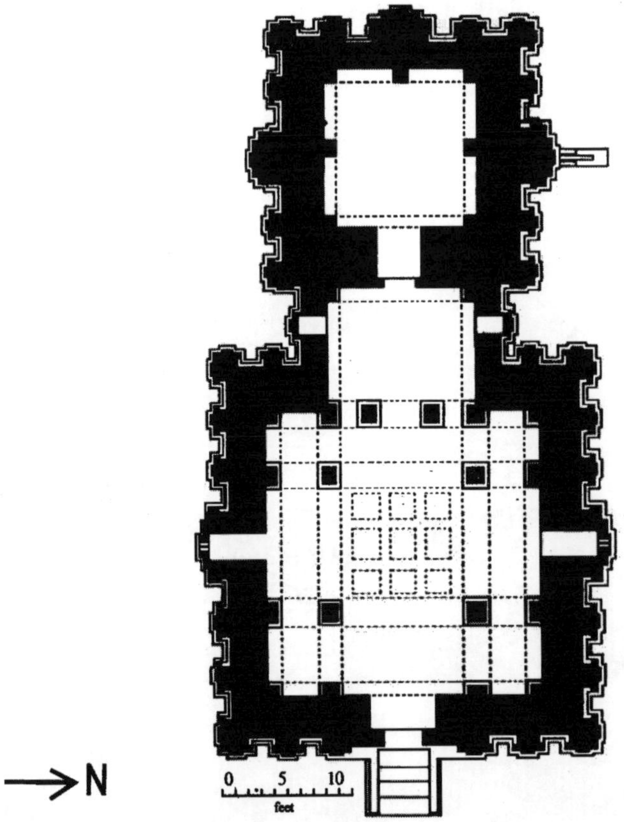

Figure 11. Avani, Lakṣmaṇēśvara temple groundplan (from *Mysore Archaeological Report*, 1935, pl. 17)

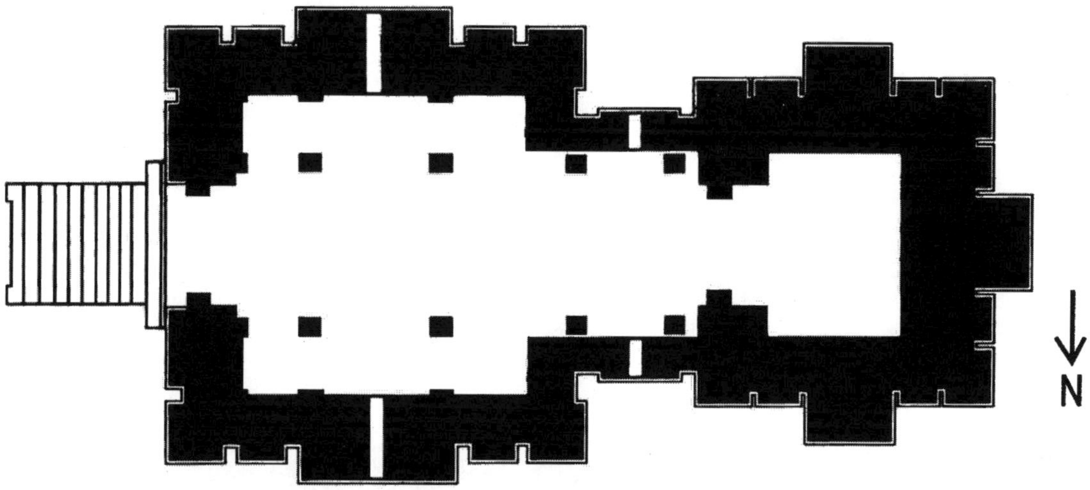

Figure 12. Kāmākṣamma temple groundplan (from Krishna Murthy, *Noḷambas*, p. 178)

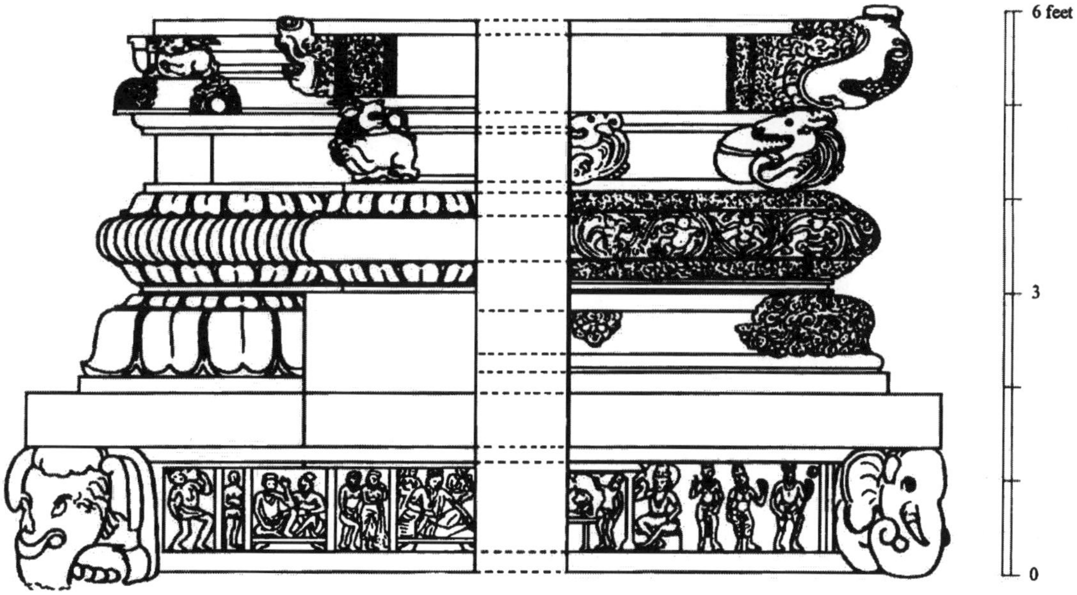

Figure 13. Kāmākṣamma temple moulding (from *Encyclopaedia of Indian Temple Architecture*, 1:108)

Glossary

abhaya-mudrā	gesture meaning 'do not fear'
adhiṣṭhāna	temple base with moulding series
agni	fire, flames
agramaṇḍapa	porch
āhūyavarada-mudrā	inviting and granting of wishes
akṣamālā	rosary
añjalī-mudrā	respect and salutation gesture; prayer
aṅkuśa	elephant goad
antarāla	vestibule before the sanctum
apsarās	female celestial associated with music and with seduction
ardhamaṇḍapa	half hall
bhadra	central wall projection
bhaṅga	bend of the body
bhūta	'elemental powers' (see *gaṇa*)
brahmakānta	rectangular pilaster
cakra	discus; wheel
catura	square; a dance pose in which both legs are bent at the knees but the left leg is higher with its toes touching the ground
caturasra	square band on *citrakhaṇḍa* pillars
caurī	fly whisk
chattra	umbrella
churī	dagger
citrakhaṇḍa	square column with panelled bands (*caturasra*)
ḍamaru	type of drum
daṇḍa	staff
danta	tooth; tusk
dēvakōṣṭha	niche intended to hold an image of a deity
dhvaja	banner; flag
dikpāla	directional guardian
dvārapāla	door guardian
ekapādāsana	standing on one foot; position to perform penance
gadā	mace or club
gajahasta	'elephant arm'; arm stretched across chest
gala	recessed moulding in temple base
gaṇa	(same as *bhūta*) dwarf attendents to Śiva
gandharva	celestial musicians
garbhagṛha	sanctum
ghaṇṭā	bell
grīvā	'neck'; portion of superstructure below cupola (*śikhara*)
gūḍhamaṇḍapa	closed hall
haṁsamālā	'garland of geese' decorative motif
hāra	necklace; cloistered parapet
jagatī	base moulding of *adhiṣṭhāna*
jāla-vātāyana	perforated window
jaṭā	hair strands
kalaśa	water pot
kalpavallī	wish-fulfilling vine; meandering lotus motif
kamaṇḍalu	water pot
kaṅkāladaṇḍa	staff with broken skeleton at top
kaṇṭha	a recess moulding
kapāla	cup; skull
kapōta	cornice
karṇa	corner wall projection
kaṭibandha	waist-band
kaṭihastamudrā	hand resting on hip
keyūra	upper armlet
khaḍga	sword
khaṭvāṅga	staff with skull at top
kheṭaka	shield
kirāta	hunter
kīrttimukha	'face of glory'; auspicious decorative motif shaped like a face
kōṣṭha	niche
kumuda	*adhiṣṭhāna* moulding (above *jagatī*), usually rounded or ridged
kuṇḍala	earring
kūṭa	square aedicula
laḍḍu	sweets commonly held by Gaṇeśa
lalita	dance pose which is the same as the *catura*, except in the

lalita the right leg is higher
lalitāsana — 'relaxation pose'; one leg rests on the seat, while the other leg hangs downward
liṅga — 'sign'; aniconic symbol of Śiva
maithuna — couple in coitus
makara — composite sea animal, mostly crocodilian
mālā — garland
maṇḍapa — hall
matsya — fish
mayūra — peacock
mekhalā — jewelled belt
mithuna — loving couple
mukuṭa — crown
muṇḍa — skull; head
nāga — snake; serpent deity
nāginī — female *nāga*
nāsī — horseshoe-shaped decorative motif
nāsikā — diminutive nāsī
nidhi — wealth deity
padma — lotus
padmapīṭha — lotus throne
padmaśākhā — *śākhā* with pattern lotus petals
padmāsana — 'lotus seat'; sitting position in which both legs are crossed and each foot rests upon the thigh of the opposite leg
pañjara — vaulted apsidal aedicula
paraśu — axe
pāśa — noose
paṭṭikā — rectilinear fillet (part of *adhiṣṭhāna*)
phaṁsanā — tiered tower
pīṭha — pedestal; throne
praṇāla — ablution drain
prastara — entablature
pratikarṇa — wall projection flanking *karṇa*
pūrṇakumbha — full or brimming pot
pustaka — book
ratnadāma — jewelled necklace
ratnaśākhā — jewelled pattern *śākhā*
ṛṣi — a sage
śākhā — door jamb
śālā — wagon-vaulted aedicula
śakti — spear; 'energy (female)'
samabhaṅga — standing without bending
śaṅkha — conch
śikhara — crowning cupola
siṁha — lion
śrīkāra — lathe-turned pillar order
stambhaśākhā — engaged pilaster jamb
sthāpati — artisan
subhadra — central offset of central wall projection
śukanāsa — antefix at the front of the superstructure
svastikāpasṛta — pose in which legs cross without touching
tapas — heat, penance
tribhaṅga — triple bend pose
triśūla — trident
upapīṭha — sub-plinth
ūrdhvajānu — dance pose in which one leg is held up high with the knee bent
utkaṭikāsana — sitting posture in which one leg is kept slantingly on the seat and the other leg hangs downward
vāhana — vehicle
vajra — thunderbolt (instrument held in hand)
varada-mudrā — gift-bestowing gesture
vidyādhara — 'bearer of wisdom'; flying celestial usually bearing a garland
vimāna — shrine portion of a temple and its superstructure
vismaya-mudrā — gesture of astonishment
viṣṇukānta — octagonal pilaster
vyākhyāna-mudrā — gesture of explanation or discourse
vyāla — composite animal, mostly leonine
yajñopavīta — sacred-thread
yāḷi — composite animal, mostly leonine

Bibliography

INSCRIPTIONS

Annual Report on Indian Epigraphy (Archaeological Survey of India), 1887-.
Annual Reports of the Mysore Archaeological Survey. Mysore: Government Press, 1906-56.
Epigraphica Andhrica. Hyderabad: Government of Andhra Pradesh, 1969-.
Epigraphica Carnatica. Bangalore: Government of Mysore, 1889-1955.
Epiqraphica Indica (Archaeological Survey of India), 1892-.
Inscriptions of the Madras Presidency. Edited by V. Rangacharya. 3 vols. Madras: Government Press, 1919.
Inscriptions of the Western Gangas. Edited by K.V. Ramesh. Delhi: Agam Prakashan, 1984.
South-Indian Inscriptions (Archaeological Survey of India), 1890-.

SECONDARY SOURCES

Ali, B.S. *History of the Western Gangas.* Mysore: University of Mysore, 1976.
Alpers, Svetlana. *The Art of Describing.* Chicago: University of Chicago Press, 1983.
Altekar, A.S. *The Rashtrakutas and their Times.* Poona: Poona Oriental Series, 1934.
Arokiaswami, A. *Kongu Country.* Madras: Madras University, 1956.
Balambal, V. *Feudatories of South India, 800-1070 A.D.* Allahabad: Chugh Pub., 1978.
Balasubrahmanyam, S. *Early Chola Art.* London: Asia Publishing House, 1967.
———. *Early Chola Temples.* Bombay: Orient Longman, 1971.
Banerjea, J.N. *The Development of Hindu Iconography.* 2nd edn. Calcutta: University of Calcutta, 1956.
———. *Pauranic and Tantric Religion.* Calcutta: University of Calcutta, 1966.
Barnett, Lionel. 'Alur Inscriptions of the Reign of Vikramaditya V. Saka 933.' *Epigraphica Indica* 16 (1921-2): 27-31.
Barrett, Douglas. *Early Cola Architecture and Sculpture.* London: Faber and Faber, 1974.
———. *Early Cola Bronzes.* Bombay: Bhulabhai Memorial Institute, 1965.
———. *Nolamba Temples at Hemavati.* Bombay: Bhulabhai Memorial Institute, 1958.
Barthakuria, A.C. *The Kapalikas.* Calcutta: Sanskrit Pustak Bhandar, 1984.
Beck, Carol., ed. *Perspectives on a Regional Culture.* New Delhi: Vikas Pub., 1979.
Bhandarkar, D.R. 'An Eklingji stone inscription and the origin and history of the Lakulisa sect.' *Journal of the Bombay Branch of the Royal Asiatic Society* 22 (1908): 151-67.
Bhattacharyya, N.N. *History of Sakta Religions.* New Delhi: Munshiram Manoharlal, 1973.
Buchanan, Susan. 'Calukya Temples: History and Iconography.' Ph.D. dissertation, Ohio State University, 1985.
Chakraborti, Haripada (trans. and intro.). *Pasupata Sutram with Panchartha-Bhasya of Kaundinya.* Calcutta: Academic Pub., 1970.
Chandra, Pramod. *On the Study of Indian Art.* Cambridge: Harvard University Press, 1983.
Coburn, Thomas. *Devi Mahatmya: The Crystallization of the Goddess Tradition.* Delhi: Motilal Banarsidass, 1985.
Cohen, Andrew. 'The King and the Goddess: The Nolamba Period Laksmanesvara Temple at Avani.' *Artibus Asiae* 52 (1992): 7-24.
———. 'Unpublished Nolamba Ceiling Panels at Hemavati.' In *Sri Nagabhinandanam,* pp. 321-4. Bangalore: Dr. M.S. Nagaraja Rao Felicitation Committee, 1995.
———. 'Why a History of Monuments from Nolambavadi.' *Artibus Asiae* 57 (1997): 17-29.
Collins, Charles. *The Iconography and Ritual of Siva at Elephanta.* Albany: State University of New York, 1988.
Cousens, Henry. *The Chalukyan Architecture of the Kanarese Districts.* Calcutta: Government of India, 1926.

Dasgupta, Surendranath. *A History of Indian Philosophy*. 5 vols. Cambridge: Cambridge University Press, 1922-5.

Davis, Richard. *Ritual in an Oscillating Universe*. Princeton: Princeton University Press, 1992.

Dayalan, D. 'The Role of War-Trophies in Cultural Contact.' *Tamil Civilization* 3 (1985): 133-7.

De Lippe, Aschwin. *Indian Mediaeval Sculpture*. Amsterdam: North Holland Pub., 1978.

Dehejia, Vidya. *Namakkal Caves*. Tamil Nadu State Dept. of Archaeology, Pub. no. 11, 1977.

———. *Yogini Cults and Temples*. New Delhi: National Museum, 1986.

Desai, Devangana. *Erotic Scupture of India*. New Delhi: Tata McGraw-Hill Pub., 1975.

Dhaky, M.A. 'Cola Sculpture.' In *Chhavi*, pp. 263-89. Banares: Bharat Kala Bhavan, 1971.

———. 'Ganga Jaina Sculpture.' In *Aspects of Jaina Art and Architecture*, pp. 195-203. Edited by U.P. Shah and M.A. Dhaky. Ahmedabad: All India Seminar on Jaina Art, 1973.

———. *The Indian Temple Forms in Karnaṭa Inscriptions and Architecture*. New Delhi: Abhinav Pub., 1977.

———. 'Nandi Images of Tamilnadu and Kannadanadu.' *Artibus Asiae* 34 (1972): 183-210.

———. 'Santara Sculpture.' *Journal of the Indian Society of Oriental Art* 4 (1971-2): 78-98.

Dikshit, G.S. *Local Self-Government in Mediaeval Karnataka*. Dharwad: Karnataka University, 1964.

Dirks, Nicholas. *The Hollow Crown*. Cambridge: Cambridge University Press, 1987.

Diwakar, R., ed. *Karnataka Through the Ages*. Bangalore: Government of Mysore, 1968.

Eschmann, Anncharlotte. 'Hinduization of Tribal Deities in Orissa: The Sakta and Saiva Typology.' In *The Cult of Jagannath and the Regional Traditions of Orissa*, pp. 79-97. Edited by A. Eschmann, *et al.* New Delhi: Manohar, 1978.

Filippe, Gian. *Some Iconographic Aspects of Siva as 'King of Dances' in Early Cola Art*. New Delhi: Star Pub., 1972.

Gaston, Anne-Marie. *Siva in Dance, Myth and Iconography*. Delhi: Oxford University Press, 1982.

Ghosh, A., ed. *Jaina Art and Architecture*. 3 vols. New Delhi: Bharatiya Jnanpith, 1975.

Gopal, B.R. *The Chalukyas of Kalyana and the Kalachuris*. Dharwad: Karnatak University, 1981.

Gopinatha Rao, T.A. *Elements of Hindu Iconography*. 2 vols. Delhi: Motilal Banarsidass, 1985 (rpt. of 1914 edn.).

Goswami, Niranjan. 'A Study of the Ugra-murtis of Siva.' Ph.D. dissertation, University of Pennsylvania, 1972.

Gururaja Rao, P. *Studies in Tuluva History and Culture*. Manipal: By the Author, 1975.

Handiqui, K.K. *Yasastilaka and Indian Culture*. Sholapur: Jaina Samskṛti Samrakshaka, 1968.

Hara, Minoru. 'Nakulisa-Pasupata-Darsanam.' *Indo-Iranian Journal* 2 (1958): 8-32.

Harle, J.C. *The Art and Architecture of the Indian Subcontinent*. Middlesex: Penguin Books, 1986.

Harper, Katherine. 'An Iconological Study on the Origins and Development of the Saptamatrkas.' Ph.D. dissertation, University of California, Los Angeles, 1977.

Heitzman, James. 'State Formation in South India, 850-1280' *The Indian Economic and Social History Review* 24 (1987): 35-61.

Hermeren, Goran. *Influence in Art and Literature*. Princeton: Princeton University Press, 1975.

Hirsh, Marilyn. 'Sources for the Figural Sculpture of Mamallapuram.' Ph.D. dissertation, New York University, Institute of Fine Arts, 1985.

Hoekveld-Meijer, G. *Koyils in the Colamandalam: Typology and Development of Early Cola Temples*. Amsterdam: Vrije Universiteit te Amsterdam, 1981.

Hocart, A.M. *Kings and Councillors: An Essay in the Comparative Anatomy of Human Society*. Edited by R. Needham. Chicago: University of Chicago Press, 1970.

Huntington, Susan. *The Art of Ancient India*. New York: Weatherhill, 1985.

Inden, Ronald. *Imagining India*. Oxford: Basil Blackwell, 1990.

Jouveau-Dubreuil, G. *Archeologie du sud de l'Inde*. 2 vols. Paris: P. Geuthner, 1914.

Kamalakar, G. 'Art and Architecture of Renandu; Cuddapah District, Andhra Pradesh.' Ph.D. dissertation, Nagarjuna University, 1984.

Karashima, Noboru. *South Indian History and Society: Studies from Inscriptions A.D. 850-1800*. Oxford: Oxford University Press, 1984.

Khandalavala, Karl. 'Two Bronzes from Karnataka.' In *Madhu: Recent Researches in Indian Archaeology and Art History*, pp. 239-41. Edited by M. S. Nagaraja Rao. Delhi: Agam Kala Prakashan, 1981.

Kinsley, David, *Hindu Goddesses*, Berkeley: University of California Press, 1986.

Kitti, M. 'Ganga, Nolambas and Banas in Kongu Country.' In *Srinidhi*, pp. 329-32. Edited by K.V. Raman, *et al.* Madras: New Era Pub., 1983.

Kramrisch, Stella. *Hindu Temple*. Calcutta: University of Calcutta, 1946; reprinted edn., Delhi: Motilal Banarsidass, 1980.

———. *Manifestations of Shiva*. Philadelphia: Philadelphia Museum of Art, 1981.

———. *The Presence of Siva*. Princeton: Princeton University Press, 1981.

Krishna Murthy, K. *Nolamba Sculptures: A Cultural Study*. Delhi: Sundeep Prakashan, 1987.

Krishna Murthy, M.S. 'The First Nolamba Coin.' *Journal of the Numismatic Society of India* 62 (1980): 130-2.

———. *The Nolambas: A Political and Cultural Study*. Mysore: University of Mysore, 1980.

Krishnarao, Bhavaraj. 'Tandikonda Grant of Ammaraja II.' *Epigraphica Indica* 23 (1935-6): 161-6.

Kriṣhna Rao, M.V. *The Gangas of Talkad*. Madras: B.G. Paul and Co., 1936.

———. 'Ganga Period Architecture.' *Quarterly Journal of the Mythic Society* 25 (1934-5): 161-81.

Krishna Sastry, H. *South Indian Images of Gods and Goddesses*. 1916; reprinted edn., New Delhi: Asian Educational Services, 1986.

———. 'Two Nolamba Inscriptions from Dharmapuri of the 9th Century A.D.' *Epigraphia Indica* 10 (1909): 54-70.

Krishnan, K.G. 'Three Inscriptions of Vira-Nolamba.' *Epigraphia Indica* 39 (1971): 13-16.

Kulandaivelan, K. 'Chalukya and Nolamba Sculptures from Trailoka.' In *South Indian Studies*, pp. 174-7. Edited by R. Nagaswamy. Madras: Society for Archaeological, Historical and Epigraphical Research, 1978.

Kulke, Hermann. 'Royal Temple Policy and the Structure of Medieval Hindu Kingdoms.' In *The Cult of Jagannath and the Regional Traditions of Orissa*, pp. 125-37. Edited by A. Eschmann, *et al*. New Delhi: Manohar, 1978.

Lakshminarayan Rao, N. 'Geneology and Chronology of the Nolamba-Pallavas.' *The Quarterly Journal of the Mythic Society* 47 (1956-7): 131-41.

Liebert, Gosta. *Iconographic Dictionary of the Indian Religions*. Leiden: E.J. Brill, 1976.

Linda, Mary. 'Medieval Kalinga Hindu Temples.' Ph.D. dissertation, University of California, Berkeley, 1986.

Lorenzen, David. *The Kapalikas and Kalamukhas: Two lost Saivite Sects*. New Delhi: Thomson Press, 1972.

Mahalingam, T.V. 'The Banas in South Indian History.' *Journal of Indian History* 28 (1950): 153-81, and 277-89.

———. 'The Nolamba Pallavas: Their Origins.' *Journal of Indian History* 36 (1958): 131-41.

Meister, Michael. 'Bithu: Individual and Idiom.' *Ars Orientalis* 13 (1982): 169-75.

———. ed. *Discourses on Siva*. Philadelphia: University of Pennsylvania, 1984.

———. ed. *Encyclopaedia of Indian Temple Architecture: South India, Lower Dravidadesa*. Vol. 1. New Delhi: American Institute of Indian Studies, 1983.

Meister, Michael and Dhaky, M.A., eds. *Encyclopaedia of Indian Temple Architecture: South India, Upper Dravidadesa*. Vol 2. New Delhi: American Institute of Indian Studies, 1986.

Michell, George. *The Architecture and Art of Southern India: Vijayanagara and the Successor States*. Cambridge: Cambridge University Press, 1995.

Mysore Gazetteer. Edited by C. Hayavadana Rao. 5 vols. Bangalore: Government Press, 1930.

Nagaraja Rao, M.S. *Kiratarjuniyam in Indian Art (with Special Reference to Karnataka)*. New Delhi: Agam Kala Prakashan, 1979.

Nagaswamy, R. *Tantric Cult of South India*. New Delhi: Agam Kala Prakashan, 1982.

Nandi, R.N. *Religious Institutions and Cults in the Deccan* Delhi: Motilal Banarsidass, 1973.

Narasimha Murthy, A.V., ed. *Archaeology of Karnataka*. Mysore: University of Mysore, 1978.

Nigam, M.L. *Sculptural Heritage of Andhradesa*. Hyderabad: Osmania University, 1975.

Nilakanta Sastri, K.A. *The Colas*. 2nd edn. Madras: University of Madras, 1955.

———. *Development of Religion in South India*. Madras: Orient Longmans, 1963

———. *A History of South India*. 4th edn. Madras: Oxford University Press, 1975.

Nilakanta Sastri and Subramaniam, T.N. 'Hemavati Pillar Inscription of Kulottungachola (III), Year 2.' *Epigraphia Indica* 31 (1956): 269-76.

Nolamba Itihasa Darshana. Tiptur: Nolamba Itihasa Parishath, 1976 (In Kannada).

O'Flaherty, Wendy. *Siva, the Erotic Ascetic*. Oxford: Oxford University Press, 1973.

———. intro. *Hindu Myths*. Middlesex: Penguin Books, 1975.

Pal, Pratapaditya. *Indian Sculpture*. Vol 2. Los Angeles: Los Angeles County Museum, 1988.

Prakash, Gyan. 'Writing Post-Orientalist Histories of the Third World: Perspectives from Indian Historiography.' *Comparative Studies in Society and History* 32 (1990): 383-408.

Rabe, Michael. 'The Monolithic Temples of the Pallava Dynasty: A Chronology.' Ph.D. dissertation, University of Minnesota, 1987.

Radcliffe, Carol. 'Early Chalukya Sculpture.' Ph.D. dissertation, New York University, Institute of Fine Arts, 1981.

Rajamanickam, M. *The Development of Saivism in South India*. Dharmapuram: Dharmapuram Adhinam, 1964.
Rajendra Prasad, B. *Art of South India: Andhra Pradesh*. Delhi: Sundeep Prakashan, 1980.
———. 'Rastrakuta Temples at Bhavanasi Sangam.' *Artibus Asiae* 34 (1972): 211-21.
———. *Temple Sculpture of Andhra Pradesh*. Hyderabad: Government of Andhra Pradesh, 1978.
Ramamurthy, K.K. 'Kshetrapalla Concept and Cult Images from South India.' In *Indian Studies*, pp. 123-9. Edited by Amita Ray, *et. al.* Delhi: Caxton, 1984.
———. 'Narrative Sculptures from Arkesvara Temple at Alur.' In *Srinidhi*, pp. 187-90. Edited by K.V. Raman, *et al.* Madras: New Era Pub., 1983.
Ramanujan, A.K., tr. *Poems of Love and War*. New York: Columbia University Press, 1985.
———. tr. *Speaking of Siva*. Baltimore: Penguin Books, 1973.
Ramesh, K.V. 'Note on Madakasira Inscription of Diliparasa, Saka 870.' *Epigraphia Indica* 33 (1958): 77-8.
———. 'Two Nolamba-Pallava Inscriptions'. *Indica* 39 (1971): 27-34.
Rea, A. *Chalukyan Architecture*. Madras: Government Press, 1896.
———. *Pallava Architecture*. Madras: Government Press, 1909.
Rice, Lewis. *Mysore and Coorg From the Inscriptions*. London: Archibald Constable and Co., 1909.
Sanford, David. 'Early Temples Bearing Ramayana Relief Cycles in the Chola area.' Ph.D. dissertation, University of California, Los Angeles, 1974.
Schwindler, Gary. 'A Proposed Methodology, based upon T.S. Kuhn's *The Structure of Scientific Revolutions*, for the Study of Medieval South Indian Stone Sculpture from the Region of Colamandalam, *c.* AD 850-1050.' *South Asia Research* 2 (1982): 35-51.
———. 'The Dating of South Indian Metal Sculptures.' Ph.D. dissertation, University of California, Los Angeles, 1975.
———. 'Sculpture in Medieval South India, *c.* 9th to 11th Century A.D.: Some New Directions.' In *Kaladarsana*, pp. 91-8. Edited by Joanna Williams. New Delhi: Oxford Press, 1981.
Seshadri, M. 'Astadikpala Figures from Aralaguppe, Mysore State.' *Journal of the Mysore University* 23 (1967): 70-1.
———. 'Sandhya Tandava.' *Artibus Asiae* 18 (1955): 117-20.
Settar, S. 'Peregrination of Medieval Artists.' In *Journal of Indian History Golden Jubilee Volume*, pp. 419-35. Trivandrum: University of Kerala, 1973.
Shulman, David. *The King and the Clown in South Indian Myths and Poetry*. Princeton: Princeton University Press, 1985.
———. *Tamil Temple Myths*. Princeton: Princeton University Press, 1980.
Sicar, D.C. *Indian Epigraphy*. New Delhi: Motilal Barnarsidass, 1965.
———. *Indian Epigraphical Glossary*. New Delhi: Motilal Barnarsidass, 1966.
Sinha, Ajay. 'Originality and Origination of Vesara Architecture.' Ph.D. dissertation, University of Pennsylvania, 1993.
Sivaramamurti, C. *The Art of India*. New York: Harry Abrams Pub., 1977.
———. *Early Eastern Chalukya Sculpture*. Madras: Government of Madras, 1957.
———. *Nataraja in Art, Thought and Literature*. New Delhi: National Museum, 1974.
———. *Nolamba Sculptures in the Madras Government Museum*. Madras: Government of Madras, 1964.
———. *A Panorama of Jain Art*. New Delhi: Times of India, 1983.
———. *Royal Conquests and Cultural Migrations in South India and the Deccan*. Calcutta: Indian Museum, 1964.
Sompath, M.D. 'New Light on Nolambas.' In *Professor K.A. Nilakanta Sastri Felicitation Volume*, pp. 165-79. Madras: Prof. K.A. Nilakanta Sastri Felicitation Committee, 1971.
Soundara Rajan, K.V. *Architecture of the Early Hindu Temples of Andhra Pradesh*. Hyderabad: Government of Andhra Pradesh, 1965.
———. 'Early Pandya, Muttarayan and Irukkuvel Architecture.' In *Studies in Indian Temple Architecture*, pp. 240-300. Edited by P. Chandra. New Delhi: American Institute of Indian Studies, 1975.
———. *Early Temple Architecture in Karnataka and its Ramifications*. Dharwad: Karnatak University, 1969.
———. *Indian Temple Styles*. New Delhi: Munshiram Manoharlal, 1972.
Spencer, George. 'Religious Networks and Royal Influences in Eleventh Century South India.' *Journal of the Economic and Social History of the Orient* 12 (1969): 42-56.
Srinivasan, K.R. *Cave Temples of the Pallavas*. New Delhi: Director General of Archaeology, 1964.
———. *The Dharmaraja Ratha and its Sculptures*. New Delhi: Abhinav Pub., 1975.
———. 'Jaina Art and Architecture under the Gangas of Talkad.' In *Aspects of Jaina Art and Architecture*,

pp. 161-84. Edited by U.P. Shah and M.A. Dhaky. Ahmedabad: All India Seminar on Jaina Art, 1973.

———. 'The Pallava Architecture of South India.' *Ancient India* 14 (1958): 131-8.

———. *Some Aspects of Religion as Revealed by Early Monuments and Literature of the South.* Madras: University of Madras, 1960.

Srinivasan, P.R. 'Sculptures in the two Rock-cut Vaisanava Cave Temples of Namakkal.' *Artibus Asiae* 24 (1961): 107-16.

Stein, Burton. 'Devi Shrines and Folk Hinduism in Medieval Tamilnad.' In *Studies in the Language and Culture of South Asia*, pp. 75-90. Edited by Edwin Gerow. Seattle: University of Washington Press, 1973.

———. *Peasant State and Society in Medieval South India.* Oxford: Oxford University Press, 1980.

———. ed. *All the Kings' Mana: Papers on Medieval South Indian History.* Madras: New Era Pub., 1984.

———. ed. *South Indian Temples.* New Delhi: Vikas pub., 1978.

Sundara A. 'A Unique Virabhadra Image from South India.' In *Srinidhi*, pp. 151-4. Edited by K.V. Raman, *et al.* Madras: New Era Pub., 1983.

———. 'Two Temples in Dharwar District and the Impact of the Lakula and Kalamukha Saiva Sects.' In *Chalukyas of Kalyana*, pp. 171-4. Edited by M.S. Nagaraja Rao. Bangalore: Mythic Society, 1983.

Tartakov, Gary, and Dehejia, Vidya. 'Sharing, Intrusions, and Influence: The Mahisasuramardini Imagery of the Calukyas and the Pallavas.' *Artibus Asiae* 45 (1984): 287-345.

Vatsyayan, Kapila. *Traditions of Indian Folk Dance.* New Delhi: Indian Book Co., 1976.

Wagoner, Phillip. 'Mode and Meaning in the Architecture of Early Medieval Telangana (C. 1000-1300).' Ph.D. dissertation, University of Wisconsin-Madison, 1986.

Whitehead, Henry. *The Village Gods of South India.* Oxford: Oxford University Press, 1921.

Index